Validation of Risk Management Models for Financial Institutions

Financial models are an inescapable feature of modern financial markets. Yet, it was over-reliance on these models and the failure to test them properly that is now widely recognized as one of the main causes of the financial crisis of 2007–2011. Since this crisis, there has been an increase in the amount of scrutiny and testing applied to such models, and validation has become an essential part of model risk management at financial institutions. The book covers all the major risk areas that a financial institution is exposed to and uses models for, including market risk, interest rate risk, retail credit risk, wholesale credit risk, compliance risk and investment management. The book discusses current practices and pitfalls that model risk users need to be aware of and it identifies areas where validation can be advanced in the future. This provides the first unified framework for validating risk management models.

DAVID LYNCH is Deputy Associate Director for Policy Research and Analytics at the Board of Governors of the Federal Reserve System. He joined the board in 2005, and his areas of responsibility include Volcker metrics, swap margin, and oversight of models for market risk capital and counterparty risk capital.

IFTEKHAR HASAN is University Professor and E. Gerald Corrigan Chair in Finance at Fordham University. He is the editor of the *Journal of Financial Stability* and is among the most widely cited academics in the world.

AKHTAR SIDDIQUE taught finance at Georgetown University after his finance Ph.D. at Duke University. He has published extensively in leading finance journals and currently works at the Office of the Comptroller of the Currency.

Validation of Risk Management Models for Financial Institutions

Theory and Practice

Edited by

DAVID LYNCH
Federal Reserve Board of Governors

IFTEKHAR HASAN
Fordham University Graduate Schools of Business

AKHTAR SIDDIQUE
Office of the Comptroller of the Currency

CAMBRIDGE
UNIVERSITY PRESS

CAMBRIDGE
UNIVERSITY PRESS

Shaftesbury Road, Cambridge CB2 8EA, United Kingdom

One Liberty Plaza, 20th Floor, New York, NY 10006, USA

477 Williamstown Road, Port Melbourne, VIC 3207, Australia

314–321, 3rd Floor, Plot 3, Splendor Forum, Jasola District Centre, New Delhi – 110025, India

103 Penang Road, #05–06/07, Visioncrest Commercial, Singapore 238467

Cambridge University Press is part of Cambridge University Press & Assessment, a department of the University of Cambridge.

We share the University's mission to contribute to society through the pursuit of education, learning and research at the highest international levels of excellence.

www.cambridge.org
Information on this title: www.cambridge.org/9781108497350

DOI: 10.1017/9781108608602

First published 2023

A catalogue record for this publication is available from the British Library.

Library of Congress Cataloging-in-Publication Data
Names: Lynch, David, 1964– editor. | Hasan Iftekhar, editor. | Siddique, Akhtar R., editor.
Title: Validation of risk management models for financial institutions : theory and practice / edited by David Lynch, Federal Reserve Board of Governors, Iftekhar Hasan, Fordham University Graduate Schools of Business, Akhtar Siddique, Office of the Comptroller of the Currency.
Description: First edition. | New York, NY : Cambridge University Press, [2022] | Includes bibliographical references and index.
Identifiers: LCCN 2022012256 (print) | LCCN 2022012257 (ebook) | ISBN 9781108497350 (hardback) | ISBN 9781108739962 (paperback) | ISBN 9781108608602 (epub)
Subjects: LCSH: Finance–Mathematical models. | Financial institutions–Mathematical models. | Risk management. | Quantitative research–Evaluation.
Classification: LCC HG106 .V35 2022 (print) | LCC HG106 (ebook) | DDC 332/.01/5118–dc23/eng/20220418
LC record available at https://lccn.loc.gov/2022012256
LC ebook record available at https://lccn.loc.gov/2022012257

ISBN 978-1-108-49735-0 Hardback

Contents

Figures

Tables

Contributors

Rebecca Alper, *Board of Governors of the Federal Reserve*

Chris Anderson, *Board of Governors of the Federal Reserve*

Francesco Campobasso, *University of Bari Aldo Moro*

Eduardo Canabarro, *Barclays (retired)*

Filippo Curti, *Federal Reserve Bank of Richmond*

Ashish Dev, *Ex Board of Governors of the Federal Reserve*

Ibrahim Ergen, *Ex Federal Reserve Bank of Richmond*

Iftekhar Hasan, *Fordham University*

Diana Iercosan, *Board of Governors of the Federal Reserve*

Hulusi Inanoglu, *Board of Governors of the Federal Reserve*

Jonathan Jones, *Office of the Comptroller of the Currency*

Nick Klagge, *Federal Reserve Bank of New York*

Sang-Sub Lee, *Office of the Comptroller of the Currency*

Feng Li, *Office of the Comptroller of the Currency*

Jose A. Lopez, *Federal Reserve Bank of San Francisco*

David Lynch, *Board of Governors of the Federal Reserve*

Dennis Mawhirter, *Board of Governors of the Federal Reserve*

David McArthur, *Board of Governors of the Federal Reserve*

Marco Migueis, *Board of Governors of the Federal Reserve*

Victor K. Ng, *Goldman Sachs*

Valerio Potì, *University College Dublin*

Bhojnarine R. Rambharat, *Office of the Comptroller of the Currency*

Debashish Sarkar, *Federal Reserve Bank of New York*

Alysa Shcherbakova, *Goldman Sachs*

Partha Sengupta, *Office of the Comptroller of the Currency*

Akhtar Siddique, *Office of the Comptroller of the Currency*

Robert Stewart, *Ex Federal Reserve Bank of Chicago*

Foreword

Modern financial institutions rely heavily on quantitative data, analysis and reporting to inform decisions on risk management, on pricing transactions, on extending credit and on establishing capital needs, among other applications. Collectively, the systems and components that link data, analysis and reporting can be referred to as quantitative "models." In practice, models undergo a life cycle of design, prototype, testing, implementation, monitoring and enhancement, perhaps with eventual replacement. A key part of this cycle is model validation, that is, review of the model, initially and over time, both by the model builders and by parties independent of model design, implementation and use. The purpose of model validation is to identify and communicate strengths and weaknesses of a given quantitative approach, and to determine whether the model is appropriate for its intended and actual use.

This book provides detailed information about model validation in the context of financial institutions. A variety of approaches are explained, compared and evaluated. As it does for models themselves, the choice of validation approach depends on the situation; there may not be a "best" practice, but there are strong practices to choose from, and experiences to guide those choices. The authors of the chapters in this book have extensive experience in the workings of financial institutions, and share here some of their unique perspectives on the many aspects of validation. This set of chapters captures a snapshot of the state of the art in a field that continues to develop.

Lest the reader have the misconception that a formal approach to model validation is a product only of efforts in the recent past, the editors demonstrate that formal thinking on the topic dates back over fifty years. Indeed, I was astonished and touched to learn from this manuscript that one of the early influential papers was published by my late father. I thank the editors for this delightful surprise, and for the opportunity to introduce this excellent volume. I am sure readers will take from this book a wealth of in-depth knowledge, and hope that they also derive some fraction of the inspiration that it gave me to make my own contributions to the field.

Christopher Finger
Associate Director, Supervision and Regulation, Board of Governors of the Federal Reserve

Acknowledgments

David acknowledges the encouragement and support from Michael Gibson and Norah Barger. Iftekhar acknowledges the continuous support from colleagues in the area of finance and the administration at the Gabelli School of Business at Fordham. Akhtar acknowledges support and encouragement over the years, especially from Campbell Harvey and Andrew Lo, as well as from colleagues in supervision and economics at the Office of the Comptroller of the Currency.

1 Common Elements in Validation of Risk Models Used in Financial Institutions*

DAVID LYNCH, IFTEKHAR HASAN AND AKHTAR SIDDIQUE

Financial institutions use of models has grown dramatically over the past few decades. The use of these models is both absolutely necessary for financial decision making and widely criticized as adding to the complexity of the financial markets. The financial crisis of 2007–2009 brought to light some of the poor modeling choices that had been made by financial institutions. Often they found themselves in terra incognita, where the models acting as their GPS for the financial markets left them stranded. A great distrust in once-trusted financial models developed. Some of the uses of poor models have been documented in news stories. Models were viewed by some as significant contributors to the problems that banks experienced during the Great Recession. Others, notably the Financial Crisis Inquiry Commission, noted the use of models, but laid the blame squarely on the people using them and the decisions they made whether guided by models or not.

Cases of models being used without adequate validation are well documented.[1] In many cases, the decision to use a model with known failings or to use a model without examining its shortcomings have led to disastrous outcomes. The human biases and failings that led to using flawed models called attention to the need for a more systematic approach to model validation.

* The views expressed in this chapter (and other chapters in the book) are those of the authors alone and do not establish supervisory policy, requirements or expectations. They also do not represent those of the Comptroller of the Currency, Board of Governors of the Federal Reserve or Bank of Finland.

[1] Examples include "Recipe for Disaster: The Formula That Killed Wall Street" Wired, Felix Salmon 2009, "Risk Management Lessons from Long Term Capital Management" European Financial Management, Phillippe Jorion, 2006.

Model risk management generally and model validation particularly have gained special attention in its aftermath. The model risk management guidance issued by US regulators (SR 11-7 from the Federal Reserve and Bulletin 2011–12 from the OCC) and European regulators (the EBA issued GL/2014/13 on Supervisory Review and Evaluation Process SREP) outline expectations from the regulators. The guidance contains perspectives on both governance and modeling. Given the regulatory requirements, validation is mandatory for almost all models used at regulated financial institutions. Even for financial institutions outside the regulated banking sector, validation of models is considered quite important.

For example, in 2018, the Securities and Exchange Commission focused on portfolio allocation models used by AEGON USA Investment Management, an asset manager with $106 billion in assets under management. The SEC issued a cease and desist order and imposed nearly $100 million in penalties against AEGON USA Investment Management, Transamerica Asset Management, Transamerica Capital and Transamerica Financial Advisors. SEC complained that the representations regarding the models were misleading because the advisers and broker-dealers "launched the products and strategies without first confirming that the models worked as intended and/or without disclosing any recognized risks associated with using the models."

To the uninitiated, the model validation process often appears to be a disorganized assortment of statistical tests and individual judgements where some aspects of a risk model are challenged and some are not. Many people within a financial organization will have a stake in the model; many of the techniques used by validators are informal and can lead to disputes between the validators and users without any clear criteria for decision making. A few attempts have been made to organize and formalize the processes within financial institutions.

Model validation has been around since the development of models. However, model validation as a formal discipline became more important with the development and increased use of more formal models. In an influential article, Naylor and Finger (1967) identify three schools of thought in approaching validation of models used in business and economics setting. These are rationalism, empiricism and positive economics. The first two schools mainly address the validity of a model's assumptions; the last addresses the validity of a model's predictions.

Rationalism, ultimately beginning with Kant's beliefs in synthetic a priori, views models as logical deductions from synthetic premises that, on their own, are not verifiable. In such an approach, validation mostly consists of examining the validity of those premises and the logical reasoning. The assumptions of a model must be clearly stated, and those assumptions must be readily accepted. Correct logical deductions from those assumptions are acceptable.

This approach seemingly makes model validation a simple process of examining the assumptions and the internal logic of the model; if these are sound the model is valid. However, this approach can take many possible sets of assumptions as valid, with several possible competing models being acceptable based on an examination of their assumptions and logic.

Under a rationalist philosophical approach, then validation is a semiformal, conversational process. A valid model is assumed to be only one of many possible ways of describing a real situation. No particular representation is superior to all others in any absolute sense, although one could prove to be more effective. No model can claim absolute objectivity, for every model carries in it the modeler's world view. In this approach, model validation is a gradual process of building confidence in the usefulness of a model; validity cannot reveal itself mechanically as a result of some formal algorithms. Validation is a matter of social conversation, because establishing model usefulness is a conversational matter.

An alternative approach to the rationalist approach is logical empiricism. In Naylor and Finger's (1967) succinct summation, validation begins with facts rather than assumptions. Observations are viewed as the primary source of truth. Empiricists regard empirical science, and not mathematics, as the ideal form of knowledge. In the words of Reichenbach (1951): "They insist that sense observation is the primary source and the ultimate judge of knowledge, and that it is self-deception to believe the human mind to have direct access to any kind of truth other than that of empty logical relations." In this view every assumption should be validated by empirical observation. More broadly, outcomes of a model are also to be validated by empirical observation.

With a logical empiricist approach then, validation is seen as a formal and "confrontational" process, in the sense that the model is confronted with empirical data. Since the model is assumed to be an objective and absolute representation of the real system, it can be either true or false. And given that the validator uses the proper validation algorithms, once the model confronts the empirical facts, its truth (or falsehood) is automatically revealed. Validity becomes a matter of formal accuracy rather than practical use.

A third school of thought on validation is based on the ability of the model to predict the behavior of the dependent variables that are treated by the model. The "Positive Economics" view is most widely associated with Milton Friedman (1953) where a model cannot be tested by comparing its assumptions with reality. A model is judged by whether its predictions are good enough for use or better than predictions from alternative models. The realism of the model's assumptions does not matter, only the accuracy of the predictions.

Finger and Naylor synthesize these three schools of thought into a single multi-stage validation process. The first stage is largely in the rationalist tradition, it involves clearly spelling out the model's assumptions and comparing them to theory, casual observations, and general knowledge. The second stage is in the empiricist tradition and involves empirically testing the model's assumptions where possible. The third stage, in the positive economics tradition, involves comparing the output of the model to the real system.

In the United States, model validation for the very complex and large models deployed in the energy domain was an important concern and several conferences organized in the late 1970s and early 1980s under the auspices of the Department of Energy and national labs were important in how model validation developed as a discipline.[2] Model validation since that time has involved the development of techniques to demonstrate the model's validity, a relaxation of the three-step approach, and an emphasis on data validity. Sargent (2011) provides an overview.

Following the three-step approach, the validation of assumptions of a model presents some difficulties. Some assumptions are to be validated on general knowledge and theory, while others are to be empirically validated. How should the model validator decide when to validate based on theory and general knowledge and when to validate based on empirical observation? Naylor and Finger provide one approach where the assumptions should be empirically tested whenever possible. This seemingly straightforward advice may prove difficult when the number

[2] See National bureau of standards (1980) for example.

of assumptions used in a complex simulation is very large or there are many models to be validated. Empirical testing is time-consuming and it may not be feasible to empirically test all assumptions.

Jarrow (2011) provides an approach to selecting which assumptions to test. He divides the assumptions into critical assumptions and robust assumptions. Conclusions of the model are not sensitive to the robust assumptions, where the implications of the model only change slightly if the assumption changes slightly. The critical assumptions are those where the implications of the model change dramatically if one of the critical assumptions change slightly. Jarrow provides the basis for a model validation process. In order to validate a model, a financial institution should (1) test all implications, (2) test all critical assumptions, (3) test all observable robust assumptions and (4) believe all non-observable robust assumptions. The model should be rejected unless all these four conditions are met.

For financial institutions, the regulatory model guidance builds on the validation approaches described above. It states "model validation is the set of processes and activities intended to verify that models are performing as expected, in line with their design objectives and business uses. Effective validation helps ensure that models are sound. It also identifies potential limitations and assumptions, and assesses their possible impact. As with other aspects of effective challenge, model validation must be performed by staff with appropriate incentives, competence, and influence." The guidance identifies three core elements;

1. evaluation of conceptual soundness including developmental evidence;
2. ongoing monitoring, including process verification and benchmarking;
3. outcomes analysis including backtesting.

The first element blends the first two steps of Naylor and Finger's three-step approach and avoids being definitive about which assumptions should be confronted with empirical facts and which assumptions are to be tested more conversationally based on theory and general knowledge. However, Jarrow's approach can provide some guidance here.

The second element, ongoing monitoring, can be viewed either in a rationalist sense or in an empirical sense. A rationalist view of ongoing monitoring is that it should be considered as a search for models that are more useful over time. Since no model is objectively the truth one should consider it a search for better assumptions and premises that provide more useful models over time. The empiricist view is that ongoing monitoring provides a set of comparisons of the model to measured variables. These comparisons provide tests of the model that allow it to be accepted or rejected.

The third element blends in the view of positive economics. How well the model describes reality as measured by its predictions takes center stage. A model that does not predict reality is not easily accepted.

It is important to note that how validation of risk management models proceeds across the various parts of a large financial institution also depends on how risk is viewed and measured in the disparate parts of the organization. Risk model validation is also affected by the development of the discipline over time. The distinct elements of how risk is perceived in different parts of the financial institution drive how risk is measured.

In general, the approaches to model validation depend on how risk is perceived. For certain risk types such as credit risk, the riskier outcome of a default is directly observable. In contrast, volatility of returns or other measures of dispersion are not easily observable. As such there are a variety of models that attempt to convert the observable outcomes into the risk measures. Models that measure portfolio risk, such as volatility and Value-at-Risk, are of the second variety.

In spite of disparate approaches taken for the risk measured for a given type of model, the underlying approaches tend to share similarities as well as suffering from similar shortcomings. Nearly all risk model validation approaches contain the three elements, albeit the relative importance of each of the elements may vary.

The model validation function is tasked with applying these core elements to each model used by a financial institution. Practitioners seem stuck using the same validation techniques that they have been using since the 1990s. At the same time, the academic literature on forecast evaluation has developed greatly over the last decades.[3] This literature provides insight on the appropriate methods to performing

[3] See the forecast evaluation chapters in the Handbook of Economic Forecasting Vol 1. (2006) Graham Elliott, Clive W. J. Granger and Alan Timmerman Eds. Elsevier.

backtesting, the comparison of model predictions with actual outcomes, and benchmarking the comparison of two models. Many of these techniques have begun to be applied to risk models by academics, but not necessarily by practitioners. In particular, forecast evaluation techniques and forecast encompassing tests developed primarily for point forecasts in the late 1990s have been adapted to cover the models used in risk management. These models include, quantile estimates like Value-at-Risk models, volatility forecasts, probability density forecasts and probability estimates of discrete events such as corporate defaults. This chapter provides a brief description of forecast evaluation and forecast encompassing, using Mincer-Zarnowitz regressions as a point of departure, showing how these statistical techniques and variants can be applied to the types of models used in risk management in large financial institutions to validate models.

1.1 Mincer-Zarnowitz Regressions

The evaluation of forecasts through regression-based techniques generally starts with Mincer and Zarnowitz (1969). The original Mincer-Zarnowitz approach is derived from the properties of optimal forecasts. The literature has established the following important properties of optimal forecasts:

(1) they are unbiased;
(2) optimal one-step-ahead forecast error is white noise and unforecastable;
(3) optimal h-step-ahead forecast errors are correlated, but at most an MA(h-1);
(4) variance of optimal forecasts increases with the forecast horizon;
(5) forecast errors should be unforecastable from all information available at the time of the forecast.

Based on these properties, the regression of the actual value on the *ex ante* forecast should have a zero intercept and a coefficient of one if the *ex ante* forecast is optimal. If the coefficients are different, it indicates systematic bias in the historical forecasts.

The procedure is fairly simple. Estimate the simple regression

$$y_{n+h} = \alpha + \beta y_{n+h|n} + e_{n+h|n}$$

That is regress, at time $n + h$, the forecasted value of y, h time periods ahead at time n using the information available at time n on the actual value of y. Then test the joint hypothesis $\alpha = 0, \text{and } \beta = 1$. If the hypothesis is rejected the forecast can be improved by adjusting the forecast using the linear equation just estimated by the Mincer-Zarnowitz regression itself to get a better forecast.

Running a Mincer-Zarnowitz regression is one way to meet the third element of the model validation guidance for US banking regulators described above. It is a form of outcomes analysis that can be applied whenever a financial institution's model generates a forecast. If one took the positive economics philosophy to an extreme, this type of testing is all that would be necessary; only the forecast matters and the realism of the model's assumptions do not.

However, there are two other elements to the validation of a model contained in US regulatory guidance. It would seem that one would have to look elsewhere to address the other elements of this guidance since at its core the Mincer-Zarnowitz regression is really a test of the models forecast. Modifications of the Mincer-Zarnowitz regression can provide insight into the other two elements contained in the regulatory guidance. While these modified regressions can help address the other two elements of the model validation guidance, it should be noted that fully addressing these elements would usually include more than just these tests.

The first element is an evaluation of the conceptual soundness of the model. As described above, this typically involves an evaluation of the assumptions of the model. A good forecast should incorporate all useful information. If there is additional information available at the time the forecast is made that could improve the forecast, then that information should be used in making the forecast. Implicitly the assumption is that this other information does not affect the forecast. One can test whether other variables are useful in making a forecast by augmenting the regression model with additional auxiliary exogeneous variables.

$$y_{n+h} = \alpha + \beta_1 y_{n+h|n} + \beta_2 x_{2|n} + \cdots + \beta_k x_{k|n} + e_{n+h|n}$$

Each of these additional variables should have no effect on the model. In this case the hypothesis to be tested is that $\alpha = 0,\ \beta_1 = 1,\ \beta_2 = 0,\ \beta_3 = 0,\ \cdots \beta_k = 0$. If some of the auxiliary exogenous variables are important, then the model can be improved by using those variables in the model producing the forecast. Furthermore, lagged variables and transformations of variables can be used as auxiliary regressors to detect whether persistence or non-linearities are important elements of the model.

The second element of the regulatory guidance includes benchmarking of the model. This generally includes a comparison of the forecast to an alternative forecast. The basic Mincer-Zarnowitz regression only includes one forecast on the right-hand side, but it would be fairly easy to expand this to include a second forecast or even more,

$$y_{n+h} = \alpha + \beta_1 y^1_{n+h|n} + \beta_2 y^2_{n+h|n} + e_{n+h|n}.$$

The superscripts 1 and 2 now refer to the two different forecasts that one is comparing in the regression. Most typically, the forecasts are unbiased so that $\alpha = 0$, and the coefficients on the forecasts are constrained to sum to 1. If we test the hypothesis that $\beta_1 = 1$ and $\beta_2 = 0$ and this hypothesis is not rejected, then we say that forecast 1 encompasses forecast 2. The second forecast adds nothing to the first forecast in its ability to make the prediction. Similarly, we can test whether forecast 2 encompasses forecast 1. Alternatively, neither forecast may encompass the other and both forecasts have important information not included in the other forecast. The encompassing regression can be seen as part of the conversational or rationalist approach to model validation where all models have validity and one is searching for more useful models over time.

The use of all these variants of the Mincer-Zarnowitz regressions can be part of a process of model improvement over time. The regressions and tests are run frequently, and the tests are used as indicators that the models need to be updated or changed. In our experience, when these types of tests are run, they are most frequently done when models are first implemented, and rarely done thereafter. As part of meeting the second element of regulators guidance on model validation, the tests should be run on a regular basis to perform ongoing monitoring of the model.

It is also important to note that the implied loss function in the original Mincer-Zarnowitz regression is a mean-squared error function. Subsequent literature has pointed out that the loss function in many forecasting contexts may not be a mean squared error function and may be asymmetric. For example, Patton and Timmerman (2006) show that the Federal Reserve's loss function on forecasts of GDP may be asymmetric. In such cases the Mincer-Zarnowitz framework has to be adjusted to accommodate the loss function that is actually used.

It is important to evaluate a model based on the loss function of the user. In many cases the loss from making an error is not well represented by a mean squared error model. In many contexts an underprediction can be more costly than an overprediction or vice versa. In these cases, the evaluation should be changed to take into account the actual form of the loss function. Elliott and Timmermann (2016) provide a thorough discussion of evaluating forecasts based on different loss functions.

Importantly, many models are estimated by minimizing something other than mean squared error in contradiction to what is assumed when using the Mincer-Zarnowitz regression to evaluate a forecast. Notably, quantile estimates, widely used for risk management, use a "check" loss function.

$$L = \tau \cdot \max(e, 0) + (1 - \tau)\max(-e, 0),$$

where τ is the quantile of interest and e is the error. Gaglione et al. (2011) provide a method for evaluating quantile estimates using quantile regression analogous to a Mincer-Zarnowitz regression. Giacomini and Komunjer (2005) provide a method for comparing two quantile forecasts and performing encompassing tests. Lopez (1999) suggests that regulators do not have a loss function for VaR models, which is a quantile estimate, based on the check function. He proposes that regulators are more concerned about losses that exceed the regulatory VaR than they are about losses within the regulatory VaR and proposes a regulatory loss function that reflects this. This provides some basis to the claim by Perignon, Deng and Wang (2008) that banks overstate their VaR models, at least during normal market times. Gordy and McNeil (2020) provide an approach to backtesting that can reflect these differences in loss functions.

In the cases of probability forecasts, often used to estimate probabilities of default, the mean squared error loss function is modified to the quadratic probability score but other loss functions surface in the literature, the logarithmic probability score and spherical probability score are examples. Clements and Harvey (2010) provide an overview of forecast encompassing tests for probability forecasts using quadratic and logarithmic probability scores.

Volatility estimates play a large role in risk management and portfolio allocation applications. In this case, the use of Mincer-Zarnowitz regressions is complicated because volatility is not directly observable. The use of proxies, such as squared returns, for volatility introduces additional noise. This means that fits to a Mincer-Zarnowitz regression are very low, which makes evaluation and encompassing tests very difficult to perform without large amounts of frequently observed data.

There are many other aspects to evaluating forecasts that are not covered here. This overview provides some insight how this econometric tool can be adapted to assist in the validation of models not just to meet regulatory requirements, but to actively seek to improve models. Even as these approaches to validation are coming into use, machine learning and artificial intelligence have brought to the fore some other aspects of model validation that are important to consider.

The advent of machine learning models and big data has raised several new validation issues related to model use in the financial industry. An important topic is the ability to explain how these large scale models arrive at their outcome. Traditional linear regression models provide a whole host of model diagnostics that allow what Efron (2020) calls attribution or significance testing. These significance tests allow an explanation of how the model arrives at a decision. Machine learning algorithms have generally sacrificed attribution to provide better predictions.

Breiman (2001) echoing a positive economics view, has taken the view that statistical modeling should start with prediction as the goal rather than a theoretic description of the data generating process. Many of the new algorithmic methods do not lend themselves to easy explanation, nonetheless good explanations need to start with good predictions. The debate seems to mirror much of the philosophical debate that opened this chapter.

Machine learning is beginning to deal with the need for explanation of the results of their prediction algorithms. The National Institute of Standards and Technology (2020) has issued a draft setting the principles for explainable Artificial Intelligence for public comment. They note that Artificial intelligence is becoming part of high stakes decision processes, and that laws and regulations in areas where these models are used require information be provided about the logic of how the decision was made and that explanations would also make artificial intelligence applications more trustworthy.

The NIST draft sets forth four principles for explainable AI. The first, characterized as the explanation principle, requires that a model delivers accompanying evidence or reasons for all outputs of the model. The second requires that the explanations be meaningful, that the explanation is understandable to individual users. The third principle requires that the explanation correctly reflects the systems process for generating the output. The last is to recognize the limits of the system so that the system only operates when there is sufficient confidence in its output. The draft notes that explanations may vary depending on the consumer. It is too much to expect a loan applicant to find the explanation that is useful to a model developer satisfying.

It is typical to consider linear regression, logistic regression and decision trees to be self-explainable. The attribution process is well understood and provides suitable explanations for why decisions are made. On the other hand, bagging, boosting, forests and neural networks are examples of modeling techniques that need further explanation and are referred to as black-box algorithms.

Certainly, there are approaches being developed to provide explanations for the black-box models that are comparable to what is provided for the self-explainable models. These generally come in two categories, global explanations and local explanations.

Global explanations are themselves models that explain the algorithm by using the black-box model to build the explanation. One global explainable algorithm is SHAP (Lundberg and Lee, 2017) based on the Shapley value from cooperative game theory. The importance of a feature is determined by its Shapley value. Additionally, partial dependence plots are often used to describe feature importance. See Friedman (2001) or Hastie, Tibshirani and Friedman (2010) for a description of partial dependence plots.

Local explanations are explanations of each decision made by a black-box model. The explanation does not need to generalize to other models. LIME, or Local Interpretable Model Agnostic Explainer, uses nearby points to build a self-explainable model. The self-explainable model is then used to provide the explanation for the black-box model.

Alternatively, and probably more applicable to explaining decisions to the user, is the use of counterfactuals (Wachter et al., 2017). In this approach the explanation provided is what inputs would have to change, and by how much, to change the outcome of the black-box model. In general, the approach is to provide the minimum change (according to some distance metric) that would change the output of the model. Thus, a loan applicant may be told that if their income was $10,000 more they would have received the loan.

While the notion of explainable models is important, the widespread use of machine learning models has raised questions of the ethical consequences of using these models to make automated decisions. In other words, if machine learning models are to be used to make consequential decisions, those decisions should be fair for different sociological groups. US courts have described two types of bias. Intended or direct discrimination would be a case of disparate treatment. A protected group is treated differently than other groups in the model. Unintentional bias occurs when a decision process has disparate impact for different groups regardless of intent. Both disparate treatment and disparate impact are illegal in the USA. See Feldman et al. (2015) for a more thorough discussion of disparate impact and the distinction between its legal and statistical description. A model could also be validated as being fair to different groups.

In the context of machine learning models, fairness has become an increasingly important issue. Kusner et al. (2018) provide a short list of definitions of fairness with respect to the treatment of protected attributes such as race or gender. Importantly we can think of several ways of making a machine learning model outcome fair. One approach is to ignore the protected attribute and not use it within the model. While this avoids disparate treatment, unintentional bias and disparate impact can still affect the treatment of individuals with different sociological attributes through variables correlated with a protected attribute.

To test disparate impact is more difficult. A naive approach may link this to the counterfactual explanation. What would happen if the protected attribute of a subject changed? Would the outcome of the model change? If not, one could view this as evidence of a lack of disparate impact. Once again, explanatory variables used in the model may serve as a proxy for a protected attribute, and changing the protected attribute does not reflect the lack of change in these underlying proxies.

Increasingly, fairness is becoming closely related to causality. Zhao and Hastie (2021) describe how causality in machine learning models is closely related to the partial dependence plots. Kusner et al. (2018) and Kilbertus et al. (2018) describe how fairness can be determined in machine learning models by a protected attribute not causing a decision in the sense of Pearl (2009). Examples are provided in both papers to describe the causal reasoning that would test for fairness in a model. In particular, they provide methods to test fairness that would allow for consideration that other variables besides the protected variable itself may be correlated with the protected variable. These have great promise in advancing the validation of the fairness of a model.

Models are being deployed in more contexts by financial institutions, and model outcomes are becoming more consequential and subject to increase scrutiny. For these reasons model validation continues to be of great importance. With the introduction of models into new areas, the task of model validation has been expanded to include more topics under the validation umbrella.

The rest of this book provides examples of validation procedures in different contexts. Since validation is difficult to separate from model development, of necessity the chapters also describe the types of models in use. As such the chapters in the book can serve as primers on the types of models that are used in the disparate risk areas such as market risk, retail credit risk, wholesale credit risk, operational risk, etc.

The book begins with several chapters on the validation of market risk models. Since the Basel Committee on Banking Supervision (1996) included backtesting as a requirement for the use of internal VaR models, the procedures have received considerable scrutiny and the models have been tested frequently. This provides a lot of experience in model validation over the years. These chapters also describe and make use of the regulatory backtesting data that has been collected by US regulators. The second part of the book consists of chapters that cover validation of lending models. The last part of the book considers difficult-to-validate models, those with long time horizons and infrequent or proxy observations, and non-traditional models.

In Chapter 2 David Lynch provides a description of what applying the full scope of tests implied by the regulatory guidance would entail for VaR modeling of trading activities. The chapter also shows how banks models fare under some tests that are implied by the regulatory guidance. Different loss functions are considered explicitly when VaR models are evaluated and compared to alternative models. Using data from 2013 to 2016, the authors find that the average exceedance rate is 0.4 percent for twenty holding companies, though there are individual banks that are as high as 2.1 percent. Thus, the results document the conservative nature of regulatory VaR models used by banks.

Chapter 3 provides a framework for adapting VaR backtesting to provide insight into backtesting failures. Conditioning backtests on circumstances of interest provides greater insight into VaR model performance. Examples of how this technique can be used are provided. It provides the techniques for getting continuous feedback on model performance under specific conditioning variables such as historical price variation, specific risk, concentration, etc. The framework introduced here can be used for other types of backtesting as well.

Chapter 4 provides an overview of testing of VaR models using probability integral transforms following Berkowitz (2001) at the trading desk level. Instead of testing just the ninety-ninth percentile, this approach tests the fit of the whole distribution of P&L. Several statistical tests for the fit of the distribution are used and compared. This provides new insight into the modeling practices at large bank holding companies. The authors find that pure exceedance-based tests can often fail to find the more nuanced model misspecifications that are uncovered via the use of probability integral transforms.

Chapter 5 provides a new test of the distribution of P&L based on empirical likelihood methods and it applies it to desk level results. The results are compared to the results of more conventional tests as well. This is an alternative to both the traditional exceedance-based tests as well as the probability integral transform-based tests used in Chapter 4. This chapter finds that relative entropy-based tests are often more discerning compared to the Anderson–Darling tests and probability integral transform (PIT) tests. Thus, empirical likelihood methods can ameliorate some of the conservatism inherent in the other metrics.

Chapter 6 reviews the performance of Bank holding company market risk models during the COVID crisis beginning March 2020. The authors first document that backtesting exceptions can predict future backtesting exceptions. Additionally, the predictability of backtesting exceptions increased during the COVID crisis. It notes that the VaR models did not capture the increase in market volatility over the crisis period particularly well; these results were previously documented in Berkowitz and O'Brien (2001) and Szerszen and O'Brien (2017). The chapter augments the typical backtesting tests with market risk factors to provide insight into the sources of backtesting failures. They find that no single market factor appeared to drive backtesting exceptions, but rather several different factors mattered. Taken together, these results show that backtesting exceptions are predictable from both recent exceptions and from recent market volatility, indicating that banks' VaR models did not react quickly enough to changes in market conditions.

Chapter 7 is on model validation in the context of stress testing, an area that is hampered because of the paucity of observations of true stress results. Klagge and Lopez provide techniques for monitoring the performance of models despite the lack of concrete stress outcomes and they provide methods to show that the models are working as intended.

Chapter 8, from Eduardo Canabarro, provides an overview of the validation of counterparty credit risk models along with how to manage them. His chapter provides the reader with the understanding of both default risk and credit valuation adjustment (CVA) risk in the context of counterparty credit risk. Canabarro provides clear explanations of the technical concepts used in this domain. He then traces the historical evolution of counterparty credit risk from its beginnings as well as how both the industry and regulators have reacted to the historical loss events such as the 1998 Russia/LTCM Crises and the 2008 Great Recession stemming from counterparty credit risk. He discusses the complex models that are deployed by the major institutions along with the shortcomings in these approaches.

Chapter 9, from Feng Li and SangSub Lee, provides a review of retail credit models and model components. The wide variety of models provide challenges for validating retail models. The chapter highlights issues regarding data techniques and data sampling issues in retail credit validation in particular. They begin with a primer on the various ways that retail credit risk models can be categorized. These include static credit and behavioral scoring models and various multi-period loss forecasting models. Then they provide details on aggregate or segmented pool-level modeling approaches such as roll-rate models versus loan-level models. Then they provide thorough descriptions of the components of the loan-level models such as the probability of default (PD) models and the link to survival models, loss given default (LGD) models and exposures. They describe modeling and validation issues arising in the various types of models in great detail as well as how to ameliorate them. As an example, they discuss in detail the use of the landmarking approach to estimate the effect of time-varying covariates.

Chapter 10 discusses the validation of the wholesale model and provides the comparative advantages and disadvantages for the various methods involved. The authors rely primarily on the expected loss approach that are commonly used at large financial institutions for both regulatory and internal risk management purposes. Given that the largest banking institutions use their obligor and facility internal risk ratings in PD and LGD quantification for Basel and also for quantification of stressed PD and LGD for CCAR and DFAST, they also address issues that arise in the validation of internal ratings systems used by banking institutions for grading wholesale loans.

Chapter 11 presents some case studies in the context of validation of wholesale models. These are of value in not only wholesale credit risk models but in other risk "stripes" as well. These describe validation for use, that is ensuring that models are validated for the use they are put to. They explain issues that can arise if models that have been developed and validated for a different purpose are repurposed. Then the case studies describe how to conduct validation of data and the distinction between internal and external data that arises in this context. The next step is validation of assumptions and methodologies. Validation of model performance is covered next with techniques such as backtesting, outcomes analysis and the use of benchmark models. The next step describes the model validation report and how to structure it.

Chapter 12 provides an overview of the issues that are encountered in the validation of models for allowance for credit losses, i.e. what is referred to as Allowance for Loan and Lease Losses. What makes them distinct is that these models typically rely on more fundamental credit loss models covered in Chapters 9 through 11. At the same time, there can be significant adaptations of the more primitive credit loss models to meet the requirements to estimate the reserves (allowances) and validation needs to take these adaptations into account. The author also compares and contrasts with CECL models. The author provides observations that would likely be quite valuable for those involved in these validations.

Chapter 13 considers the validation of operational risk models, in particular the loss distribution approach used for capital models and the regression models that are often used for stress testing. They explore the challenges associated with these models, such as the small historical length of operational risk datasets, the fat-tailed nature of operational losses, and the difficulties assigning dates to operational loss events. They propose possible approaches for robust regression modeling, such as the use of external data. They then discuss back-testing and benchmarking of operational risk models and present practical examples of benchmarks used by US regulators to benchmark operational risk models.

Chapter 14 presents a framework grounded in statistical decision theory to assess model adequacy through utility functions, offering an additional approach to supplement common model assessment criteria. Model users rely on standard measures of statistical goodness-of-fit such as AIC to evaluate models, but selecting (and subsequently validating) a model may not be straightforward if, for example, the differences in comparative metrics are marginal as this can amplify uncertainty in a model choice.

Chapter 15 provides an overview of the validation of enterprise level economic capital model. It provides an evaluation of the model against actual outcomes, despite the lack of data for models of this type. The model is evaluated under different loss functions. The chapter relies on all three methods of aggregation that are commonly practiced, namely 1) variance–covariance approach, 2) copula approach and 3) scenario-based aggregation. The authors propose an empirical statistical framework to test the performance of alternative benchmark models for economic capital estimation. They compare different copula functions and find that the T4 copula performs better than other copulas with the hypothetical bank holding company data used.

Chapter 16 provides a view on validation of interest rate risk models that is entirely in the rationalist tradition. The outcomes are largely unobservable and there is little in the way to choose among ways to model the sensitivity of deposits and other products to interest rates. The approach is then to confirm that the products are modeled correctly in the chosen framework.

Chapter 17 provides a discussion on the validation of asset management models, where the output from a model interacts quite heavily with expert judgment. These include portfolio allocation models. This is primarily descriptive rather than an empirical illustration.

References

Berkowitz, J. (2001). Testing density forecasts, with applications to risk management, *Journal of Business and Economic Statistics*, 19(4), 465–474.

Berkowitz, J. and O'Brien, J. (2002). How accurate Are Value-at-Risk models at commercial Banks? *The Journal of Finance*, 57(3), 1093–1111.

Breiman, L. (2001). Statistical modeling: The two cultures, *Statistical Science*, 16, 199–231.

Carson, E.R. and Flood, R.L. (1990). Model validation: Philosophy, methodology and examples, *Transactions of the Institute of Measurement and Control*, 12(4), 178–185. DOI:10.1177/014233129001200404.

Efron B. (2020). Prediction, estimation, and attribution, *Journal of the American Statistical Association*, 115(530), 636–655, DOI: 10.1080/01621459.2020.1762613.

Elliot, G., Granger Clive W. J. and Timmerman Alan. Eds. (2006). *Handbook of Economic Forecasting*, Vol. 1. Elsevier.

Elliott, G. and Timmermann, A. (2016). *Economic Forecasting*. Princeton University Press.

Friedman, J. H. (2001). Greedy function approximation: A gradient boosting machine, *Annals of Statistics*, 29, 1189–1232.

Gaglianone,W. P., Lima, L. R., Linton, O. and Smith, D. R. (2011). Evaluating Value-at-Risk models via quantile regression. *Journal of Business and Economic Statistics*, 29(1), 150–160.

Giacomini, R., Komunjer, I., (2005). Evaluation and combination of conditional quantile forecasts. *Journal of Business and Economic Statistics*, 23, 416–431.

Gordy, M. and McNeil, A. (2020). Spectral backtests of forecast distributions with application to risk management, *Journal of Banking and Finance*, July, Volume 116. Available at: https://doi.org/10.1016/j.jbankfin.2020.105817.

Hastie, T., Tibshirani, R. and Friedman, J. (2009). *Elements of Statistical Learning*, New York: Springer.

Jacobs, Michael and Inanoglu, Hulusi. (2009). Models for risk aggregation and sensitivity analysis: An application to bank economic capital, *Journal of Risk and Financial Management*, 2(1), 118–189.

Jarrow R. (2011). Risk management Models: Construction, *Testing, Usage Journal of Derivatives*, 18(4), 89–98.

Kilbertus, N., Carulla, M. R., Parascandolo, G., Hardt, M., Janzing, D. and Scholkopf, B. (2017). Avoiding discrimination through causal reasoning, in *Advances in Neural Information Processing Systems*, 656–666.

Kusner, M. J., Loftus, J., Russell, C. and Silva, R. (2017). Counterfactual fairness, in *Advances in Neural Information Processing Systems*, 4066–4076.

Lopez, A. J. (1999). Regulatory evaluation of Value-at-Risk models. *Journal of Risk*, 1, 37–64.

Lundberg, S. M. and Lee, S.-I. (2017). A unified approach to interpreting model predictions. In Guyon, I., Luxburg, U. V., Bengio, S., Wallach, H., Fergus, R., Vishwanathan, S., and Garnett, R., eds., *Advances in Neural Information Processing Systems*, 30, 4765–4774. Curran Associates, Inc.

Mincer, J. and Zarnowitz V. (1969). The evaluation of economic forecasts. In J. Mincer (ed.) *Economic Forecasts and Expectations*. National Bureau of Economic Research, New York.

Naylor, Thomas H. and Finger, J. M. (1967). Verification of computer simulation models, *Management Science* , Oct., Vol. 14, B92–B106.

O'Brien J. and Szerszen P. (2017). An evaluation of bank measures for market risk before during and after the financial crisis, *Journal of Banking & Finance*, 80, July, 215–234.

Patton, A. and Timmermann, A. *Testing forecast optimality under unknown loss, working paper*, University of California San Diego, 2006.

Pearl, J. (2009). *Causality: Models, Reasoning and Inference*. Cambridge University Press.

Pérignon, C., Deng, Z. Y. and Wang, Z. Y. (2008). Do banks overstate their Value-at-Risk? *Journal of Banking and Finance*, 32, 783–794.

Phillips, Jonathon P., Hahn, Carina A., Fontana, Peter C., Broniatowski, David A. and Przybocki, Mark A. (2020). *Four Principles of Explainable Artificial Intelligence* National Institute of Standards and Technology, Draft.

Popper, Karl, *The Logic of Scientific Discovery*, Julius Springer, Hutchinson & Co, 1959.

Reichenbach, Hans, *The Rise of Scientific Philosophy*, University of California Press, 1951.

Ribeiro, M. T., Singh, S. and Guestrin, C. (2016). Why should I trust you?" Explaining the predictions of any classifier. In *KDD 2016: Proceedings of the 22nd ACM SIGKDD Conference on Knowledge Discovery and Data Mining*, San Francisco, CA, USA. ACM.

Sargent, Robert G. (2011). Verification and validation of simulation models, Proceedings of the 2011 Winter Simulation Conference.

Validation and assessment of energy models: Proceedings of a symposium held at the National Bureau of Standards, Gaithersburg, MD, May 19–21, 1980.

Wachter, S., Mittelstadt, B. and Russell, C. (2017). Counterfactual explanations without opening the black box: Automated decisions and the GDPR. *Harvard Journal of Law and Technology*, 31, 841.

Zhao, Qingyuan and Hastie, Trevor. (2021). Causal interpretations of black-box models, *Journal of Business & Economic Statistics*, 39(1), 272–281, DOI:10.1080/07350015.2019.1624293.

2 *Validating Bank Holding Companies' Value-at-Risk Models for Market Risk*

DAVID LYNCH*

2.1 Introduction

The Basel Committee on Banking Supervision established the use of Value-at-Risk (VaR) models for capitalizing banks' trading activities in 1996. At the same time as they introduced VaR models for regulatory capital, they required that banks backtest their VaR models using a stoplight test based on the Kupiec (1995) testing procedure. If a bank's loss exceeds their VaR forecast made the previous day, then there is an exception. Banks must apply a multiplier to their VaR, which increases with the number of exceptions they experienced over the past year, in order to determine their capital requirements. For this reason, backtesting has played an especially important role in validating VaR models for market risk. More recently, the Basel Committee on Banking Supervision has switched to the use of expected shortfall (BIS 2019) with expected implementation in 2025.

This emphasis on the role of backtesting VaR models in capital determinations has been an important element of model validation for market risk models, and there is no doubt that it will continue to play an important role. However, there are other elements of validating VaR models that financial institutions should pay attention to, but have not emphasized given the importance of backtesting in the regulatory framework. Academic analysis has improved the tools available for model validation of trading models, including backtesting, and these tools should be applied within financial institutions.

In addition to the Basel backtesting requirements, the US banking agencies have issued guidance on model validation that contains three key components.[1] This guidance applies to all models, including

* Federal Reserve Board. The views expressed in this paper are the author's own and do not represent the views of the Board of Governors or the Federal Reserve System.

[1] Note FRB OCC and EU requirements.

trading models. The Basel requirements on backtesting are simply more specific on this single aspect regarding the validation of capital models for trading. The guidance covers three types of testing that should be performed by banks. First, banks must assess the conceptual soundness of the model. This includes reviewing data, assumptions and techniques used in the model, and performing sensitivity analysis on those elements of the model where warranted. Second, the banks must perform an outcomes analysis, which could include backtesting. The third aspect is the benchmarking of models or a comparison of the model to other models. Banks have traditionally emphasized backtesting for their trading activities, but the other aspects of model validation are applicable to trading as well.

In this chapter, we provide a short overview of the VaR models commonly used at banks. We then review how these three aspects of validation can be applied to VaR models of banks' trading activities. In the case of backtesting and benchmarking we show how banks' VaR models fare under some of the backtesting and benchmarking tests.

2.2 VaR Models

There are many treatments that describe the implementation of VaR models. Jorion (2006), Christoffersen (2012), Andersen et al. (2006) are examples of how to construct a VaR model. Nieto and Ruiz (2016) provide an overview of both VaR models and their testing. The summary description of VaR models here is to provide background for understanding the validation of those models at financial institutions. For these purposes VaR is defined as follows:

$$P\left(\Delta V_{P,t+N} \leq -VaR_{t+N}^{1-c} \vert \mathcal{F}_t\right) = 1 - c.$$

The probability that the change in the value of portfolio $P, \Delta V_{P,t+N}$, from t to $t+N$ is less than or equal to the negative of the VaR using the information $\mathcal{F}_t$ available at time t is equal to $1-c$, where c is the coverage level of the VaR.[2] Under the Basel requirements from 1996, N is 10 days and c is 99% (thus the superscript to the VaR represents

[2] VaR models are usually defined by their coverage ratio, the probability that the financial institution will not experience a loss larger than the VAR rather than the probability of seeing an exception 1–*c*. Furthermore, VaR is usually reported as a positive number even though it represents a loss.

the probability that a loss exceeds the negative value of VaR, in this case 1%). The change in the value of the portfolio is the sum of the changes in the value of the portfolio components or positions:[3]

$$\Delta V_{P,t+N} = \sum_{i\epsilon P} \Delta V_{i,t+N}.$$

In most types of VaR models, a pseudo history of changes in the value of the portfolio is necessary. Generally, that history is constructed of one-day changes in value of the portfolio so that $N = 1$ and the history is constructed based on the composition of the current portfolio V, at time T. In this case the pseudo history is described by

$$\left\{\Delta V_t^T\right\}_{t=1}^{T} \equiv \left\{\sum\nolimits_{i\epsilon P} V_{iT} r_{it}\right\}_{t=1}^{T},$$

where r_{it} are the returns on each date in the history for the positions. The construction of this pseudo history is not a trivial task and more will be said about this later. In fact, supervisory reviews spend a lot of effort ensuring that this pseudo history is accurate.

The most straightforward way to turn this pseudo history into a VaR model is to use it to generate a distribution of returns and select the return representing the appropriate quantile for the VaR model. This is the historic simulation method:

$$HS - VaR_{T+1}^{1-c} = -Q_{1-c}\left(\left\{\Delta V_t^T\right\}_{t=1}^{T}\right).$$

One orders the valuation change of the pseudo history from lowest to highest and selects the c^*T ranked return, interpolating if necessary. Pritsker (1997) provides a critique of the use of historic simulation, noting that it is not very responsive to recent volatility in portfolio valuations, and Escanciano and Pei (2012) provide a critique of unconditional backtesting of historic simulation. Nonetheless, historic

[3] Academic papers usually perform analysis on the returns or log returns of a portfolio. Practitioners usually perform analysis on the change in value of the portfolio – its profit or loss. We emphasize the analysis on the profit or loss in this chapter rather than returns so that it is more directly applicable to practitioners at financial firms and can be applied to data reported by banks. This does not come without difficulties, notably all tests require that the variable of interest is i.i.d or that the variable be transformed to i.i.d. When P&L is used directly, and banks change their trading portfolio frequently, the use of P&L without transformation violates this condition.

simulation remains the most widely used method of computing VaR at commercial banks.

To address the lack of responsiveness, GARCH models are often used to make the volatility of the portfolio valuation changes depend on recent changes in the pseudo history. In this case

$$\Delta V_{P,t+1} = \mu_t + \sigma_t z_t \quad z_t \sim g(0,1) \tag{2.1}$$

and

$$\sigma_t^2 = \omega + \sum_{j=1}^{p} \alpha_j \Delta V_{t-j}^2 + \sum_{k=1}^{q} \beta_k \sigma_{t-k}^2, \tag{2.2}$$

with the parameters estimated from the pseudo history. g is the general probability density function with mean 0 and variance of 1, which is not necessarily the normal distribution. The Garch VaR is then determined by

$$G_{p,q} - VaR_{T+1}^{1-c} = \sigma_{T+1} G_c^{-1} - \mu_t. \tag{2.3}$$

Oftentimes, μ_t is assumed to be zero. G_c^{-1} is the inverse cumulative density function of g evaluated at c, or, equivalently, the cth quantile of G. An important special case of the GARCH VaR is riskmetrics VaR (Riskmetrics 1997), where g is assumed to be a standard normal distribution and a restricted ARCH (1,1) is used to estimate the variance of the pseudo history of changes in the portfolio value.

$$\sigma_t^2 = \lambda\, \sigma_{t-1}^2 + (1-\lambda) \Delta V_{t-1}^{T^2},$$
$$RM - VaR_{T+1}^{c} = \sigma_{T+1} \Phi_c^{-1},$$

where Φ_c^{-1} represents the cth quantile of the standard normal distribution. A drawback of the GARCH approach is that one has to specify the distribution of z_t. To avoid making this distributional assumption one can get the cth quantile from the pseudo history of shocks z_t. One orders the shocks and selects the 1 – cth smallest. This is the filtered historic simulation (FHS) method of Barone-Adesi et al. (1999). The FHS Value-at-Risk is given by

$$F_{p,q} - VaR_{T+1}^{1-c} = -\sigma_{T+1} Q_{1-c}(\{z_t\}) - \mu_{T+1} \tag{2.4}$$

which is essentially taking the (1–C)*T lowest z_t and multiplying it by the current volatility from the GARCH model to calculate the VaR. The FHS method allows the model to capture the dependence in volatility without making a distributional assumption regarding the error terms.

These are the main methods to estimate a VaR using a univariate approach. In many cases a more disaggregated approach is desireable and rather than estimate a univariate model, a multivariate model is estimated, with the pseudo history decomposed into the pseudo history of the portfolios' individual positions. This requires estimating the volatility of each individual position as well as the correlation between the positions in the portfolio. This can become intractable quite quickly as the number of positons in the portfolio grows. See Andersen et al. (2006) or Christoffersen (2012) for an exposition of extending the univariate approaches described here to a multivariate model.

2.3 Conceptual Soundness

The banking guidance on model validation requires a review of conceptual soundness of the model. This requires the validator to determine whether the model assumptions, techniques and data used are appropriate. In most cases this is accomplished through a narrative provided by the validator. As one builds a large-scale VaR model, numerous modeling decisions are made. Model Validation is a review of those decisions and an assessment of those choices and how realistic they are. At its core, a very basic decision is whether the model is suitable for the purpose it is developed for. In the case of VaR models, their basic purpose is to help the firm manage the risk of its positions; they have other uses such as for capital calculations, but these are perhaps ancillary to the risk management purpose.

In an early evaluation of VaR models, Berkowitz and O'Brien (2002) compared banks' VaR models to a simple model based on a GARCH model of the actual profit and loss (P&L) of firms. They found that the GARCH model of actual P&L outperformed the VaR model used by the commercial banks. It would be tempting to conclude that the GARCH on actual P&L should be used in favor of the banks' VaR models. Lo (2001) and Jorion (2007) have an exchange regarding VaR models that illustrates the danger of using a P&L-based VaR for a dynamic portfolio. Lo describes the profitability and risk of a hypothetical hedge fund and capital decimation partners, and shows that it appears to make good returns on low risk based on those profitability numbers. The dynamic strategy consists of selling out of the money puts. The risk measures do not recognize the dynamic nature of the portfolio. Jorion shows how the risk measures would change if the VaR incorporated positional information, essentially recomputing the pseudo history of the change in the portfolio values whenever the portfolio changes to reflect the change in positons. Doing this more accurately reflects the riskiness of selling deep out of the money puts and reflects when the portfolio becomes more risky due to a change in positions.

For a risk manager and for traders in general, it is important to reflect how a change in the firm's positions is reflected in VaR. Consider a risk manager who has told a trader to reduce the risk of their portfolio measured by VaR. The trader dutifully reduces their positons. If the risk manager bases the risk on the actual P&L history, the reduction in positions does not result in a reduction in VaR since the actual P&L history is unaffected by the change in positions. On the other hand, a VaR model that is based on the pseudo history of P&L described above would show a reduction of risk as the positions (V_T) would have changed. This highlights a crucial aspect of VaR modeling; its key purpose is to show how risk changes when positions change. VaR models that cannot be used to show how risk changes when positions change are not "fit for purpose" and thus fail a crucial conceptual soundness test in the model validation process.

Beyond the consideration of how the model will be used, the conceptual soundness of the model can be considered using more quantitative tests. These include sensitivity analysis that can show the effect of data limitations or choices and provide statistical confidence intervals around VaR estimates. These can answer fundamental questions regarding the performance of the VaR model and can also assess the severity of data problems and estimation errors. These two tests shed light on the degree to which the model can be used to help manage positions.

2.4 Sensitivity Analysis

Since the model is designed to show risk changes when positions change, it would be important to check the sensitivity of the VaR model to changes in positions. Garman (1997), Hollerbach (2003), Tasche (2000) and Gourieroux et al. (2000) describe methods to decompose and perform sensitivity analysis for VaR models. In the context of the models described above, this provides a way to check the assumptions or simplifications made in developing the pseudo history of the portfolios' value changes. This is especially true for the omissions in the pseudo history. One would like to know that the simplification or omission did not materially affect the VaR model's output. In fact, supervisors around the world have begun to have financial institutions track and quantify the risks that are not included in their VaR model and to track their use of data proxies. Generally the methods to quantify and track these omitted risks are ad hoc. However, sensitivity analysis provides a consistent framework for making the assessment.

Value-at-Risk is linear homogeneous in positions. It therefore satisfies the Euler equation

$$VaR(V_{PT}) = \sum_{i \in P} \frac{\partial VaR}{\partial V_{iT}} V_{iT}.$$

Each term on the right-hand side is known as the component VaR and the derivative, $\partial VaR/\partial V_{it}$, is known as the marginal VaR. The marginal VaR shows how VaR would change due to a small change in the size of the position and is related to the regression coefficient of a regression of the change in value of the whole portfolio on the change in the value of the position:

$$\Delta V_{it} = \alpha + \beta_i \Delta V_{Pt} + \varepsilon_t, \tag{2.5}$$

which leads to a formula for each component VaR based on the position

$$component_i VaR(V_{PT}) = VaR(V_{PT}) w_i \beta_i.$$

Thus, the sensitivity of VaR to the position is dependent on the share of the position in the portfolio, w_i, and the sensitivity of the position value to the overall portfolio value. If the financial institution has a concern regarding some choice it has made regarding the valuation of a particular position, this analysis can help show how sensitive the VaR is to the valuation choice.

This framework provides some mechanism to assess the importance of a position in the VaR. However, it can be difficult to apply in circumstances that frequently occur at trading institutions. First, Equation 2.5 requires that you have a full time series of the change in value of the positions. Often the financial institution wants to know the impact of the position because this valuation data is missing or scarce.

Equation 2.5 may be difficult to estimate due to the data scarcity. A proxy may be used, but a proxy may not be as volatile as the original position or may be less correlated with the portfolio than the original position and thus understates the contribution to VaR. With scarce data, the regression approach described is difficult to implement. Tasche (2000) and Hallerbach (2003) provide a method for when the regression approach will not work that is especially easy to implement when using historic simulation.

Tasche and Hollerbach show that linear homogeneity implies

$$VaR_{PT} = \Delta V^*_{PT} = \sum_{i \in P} E\left(\Delta V_{iT} | \Delta V_{PT} = \Delta V^*_{PT}\right),$$

when the VaR is determined by a scenario where ΔV^*_{PT} is the change in portfolio value. This change in portfolio value can be decomposed into the sum of the expected changes in value of the positions in the portfolio, conditional on realizing the change in value of the whole portfolio equal to the VaR. The component VaR for each position can be estimated by the change in value each position would have experienced on the day that determines the historic simulation VaR scenario. In the case of a "missing" position this reduces the problem of estimating the component VaR to observing how much it would have lost on the day that determines the VaR. This single observation is less reliable than an estimate based on multiple observations, so the average of the ordered observations near the HS-VAR may be used instead.

This is the nature of estimating the omitted risks in VaR. If you have sufficient data to estimate it accurately, it is likely that the omitted risk would be included already. If you don't have much data, it isn't in the VaR and it is difficult to make a precise estimate of how sensitive the overall VaR is to the omission. The process is quite general and can be applied in many cases where there is an omission from the valuation of the portfolio. For example, the portfolio valuation may rely on a Taylor series expansion with only the first few terms used. The omission of the "next" higher order term may be estimated in an analogous fashion.

In practice, the sensitivity depends on the portfolio composition. The portfolio composition of a large trading organization may change rapidly. For this reason many supervisors ask for the risk not in VaR to be estimated based on both the component VaR and the stand alone VaR so that they get a sense of the effect of the omission that is independent of the portfolio.

This process of examining the pseudo history of changes in the portfolio value can be viewed as an application of the validation process described by Jarrow (2011) whereby the model is examined to see if it is sensitive to changes in assumptions. In this case the assumption that particular positions or risk factors being omitted is immaterial is being tested by this sensitivity analysis. The process also provides a more rigorous way of prioritizing changes to the model to include more risk factors or higher order terms.

2.5 Confidence Intervals for VaR

When estimating a Value-at-Risk figure for a portfolio it is natural to ask about the accuracy of the estimate. The statistical way to answer this question is to place confidence intervals around the estimate whereby the true value of the VaR estimate should be within the confidence interval a stated high percentage of the time. This provides an assessment of the estimation risk in the VaR. In many contexts an assessment of the estimation risk is standard and widely expected. However, despite VaR being an inherently statistical framework, most financial institutions do not calculate the confidence levels for their VaR estimates. This is strange and it seems that it would be an important aspect of model validation of VaR models and a test that should be carried out routinely. Jorion (1996) describes a method for estimating the confidence interval of a VaR model based on the asymptotic standard error of a quantile.

$$SE\left(VaR_{PT}^{1-c}\right) = \sqrt{\frac{c(1-c)}{Tf\left(VaR_{PT}^{1-c}\right)^2}}$$

This is a seemingly straightforward calculation with VaR, T, and c known. The main issue is evaluating the probability density function at the VaR estimate. In most cases one would impose a distributional assumption on the change in portfolio values and proceed to calculate confidence intervals. However, it is a stylized fact that financial returns are non-normal so imposing a normal distribution would probably be a mistake. Furthermore, as Jorion notes, it may be desirable to base the confidence interval on more than the single point of the quantile estimate and instead estimate the confidence interval based on a calculation of the variance of the distribution of pseudo returns. The trick in applying a formula like the one proposed by Jorion is clearly in determining *f()* and one could proceed along those lines. Alternatively, one could apply a more non-parametric approach. Two approaches in the academic literature are the use of order statistics (Dowd 2006) or the use of bootstrap techniques (Christoffersen and Goncalves 2006).

The use of order statistics starts with the pseudo history of portfolio value changes, $\{\Delta V_t^T\}_{t=1}^T$ and reorders them from lowest to highest so that $\Delta V_{(1)}^T \leq \Delta V_{(2)}^T \leq \Delta V_{(3)}^T \ldots \leq \Delta V_{(T)}^T$. The probability that at least r of the observations in the sample do not exceed a specified ΔV is given by the distribution

$$G_r(\Delta V) = \sum_{j=r}^{T} \binom{T}{j} [F(\Delta V)]^j [1 - F(\Delta V)]^{n-j}$$

where $F(\Delta V)$ is the cumulative density function of the observations of the change in portfolio value. Since VaR is one particular value of ΔV the formula applies to the negative of VaR. To create 90% confidence intervals around VaR one sets G_r(VaR) equal to 0.05 and 0.95 to create the lower and upper bound of the confidence interval, with r set to 0.05T and 0.95T respectively. One then numerically solves for F_l for the lower bound and F_u for the upper bound.

How one proceeds from that point depends on the type of VaR model. For a historical simulation VaR, one takes the confidence interval as $\left(\Delta V_{(F_l \Delta \cdot T)}^T, \Delta V_{(F_u \Delta \cdot T)}^T\right)$ from the ordered pseudo history. For a GARCH model one uses the estimated variance and distributional assumptions to specify $F(\Delta V)$. The ΔV that corresponds to the upper and lower bound is then taken from that function.

Christoffersen and Goncalves (2005) propose to use bootstrap procedures to calculate confidence intervals for VaR estimates and provide methods for historic simulation, GARCH(1,1), and filtered historic simulation methods. These procedures are fairly straightforward to apply for univariate estimates, although potentially computationally expensive.

To bootstrap 90% confidence intervals for a historic simulation VaR, one draws observations from the pseudo history $\{\Delta V_t^T\}_{t=1}^T$ with replacement to generate a bootstrapped pseudo history $\{\Delta V_t^{S_1}\}_{t=1}^T$. The VaR is then calculated from the bootstrapped sample,

$$HS - VaR^{1-c}_{S_1+1} = -Q_{1-c}\left(\left\{\Delta V^{S_1}_t\right\}^T_{t=1}\right).$$

Repeat this procedure generating a bootstrap sample S_i and a VaR for the bootstrap sample, B times to generate $HS - VaR^{1-c}_{S_i+1}$ for $i = 1$ to B. The distribution of VaRs is the sampling distribution and the confidence interval can be calculated directly from the ordered VaR values as the fifth percentile and ninety-fifth percentile of the bootstrapped VaRs. More generally, to calculate a confidence interval of CI, the confidence interval will be given by:

$$\left[Q_{CI/2}\left(\left\{HS - VaR^{1-c}_{(i)}\right\}^B_{i=1}\right), Q_{1-CI/2}\left(\left\{HS - VaR^{1-c}_{(i)}\right\}^B_{i=1}\right)\right] \tag{2.6}$$

This approach to calculating confidence intervals is nonparametric like the calculation of historic simulation VaR itself. However, it does assume independence of the changes in portfolio value over time and thus does not reflect possible dependence in returns over time.

The GARCH VaR accounts for the dependence of changes in portfolio values. The bootstrap approach must be designed to mimic the dependence properties of these changes and it is easiest to resample from an IID series to generate the bootstrap sample. In the case of a GARCH VaR model, z_t in Eq. 2.1 is IID and Eqs. 2.1 and 2.2 are used to generate samples of $\Delta V_{P,s_i}$ and σ_{s_i}.

It would be tempting to calculate the bootstrapped VaR for the sample from Eq. 2.3 directly. However, Eq. 2.3 is subject to estimation risk and we would also like to account for that in the bootstrapped confidence level. To do this, Eq. 2.2 is re-estimated for the bootstrapped sample using $\Delta V_{P,s_i}$. New estimates of $\Delta V^*_{P,s_i}$ and $\sigma^*_{s_i}$ are generated based on a re-estimated equation. The GARCH VaR for the samples are then re-calculated based on this.

$$G_{p,q} - VaR^{1-c}_{T+1} = \sigma^*_{T+1} G^{-1}_c - \mu \tag{2.7}$$

This process is repeated B times and the confidence interval CI as it was for historic simulation

$$\left[Q_{CI/2}\left(\left\{G_{p,q} - VaR^{1-c}_{(i)}\right\}^B_{i=1}\right), Q_{1-CI/2}\left(\left\{G_{p,q} - VaR^{1-c}_{(i)}\right\}^B_{i=1}\right)\right] \tag{2.8}$$

In the case of a Filtered Historic Simulation model, one does not make the parametric assumption in Eq. 2.7. Instead, one also keeps re-estimated residuals $z^*_{s_i}$ and recalculates the VaR for each sample according to Eq. 2.4. The confidence interval is then calculated similarly to Eqs. 2.6 and 2.9.

More recently, methods of providing confidence intervals for VaR models using the empirical likelihood have been proposed. Chan et al. (2007) provide a method for GARCH models. Gong Li and Peng (2009) provide a method for ARCH models.

As a basis of comparison, in Table 2.1 we calculate confidence intervals for one-day 99% VaR based on the returns of the S&P 500. We look at different methods to compute the VaR (historic simulation, GARCH, and FHS) and different methods to compute the confidence intervals over different time intervals to compare the methods. The time periods used are a recent one-year time period, a longer time period, a one-year stress period, and a three-year stress period.

The results indicate first that confidence intervals are not symmetric and, as expected, that more data used to estimate VaR leads to tighter confidence intervals. Second for Historic simulation VAR, while there is a difference in the confidence intervals calculated using order statistics and the bootstrap, there does not appear to be convincing evidence that one method or the other produces tighter confidence intervals on a consistent basis. Historic simulation VaR has particularly wide confidence intervals during stress periods. Most notable are the narrow confidence intervals for filtered historic simulation, suggesting that it provides more efficient estimates of VaR.

Few Bank Holding Companies routinely calculate confidence intervals for their VaR estimates. This is somewhat puzzling since the methods for computing them are well established and there is significant value in determining the accuracy of a VaR model. We do not have the pseudo history of banks' own P&L used to calculate their VaRs. Following Berkowitz and O'Brien, we can use the VaR calculated on the profit and loss of the banks' trading portfolio (the change in value of the portfolio of trading positions held at the end of the previous day) as a comparison rather than use the pseudo history of the P&L. As discussed earlier, this VaR is not suitable for risk management, but can be useful as a description of the accuracy of Bank Holding companies' VaR estimates based on P&L. Table 2.2 shows a comparison of confidence interval estimates for two VaRs calculated

Table 2.1. *Confidence intervals for one-day 99% VaR under different methods.*

VaR method	Cl method	N	Date range	VaR	95% Cl		Cl as a percentage of VAR	
HS	Bootstrap	250	5/2016–5/2017	1.725	1.347	1.98	21.9	14.8
HS	Bootstrap	9424	1/1980–5/2017	2.878	2.727	3.138	5.2	9.0
HS	Bootstrap	253	8/2008–8/2009	8.439	5.536	10.58	34.4	25.4
HS	Bootstrap	755	8/2006–8/2009	5.662	4.103	6.271	27.5	10.8
HS	Order	250	5/2016–5/2017	1.725	1.358	1.761	21.3	2.1
HS	Order	9424	1/19 80–5/2017	2.878	2.729	3.137	5.2	9.0
HS	Order	253	8/2008–8/2009	8.439	5.008	10.24	40.7	21.3
HS	Order	755	8/2006–8/2009	5.662	4.001	6.171	29.3	9.0
Garch	Order	250	5/2016–5/2017	1.109	0.846	1.152	23.7	3.9
Garch	Order	9424	1/19 80–5/2017	1.11	0.903	1.252	18.6	12.8
Garch	Order	253	8/2008–8/2009	2.91	2.443	3.3	16.0	13.4
Garch	Order	755	8/2006–8/2009	2.815	2.579	3.101	8.4	10.2
FHS	Order	250	5/2016–5/2017	1.205	1.188	1.222	1.4	1.4
FHS	Order	9424	1/19 80–5/2017	1.324	1.314	1.334	0.8	0.8
FHS	Order	253	8/2008–8/2009	3.109	3.001	3.136	3.5	0.9
FHS	Order	755	8/2006–8/2009	3.239	3.158	3.284	2.5	1.4

Table 2.2. ***One-day 99% VaR confidence intervals on Hypothetical P&L as a percentage of the VaR estimate.***

	Lower bound			Upper bound		
VaR method	Minimum (%)	Median (%)	Maximum (%)	Minimum (%)	Median (%)	Maximum (%)
HS	8.50	19.60	50.90	7.20	15.92	34.00
GARCH(1,1)	0.01	1.20	7.40	0.10	2.30	9.70

on banks' history of actual P&L. The results indicate much narrower confidence intervals for the Garch VaR than for Historic simulation VaR. While not conclusive, these results suggest that filtered historic simulation would provide improved estimates of VaR for banks that do not use that technique.

2.6 Backtesting

The second aspect of model validation is to compare predicted outcomes to realized outcomes, otherwise known as backtesting. Banks have been backtesting their VaR models for their trading portfolios since 1996 when backtesting was included by the Basel Committee in regulatory capital requirements. Berkowitz and O'Brien (2002) summarize the early results of backtesting VaR models by banks. They found the VaR modeling to be lacking, notably that banks' losses that exceeded VaR occurred infrequently and occurred in clusters, demonstrating dependence. Perignon and Smith (2006, 2010a, 2010b) find similar results and provide possible explanations for the conservative VaR models. Szerszen and O'Brien (2017) find that Banks VaR models were conservative both before and after the financial crisis, but were not conservative during the financial crisis.

This testing is predicated on banks reporting their backtesting results either to their supervisors or publicly. In most cases, banks have reported their actual profit and loss values. In making the comparison of *ex ante* VaR to *ex post* profit and loss, the profit and loss includes components of profit and loss that perhaps should not be included in the backtest. Fresard, Perignon and Wilhelmsson (2011) describe the effect of including fee income, commissions and other components on backtesting results in a simulation model and include this as a possible explanation for the backtests showing the VaR models are conservative. More recently US bank holding companies operating under the Basel 2.5 trading requirements have reported at the subportfolio level comparsons of VaR to the profit or loss that banks would experience if they had held their portfolios at the end of the previous day fixed and held it for one day. In this regard the test has improved in that the profit and loss used for the comparison is closer to what banks VaR models are designed to capture. For example, fees and commissions are not expected to be part of the VaR model and should not be part of the profit and loss that a bank backtests against either if one is testing the accuracy of the model. Much of the research conducted on actual 'backtesting include these components in the banks' profit and loss.

Kupiec (1995) and Christoffersen (1998) provide the early work on backtesting procedures. At its simplest, backtesting starts with the observation that a VaR with 99% coverage should on average see a violation of VaR 1% of the time. This is the basis of the unconditional coverage test of Kupiec and the BCBS backtesting procedures. Christoffersen includes a test of independence and conditional coverage. The test for conditional coverage is a test that a (conditional) VaR with 99% coverage if properly specified should have a probability of a violation of VaR 1% of the time at any point in time, not just on average.

To create the test for VaR evaluation, one needs to count the number of times that a loss exceeds the VaR threshold. Specifically, one creates the indicator variable for exceedances that takes a value of 1 when VaR is exceeded and is zero otherwise.

$$I_{t+1} = \begin{cases} 1 \text{ if } \Delta V_{P,t+1} < -VaR_t^{1-c} \\ 0 \text{ otherwise} \end{cases}$$

The test for unconditional coverage is a test of whether the probability of violation is equal to 1 minus the coverage rate of the VaR.

$$P(I_{t+1} = 1) = 1 - c$$

It does not depend on the information at time t. In contrast, the test for conditional coverage is a test of whether the probability of a violation is one minus the coverage rate taking into account all information available at time t.

$$P(I_{t+1} = 1|\mathcal{F}_t) = 1 - c$$

The null hypothesis for the unconditional backtest is that the indicator variable is independently and identically distributed over time as a Bernoulli variable. We denote the number of times that the indicator takes a value of zero and one as T_0 and T_1 (which sum to the backtesting sample T) and then the likelihood function for an observed fraction of violations π in the unconditional test is

$$L(\pi) = (1 - \pi)^{T_0}(\pi)^{T_1}.$$

The fraction of violations is estimated from the backtesting sample as T_1/T and this is compared to the expected number of violations, 1 − c from the VaR model in a likelihood ratio test.

$$LR_{uc} = -2\ln\left[L(1-c)/L(T_1/T)\right] \sim \chi_1^2$$

This provides a test of the whether the model has the correct coverage on average. However, if the violations cluster around a point in time, then the risk of extreme losses during a time when the exceedences are more likely would be problematic. If the exceedences were independent over time, then there would be no clustering and no concern over the effect of clustering.

Christoffersen (1998) provides a test of independence that serves as a bridge to a test of conditional coverage, which is a joint test of proper coverage and independence. Christoffersen considers a first order markov chain as the model of the dependence structure. In this case, the violations can be described by a simple transition probability matrix where π_{ij} is the probability of being in state j today conditional on being in state i the previous day.

$$\Pi_1 = \begin{bmatrix} \pi_{00} & \pi_{01} \\ \pi_{10} & \pi_{11} \end{bmatrix} = \begin{bmatrix} 1 - \pi_{01} & \pi_{01} \\ 1 - \pi_{11} & \pi_{11} \end{bmatrix}$$

The test for independence is that $\pi_{01} = \pi_{11} = T_1/T$ where T_1 qnd T have the same meaning as in the unconditional backtest, so that past exceedences do not affect the current probability of an exceedance. Extending the notation from the unconditional backtest, let T_{ij} where i, $j = 0{,}1$ represent the number of observations in the sample with a j followed by an i. The maximum likelihood estimates for π_{01} and π_{11} and the likelihood function are:

$$\hat{\pi}_{01} = {}^{T_{01}}\!/_{(T_{00}+T_{01})}$$
$$\hat{\pi}_{11} = {}^{T_{11}}\!/_{(T_{10}+T_{11})}$$
$$L_c(\Pi_1) = (1-\pi_{01})^{T_{00}}\pi_{01}{}^{T_{01}}(1-\pi_{11})^{T_{10}}\pi_{11}{}^{T_{11}}.$$

The likelihood ratio test for independence is then given by

$$LR_{ind} = -2ln\left[{}^{L\left(\frac{T_1}{T}\right)}\!/_{L_c(\hat{\Pi}_1)}\right] \sim \chi_1^2,$$

where $L_c(\hat{\Pi}_1)$ uses the maximum likelihood estimates described above. The test does not consider whether the coverage level is correct. The test for conditional coverage combines the unconditional coverage test and the independence test and conducts the joint test of whether the number of violations is correct and if the violations are independent. In this case we test whether $\pi_{01} = \pi_{11} = 1 - c$. The likelihood ratio test for conditional coverage is

$$LR_{cc} = -2ln\left[{}^{L(1-c)}\!/_{L_c(\hat{\Pi}_1)}\right] \sim \chi_2^2,$$

and we note that $LR_{cc} = LR_{uc} + LR_{ind}$.

Pajhede (2017) provides a discussion of generalizing the conditional coverage test. Notably the idea of allowing for greater than first order dependence in the transition probability matrix is explored. Testing for *Kth* order dependence would entail increasing the number of estimated parameters that would quickly become intractable without some restrictions. To overcome this issue, Pajhede expands the window over which the previous exceedances affect today's probability of an exceedance. Instead of just counting the previous day the exception counts over the previous K days. In this case π_{01} represents the probability of an exceedance given that there were no exceedances over the previous K days and π_{11} represents the probability of an exceedance conditional on there being at least one exceedance in the previous K days. This is one particular way of expanding the dependence structure and others could be envisioned. More generally if one is considering testing for higher order dependence a Ljung–Box test could be run. Although this only tests for independence not for coverage.

Engle and Manganelli (2004) provide a dynamic quantile (DQ) test for a linear probability model that is fairly simple to implement, allows for dependence in the exceedances and allows tests of whether other information might significantly improve the VaR model. The test statistic is

$$DQ = \frac{\left(Hit'_t x_t \left[x'_t x_t\right]^{-1} x'_t Hit_t\right)}{T(1-c)c} \sim \chi^2_q,$$

where the de-meaned indicator function $Hit_t = I_t - (1 - c)$ and X_t is a vector of variables available at time $t - 1$ including lagged values of the Hit function.

Clements and Taylor (2003), Patton (2006) and Berkowitz et al. (2011) convert the DQ test to logistic regression-based test to account for the fact that the indicator function is a limited dependent variable. We call this the logistic dynamic quantile test (LDQ). A model of the nth-order auto regression is given by:

$$I_t = \alpha + \sum_{k=1}^{n} \beta_{1k} I_{t-k} + \sum_{k=1}^{n} \beta_{2k} g(I_{t-k}, I_{t-k-1}, \ldots, \Delta V_{t-k}, \Delta V_{t-k-1}, \ldots,) + u_t.$$

Other variables known at time $t - 1$ may also be included. A likelihood ratio test can then be constructed to test the significance of the beta coefficients while the significance of each beta parameter can be tested via Wald test. A test of independence (that could include tests of greater than first order dependence) and that the VaR model has been properly conditioned on available information is a test of whether

$$P(I_t = 1) = {}^{e^\alpha}\!/_{1+e^\alpha}.$$

To test whether the model has both correct conditional coverage and is independent we test whether

$$P(I_t = 1) = {}^{e^\alpha}\!/_{1+e^\alpha} = 1 - c.$$

These regression-based approaches are especially easy to implement and Berkowitz et al. (2011) find that the LDQ test has significant power advantages over other tests that they compared it to.

Gaglianone et al. (2011) propose a test based on a quantile regression. It can be thought of as an extension of a Mincer Zarnowitz (1969) regression test to predicted quantiles where VaR is regressed on the change in portfolio value. To test a VaR model the regression setup is:

$$\Delta V_t^t = \alpha_0^{1-c} + \alpha_1^{1-c} VaR_{t-1}^{1-c} + \varepsilon_t.$$

In this quantile regression the hypothesis of a good VaR model is a test that α_0 is equal to zero and α_1 is equal to one. A value of α_0 different than zero indicates a biased VaR estimate and also that the VaR is consistently either too high or too low. A value of α_1 greater than one indicates that high values of VaR underpredict the quantile of the change in portfolio value. One could augment this equation with additional variables known at time t–1, all of which should have coefficients equal to zero.

In performing these tests, the choice of significance level is driven by the tradeoff of the possibility of making a type I error (rejecting a correct model) or making a type II error (failing to reject an incorrect model) Increasing the significance level increases a type I error but reduces the type II error. The case can be made that type II errors are expensive in risk management so accepting a lower confidence level than in academic work would be appropriate.

It is rare to have a large number of observations when performing backtesting. Having a large number of violations is even rarer. Christoffersen (2012) and Berkowitz et al. (2011) advocate the use of Dufour's (2006) Monte Carlo simulated P-values rather than using p-values from the asymptotic (generally chi-squared) distribution. This procedure ensures a correctly sized test in small samples and addresses the small sample issue as well as it can be addressed. Kupiec (1995) and others describe the low power of backtests and how large samples are needed to reject incorrect models. Bringing in more information to assess the model as is done in the QR, LQR and VQR tests helps address this power issue.

2.7 Results of the Backtests

We run these tests on the trading portfolios of bank holding companies that are subject to the market risk rule in the United States. Prior to 2013, banks compared VaR to actual P&L, where actual profit and loss would include fees, commissions, and intraday trading revenue, among other items. This tended to increase P&L above the simple change in value of the portfolio that was held at the end of the previous trading day, although in a few instances it would reduce the profit and loss. Indeed, a problem that can be encountered at trading banks is where a trading desk is losing money on its portfolio, but the fees and commissions obscure the losses on the portfolio and make it appear that the desk inventory is profitable. Current rules for backtesting do not include these items in the reported profit and loss. Banks now report the change in value of the portfolio they held at the end of the previous trading day, which is what the bank's VaR model is trying to capture. In this sense this is the appropriate test of the VaR model itself, although it could be argued that the appropriate test from a supervisory standpoint would include the banks' ability to earn other sources of revenue as well.

The data used cover the period from the second half of 2013 to 2016. Banks in the sample were subject to the market risk rule over substantially the whole time period, but a few became subject to the market risk rule at a slightly later date. The data we present covers twenty Bank Holding companies who reported backtesting data for at least 499 trading days and up to 647 trading days. The banks provide their 1 day 99% VaR and their profit and loss for each trading day.

Table 2.4 shows the results of the unconditional coverage test, the conditional coverage test, the DQ test, the LDQ test, and the VQR test.

The aggregate results are summarized in Table 2.3. The exceedance rate over the time period shows that firms are on average conservative in their VaR estimates with an average exceedance rate of 0.4%, below the 1% exceedance rate that would be expected. Since 2013–2016 was a benign period for markets, overall this is consistent with the observation that VaR models are generally conservative during benign periods, although clearly some firms were not conservative with the highest exceedance rate being 2.1%, double the expected rate.

Table 2.4 presents the results of specific tests described above using a two-sided confidence interval so that banks may fail because their model is either too conservative or too aggressive. No additional explanatory variables are included. The unconditional coverage test,

Table 2.3. *Summary statistics on backtesting data for 99% VaR.*

Number of firms	20
Firms with zero exceedences	5
Average exceedence rate	0.4%
Maximum exceedance rate	2.1%

Table 2.4. ***Results of backtesting.***

	UC	CC	DQ	LDQ	VQR
Number of firms that fail at 90% confidence	4	3	2	3	19
Number of non-conservative fails	1	1	1	2	8
Minimum P-value	0.0003	0.0015	0.0000	0.0011	
Maximum P-value	0.5972	0.8354	0.9999	0.9004	
Average P-value	0.1627	0.2605	0.6945	0.4472	

the conditional coverage test, the dynamic quantile test, and the logistic dynamic quantile test all performed similarly, with a small number of firms failing the test, and just one or two failing because the model was aggressive. The VaR quantile regression test failed nineteen of the Bank holding companies' VaR models. It appears to be a much more stringent test, perhaps also affected more by the non-stationarity of the portfolio.

The tests described summarize the tests that use the indicator variable for an exceedance since most testing in practice uses this indicator. Both because of their simplicity and because of their use in regulations. The more stringent quantile test is included for comparison. The quantile test shows rather poor performance. In some ways the use of the indicator function as a regulatory evaluation of the model could have changed the behavior of Bank Holding Companies, causing them to alter their models to pass the test, perhaps at the expense of performance on other tests.

Other types of tests have been proposed, for example, the duration based tests (Christofferson and Pellitier, 2004) but these are largely unused for evaluating models in practice. More recently, Gordy and McNeil (2020) propose extensions using probability integral transforms that weights parts of the distribution to allow the user to choose what parts of the distribution to weight more heavily in the backtest.

2.8 Benchmarking

Perhaps the most neglected aspect of model validation in market risk is benchmarking. While many banks will run a new model in parallel with an old model for a short period of time to check if it is well behaved, there is rarely any formal comparison between a bank's model and an alternative model. In some sense this is understandable; it is time-consuming and resource-intensive to build a single VaR model at a bank. Building two models simply compounds the problem. However, during the time a bank aims to replace a VaR model or at least upgrade part of a VaR mode there is a period of time during which the bank can perform this comparison at low cost. The most common practice is simply to plot the two VaR models over time. There rarely is anything useful to say about the models from these plots other than one model seems more conservative than the other or that they seem to behave about the same. Turning this comparison into more formal tests would be an improvement in model validation. The literature for comparing models on their predictive ability is well developed. Komunjer (2013) provides a comprehensive overview of all forms of evaluating quantile forecasts including VaR models.

Two aspects of benchmarking hinder the application of statistical tests comparing two models. The first is that trading portfolios change frequently so that errors are not independent and identically distributed. This seems to be particularly problematic for regression-based tests. Christoffersen et al. (2001) propose methods to overcome this but restrict this to distributions that are location scale models so that the quantile is a linear function of the volatility. The second aspect has already been mentioned, that banks rarely have two VaR models available to compare. Berkowitz and O'Brien (2002) overcome this issue by estimating a GARCH (1,1) VaR model on the profit and loss from trading by the bank. This data is available to all banks. As indicated in the section on conceptual soundness, there are reasons why a bank would not use a VaR model based on GARCH on the profit and loss for risk management, but it is a ready source of comparison for banks, and, as has been shown, it is a difficult benchmark to beat.

In comparisons of forecast accuracy, the starting point is Diebold and Mariano (1995). This paper did not explicitly consider the case of quantile forecasts but set the groundwork for comparisons of all types of forecasts. An important point made in the paper is that evaluation should depend on the loss function of the forecaster. This may or may not take on the typical mean squared error loss evaluation that is used for point forecasts. For example, Lopez (1996) introduces the regulatory loss function. Since capital is based on the VaR model, the regulator is more concerned about cases where the loss exceeds the VaR rather than cases where the bank's VaR exceeds the P&L. More concretely for any observation the loss, l_{t+1}, (since VaR is a positive number even though it represents a loss) can be described as:

$$l_{t+1} = \begin{cases} \left(\Delta V_{P,t+1} + VaR_t^{1-c}\right)^2 \; if \; \Delta V_{P,t+1} < -VaR_t^{1-c} \\ 0 \; otherwise \end{cases}$$

This regulatory criterion clearly favors conservatism in the estimate of VaR since only exceedances are penalized. Alternatively, the quantile could be evaluated based on accuracy using the same "check" function as is used to estimate a quantile regression. In this case the loss is:

$$l'_{t+1} = \left((1-c) - \mathbf{1}\left(\Delta V_{P,t+1} < -VaR_t^{1-c}\right)\right) \cdot \left(\Delta V_{P,t+1} + VaR_t^{1-c}\right)$$

Sarma et al. (2003) uses the sign test described in Diebold and Mariano to evaluate VaR models estimated on the S&P 500 and India's NSE-50 index. The sign test is a test of the median of the distribution of the loss differential between two competing models. The loss differential between two models, i and j, is $z_t = l_t^i - l_t^j$. The sign test is then given by:

$$\frac{\sum_{i=t+1}^{t+N} 1(z_t > 0) - 0.5N}{\sqrt{0.25N}} \sim N(0,1)$$

Rejecting the null hypothesis would indicate that model i is a significantly better model under the loss function considered. The sign test is easy to implement so there is little reason for banks not to make their comparisons more formal using this test.

The backtesting data described above allows a comparison of a bank's VaR model (positional VaR) to a VaR model based on running a GARCH (1,1) model on the bank's P&L (P&L VaR). Both are calculated as a one-day VaR at 99% coverage. The sign test is used to compare the models based on the regulatory loss function and based on the check loss function. When the regulatory loss function is used the positional VaR model significantly outperforms the P&L VaR in every case. This demonstrates the conservative nature of banks' positional VaR models, often attributed to the effect of regulatory oversight (Perignon Deng and Wang 2008).

When the positional VaR and P&L VaR are compared on accuracy using the check loss function, the P&L VaR outperforms the positional VaR at sixteen out of nineteen banks. Only one bank's positional VaR outperformed the P&L VaR; for the remaining two banks the difference was insignificant. It is clear that banks' VaR models are designed to be conservative; the conservative nature of the positional VaR models may hinder their ability to outperform the P&L VaR models on accuracy.

2.9 Conclusion

The tests described above provide a demonstration of how bank holding companies may make concrete the types of validation that regulators seek. US regulators expect tests of conceptual soundness, outcomes analysis and benchmarking. This chapter makes concrete how these tests can be done in the context of VaR models.

The fundamental review of the trading book BIS (2019) replaces the use of VaR models to determine regulatory capital with expected shortfall models. In many cases there is a direct translation of tests used for VaR models to those used for expected shortfall models. Both Dowd and Christoffersen and Goncalves describe how confidence intervals for expected shortfall can be provided. Hollerbach and Tasche provide examples of how to estimate the effect of missing risk factors in expected shortfall models. A relatively simple method for backtesting for expected shortfall models is described in Du and Escanciano (2016). The sign test for comparing models can also be extended to expected shortfall models.

References

Andersen, T. G., Bollerslev, T., Christoffersen, P. F. and Diebold, F. X. (2006). Volatility and correlation forecasting. In Elliott, G., Granger, C. W. J., and Timmerman A. (Eds.), *Handbook of Economic Forecasting*, Vol. 1, Amsterdam: North-Holland, 777–878.

Barone-Adesi, G., Giannopoulos, K. and Vosper, L. (1999). VaR without correlations for portfolios of derivative securities. *Journal of Future Markets*, 19(5), 583–602.

Berkowitz, J., Christoffersen, P. and Pelletier, D. (2011). Evaluating Value-at-Risk models with desk-level data. *Management Science*, 57(2), 2213–2227.

Berkowitz, J. and O'Brien, J. (2002). How accurate are Value-at-Risk models at commercial banks? *Journal of Finance*, 57, 1093–1111.

BIS (2019). Minimum Capital Requirements for Market Risk. Basel Committee on Banking Supervision.

Chan, N. H., Deng, S.-J., Peng, L. and Xia, Z. (2007). Interval estimation of Value-at-Risk based on GARCH models with heavy-tailed innovations. *Journal of Econometrics*, 137(2), 556–576.

Christoffersen, P. F. (1998). Evaluating interval forecasts. *International Economic Review*, 39, 841–862.

(2012). *Elements of Financial Risk Management* (2nd ed.). Amsterdam: Academic Press.

Christoffersen, P. F. and Goncalves, S. (2005). Estimation risk in financial risk management. *Journal of Risk*, 7, 1–28.

Clements, M. P. and Taylor, N. (2003). Evaluating interval forecasts of high frequency financial data. *Journal of Applied Econometrics*, 18, 445–456.

Dowd, K. (2006). Using order statistics to estimate confidence intervals for probabilistic risk measures. *Journal of Derivatives*, 14(2), 77–81.

Du, Z. and Escanciano, J. C. (2016). Backtesting expected shortfall: Accounting for tail risk. *Management Science*, 63(4), 940–958.

Dufour, J.-M. (2006). Monte Carlo tests with nuisance parameters: A general approach to finite-sample inference and nonstandard asymptotics. *Journal of Econometrics*, 133(2), 443–477.

Engle, R. F. and Manganelli, S. (2004). CAViaR: Conditional autoregressive value at risk by regression quantiles. *Journal of Business and Economic Statistics*, 22(4), 367–381.

Escanciano, J. C. and Pei, P. (2012). Pitfalls in backtesting historical simulation VaR models. *Journal of Banking and Finance*, 36, 2233–2244.

Frésard, L., Pérignon, C. and Wilhelmsson, A. (2011). The pernicious effects of contaminated data in risk management. *Journal of Banking and Finance*, 35(10), 2569–2583.

Gaglianone, W. P., Lima, L. R., Linton, O. and Smith, D. R. (2011). Evaluating Value-at-Risk models via quantile regression. *Journal of Business and Economic Statistics*, 29(1), 150–160.

Garman, M. (1997). Taking VaR to pieces. *Risk*, 10(10), 70–71.

Gong, Y., Li, Z. and Peng, L. (2010). Empirical likelihood intervals for conditional Value-at-Risk in ARCH-GARCH models. *Journal of Time Series Analysis*, 31(2), 65–75.

Gordy, M. B. and McNeil, A. J. (2020). Spectral backtests of forecast distributions with application to risk management. *Journal of Banking and Finance*, 116, 1–13.

Gourieroux, C., Laurent, J. P. and Scaillet, O. (2000). Sensitivity analysis of Values at Risk. *Journal of Empirical Finance*, 7(3), 225–245.

Hallerbach, W. (2003). Decomposing portfolio Value-at-Risk: A general analysis. *Journal of Risk*, 2(5), 1–18.

Jarrow, R. A. (2011). Risk management models: Construction, testing usage. *Journal of Derivatives*, 18(4), 89–98.

Jorion, P. (1996). Risk2: Measuring the risk in value at risk. *Financial Analysts Journal*, 52, 47–56.

(2006). *Value-at-Risk: The new benchmark for managing financial risk* (3rd ed.). New York: McGraw-Hill.

(2007). Risk Management for Hedge Funds with Position Information. *Journal of Portfolio Management*, 34(1), 127–134.

(2009). Risk management lessons from the credit crisis. *European Financial Management*, 15(5), 923–933.

Kupiec, P. (1995). Techniques for verifying the accuracy of risk measurement models. *Journal of Derivatives*, 2, 173–184.

Lo, A.W. (2001). Risk management for hedge funds: Introduction and overview. *Financial Analysts Journal*, 57(6), 16–33.

Mincer, J. and Zarnowitz, V. (1969). The evaluation of economic forecasts and expectations. In J. Mincer (Ed.), *Economic Forecasts and Expectations*. New York: National Bureau of Economic Research.

Nieto, M. R. and Ruiz, E. (2016). Frontiers in VaR forecasting and backtesting. *International Journal of Forecasting* 32, 475–501.

O'Brien, James and Szerszeń, Paweł J. (2017). An evaluation of bank measures for market risk before, during and after the financial crisis. *Journal of Banking & Finance, Elsevier*, vol. 80(C), 215–234.

Pajhede T. (2017). Backtesting Value at Risk: A generalized Markov test. *Journal of Forecasting*, 36(5), 597–613.

Patton, A. (2006). Modelling asymmetric exchange rate dependence. *International Economic Review*, 47, 527–556.

Pérignon, C., Deng, Z. Y. and Wang, Z. Y. (2008). Do banks overstate their Value-at-Risk? *Journal of Banking and Finance*, 32, 783–794.

Pérignon, C. and Smith, D. R. (2008). A new approach to comparing VaR estimation method. *The Journal of Derivatives*, 16(2), 54–66.

(2010a). Diversification and Value-at-Risk. *Journal of Banking and Finance*, 34, 55–66.

(2010b). The level and quality of Value-at-Risk disclosure by commercial banks. *Journal of Banking and Finance*, 34, 362–377.

Pritsker, M. (1997). The hidden dangers of historical simulation. *Journal of Banking and Finance*, 30(2), 561–582.

Riskmetrics (1997). *Riskmetrics: Technical Document* (4th ed). J.P. Morgan/ Reuters.

Tasche, D. (2000). *Risk Contributions and Performance Measurement. Working paper*, Munich University of Technology.

3 A Conditional Testing Approach for Value-at-Risk Model Performance Evaluation

VICTOR K. NG

3.1 Introduction

This chapter presents a general approach to evaluate the empirical performance of a VaR model. The approach leverages data used in standard backtesting, filtering on a number of selected conditioning variables to perform tests on specific properties of the model by restricting to subsamples in which the chosen criteria hold true.

This simple but general approach can be used to test a wide range of model properties and across many product areas. These include the ability of the model to capture specific risk, historical price variation, and concentration, model performance during stress periods, the importance of missing risk factors, quality of model for already captured risk factors, missing seasonality, as well as model performance during days with economic announcements (event days). The test results can point to specific weaknesses the VaR model has, and therefore facilitates the identification of potential areas of improvement.

These different tests are constructed by choosing one or more conditioning variables and corresponding criteria for the selections of dates on which the criteria specified for the chosen conditioning variables are met.

We will first present the general test framework and then go into specific choices of conditioning variables and criteria for a set of properties we want to test.

3.2 The General Framework

3.2.1 *Conditional Backtesting*

The simplest form of backtesting involves specifying a particular confidence level, α, and a test sample of T days. The backtest then involves comparing daily P&L to VaR at the chosen confidence level. The test statistics are the number of days (n) on which P&L is worse than predicted by VaR.

Specifically, under standard backtesting,

$$n = \text{count}(P\&L(t) < -\text{VaR}(\alpha, \text{t});\ \text{t} = 1, \ldots, T)$$

n follows a binomial distribution with

$$\text{Mean}(n) = (1 - \alpha)\ *\ T$$

$$\text{Stdev}(n) = \sqrt{(T * \alpha * (1 - \alpha))}$$

Based on the distribution and a chosen level of significance "q" (e.g. $q = 5\%$), we can consider the number of exceptions statistically significant if the p-value of n is less than q.

For a large T (as defined below), n is well approximated by the normal distribution. As such the 5% confidence interval (right tail) of n can be written as:

$$CI95 = (1 - \alpha) * T + 1.645 * \sqrt{(T * \alpha * (1 - \alpha))}$$

If n is larger than $CI95$, then we consider the number of exceptions statistically significantly larger than expected. By larger T, we use the criterion that: Max $[T * (1 - \alpha), T * \alpha] >= 1$. That is, for $\alpha = 0.99$, one would need at least 100 observations to use the normal confidence bound.

While the standard approach is useful in the evaluation of model performance in general, it fails to provide insights as to how the model performs relative to the specific properties of interest.

The conditional backtesting approach discussed below is an attempt to overcome this weakness by only performing tests on days for which some set of criteria on a number of conditioning variables are met.

It is important to note that the test will be moot if the choice of conditioning variables and criteria is such that there are only very few days satisfying such criteria. Those cases represent hypotheses that cannot be tested at the chosen confidence level without more data. We need a longer sample to allow for more days satisfying the criteria to be included before the test can be performed. Alternatively, one can lower the confidence level α at which the test is performed. (e.g. use 95% VaR when there is not enough observation to conduct a statistically meaningful test using the 99% VaR.

Let $X_k(t)$, be the time t value of the kth conditioning variable and $C(j, X_k(t); k = 1, \ldots, K)$ be an indicator function which takes a value of 1 on day t when the jth criterion on the K conditioning variables is met. Note that a criterion can be as simple as $X_k(t) < \text{average}(X(t), t = 1, \ldots, T)$. A criterion can also involve more than one conditioning variable.

The conditional backtesting framework is essentially backtesting over a subsample which can include non-consecutive days on which the criteria are met. Specifically, under the framework we have:

$$n_c = \text{count}(\text{P\&L}(t) < \text{VaR}(\alpha, t)\ ;\ \text{for } C(j, X_k(t); k = 1, \ldots K) = 1$$

for all $j = 1,\ldots,J$ and $t = 1,\ldots,T$

$$T_c = \text{count}\big(C(j, X_k(t);\ k = 1, \ldots, K) = 1 \text{ for all } j = 1, \ldots, J \text{ and } t = 1, \ldots, T\big)$$

Then, under the null hypothesis that model performance is not affected by the conditioning, nc follows a binomial distribution with

$$\text{Mean}(n_c) = (1 - \alpha) * T_c$$
$$\text{Stdev}(n_c) = \sqrt{(T_c * \alpha * (1 - \alpha))}$$

Since $T_c < T$, T_c might not satisfy the criterion of $Max[\ T_c{}^* \alpha,\ T_c{}^* (1 - \alpha)\ ] >= 1$ at $\alpha = 0.99$.

While one might be able to use the actual binomial percentiles rather than the normal confidence interval, the fundamental issue is that one cannot really test a model at the 99% level when there are not even 100 observations. This means one would need to be careful about the construction of the test, the length of the sample, as well as the VaR percentile to be tested for the test to be meaningful.

If T_c is small, we would need to look at a lower percentile (e.g., 95% VaR) than the 99%. Alternatively, one might need a bigger sample in order to have a larger T_c.

If the p-value of n_c is smaller than the confidence level q, then we can consider the number of exceptions statistically significant. For a sufficiently large sample where α and T_c are such that $\text{Max}[\ T_c\, \alpha,\ T_c(1 - \alpha)\ ] >= 1$, the upper bound of the 95% confidence interval of nc is given by:

$$\text{CI95}(n_c) = (1 - \alpha)T_c + 1.645\sqrt{(T_c\alpha(1 - \alpha))}.$$

If n_c is larger than $CI95(n_c)$, then we consider the number of exceptions statistically significantly larger than expected and the null hypothesis is rejected.

In addition to testing subsample performance, in some cases it would be useful to test relative performance in different subsamples. Specifically, model performance in the subsample where the conditioning criteria hold versus model performance in the remaining subsample where the conditioning criteria do not hold.

In this case, let $T_x = \text{count}(C(j, X_k(t);\ k = 1, \ldots, K) = 0$ for at least one j and $t = 1,\ldots,T)$. Also let,

$$n_x = \text{count}(\text{P\&L}(t) < \text{VaR}(\alpha, \text{t});\ for\ C(j, X_k(t); k = 1, \ldots K) = 0,$$

for at least one j and $t = 1,\ldots,T$)

$$\text{Mean}(n_x) = (1 - \alpha) * T_x$$

$$\text{Stdev}(n_x) = \sqrt{(T_x * \alpha * (1 - \alpha))}.$$

Since the days satisfying the criteria and days not satisfying the criteria are disjointed, $n_d = n_c - n_x$ would have the following summary statistics:

$$\text{Mean}(n_d) = (1 - \alpha) * (T_c - \text{T}_x)$$

$$\text{Stdev}(n_d) = \sqrt{((T_c + \text{T}_x) * \alpha * (1 - \alpha))}$$

Under the null hypothesis that $n_c = n_x$ (that is, the model does not have different performance in the two samples, then the 95% confidence bound under the normal distribution approximation is:

$$\text{CI95}(n_d) = (1 - \alpha) * (T_c - \text{T}_x) + 1.645 * \sqrt{((T_c + \text{T}_x) * \alpha * (1 - \alpha))}.$$

So, we can reject the null hypothesis that $n_d = 0$ if:

$$n_d > CI95(n_d).$$

3.2.2 Conditional Volatility Test

The conditional testing framework can also be applied to volatility testing. Specifically, one can test if the model captures the variability of P&L at the subsample defined by the conditioning variables and corresponding criteria.

First, let us go through the original case without any conditioning. Let EVol be the expected one-day-ahead P&L volatility as predicted by the VaR model. Under the assumption that the VaR model correctly captures the volatility of P&L, P&L normalized by EVol should have a standard deviation equal to one.

$$\text{Stdev}[z(t)] = 1; \text{ where } \mathrm{z}(t) = \text{PnL}(t)/\text{EVol}(t).$$

The standard error of the standard deviation estimate is given by:

$$\text{Stderr} = 1/\sqrt{(2 * T)}.$$

Based on the standard error estimate, we can test if the standard deviation of z is statistically significantly different from 1 using the Wald test.

The case with conditioning is nothing more than performing the volatility test using a subsample as defined by the conditioning variables and the corresponding criteria. Let, $z_c(t)$ be the conditional normalized P&L on date t at which all J criteria on the K conditioning variables are satisfied.

$$z_c(t) = \text{PnL}(t) * \left\{\prod j = 1,\ldots,J[C(j, \mathrm{X}_k(t);\ \mathrm{k} = 1,\ldots K))]\right\}/\text{EVol}(t).$$

Let T_c be the conditional sample size as defined previously.

Under the null hypothesis that the VaR model captures volatility correctly irrespective of the conditioning, then the standard deviation of $z_c(t)$ should equal one for all t satisfying the criteria. That is:

$$\text{Stdev}(z_c(t)) = 1$$

Since the VaR model does not make any assumption about expected return, the standard deviation of z_c is estimated as:

$$\text{EstStdevz}_c = \sqrt{\left(\sum\left(z_c(t)^2\right)/(T_c)\right)}.$$

The corresponding standard error of the standard deviation estimate is calculated as:

$$\text{Stderrz}_c = 1/\sqrt{(2 * T_c)}.$$

With the standard deviation estimate and the corresponding standard error, we can test if the standard deviation of z is statistically significantly different from one employing the Wald test.

3.3 Test Design

As discussed above, a test is constructed by choosing the conditional variables and criteria useful for testing the particular model property of interest. Below are some examples:

3.3.1 Specific Risk

Specific risk is most important / visible on days without big market wide moves. Given this insight, under the null hypothesis that the model adequately captures specific risk, we should not see statistically significantly more exceptions on days with little general market moves.

We can measure the degree of general market movement using market wide indices. In the case, of equity, if we are looking at equity price risk in the US, we can use the S&P500 as a conditioning variable. Alternatives are the Nasdaq (if we were to focus on the OTC population) or the Russell 2000 (if we were to focus on small stocks). For Europe, it can be the Stoxx50. For Japan it can be the Nikkei 225. For Hong Kong, it can be the HangSeng Index etc.

If we are looking at the equity volatility market, then the VIX can be a reasonable choice of a volatility market conditioning variable.

If we are looking at the credit market, one can use the CDX or the Itraxx Indices as conditioning variables.

Defining dates with little market movement involves a tradeoff between precision and the number of observations in the subsample that satisfies the selected criteria on the conditioning variables. One simple choice is to focus on days when the index moves by less than one standard deviation. One can make it half a standard deviation making it closer to little market movement. However, this comes with fewer observations in the subsample which could result in testing at lower confidence levels, unless we started off with a larger sample.

3.3.2 Historical Price Variation

Another interesting attribute to test is whether the VaR model is able to capture historical price variation when estimating the risk of loss. Since the focus of this criterion is on volatility, the most relevant test to be applied is the volatility test. However, it is important to recognize that VaR models are not designed to measure expected gains.

Given the focus of VaR models is on the possibilities of loss, the most relevant test is on the loss side of the distribution. This is essentially a conditional volatility test with the P&L itself being the conditioning variable. The criterion of observation selection is that P&L(t) < 0.

The conditional testing approach can also be used to test if historical price variation adequately captures in the presence of seasonality in volatility. For example, for some energy products, there can be differences between winter months and summer months. To control for seasonality, one can use as a conditioning variable an indicator that gives a value of 1 for any t that belongs to one season while 0 for others.

3.3.3 Concentration

It is important for a VaR model to capture concentration yet it is not easy to test if a model adequately captures concentration. It is bad if the model suggests that there is a lot of diversification benefit when there is in fact little diversification benefit. With the conditional testing approach, one can test if the model performs poorly when the model suggests there is more diversification benefit.

The diversification benefit of a portfolio can be defined as the the difference between its VaR and the sum of the VaR of all its sub-portfolios. The diversification benefit, thus defined, can then be defined as a conditioning variable. The testing criterion is above average diversification benefit.

This test can be constructed as a relative backtesting performance test on the significance of the difference in the number of exceptions in the half of the sample with above average diversification benefit versus the other half with below average diversification benefit.

3.3.4 Market Stress/Adverse Environment

Another interesting attribute to test is whether the VaR model is robust to market stress. This is naturally set up as a conditional test. The conditioning variable can simply be pre-specified indicators with externally chosen stress periods. One can also define an adverse stress environment as one with high volatility. Under this definition, one can use rolling (moving window) estimates of market volatility as a conditioning variable and have a criterion being the top quartile of volatility. An alternative is to use VIX as the conditioning variable.

We can also define an adverse environment as one where the asset market has performed very poorly. For example, for equity, one can look at return relative to the 200 days moving average of asset price as a conditioning variable, and pick days with returns in the lowest quartile. For credit, one can use spread levels such as that of the CDX or Itraxx Indices as conditioning variables and have a criterion that picks days with spread levels in the highest quartile.

3.3.5 Events

Testing the model's ability to capture events is difficult as there are all kinds of events. It is almost impossible to perform meaningful statistical tests on model performance relative to extremely rare events. It is really a matter of whether it did well or not on the occasion. A test is also not well defined without specifying the type of events.

The type of events that can be tested are recurring but not too rare. For example, certain relatively frequent economic announcements. Even then, more than one year of data might be needed and only low confidence level VaR tests or volatility tests could be run. The conditioning variable is just a date indicator that takes a value of 1 on the event-date or a short window around the event-date.

3.4 Summary

In this chapter we presented a conditional testing approach for the testing of a VaR model. By choosing different conditional variables and criteria, we can adapt the test for the testing of different properties of the VaR model. This allows us to identify weaknesses of a VaR model and therefore areas for enhancement. Having a good feedback mechanism to continuously inform the users and model developers of model performance is crucial for the use of a model. Over time, model weaknesses could emerge when there are structural changes in the market environment. It is important to be able to identify these weaknesses as they emerge and have the model updated before it leads to incorrect decision. The technique presented in this chapter provides a general approach for building feedback mechanisms.

4 *Beyond Exceedance-Based Backtesting of Value-at-Risk Models: Methods for Backtesting the Entire Forecasting Distribution Using Probability Integral Transform*

DIANA IERCOSAN, ALYSA SHCHERBAKOVA, DAVID MCARTHUR AND REBECCA ALPER

"Once more unto the breach, dear friends, once more;"

William Shakespeare (Henry V)

4.1 Introduction

Banks are required to develop sophisticated and reliable models of market risk inherent in their trading portfolios. These models have multiple uses, including determination of regulatory capital requirements, monitoring and limiting of trader risk taking, as well as banks' internal management of risk. Many of these uses, and in particular determination of regulatory capital requirements, focus on the calculation of the portfolio's Value-at-Risk (VaR), which quantifies the portfolio's downside risk. More precisely, VaR is a mathematical concept that measures the loss that a given portfolio is expected not to exceed over a specific time interval and at a predetermined confidence level.

Regulatory capital requirements depend on the one-day VaR with a 99% confidence level. Simply put, a one percent VaR of $1,000,000 over a one-day horizon implies that a one-day realized loss on a portfolio is expected to exceed $1,000,000 one percent of the time and remain below the $1,000,000 threshold the remaining 99% of the time. In the context of regulatory oversight, assuming a one-day horizon with a 99% confidence level, if the risk model is accurate, then, each day, there will be an exactly 1% probability that the next day's profit and loss (P&L) will be a realized loss greater than the VaR measure estimated by the model.

There is a vast literature on the statistical properties of VaR models. Jorion (2002) provided a comprehensive survey and analysis of various

VaR model specifications in the first edition of his book which described VaR as the "the new benchmark for controlling market risk." Other analysis showing forecast performance used hypothetical portfolios Marshall and Siegel (1997) and Pritsker (1997). Moreover, Berkowitz and O'Brien (2002) showed empirical results on the performance of banks' actual trading risk models by examining the statistical accuracy of their regulatory VaR forecasts for a sample of large trading banks. Berkowitz et al. (2016) showed acuracy of forecasts of VaR models for a small sample of desks. The contribution of this chapter is twofold: it describes how banks' VaR models fare in backtesting at 99% and introduces tests of the whole distrubution; and it shows how banks fare on those tests at a firm-wide aggregated level, but also at a disaggregated portfolio level.

Backtesting has proven to be a key tool in the validation of risk models by comparing realized outcomes to the model's forecast for those outcomes. Strictly speaking, backtesting is a statistical procedure where the precision of a portfolio's VaR estimates are systematically compared to corresponding realized P&L outcomes. As such, a disciplined backtesting regime ensures that models remain properly constructed for internal risk management purposes and calculation of regulatory capital.

Since the mid 1990s various methods for backtesting have been proposed. A standard backtesting practice is to count instances when daily P&L is lower than the *ex ante* VaR (i.e., portfolio loss exceeds its estimated VaR). These instances are also known as VaR exceedances, exceptions or breaches.

In addition to exceedance counts, recent quantitative literature has placed significant emphasis on the calculation of the probability integral transform (PIT), often called the "p-value", associated with the VaR model P&L as an integral component of a robust backtesting process. The PIT was introduced by Diebold et al. (1998) for backtesting of density forecasts and represents the cumulative probability of observing a loss greater than the current P&L realization based on the previous day's VaR model forecast. When PITs are well estimated they provide information on the accuracy of the risk model at any percentile of the forecast distribution.

According to Christoffersen (1998), any backtesting of a VaR model that accurately reflects the actual distribution of the P&L is expected to have two distinct properties:

1. unconditional coverage;
2. and independence.

The unconditional coverage property restricts the number of exceedances which may be observed in a given time period at a determined statistical significance level (again, in the regulatory context, this is a one-day horizon with a 99% confidence level). This property was investigated by Kupiec (1995) who defined a statistical test. Unconditional coverage is analogous to the uniformity distributional property of a series of PITs. If the risk is adequately modeled, the exceedances at 1% VaR should be observed 1% of the time, exceedances at 3% VaR should be observed 3% of the time, etc. In other words, the series of probabilities of observing each P&L outcome in relation to VaR should be uniformly distributed over a zero to one interval, *U(0,1)*.

The independence property asserts that the observed exceedances should be independent from one another, and each observed exceedance should not be informative of future exceedances. Operationally, if a risk model is perfectly accurate, a series of PITs are *i.i.d. U(0,1)*, Rosenblatt (1952).

Deviations from these properties indicate that the model is likely to be misspecified, with that misspecification taking on a conservative or an aggressive manner. Conservative misspecification implies that the model distribution is too wide, and P&L observed is small, clustering in the middle of the distribution (i.e., the model parameters are too conservative to accurately model market dynamics). Aggressive misspecification implies that the model distribution is too narrow and we often see realized P&L in the tails of the distribution.

A number of statistical tests have been developed to analyze the performance of VaR models. These tests are based on evaluating the degree to which the model exhibits the two properties described above either individually or jointly. This chapter provides a comprehensive overview of the range of tests available to assess VaR model fit and performance.

First, we investigate results from a set of tests used to assess unconditional coverage, conditional coverage, and independence properties of the realized VaR exceptions. Second, we present a comprehensive overview of tests used to assess the uniformity and independence properties of a series of PIT estimates generated from real-world risk models. The analysis includes tests based on the empirical CDF (e.g. Kolmogorov–Smirnov; Cramér–Von Mises; and Anderson–Darling) as well tests of dependence based on regression analysis of the observed PITs. In this chapter we assess the accuracy and possible misspecification of VaR models, and offer a comparison of backtesting results using PITs over exceedances for the same sample of real portfolios.

4.2 Data

Under Basel III Subpart F (Market Risk) Section 205, paragraphs (c)(1)–(c)(3), US financial institutions are required to submit backtesting information for each subportfolio, for each business day, on an ongoing basis beginning January 2013. We apply the tests catalogued in this chapter to a sample of these backtesting results. Our data starts on January 1, 2013 and ends on December 31, 2015. The data used in the analysis was collected as part of the ongoing Basel III regulatory reporting for market risk. The VaR model performance results are aggregated in order to preserve anonymity of individual firms, but are also disaggregated by the type and geographical region of the financial products being modeled. The sample consists of 20 US financial firms with significant asset concentrations in the trading book, a total of 597 distinct, non-overlapping subportfolios, with a mean of 591 days and median of 707 days of data for each subportfolio. Each firm defined its subportfolios based on the firm's internal risk management practice and aligned subportfolio definitions with existing business practices. For each day and each subportfolio, firms reported to their supervisors a one-day regulatory VaR, calibrated to a 99% confidence level, one-day clean P&L (i.e. the net change in the price of the positions held in the subportfolio at the end of the previous business day), and the corresponding PIT. Clean P&L is a hypothetical P&L excluding new trades and fees that are not accounted for in the VaR model.

The analysis is based on the premise that if the risk model produces an accurate daily forecast distribution for the portfolio P&L, $F_t()$, then after observing the daily realization of the portfolio P&L, PL_{t+1}, we can calculate the risk model's probability of observing a loss below the actual P&L, known as Probability Integral Transform denoted by p_{t+1},

$$p_{t+1} = F_t(PL_{t+1}). \tag{4.1}$$

From the daily VaR and P&L series we can infer exceedances and assess model performance using these observations. Mathematically, the sequence of VaR_t exceedances is defined as,

Table 4.1. ***Subportfolio count by product composition.***

Product	Count single	Count multiple
SovereignBonds	6	266
CorporateBonds	8	177
MuniBonds	3	44
AgencyMBS	1	47
NonAgencyMBS	–	44
CMO	–	40
InterestRates	30	382
FX	43	305
Commodities	23	64
OtherProductType	15	190

$$I_{t+1} = \begin{cases} 1, & \text{if } R_{t+1} < VaR_t(p) \\ 0, & \text{else} \end{cases} \tag{4.2}$$

where 1 indicates a VaR breach or hit on day $t + 1$.

The analysis of the series of breaches or PIT is based on data aggregated across subportfolios grouped by, (i) single product and (ii) multiple product, according to subportfolio characteristics. "Single" product refers to subportfolios identified as consisting predominantly of a single product type. "Multiple" product refers to all portfolios in which a given product was present, regardless of materiality of its representation among other products in that portfolio. Table 4.1 illustrates the composition of the sample and summarizes the count of single (i.e., unique) and multiple product subportfolios.

4.3 Graphics of the Exceedance Count and Distribution of PITs

Analysis of the VaR model performance is done on the subportfolio level using the backtesting results from the most granular and distinct subportfolios. Analysis is also performed on the combined top-of-the-house backtesting data reported by firms. The analysis is based on the distribution of exceedance counts, and on the distributional properties of PITs associated with subportfolio backtests. As we discussed in the introduction, realized exceedances provide information on the performance of the VaR model at a single percentile, while reported PITs provide

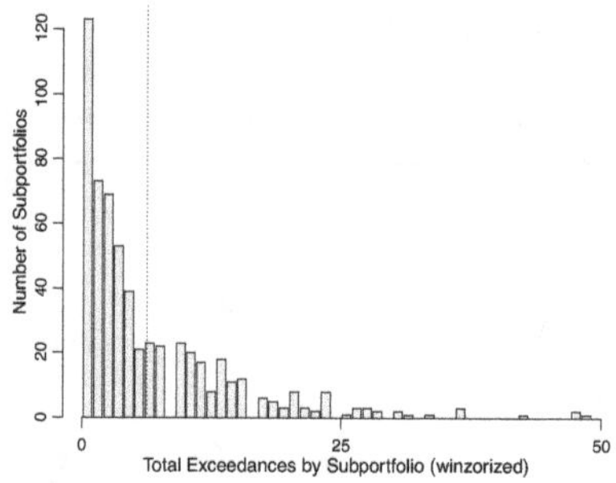

Figure 4.1a Total exceedances by subportfolio (winzorized).

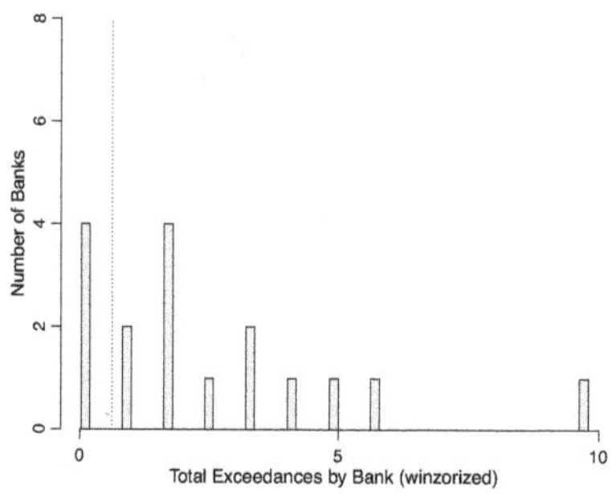

Figure 4.1b Top of the house exceedances by bank (winzorized).

information on the quality and robustness of the model used for the daily forecasting of the full distribution of portfolio P&L.

As we are assessing regulatory VaR models, a priori, we expect to observe 1% exceedances, and we expect the series of PITs to be uniformly distributed. In what follows, we rely on a qualitative assessment of how closely a firm's methodology supports these expectations. We expect that the degree to which actual distribution of PITs differs from uniform may provide information regarding the model's ability to accurately and reliably assess risk of a given portfolio of instruments.

The charts presented in this section were produced using distinct subportfolios submitted by a number of financial institutions in the sample. The first histogram (Figure 4.1) illustrates risk model performance in terms of the number of exceedances. The vertical line indicates the expected number of exceedances based on one percentile confidence level (i.e., about 6 exceedances given our time series of approximately

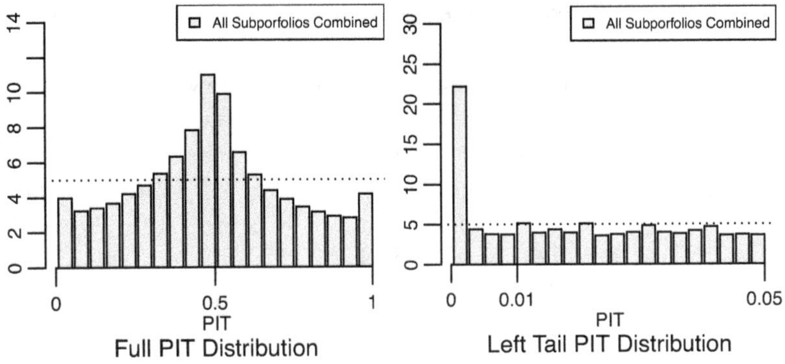

Figure 4.2a PIT distribution.

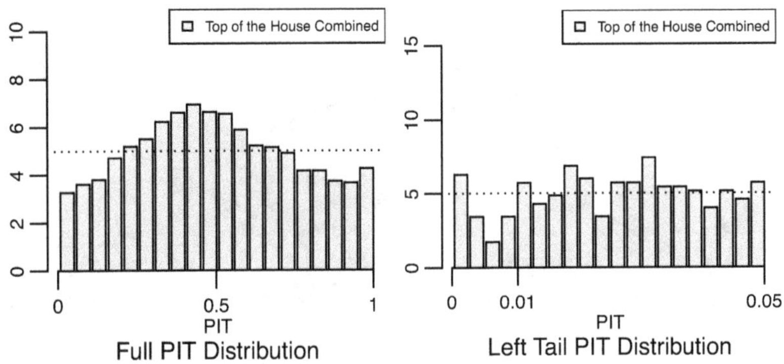

Figure 4.2b Top of the house PIT distribution.

625 daily observations for each subportfolio). Subportfolios to the left of the line produced reasonable backtesting results (i.e., demonstrating fewer than 6 exceedances), while subportfolios to the right of the line have an excess number of exceedances, thus failing VaR backtesting. Note, ten subportfolios exhibited more than fifty exceptions each in the 625 day time interval and were excluded from the histogram for illustration purposes.

The next histograms in Figure 4.2a and 4.2b illustrate the deviation from uniformity observed in the distribution PITs aggregated across all subportfolios and across all entire firm portfolios, respectively. That is, for the purpose of this illustration, all PITs were combined into a single series and graphed. The distorted shape of the distributions indicates that when considered in aggregate, models are fairly conservative in the body of the forecast distribution (i.e., humped shape). Figure 4.2a depicts the distribution of subportfolio PITs and shows that the tails of these risk models are thinner than is required by the realizations of P&L (i.e., visible spikes at each end of the distribution). The conditional histogram on the right focuses on the 5% of the left tail, demonstrating that the estimation at 1% is conservative across all subportfolios, but the tail is understated for extreme realizations. Nevertheless Figure 4.2b shows less deviation from uniformity in the loss tail for firm-wide risk models, indicating more adequate modeling of losses at the top of the house.

The quantile–quantile (Q–Q) plots of the series of PITs are provided below in Figure 4.3a and 4.3b. The first Q–Q plot of PITs highlights that

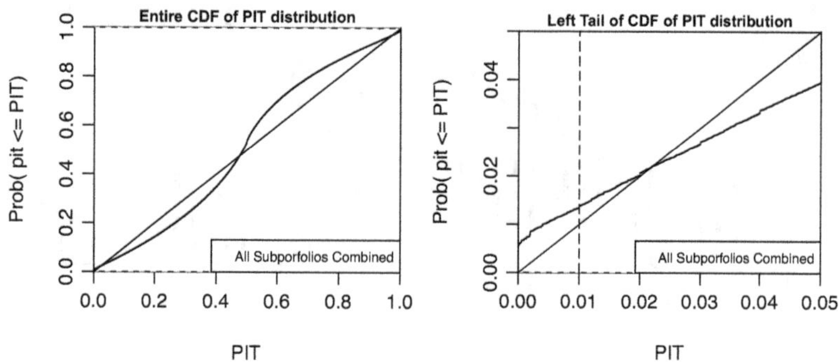

Figure 4.3a CDF of PIT distribution.

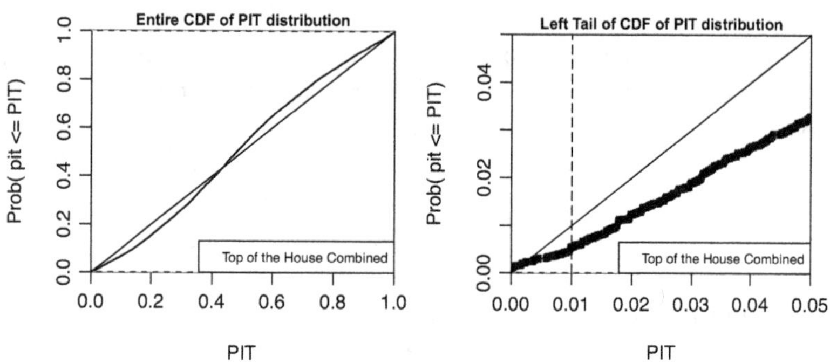

Figure 4.3b Top of the house CDF of PIT distribution.

risk models are built to be conservative generally. However, the second Q–Q plot in Figure 4.3a highlights the fact that risk models underestimate losses in the far left tail at subportfolio level, which is not confirmed in Figure 4.3b that shows results for aggregate firm level.

4.4 Quantifying Deviations from Uniformity of Distribution of PITs

Numerical methods quantify deviations from uniformity in terms of mean, median, standard deviation, skewness and kurtosis of the distribution of PITs. The histograms in Figure 4.4a illustrate the statistical properties of subportfolios in our sample. Similarly, moments of the distribution of PITs for each firm are plotted in Figure 4.4b.

The vertical line in each histogram indicates an expected mean, median, standard deviation, skewness and kurtosis of a Uniform $[0, 1]$ distribution. The histograms in Figure 4.4a clearly illustrate that VaR models generally produce distributions that overstate variance and understate kurtosis. Further, we observe deviations from the expected mean, as well as evidence of skewness in either positive or negative direction. Note, nine subportfolios exhibited kurtosis in excess of fifteen and, for illustration purposes, were excluded from histograms provided in this section. Figure 4.4b shows less dispersion in moments of the firm-wide PITs than for the subportfolio level, and with considerably smaller kurtosis.

4.5 Misspecification Tests Based on Exceptions

Standard backtesting practices are rooted in tests of unconditional coverage and independence of VaR exceedances. These tests rely on the assumption that exceedances should be independent and occur precisely the number of times corresponding to the confidence level of the calculated VaR (i.e., for a 99% VaR, exceedances are expected to occur 1% of the time).

The *unconditional coverage test* introduced by Kupiec (1995) examines whether the theoretical confidence level matches the empirical probability of an exceedance. In other words, given a 1% VaR backtest, we expect to observe a VaR violation 1% of the time. If, instead, exceedances are observed more frequently, our conclusion is that the VaR systematically underestimates risk at the 1% level.

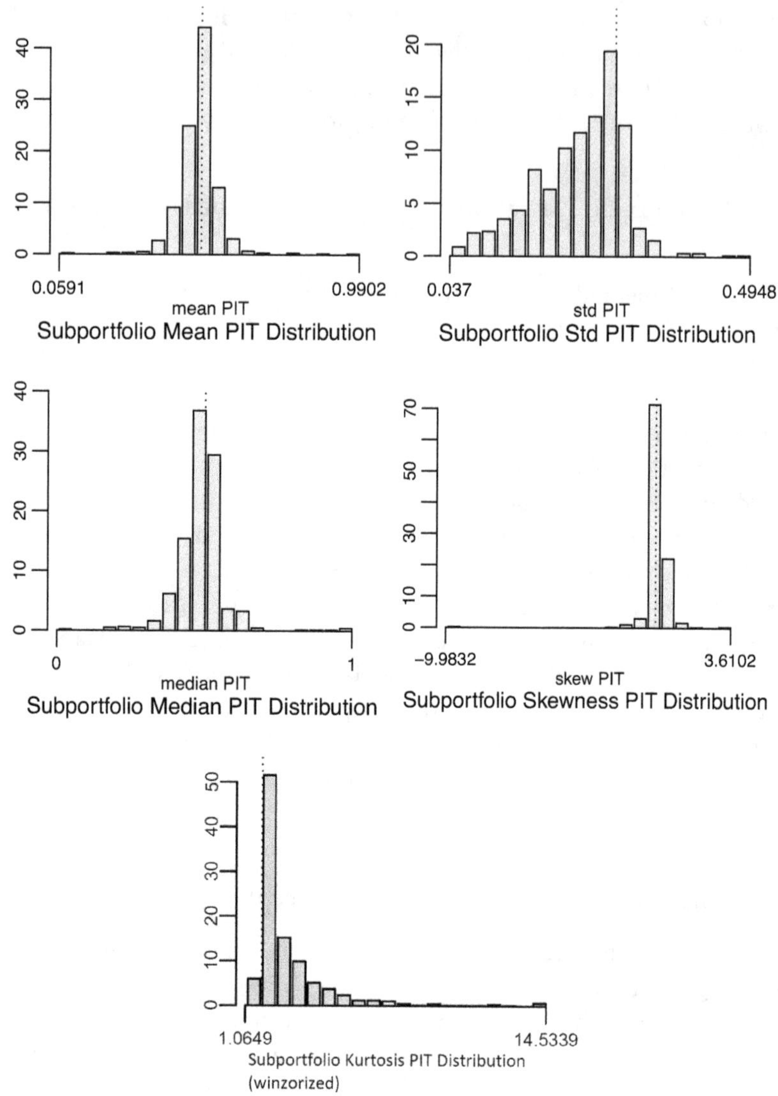

Figure 4.4a Subportfolio moments of the distribution of PITs.

In the Kupiec proportion of failures test, the null hypothesis assumes that the series of observed exceptions I_t (also referred to as the "hit" series) follows a Bernoulli distribution with a success probability parameter p such that,

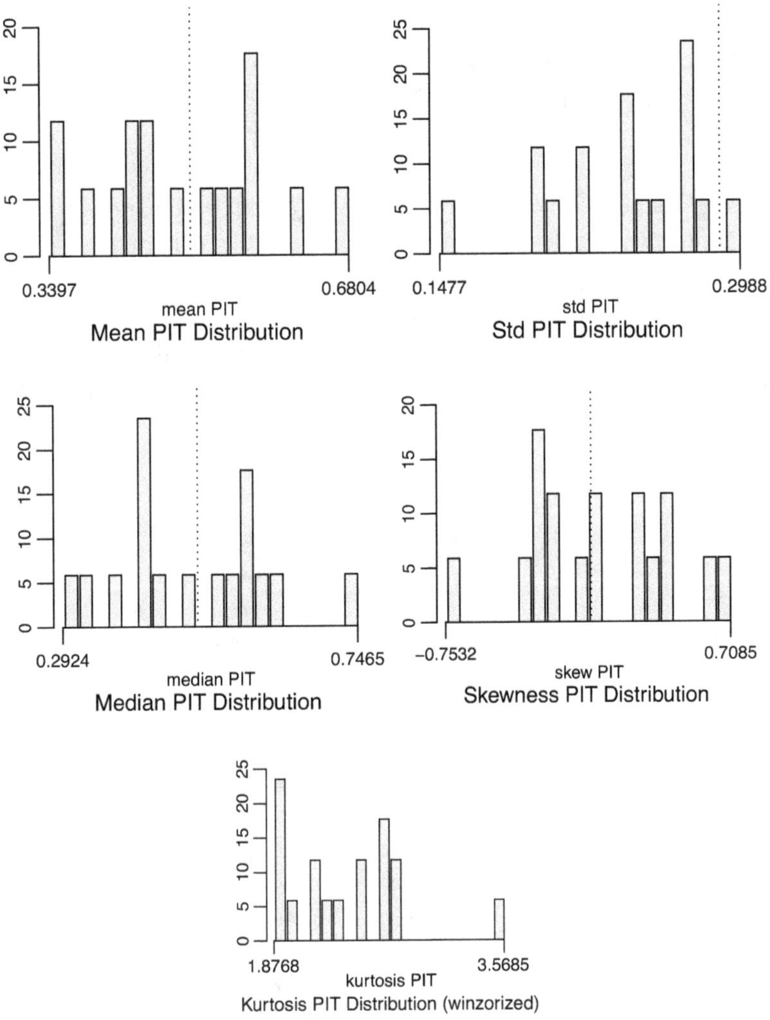

Figure 4.4b Top of the house moments of the distribution of PITs.

$$I_t \sim \text{i.i.d. } Bernoulli(p)$$

This null is tested against an alternative that the observed success probability of the Bernoulli distribution is different from the assumed probability p,

$$I_t \sim Bernoulli(\pi)$$

Mathematically, the test for unconditional coverage (denoted as *(uc)*) is states as follows,

$$H_{0,uc} : \pi = p$$

The likelihood function for a sample of T i.i.d. observations from a Bernoulli variable, I_t, with known probability p is written as

$$L(I,p) = p^{T_1}(1-p)^{T-T_1}. \tag{4.3}$$

where T_1 is the number of ones in the sample. The likelihood function for an i.i.d. Bernoulli with unknown probability parameter, π_1, to be estimated is

$$L(I,\pi_1) = \pi_1^{T_1}(1-\pi_1)^{T-T_1}. \tag{4.4}$$

The maximum-likelihood (ML) estimate of π_1 is

$$\hat{\pi}_1 = T_1/T \tag{4.5}$$

and we can thus write a likelihood ratio test of unconditional coverage as

$$LR_{uc} = 2(ln\ L(I,\hat{\pi}_1) - ln\ L(I,p)). \tag{4.6}$$

The number of subportfolios for which we do not reject the null at the 1% confidence level is 401, which represents 67% of the sample. Out of the 196 subportfolios that failed the unconditional coverage test, there are 83 subportfolios with zero exceedances. Table 4.2 summarizes results of the Kupiec test by providing counts and shares of subportfolios which pass (fail to reject the null hypothesis) categorizing subportfolios by product. VaR models of muni bonds, single-name credit default swaps (CDS), and tranched products appear to perform very well relative to other products both, for single product portfolios as well as for combinations of products. However, the small sample size of these categories reduces the statistical significance of this conclusion. Instead, if we consider products consisting of larger subportfolio groups, we note that linear equities, interest rate products, FX and commodities have passage rates of 70% for single and in excess of 64% for multiple product categories, implying that, relatively speaking, these products lend themselves to more "accurate" modeling.

Table 4.2. ***Count and percent of subportfolios pass the Kupiec test.***

Product	Count single	Count multiple	Percent single	Percent multiple
SovereignBonds	6	175	100	66
CorporateBonds	6	118	75	67
MuniBonds	3	32	100	73
AgencyMBS	0	25	0	53
NonAgencyMBS	–	26	–	59
CMO	–	21	–	52
IndexCDS	1	118	50	71
SingleNameCDS	2	131	100	71
Tranched	1	43	100	70
LinearEquities	14	109	70	64
NonlinearEquities	1	90	100	66
ExoticEquities	–	31	–	60
InterestRates	21	256	70	67
FX	31	213	72	70
Commodities	17	43	74	67
OtherProductType	9	128	60	67

It's important to point out the limitations of the unconditional coverage test, most notable of which is that the test ignores the time variation in the data. This limitation is mitigated through the independence test proposed by Christoffersen (1998) and noted by Berkowitz and O'Brien (2002). Rather than focusing on the expected vs observed fraction of violations, Christoffersen focuses on whether the observed violations cluster or evenly spread out over time. The *independence test* assumes that the sequence of exceptions follows a first-order Markov process with a switching probability matrix such that,

$$\Pi = \begin{bmatrix} 1 - \pi_{01} & \pi_{01} \\ 1 - \pi_{11} & \pi_{11} \end{bmatrix}$$

where π_{ij} is the probability of an i on day $t-1$ being followed by a j on day t. The test of independence (denoted as *ind*) is specified as,

$H_{0,ind} : \pi_{01} = \pi_{11}.$

The likelihood ratio for the test of the null independence hypothesis can be computed using the likelihood function

$$L(I, \pi_{01}, \pi_{11}) = (1 - \pi_{01})^{T_0 - T_{01}} \pi_{01}^{T_{01}} (1 - \pi_{11})^{T_1 - T_{11}} \pi_{11}^{T_{11}}, \quad (4.7)$$

where T_{ij} denotes the number of observations with a j following an i, and T_i is the number of i (i.e., is the number of ones or zeros in the sample).

The ML estimates are

$$\hat{\pi}_{01} = T_{01}/T_0 \quad (4.8)$$

$$\hat{\pi}_{11} = T_{11}/T_1 \quad (4.9)$$

and the independence test statistic is

$$LR_{ind} = 2(ln\ L(I, \hat{\pi}_{01}, \hat{\pi}_{11}) - ln\ L(I, \hat{\pi}_1)). \quad (4.10)$$

The number of subportfolios for which we fail to reject the null of the Christoffersen independence test at the 1% confidence level is 551, which represents 92% of the total number of subportfolios. Table 4.3 summarizes the results of the test (i.e., counts of subportfolios which fail to reject the null) categorizing the subportfolios by product. Here too, linear equities, interest rate products, FX and commodities appear to have high pass rates, in excess of 85% for single products and exceeding 94% for subportfolios containing multiple products.

We previously mentioned that an accurate VaR measure must exhibit the properties of unconditional coverage AND independence. It follows that in order to assess accuracy, a model must be evaluated against these tests jointly. The unconditional coverage and independence tests can be combined to test a sequence for *conditional coverage* (denoted *cc*). Empirically, this is represented as,

$H_{0,cc} : \pi_{01} = \pi_{11} = p.$

The likelihood ratio for the test of the null of conditional coverage hypothesis can be computed using the previous likelihood function and adding the coverage restriction:

$$LR_{cc} = 2(ln\ L(I, \hat{\pi}_{01}, \hat{\pi}_{11}) - ln\ L(I, p)). \quad (4.11)$$

The independence and conditional coverage tests are carried out conditioning on the first observation. The tests are asymptotically

Table 4.3. *Count and percent of subportfolios that pass the independence test.*

Product	Count single	Count multiple	Percent single	Percent multiple
SovereignBonds	6	251	100	94
CorporateBonds	8	163	100	92
MuniBonds	0	34	0	77
AgencyMBS	0	43	0	91
NonAgencyMBS	–	41	–	93
CMO	–	36	–	90
IndexCDS	2	161	100	96
SingleNameCDS	2	174	100	95
Tranched	1	59	100	97
LinearEquities	15	156	75	92
NonlinearEquities	1	127	100	93
ExoticEquities	–	50	–	96
InterestRates	29	357	97	93
FX	42	287	98	94
Commodities	22	63	96	98
OtherProductType	13	175	87	92

distributed as chi-square with degree of freedom one for the *uc* and *ind* tests and two for the *cc* test. But we will rely on finite sample p-values below.

Practically, the test checks whether the proportion of violations following an exceedance is the same as the proportion of violations following a non-exceedance, while simultaneously determining whether each of these proportions is significantly different from the pre-determined confidence level (here, 1%).

The number of subportfolios for which we fail to reject the null of conditional coverage at the 1% confidence level is 422, which represents 71% of the sample. Table 4.4 summarizes the test results (i.e., fail to reject the null) categorizing the subportfolios by product. As with individual tests of unconditional coverage and independence, linear equities, interest rate products, FX and commodities continue to outperform other products when it comes to passage rates.

While joint tests may perform well at identifying instances where both properties have been violated, they have significant limitations

Table 4.4. ***Count and percent of subportfolios that pass the conditional coverage test.***

Product	Count single	Count multiple	Percent single	Percent multiple
SovereignBonds	6	190	100	71
CorporateBonds	7	125	88	71
MuniBonds	0	27	0	61
AgencyMBS	0	30	0	64
NonAgencyMBS	–	29	–	66
CMO	–	26	–	65
IndexCDS	2	127	100	76
SingleNameCDS	2	138	100	75
Tranched	1	50	100	82
LinearEquities	13	118	65	69
NonlinearEquities	1	91	100	66
ExoticEquities	–	35	–	67
InterestRates	20	274	67	72
FX	34	228	79	75
Commodities	18	49	78	77
OtherProductType	9	137	60	72

in their ability to detect misspecifications when only one of the two properties is violated.

While independence and conditional coverage tests are considered to have greater discriminatory power than unconditional coverage tests, it is important to recognize that they too have significant drawbacks. Specifically, the Christoffersen test does not allow for the possibility that independence may be violated at a distance greater than one lag. While it may be true that yesterday's exceedance has no information about the probability of observing an exceedance today, the test provides no information about the dependence of breaches one week apart. Or whether exceedances occurring one month apart are independent from one another.

In addition to Kupiec and Christoffersen, other tests have been emphasized for their ability to identify misspecified models. Among others, these include the *Ljung–Box test* (1978) which examines the autocorrelation properties of hits and Chrisoffersen and Pelletier (2004) test of independence of time between exceptions.

Table 4.5. ***Count and percent of subportfolios that pass the Ljung–Box test.***

Product	Count single	Count multiple	Percent single	Percent multiple
SovereignBonds	5	161	83	83
CorporateBonds	6	110	75	81
MuniBonds	0	27	0	71
AgencyMBS	0	20	0	71
NonAgencyMBS	–	16	–	73
CMO	–	16	–	70
IndexCDS	1	99	100	88
SingleNameCDS	2	112	100	85
Tranched	1	38	100	90
LinearEquities	11	122	58	81
NonlinearEquities	1	96	100	82
ExoticEquities	–	35	–	85
InterestRates	22	245	92	83
FX	36	226	92	85
Commodities	18	52	90	93
OtherProductType	9	120	69	81

Ljung–Box test allows us to jointly test whether m number of lags are zero. To do so, we need to calculate the following test statistic,

$$Q = T(T+2)\sum_{k=1}^{m}\frac{r_k^2}{T-k} \tag{4.12}$$

which is asymptotically chi-square with m degrees of freedom.

The null of Ljung–Box test assumes no autocorrelation of exceedances. The number of subportfolios for which we fail to reject the null of autocorrelation at a single lag at 1% confidence level is 387, which represents 82% of the total number of subportfolios. Table 4.5 summarizes the test results (i.e., fail to reject the null) categorizing the subportfolios by product. FX appears to demonstrate a strongest performance relative to other products for both, single as well as multiple product categories.

The Ljung–Box test can be extended as in Berkowitz et al. (2011) to include other available information as predictors of exceedances, providing further evidence that the risk model has been misspecified, in this case by not incorporating all relevant past information. As in Berkowitz et al., we estimate a linear probability model (LPM) and logit regressions of the exceedances on their lags and, additionally, lagged VaR or lagged P&L. Both regressions use a binary outcome variable based on exceedances. For linear probability model regressions, errors are assumed to have zero conditional mean, but there is no explicit parametric assumption on their distribution.

While LPM is simple to estimate and constitutes a robust check of the independence property, it has non-trivial drawbacks. For instance, the error term of a binary variable has a Bernoulli structure, the LPM can yield values of predicted values of the dependent variable outside of the $[0, 1]$ interval, and it imposes linearity on the relationship between the dependent variable and the right-hand side variables. In light of these limitations, a more appropriate model specification for the error structure is the logistic distribution where expectation of an exceedance is,

$$E[I_{t+1}|X_t] = p_t = logit^{-1}(\beta \cdot X_t) = \frac{1}{1 + e^{-\beta \cdot X_t}} \tag{4.13}$$

where I_{t+1} is the indicator variable if the subportfolio observered a breach on date $t+1$, while X_t is the information available to risk manager at the time of the model forecast, i.e., past exceedances I_t, I_{t-1}, etc., past portfolio returns PL_t, PL_{t-1}, etc., and past information sets that were included in previous VaR models VaR_t, VaR_{t-1}.

In our analysis, we focused on estimating models with a single lagged explanatory variable and tested whether the β coefficients are statistically significantly different from zero. Observing significant coefficients indicates that the forecasting model for losses does not respond sufficiently fast to the observed changes in market environment. The results of these tests are summarized in Table 4.6, which provides the counts of subportfolios with significant coefficients at a 1% confidence level for various specifications of the Linear Probability and Logit models. For example, the first logit specification includes lag exceedances and lag VaR as explanatory variables. Out of 597 logit regressions, fifty-four regressions had a significant coefficient on lag exceedances and thirty-six had a significant coefficient on lag VaR. For seven regressions both lag exceedence and lag VaR were significant.

Table 4.6. ***Logit and LPM regressions of exceedances on lagged VaR or lagged P&L.***

	Logit (1)	Logit (2)	Logit (3)	LPM (1)	LPM (2)	LPM (3)
Lag Exceedance	54	45	68	83	84	87
Lag VaR	36	–	–	45	–	–
Lag PnL	–	33	–	–	54	–
Both Lags	7	4	–	17	18	–
Neither Lags	514	523	529	361	352	385
N	597	597	597	472	472	472

In a seminal work, Christoffersen and Pelletier (2004) demonstrated that the tests described thus far can lack power. In order to increase the robustness of results, Christoffersen and Pelletier proposed a duration test, which assesses the information content of time between observed exceedances. Broadly, the intuition behind the duration-based tests is that the clustering of violations will result in an excessive number of relatively short and relatively long durations, where no exceptions are observed, corresponding to market turbulence and market calm, respectively. Ideally, the time duration between VaR exceedances should not cluster, implying that in a correctly specified risk model, the no-exception duration should have no memory. This Christoffersen and Pelletier duration test will be able to identify models with dependent exceptions, but also models that do not producce a sufficient number of expected exceptions.

Duration between exceedances is defined as

$$D_i = t_i - t_{i-1}. \tag{4.14}$$

Using the Bernoulli distribution property, the probability of a breach in the next period is exactly equal to

$$Pr(D_i = 1) = Pr(I_{t+1} = 1) = p. \tag{4.15}$$

It follows that the probability of a breach in d periods can be defined as,

$$Pr(D_i = d) = Pr(I_{t+1} = 0, I_{t=2} = 0, \ldots, I_{t+d} = 1), \tag{4.16}$$

and since

$$I_{t+1} \sim \text{iid}\,(p, p(1-p)), \tag{4.17}$$

we have

$$Pr(D_i = d) = (1-p)\ldots(1-p)(p) = (1-p)^{d-1}p. \tag{4.18}$$

For a correctly specified model, with no dependence between exceedances, the distribution for duration is exponential,

$$f_{exp}(D;p) = pe^{-pD}. \tag{4.19}$$

We test the null against the alternative hypothesis that duration has a Weibull distribution,

$$f_W(D;a,b) = a^b bD^{b-1}\,exp^{\,-(aD)^b}. \tag{4.20}$$

Statistically, the independence of the duration test can be summarized as follows,

$$H_o : b = 1 \text{ and } a = p; H_a : b \neq 1 \text{ or } a \neq p. \tag{4.21}$$

A total of 77 subportfolios fail the duration test at the 1% confidence level, implying that in effect, the conditional expected duraton between violations is not constant. The fraction of failed supportfolios represents 13% of the overall sample.

4.6 Misspecification Tests Based on the Distribution of PITs

In the previous section, we discussed the backtesting of VaR models using the "hit" series of exceedances. While this approach to backtesting allows a simplistic assessment of model quality, we can enhance the precision of our estimates of model accuracy and fit by using more sophisticated backtesting approaches. We are referring to the practice of backtesting with PITs and assessing their entire distribution for properties of independence and uniformity.

A wide range of goodness-of-fit tests (e.g., Kolmogorov–Smirnov, Anderson–Darling, Cramér–von Mises) can be used to assess the uniformity of the distribution of PITs. *Kolmogorov–Smirnov test* (KS) is a widely used nonparametric test that evaluates the goodness-of-fit by comparing the empirical distribution function of a sample with some reference distribution function. Operationally, the KS statistic quantifies the distance between the empirical CDF of the sample and the CDF of the reference distribution.

Table 4.7. ***Count and percent of subportfolios that pass the Kolmogorov–Smirnov test.***

Product	Count single	Count multiple	Percent single	Percent multiple
SovereignBonds	1	42	17	16
CorporateBonds	0	22	0	12
MuniBonds	1	9	33	20
AgencyMBS	0	1	0	2
NonAgencyMBS	–	2	–	5
CMO	–	1	–	2
IndexCDS	1	25	50	15
SingleNameCDS	1	31	50	17
Tranched	0	10	0	16
LinearEquities	7	36	35	21
NonlinearEquities	0	26	0	19
ExoticEquities	–	11	–	21
InterestRates	11	75	37	20
FX	16	73	37	24
Commodities	8	14	35	22
OtherProductType	1	33	7	17

As in the previous section, the reference distribution function against which PIT distribution is compared is the continuous uniform distribution over the $[0, 1]$ interval and the KS test allows us to determine whether the data is in fact drawn from the distribution in question. The KS test statistic is defined as,

$$D = \max_j\{\text{abs}(z_j - A_j)\} \tag{4.22}$$

where z_j is the theoretical CDF under the null, A_j the empirical CDF and D is equal to zero under the null hypothesis.

The number of subportfolios for which we fail to reject null of the Kolmogorov–Smirnov test at 1% confidence level is 123, which is approximately 21% of the entire sample. The low number of subportfolios that "pass" the KS test is not surprising given the deviation from uniformity that we observed by representing the PIT statistics as histograms in Section 4.3. Table 4.7 summarizes the count and percentage of subportfolios for which we fail to reject the null of uniformity.

We should note that a limitation of the KS test is its lack of sensitivity at the extremes of the distribution. That is, while the test is effective in detecting differences in central masses of the two distributions, it is not reliable when it comes to comparison of the tails. *Anderson–Darling test* (A-D) is a modification of the Kolmogorov–Smirnov test that corrects for this limitation. Unlike the KS test, A-D puts more weight on the tails of the distribution, yielding more power in the presence of distributional biases. A majority of financial institutions use a tail metric as a risk measure, e.g. 99% VaR. Therefore, any misspecification in the tail of the distribution of the risk model will be better identified by the A-D test.

Statistically speaking, Anderson–Darling tests are to assess if the data are independently and identically distributed from a specific distribution. Here, we are interested in assessing whether the subportfolio PITs may be from a uniform $[0, 1]$ distribution, which is reflected in the null hypothesis. Out alternative hypothesis is that the empirical CDF of PITs is a function other than uniform.

The A-D test statistic is calculated as

$$A^2 = -n - \frac{1}{n}\sum_{j=1}^{n}(2j-1)\left[log(z_j) + log(1 - z_{-j})\right] \tag{4.23}$$

where n is the number of observations. As with the KS, the test statistic is equal to zero under the null hypothesis.

The number of subportfolios for which we fail to reject null of the Anderson–Darling test at 1% confidence level is 65, a mere 11% of the total number of subportfolios. It is clear that as the power of the test increases, we are able to find fewer subportfolios which exhibit the desired properties, summarized also by product in Table 4.8.

Cramér–von Mises test is another variation of the Kolmogorov–Smirnov test. However, rather than using the supremum, it relies on the mean squared deviation of the distribution. Cramér–von Mises tests the goodness-of-fit relative to the continuous uniform distribution $[0, 1]$. Here, too, we assume that the values are independent, identically distributed random values. The null hypothesis is that the empirical CDF is cumulative uniform, while the alternative hypothesis is that the distribution is some other function.

Cramér–von Misses test statistic is calculated as follows,

Table 4.8. ***Count and percent of subportfolios that pass the Anderson–Darling test.***

Product	Count single	Count multiple	Percent single	Percent multiple
SovereignBonds	1	26	17	10
CorporateBonds	0	13	0	7
MuniBonds	0	3	0	7
AgencyMBS	0	1	0	2
NonAgencyMBS	–	2	–	5
CMO	–	1	–	2
IndexCDS	0	13	0	8
SingleNameCDS	0	17	0	9
Tranched	0	7	0	11
LinearEquities	6	16	30	9
NonlinearEquities	0	10	0	7
ExoticEquities	–	5	–	10
InterestRates	7	40	23	10
FX	8	36	19	12
Commodities	5	7	22	11
OtherProductType	1	19	7	10

$$W^2 = \sum_{j=1}^{n} \left[z_j - (2j-1)/2n\right]^2 + (1/12n). \tag{4.24}$$

As with the KS, it is equal to zero under the null hypothesis.

The number of subportfolios for which we fail to reject null of CVM test at 1% confidence level is 123, 21% of the total number of subportfolios. Table 4.9 shows the results with single name CDS, interest rates and FX exhibiting stronger passing rates than other products.

To parallel the independence test of exceedances, we proceed by assessing the *independence* of the PIT realizations. For this, we transform PITs into standard normal variables to avoid problems of inference due to bounded support, see Berkowitz (2001). Their independence is then assessed by fitting a linear regression of transformed PITs on their lags as well as lagged values of the P&L. Table 4.10 summarized the counts of subportfolios with statistically significant coefficients on the lagged variables at a 1% confidence level.

Table 4.9. *Count and percent of subportfolios that pass the Cramér–von Mises test.*

Product	Count single	Count multiple	Percent single	Percent multiple
SovereignBonds	1	48	17	18
CorporateBonds	0	22	0	12
MuniBonds	1	10	33	23
AgencyMBS	1	3	100	6
NonAgencyMBS	–	3	–	7
CMO	–	3	–	8
IndexCDS	1	27	50	16
SingleNameCDS	1	32	50	17
Tranched	0	11	0	18
LinearEquities	7	36	35	21
NonlinearEquities	0	27	0	20
ExoticEquities	–	11	–	21
InterestRates	13	83	43	22
FX	16	78	37	26
Commodities	8	13	35	20
OtherProductType	1	34	7	18

Table 4.10. *Linear regression of transformed PITs on lagged transformed PIT and lagged P&L.*

	AR1	AR conditioned
Lag Trans PIT	218	154
Lag PnL	–	108
Both Lags	–	79
Neither Lags	379	414
N	597	597

Conditional uniformity of the distribution of PITs can be visually assessed by plotting pairs of PITs and lagged PIT values for all subportfolios. The scatter plot, in Figure 4.5, provides graphical evidence for the goodness-of-fit and identifies pairs of PIT and lagged PIT values that do not follow the independence and uniformity properties of an

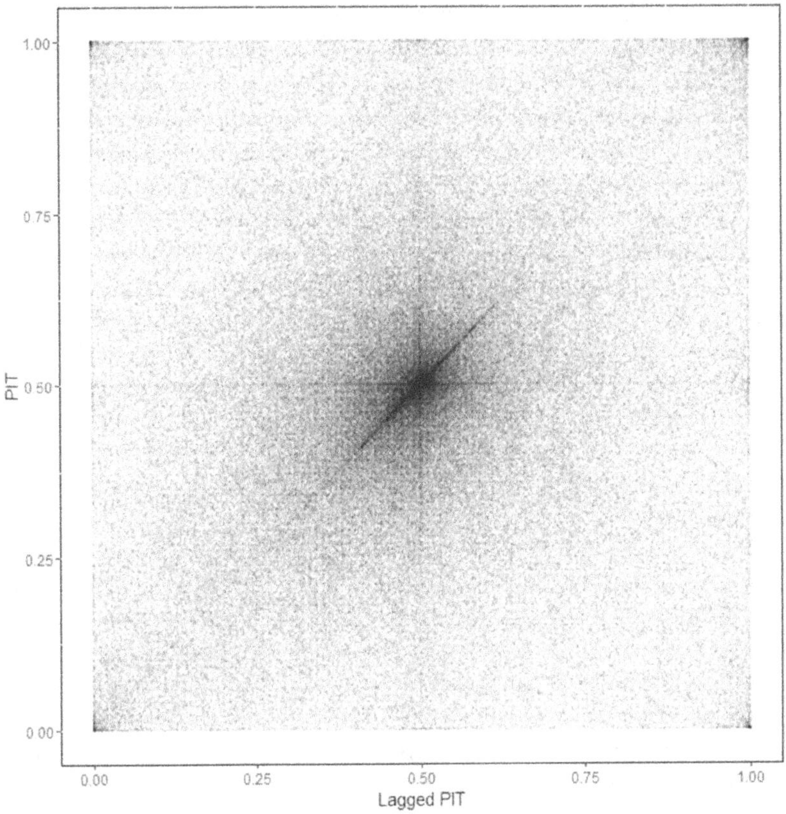

Figure 4.5 PITs vs lagged PITs by subportfolios.

accurate model. We observe significantly more mass in the center and very extremes of the distribution, suggesting dependence and lack of uniformity in the bivariate distribution.

4.7 Conclusion

Exceedance-based backtesting of risk models and, in particular, VaR models, is a well established methodology for which the financial firms have appropriately adapted their models. For example, we found that 67% of the sample passes the unconditional coverage test and moreover, if we are to disregard subportfolios with zero exceedances 78% subportfolios "pass" the unconditional coverage test. When performing an independence test based on logit regressions of exceedances,

11% of subportfolios had auto correlated exceedances. However, pure exceedance analysis fails to identify the more nuanced model misspecifications, as highlighted by the enhanced backtesting based on PITs. When performing distributional tests for uniformity we find that only 21% of the entire sample pass the Kolmogorov–Smirnov test. Moreover, when checking for independence of PITs based on autoregressive estimations, we found a larger portion of subportfolios, 37% that exhibited dependence in PITs. Overall, banks perform better on exceedence tests than on tests of distribution. This could be because risk models are designed to be more conservative and contain regulatory add ons.

References

Berkowitz, J. (2001). Testing density forecasts, with applications to risk management. *Journal of Business and Economic Statistics*, 19(4), 465–474.

Berkowitz, J. and O'Brien, J. (2002). How Accurate Are Value-at-Risk Models at Commercial Banks. *Journal of Finance*, 57(3), 1093–1111.

Berkowitz, J., Christoffersen, P. and Pelletier, D. (2016). Evaluating Value-at-Risk models with desk-level data. *Management Science*, 57(12), 2213–2227.

Campbell, S. (2006). A review of backtesting and backtesting procedures. *Journal of Risk*, 9(2), 1–17.

Christoffersen, P. (1998). Evaluating interval forecasts. *International Economic Review*, 39, 841–862.

Christoffersen, P., Hahn, J. and Inoue A. (2001). Testing and comparing Value-at-Risk measures. *Journal of Empirical Finance*, 8, 325–342.

Christoffersen, P. and Pelletier, D. (2004). Backtesting Value-at-Risk: A duration-based approach. *Journal of Financial Econometrics*, 2(1), 84–108.

Diebold, F., Gunther, T., and Tay, A. (1998). Evaluating density forecasts with applications to financial risk management. *International Economic Review*, 39(4), 863–883.

Federal Register (2013). Market Risk Capital Rule; Vol. 78 No. 198.

Jorion, P. (2002). How informative are Value-at-Risk disclosures. *The Accouting Review*, 77(4), 911–931.

Kupiec P. (1995). Techniques for verifying the accuracy of risk management models. *Journal of Derivatives*, 3, 73–84.

Ljung, G. and Box, G. (1978). On a measure of a lack of fit in time series models. *Biometrika*, 65(2), 297–303.

Marshall, C. and Siegel, M. (1997). Value-at-Risk: Implementing a risk measurement standard. *Journal of Derivatives*, 4, 91–111.

Noceti, P., Smith, J., and Hodges, S. (2003). An evaluation of tests of distributional forecasts. *Journal of Forecasting*, 22(6–7), 447–455.

Pritsker, M. (1997). Evaluating Value-at-Risk methodologies: Accuracy versus computational time. *Journal of Financial Services Research*, 12, 201–242.

Rosenblatt, M. (1952). Remarks on a multivariate transformation. *Annals of Mathematical Statistics*, 23, 470–472.

5 *Evaluation of Value-at-Risk Models: An Empirical Likelihood Approach**

DAVID LYNCH, VALERIO POTÌ, AKHTAR SIDDIQUE AND FRANCESCO CAMPOBASSO

5.1 Introduction

Within the broader risk management function at financial institutions, the aim of risk model validation is to assess the goodness of the risk model in forecasting features of the distribution of future returns on a given portfolio, whether static or dynamic in its composition, of financial assets and liabilities.

Often, when the measure of risk exposure is Value-at-Risk (VaR) at a given confidence level, the feature of interest is a specific quantile. More generally, when the measure of interest is the conditional VaR (or Expected Shortfall), the feature of interest is the tail of the distribution beginning at a given quantile.[1]

We can identify two conceptually distinct approaches to VaR model evaluation, namely backtesting (i.e. analyses of exceedances) and scenario analysis. Backtesting is based on historical scenarios; it is necessarily backward-looking and assumes stationarity of the data generating process (DGP) of portfolio returns. Stress testing is based instead on conjectured scenario, it is in principle forward-looking and, also in principle, can cope with structural breaks of the DGP. For inference, both backtesting and stress testing need to impose some distributional assumptions.

There is also a third possible approach to model validation. This relies on shrinkage estimators and shrinks either historical or expert-generated

* The views expressed in this chapter are those of the authors alone and do not establish supervisory policy, requirements or expectations. They also do not represent those of the Comptroller of the Currency or Board of Governors of the Federal Reserve.

[1] In this assessment, implicitly or explicitly, the goodness is defined as based on a set of criteria. We may refer to these criteria as reflecting the loss function implicitly or explicitly assumed by the analyst in carrying out the model validation exercise. This loss function should reflect what the posited decision maker dislikes or is assumed to dislike and should be coherent with the loss function implied by the chosen risk measure (i.e., the statistic used to measure risk) that is the object of measurement in the risk model of the bank.

scenarios (probabilities) in a way motivated by economic theory, e.g., asset pricing theory. The technical tools for this are either Bayesian shrinkage estimators or information theoretic ones, especially Empirical Likelihood (EL) (Owen 2001) estimators. At first glance, Empirical Likelihood-based estimators would fit the evaluation of VaR models well, since EL-based approaches are most useful when the distribution of the quantity or statistic of interest is unknown. Kitamura (2006) provides a good overview of empirical likelihood methodologies.

In what follows, we first review backtesting methodologies based on evaluating density forecasts. Lopez (1998) provides a good overview of the VaR model evaluation literature. We focus on tests, initially suggested by Diebold et al. (1998) and then further formalized by Berkowitz (2001), of whether the PITs (probability integral transforms) of portfolio returns are drawn from a uniform distribution. As Diebold et al. (1998) explains, PITs can be seen as encompassing the unconditional and conditional coverage tests using the more popular interval forecasts such as described in Christoffersen (1998).[2] Then, after briefly discussing the limitations in terms of power of this approach, we outline an alternative test for evaluating density forecasts. We also outline a method to infer the risk exposure, by assessing whether some measure of interval forecast error (e.g., distance between the empirical distribution of the PITs and the posited uniform distribution) is related to some measure of risk exposure, such as the volatility of given risk factors. Our intention is to carry out this analysis over time, over rolling windows of observations, as well as over the entire sample period. We will then outline and discuss scenario-based model validation and sketch a possible compromise between backward-looking backtesting and forward-looking scenario analysis based on Bayesian shrinking and methods drawn from the information theoretic tradition.

5.2 PIT-Based Backtesting

A well-known approach to VaR model backtesting, based on a result proven by Rosenblatt (1952) and subsequently applied to a risk

[2] Gordy and McNeil (2018) derive a class of backtests for forecast distributions in which the test statistic is a spectral transformation that weights exceedance events by a function of the modeled probability levels.

modelling setting by Diebold et al. (1998) and Berkowitz (2001), is to test whether the PITs of the portfolio returns, where the integral transform is given by the cumulative density function that describes the portfolio returns according to the VaR model, are drawn from a uniform distribution over the interval $(0, 1)$. In a nutshell, this is a test of whether the density forecast underpinning the VaR estimate is close to the empirical density of portfolio returns. As such, it can be seen as a conditional coverage test for intervals defined by a range of quantiles, rather than by just one quantile as in typical tests of coverage of interval forecasts (Christoffersen 1998). The range of intervals is effectively defined by the partitions (the set of "bins") of the support of the uniform distribution that is used as support of the empirical distribution of the PITs. As such, in principle, it encompasses tests for unconditional coverage of interval forecasts, though it can also be extended to encompass conditional coverage tests (Christoffersen 1998).

We first compare and contrast a number of tests of the null hypothesis that the PITs are drawn from a uniform distribution over the interval $(0, 1)$, to which we refer as *tests based on the distribution of the PITs*. We then propose an alternative approach where we test the null hypothesis that the observations (the portfolio returns) occur with probabilities implied by the VaR model (henceforth, the *implied probabilities*) against the alternative that they occur with probabilities given by their empirical distribution. We refer to this test as a first instance of *tests based on the probabilities implied by the PITs.*

5.2.1 Tests Based on the Distribution of PITs

In this type of test, the null hypothesis is that, in any given set (window) of observations (whether this is the full sample or a rolling window), the PITs are drawn from a known distribution. Formally, consider the sequence of rates of returns, $\left\{y_{t,t+h}, t = 1, 2, \ldots, \tau\right\}$, from holding a given portfolio for h periods, between time t and time $t + h$, $h \geq 1$. Each can be seen as a realization of the corresponding random variable in the sequence $\left\{Y_{t,t+h}, t = 1, 2, \ldots, \tau\right\}$. Assuming that these random variables are measurable with respect to information available at time t, the predictive density, also with a horizon of h periods, of each of these rates of return is denoted as follows:

$$f_{Y|I_t} := f(Y_{t,t+h}|I_t). \tag{5.1}$$

Here, I_t denotes information available at time t. Under this density, a forecast of $Y_{t,t+h}$ h-period ahead is given at time t by

$$\hat{Y}_{t,t+h} = E(Y_{t,t+h}|I_t) = \int_{-\infty}^{\infty} f_{Y|I_t}(x)dx. \tag{5.2}$$

Denote also the corresponding cumulative density function (CDF, henceforth) as follows:

$$F_{Y|I_t}(y) := \int_{-\infty}^{y} f_{Y|I_t}(x)dx. \tag{5.3}$$

The predictive density can be used to compute different risk measure estimates. For example, for a portfolio worth 1 unit of the numeraire currency at time t, the time-t VaR at the confidence level $1 - \alpha$ over the subsequent h-period horizon is a quantile of (Eq. 5.3),[3] i.e.

$$VaR_{Y|I_t,1-\alpha} = F^{-1}_{Y|I_t}(\alpha). \tag{5.4}$$

As another example, the conditional VaR (CVaR), also known as Expected Shortfall (ES), is

$$CVaR_{Y|I_t,1-\alpha} = \int_{-\infty}^{VaR_{Y,1-\alpha}} f_{Y|I_t}(x)dx. \tag{5.5}$$

For a sample of rates of return observations, $\left\{y_{t,t+h}, t = 1, 2, \ldots, \tau\right\}$ with density as in (Eq. 5.1), the corresponding PITs are

$$PIT_t = F_{Y|I_t}(y_t). \tag{5.6}$$

Assume now that $f_{Y|I_t}(y) = f_{Y|I_s}(y) = \forall t, s \in \{1, 2, \ldots, \tau\}$ and for all $y \in \mathbb{R}$ (i.e., for all y in the support of the densities in (Eq. 5.7) and, therefore, for all possible observable values of the portfolio rate of return). That is, assume that the predictive density is the same for all periods in the sample under consideration, which amounts to ruling out return predictability and/or heteroskedasticity, in addition to assuming weak stationarity (i.e., ruling out structural breaks as well

[3] Strictly speaking, this is the definition of the so called absolute VaR, whereas we are often interested in a relative version thereof, where $Y_{t,t+h}$ is not the rate of return on the portfolio but rather a measure of abnormal return, namely the rate of return

as, of course, stochastic trends). Then, as observed by Diebold et al. (1998) and Berkowitz (2001), based on a fundamental result demonstrated by Rosenblatt (1952), the distribution of the PITs is uniform over the support given by the interval $(0,1)$, under the under the null hypothesis that (Eq. 5.1) is the true density. That is, under this null,

$$PIT_t \sim U(0,1) \tag{5.7}$$

In particular, under this null, it follows that the VaR model that generates the PITs has correct unconditional coverage for all forecast intervals and, therefore, for all confidence levels of the VaR estimate. Hence, testing the null that (Eq. 5.7) holds encompasses tests of unconditional coverage.

To define a test procedure that encompasses also tests of conditional coverage, we need to chain up the conditional densities in (Eq. 5.1) to compute the unconditional density and cumulative density functions for the sample period under consideration, i.e.

$$f_Y := f(Y_{1,1+h}, Y_{2,2+h}, \ldots, Y_{\tau,\tau+h}) = \int_{-\infty}^{+\infty}\int_{-\infty}^{+\infty} f_{Y|I_t}(x) f_{Z_t}(z_t) dz_t dx. \tag{5.8}$$

Here, $\{f_{Z_t}(z_t)\}_{t=1,\ldots,\tau}$ is a sequence of functions of z_t, each measurable with respect to I_t, that generates the sigma field of $\{I_t\}_{t=1,\ldots,\tau}$. The corresponding cumulative density function is then:

$$F_Y(y) := \int_{-\infty}^{y} f_Y(x) dx. \tag{5.9}$$

For a sample of rates of return observations, $\{y_{t,t+h}, t = 1,2,\ldots,\tau\}$ with density as in (Eq. 5.8), the corresponding PITs are

$$PIT_t = F_Y(y_t). \tag{5.10}$$

For these PITs, the result demonstrated by Rosenblatt (1952) implies that, under the null hypothesis that (Eq. 5.8) is the true density, (Eq. 5.7) is again true, just like in the unconditional case. Under this null, the VaR model that generates the PITs has correct conditional, as well as unconditional, coverage for all forecast intervals and, therefore, for all confidence levels of the VaR estimate. Hence, testing the null that (Eq. 5.7) holds encompasses tests of both unconditional and conditional coverage.

Inference on whether (Eq. 5.7) holds when the PITs are given by either (Eq. 5.6) or (Eq. 5.10) is traditionally conducted with the Kolmogorov–Smirnov test (Kolmogorov 1933; Smirnov 1948) and the Anderson–Darling test (Anderson and Darling 1952). In both tests, the test statistic is a measure of distance between the empirical distribution of the PITs and the distribution under the null hypothesis, given by (Eq. 5.7). The two tests differ in the choice of distance measure and, therefore, in the implicit choice of loss function about which the decision maker who uses the test most cares.

The test statistic of the one-sample Kolmogorov–Smirnov test,[4] in our context, is the maximum absolute difference between the empirical CDF of the PITs, $\hat{F}_{PIT}(x)$, and their hypothesized CDF, namely the CDF of the uniform distribution with support (0, 1), $F_{PIT}(x)$:

$$KS = \max_{\substack{x=PIT_t,\\ t=1,2,\ldots,\tau}} \left(\left| \hat{F}_{PIT}(x) - F_{PIT}(x) \right| \right). \tag{5.11}$$

This test, therefore, rejects the null if there is a clustering of the PITs around certain values, so that their empirical frequency differs enough from the frequency under the uniform distribution. This means that, say, a VaR model will fail a backtesting based on this test even if there are not too many exceedances at any conventional significance level, but simply because some quantile is more frequent than we may expect based on the DGP underpinning the VaR estimate. Under appropriate regularity conditions, $\sqrt{\tau} KS_\tau$ converges to the Kolmogorov distribution, which permits calculation of p-values and statistical inference on the null hypothesis.

In the case of the Anderson–Darling test, the test statistic belongs to the family of quadratic empirical distribution function statistics, which measure the distance between the hypothesized distribution, $F_{PIT}(x)$, and the empirical CDF, $\hat{F}_{PIT}(x)$, of the PITs as

$$AD = \tau \int_{-\infty}^{+\infty} \left(\hat{F}_{PIT}(x) - F_{PIT}(x) \right)^2 w(x) dF(x) \tag{5.12}$$

[4] The one-sample Kolmogorov–Smirnov test is a nonparametric test of the null hypothesis that the population CDF of the data is equal to the hypothesized CDF. The two-sided test for unequal CDF functions tests the null hypothesis against the alternative that the population CDF of the data is not equal to the hypothesized CDF (in our case, this is the uniform CDF).

over the ordered sample values, x_i, $i = 1, 2, \ldots, \tau$, where $x_i = PIT_t$ for some i and $t \in \{1, 2, \ldots, \tau\}$, $x_i \le x_{i+1}$ and $\{x_i = x_j\} \Rightarrow \{PIT_t = PIT_s\}$ for some $t \ne s$.

Here, the weight function $w(x)$ is

$$[F_{PIT}(x)(1 - F_{PIT}(x))]^{-1}$$

which places greater weight on the observations in the tails of the distribution, thus making the test more sensitive to outliers and better at detecting departure from the hypothesised distribution in the tails of the empirical distribution. In our case, as before, the hypothesised distribution under the null is $U(0,1)$. This test, therefore, rejects the null if there is a clustering of the PITs in either tail. This means that, say, a VaR model will fail a backtesting based on this test not only if there are too many exceedances at a given conventional significance level, but also when there are too few. The distribution of the *AD* statistic under our null hypothesis is on-standard and, in our application, we use the estimate thereof produced by Monte Carlo simulation (the default in Matlab).

As an alternative to both the Kolmogorov–Smirnov test and the Anderson–Darling test, we propose a test based on a distance between the empirical density function and the density of the uniform distribution over the $(0,1)$ support. Drawing inspiration from Post and Potì (2017), the measure of distance we use is the relative entropy and, accordingly, we define the test statistic as a log-likelihood ratio:

$$RE = -2 \ln \frac{\prod_{t=1}^{\tau} \hat{f}_{PIT}(PIT_t)}{\prod_{t=1}^{\tau} f_{PIT}(PIT_t)} = -2 \times \sum_{t=1}^{\tau} \frac{\ln\left(\hat{f}_{PIT}(PIT_t)\right)}{\ln\left(f_{PIT}(PIT_t)\right)}. \tag{5.13}$$

Here, $\hat{f}_{PIT}(x)$ are the empirical densities and $f_{PIT}(PIT_t)$ are the ones under the null hypothesis, namely the ones from the $U(0,1)$ distribution. To estimate $\hat{f}_{PIT}(x)$, we allocate the PITs to $S \le \tau$ measurement classes ("bins"), ω_s with $s \in \{1, 2, \ldots, S\}$, and use the empirical frequencies of these measurement classes as the estimate of the corresponding probabilities,

$$p_s = \frac{\sum_t I(PIT_t \in \omega_s)}{\tau}. \tag{5.14}$$

Here, $I(.)$ is an indicator function that takes value one if the argument is true and value zero otherwise. Hence, assuming that the empirical density within each class is constant, we rewrite the empirical counterpart of the likelihood ratio as follows:

$$\widehat{RE} = -2 \times \sum_{s=1}^{S} \frac{\ln (p_s)}{\ln \left(\frac{1}{S}\right)}. \tag{5.15}$$

Because $\frac{1}{S}$ is the probability of each measurement class under the hypothesis that the PITs are distributed according to a $U(0,1)$ law and the p_s are consistent estimates of the empirical probability of the measurement classes under the empirical density, Wilk's theorem (Wilks 1938) directly implies that, under our null hypothesis (i.e., that the PITs are uniformly distributed), $\widehat{RE}$ is distributed as a Chi-squared random variable with one degree of freedom, i.e.

$$\widehat{RE} \sim \chi_1^2$$

5.3 Empirical Study

To compare and contrast the three tests considered above (Kolmogorov–Smirnov test and the Anderson–Darling test, on the one hand, and our new test, on the other), we use anonymized PIT data collected by the Federal Reserve on 150 trading desks. The data frequency is daily and the sample period is from 2013 to 2015.

For each desk, we conduct one and two-tailed Kolmogorov–Smirnov tests, the Anderson–Darling test (two-tailed) and one and two-tailed cross-entropy tests. In particular, the two tailed cross-entropy test includes in the sample all PITs whereas the first and second of the one-tailed tests include only the lowest 25% of the PITs and the lowest 50% of the PITs, respectively.

The values of the test statistics are reported in Table 5.1a, 5.1b and 5.1c whereas the corresponding p-values under the null hypothesis of each test are reported in Table 5.2a, 5.2b and 5.2c, respectively (we had to resort to three separate tables each for the critical values and the p-values to be able to report them for all 150 desks in our sample). The cells left blank are those for which, for the corresponding desk, not enough data was available to compute the statistic and/or to validly

Table 5.1a. *Test statistics (Desks 1–50).*

Desk id	KS one-tailed	KS two-tailed	AD	RE lowest 25%	RE lowest 50%	RE two-tailed
1	0.01	0.10	Inf	1.77	2.23	6.19
2	0.21	0.31	Inf	28.46	33.04	33.26
3	0.21	0.31	Inf	29.31	33.79	34.01
4	0.35	0.35	Inf	5.97	5.97	5.97
5	0.35	0.35	Inf	5.97	5.97	5.97
6	0.02	0.14	Inf	6.48	16.57	12.92
7	0.03	0.06	Inf	5.12	8.49	8.63
8	0.05	0.05	Inf	4.74	8.87	4.72
9	0.00	0.16	Inf	3.15	10.15	9.37
10	0.03	0.12	Inf	5.96	5.96	5.96
11	0.03	0.11	Inf	7.83	7.03	10.61
12	0.01	0.11	Inf	17.12	10.95	6.47
13	0.10	0.10	Inf	6.65	6.65	6.65
14	0.02	0.08	Inf	16.31	11.51	7.55
15	0.08	0.16	Inf	6.71	10.74	10.74
16	0.02	0.08	Inf	6.04	10.11	10.11
17	0.12	0.12	Inf	4.42	12.99	8.10
18	0.03	0.03	Inf	15.97	7.85	4.81
19	0.12	0.14	Inf	6.78	15.46	23.07
20	0.12	0.12	Inf	5.73	9.49	9.65
21	0.06	0.06	Inf	12.84	7.59	663
22	0.15	0.15	Inf	3.36	4.67	7.15
23	0.06	0.11	Inf	8.51	5.07	4.79
24	0.09	0.13	Inf	11.82	10.00	18.77
25	0.14	0.16	Inf	7.31	15.10	15.56
26	0.17	0.17	Inf	8.99	11.30	11.30
27	0.15	0.15	Inf	8.90	26.55	23.16
28	0.06	0.14	Inf	3.81	3.81	3.81
29	0.03	0.03	Inf	11.60	9.60	9.60
30	0.05	0.05	Inf	15.18	6.24	5.70
31	0.06	0.06	Inf	4.76	4.76	4.76
32	0.06	0.06	Inf	2.93	2.93	2.93
33	0.01	0.08	Inf	4.12	4.12	4.12
34	0.25	0.25	Inf	8.21	8.99	22.21
35	0.22	0.22	Inf	11.74	14.06	50.80
36	0.29	0.29	Inf	9.57	12.66	12.66
37	0.20	0.25	Inf	15.97	15.97	15.97

Table 5.1a. (*cont.*)

Desk id	KS one-tailed	KS two-tailed	AD	RE lowest 25%	RE lowest 50%	RE two-tailed
38	0.23	0.23	Inf	5.54	10.69	20.42
39	0.20	0.20	Inf	8.66	11.22	11.22
40	0.27	0.27	Inf	9.65	17.22	30.86
41	0.27	0.27	Inf	16.98	25.95	25.95
42	0.20	0.22	Inf	8.05	7.02	15.60
43	0.21	0.22	Inf	7.24	16.27	16.27
44	0.17	0.18	Inf	8.47	8.47	8.47
45	0.18	0.18	Inf	8.38	8.38	8.38
46	0.10	0.10	Inf	9.21	19.41	14.08
47	0.15	0.15	Inf	14.05	12.61	13.27
48	0.09	0.12	Inf	7.07	26.04	15.69
49	0.31	0.31	Inf	6.93	10.97	10.97
50	0.07	0.07	Inf	7.83	7.83	7.83

Table 5.1b. ***Test statistics (Desks 51–100).***

Desk id	KS one-tailed	KS two-tailed	AD	RE lowest 25%	RE lowest 50%	RE two-tailed
51	0.17	0.17	Inf	19.14	12.52	14.22
52	0.20	0.20	Inf	5.94	21.52	19.95
53	0.17	0.17	Inf	17.52	12.31	14.03
54	0.01	0.07	Inf	2.14	8.12	3.70
55	0.00	0.05	Inf	4.20	8.34	4.25
56	0.08	0.08	Inf	6.91	8.63	8.63
57	0.05	0.07	Inf	5.77	5.77	5.77
58	0.06	0.07	Inf	3.70	4.42	8.98
59	0.06	0.09	Inf	3.83	14.24	14.24
60	0.01	0.07	Inf	13.08	7.66	6.10
61	0.05	0.06	Inf	7.46	5.97	5.97
62	0.01	0.16	Inf	7.55	7.55	7.55
63	0.03	0.17	Inf	1.84	1.84	1.84
64	0.10	0.10	Inf	2.80	6.00	7.66
65	0.27	0.27	Inf	9.45	45.08	29.03
66	0.33	0.33	Inf	7.84	11.48	28.95

Table 5.1b. (*cont.*)

Desk id	KS one-tailed	KS two-tailed	AD	RE lowest 25%	RE lowest 50%	RE two-tailed
67	0.08	0.11	Inf	9.38	24.69	13.46
68	0.06	0.14	Inf	12.21	7.72	7.72
69	0.11	0.11	Inf	2.16	10.49	7.76
70	0.17	0.17	Inf	3.60	10.72	10.72
71	0.01	0.11	Inf	12.27	7.59	8.24
72	0.01	0.24	Inf	22.68	9.02	9.02
73	0.04	0.04	Inf	5.29	3.81	3.81
74	0.06	0.06	Inf	4.14	9.66	8.00
75	0.08	0.08	Inf	3.18	8.88	7.05
76	0.08	0.08	Inf	4.67	10.59	4.86
77	0.07	0.07	Inf	4.78	14.66	14.66
78	0.07	0.09	Inf	7.07	14.06	13.03
79	0.08	0.08	Inf	6.48	6.48	6.48
80	0.08	0.08	Inf	6.48	6.48	6.48
81	0.17	0.17	Inf	2.70	5.56	22.15
82	0.14	0.14	Inf	5.71	10.14	10.91
83	0.15	0.15	Inf	5.70	10.23	10.80
84	0.13	0.14	Inf	2.12	4.66	6.04
85	0.20	0.20	Inf	19.33	34.20	38.00
86	0.20	0.20	Inf	19.33	34.20	38.00
87	0.26	0.26	Inf	10.35	20.39	37.86
88	0.25	0.27	Inf	13.89	40.37	40.37
89	0.23	0.23	Inf	8.63	8.88	16.91
90	0.24	0.24	Inf	10.01	18.16	17.77
91	0.30	0.30	Inf	9.82	9.82	9.82
92	0.10	0.10	Inf	8.14	14.60	15.69
93	0.08	0.08	Inf	9.22	8.22	7.80
94	0.24	0.30	Inf	7.74	11.61	20.25
95	0.41	0.44	Inf	3.95	11.95	11.95
96	0.15	0.30	Inf	8.65	11.59	24.02
97	0.26	0.42	Inf	9.77	12.84	7.49
98	0.05	0.15	Inf	6.63	6.84	13.47
99	0.09	0.13	Inf	6.36	8.30	8.30
100	0.30	0.30	Inf	8.61	19.62	19.62

Table 5.1c. *Test statistics (Desks 101–150).*

Desk id	KS one-tailed	KS two-tailed	AD	RE lowest 25%	RE lowest 50%	RE two-tailed
101	0.00	0.22	Inf	5.55	16.18	18.24
102	0.00	0.16	Inf	3.01	10.27	9.71
103	0.11	0.18	Inf	9.23	13.66	28.25
104	0.10	0.16	Inf	14.69	10.20	10.20
105	0.00	0.08	Inf	2.91	12.43	5.09
106	0.01	0.06	Inf	14.57	8.91	4.92
107	0.00	0.13	Inf	2.71	9.71	7.84
108	0.01	0.13	Inf	6.87	6.02	6.02
109	0.01	0.17	Inf	18.30	10.58	11.84
110	0.02	0.13	Inf	5.40	8.42	9.03
111	0.00	0.16	Inf	4.33	10.27	9.52
112	0.07	0.24	Inf	8.96	17.02	16.57
113	0.06	0.21	Inf	7.06	18.62	13.64
114	0.02	0.14	Inf	5.81	13.96	13.81
115	0.01	0.17	Inf	2.40	15.87	12.43
116	0.02	0.06	Inf	3.80	7.30	5.66
117	0.01	0.10	Inf	5.47	2.62	2.62
118	0.09	0.09	Inf	3.18	17.04	12.43
119	0.01	0.13	Inf	11.22	12.30	12.54
120	0.00	0.11	Inf	4.41	10.34	10.67
121	0.00	0.17	Inf	4.46	9.63	12.63
122	0.00	0.17	Inf	4.19	11.78	15.87
123	0.00	0.17	Inf	11.43	7.21	11.56
124	0.12	0.26	Inf	8.17	12.23	11.79
125	0.17	0.27	Inf	5.00	17.77	13.39
126	0.39	0.39	Inf	33.90	21.81	21.81
127	0.06	0.07	Inf	5.37	3.18	3.18
128	0.06	0.12	Inf	21.26	6.42	6.42
129	0.06	0.12	Inf	21.26	6.42	6.42
130	0.25	0.25	Inf	16.53	36.57	56.05
131	0.28	0.28	Inf	8.73	22.89	69.38
132	0.24	0.32	Inf	7.68	39.68	39.10
133	0.36	0.45	Inf	0.64	0.64	43.08
134	0.40	0.40	Inf	18.59	18.59	18.59
135	0.11	0.21	Inf	6.25	10.75	10.75
136	0.13	0.15	Inf	12.90	12.90	12.90

Table 5.1c. (*cont.*)

Desk id	KS one-tailed	KS two-tailed	AD	RE lowest 25%	RE lowest 50%	RE two-tailed
137	0.02	0.16	Inf	10.20	8.73	8.73
138	0.00	0.21	Inf	8.11	8.79	8.79
139	0.17	0.22	Inf	27.29	24.10	24.10
140	0.05	0.05	Inf	5.90	11.45	11.45
141	0.24	0.24	Inf	8.17	14.71	14.71
142	0.16	0.19	Inf	11.98	9.49	9.49
143	0.15	0.15	Inf	9.27	19.14	19.14
144	0.26	0.26	Inf	7.99	24.47	24.47
145	0.01	0.13	Inf	15.11	8.71	8.71
146	0.03	0.03	Inf	1.83	1.88	1.88
147	0.05	0.08	Inf	3.86	13.91	13.91
148	0.07	0.08	Inf	6.29	9.55	9.55
149	0.24	0.24	Inf	6.96	7.01	7.01
150	0.01	0.10	Inf	14.68	15.20	15.20

Table 5.2a. *p-values (Desks 1–50).*

Desk id	KS one-tailed	KS two-tailed	AD	RE lowest 25%	RE lowest 50%	RE two-tailed
1	0.879	0.000	0.000	0.183	0.136	0.013
2	0.000	0.000	0.000	0.000	0.000	0.000
3	0.000	0.000	0.000	0.000	0.000	0.000
4	0.000	0.000	0.000	0.015	0.015	0.015
5	0.000	0.000	0.000	0.015	0.015	0.015
6	0.679	0.000	0.000	0.011	0.000	0.000
7	0.421	0.056	0.000	0.024	0.004	0.003
8	0.018	0.028	0.000	0.030	0.003	0.030
9	0.988	0.000	0.000	0.076	0.001	0.002
10	0.826	0.056	0.000	0.015	0.015	0.015
11	0.230	0.000	0.000	0.005	0.008	0.001
12	0.851	0.000	0.000	0.000	0.001	0.011
13	0.060	0.121	0.000	0.010	0.010	0.010
14	0.549	0.004	0.000	0.000	0.001	0.006
15	0.043	0.000	0.000	0.010	0.001	0.001
16	0.799	0.057	0.000	0.014	0.001	0.001

Table 5.2a. (*cont.*)

Desk id	KS one-tailed	KS two-tailed	AD	RE lowest 25%	RE lowest 50%	RE two-tailed
17	0.000	0.000	0.000	0.036	0.000	0.004
18	0.203	0.403	0.000	0.000	0.005	0.028
19	0.000	0.000	0.000	0.009	0.000	0.000
20	0.000	0.000	0.000	0.017	0.002	0.002
21	0.001	0.003	0.000	0.000	0.006	0.010
22	0.000	0.000	0.000	0.067	0.031	0.007
23	0.078	0.000	0.000	0.004	0.024	0.029
24	0.000	0.000	0.000	0.001	0.002	0.000
25	0.000	0.000	0.000	0.007	0.000	0.000
26	0.000	0.000	0.000	0.003	0.001	0.001
27	0.000	0.000	0.000	0.003	0.000	0.000
28	0.418	0.013	0.000	0.051	0.051	0.051
29	0.635	0.971	0.000	0.001	0.002	0.002
30	0.052	0.104	0.000	0.000	0.012	0.017
31	0.237	0.469	0.000	0.029	0.029	0.029
32	0.241	0.475	0.000	0.087	0.087	0.087
33	0.935	0.405	0.000	0.042	0.042	0.042
34	0.000	0.000	0.000	0.004	0.003	0.000
35	0.000	0.000	0.000	0.001	0.000	0.000
36	0.000	0.000	0.000	0.002	0.000	0.000
37	0.000	0.000	0.000	0.000	0.000	0.000
38	0.000	0.000	0.000	0.019	0.001	0.000
39	0.000	0.000	0.000	0.003	0.001	0.001
40	0.000	0.000	0.000	0.002	0.000	0.000
41	0.000	0.000	0.000	0.000	0.000	0.000
42	0.000	0.000	0.000	0.005	0.008	0.000
43	0.000	0.000	0.000	0.007	0.000	0.000
44	0.001	0.000	0.000	0.004	0.004	0.004
45	0.000	0.000	0.000	0.004	0.004	0.004
46	0.000	0.000	0.000	0.002	0.000	0.000
47	0.000	0.000	0.000	0.000	0.000	0.000
48	0.000	0.000	0.000	0.008	0.000	0.000
49	0.000	0.000	0.000	0.008	0.001	0.001
50	0.264	0.518	0.000	0.005	0.005	0.005

Table 5.2b. *p-values (Desks 51–100).*

Desk id	KS one-tailed	KS two-tailed	AD	RE lowest 25%	RE lowest 50%	RE two-tailed
51	0.000	0.000	0.000	0.000	0.000	0.000
52	0.000	0.000	0.000	0.015	0.000	0.000
53	0.000	0.000	0.000	0.000	0.000	0.000
54	0.841	0.002	0.000	0.143	0.004	0.054
55	0.988	0.057	0.000	0.040	0.004	0.039
56	0.074	0.117	0.000	0.009	0.003	0.003
57	0.567	0.466	0.000	0.016	0.016	0.016
58	0.002	0.000	0.000	0.054	0.035	0.003
59	0.185	0.065	0.000	0.050	0.000	0.000
60	0.911	0.001	0.000	0.000	0.006	0.014
61	0.332	0.464	0.000	0.006	0.015	0.015
62	0.965	0.001	0.000	0.006	0.006	0.006
63	0.764	0.001	0.000	0.175	0.175	0.175
64	0.000	0.000	0.000	0.094	0.014	0.006
65	0.000	0.000	0.000	0.002	0.000	0.000
66	0.000	0.000	0.000	0.005	0.001	0.000
67	0.000	0.000	0.000	0.002	0.000	0.000
68	0.109	0.000	0.000	0.000	0.005	0.005
69	0.000	0.000	0.000	0.142	0.001	0.005
70	0.000	0.000	0.000	0.058	0.001	0.001
71	0.891	0.000	0.000	0.000	0.006	0.004
72	0.898	0.000	0.000	0.000	0.003	0.003
73	0.424	0.785	0.000	0.021	0.051	0.051
74	0.029	0.058	0.000	0.042	0.002	0.005
75	0.000	0.000	0.000	0.074	0.003	0.008
76	0.000	0.000	0.000	0.031	0.001	0.028
77	0.083	0.165	0.000	0.029	0.000	0.000
78	0.006	0.000	0.000	0.008	0.000	0.000
79	0.144	0.287	0.000	0.011	0.011	0.011
80	0.144	0.287	0.000	0.011	0.011	0.011
81	0.000	0.000	0.000	0.100	0.018	0.000
82	0.000	0.000	0.000	0.017	0.001	0.001
83	0.000	0.000	0.000	0.017	0.001	0.001
84	0.000	0.000	0.000	0.146	0.031	0.014
85	0.000	0.000	0.000	0.000	0.000	0.000
86	0.000	0.000	0.000	0.000	0.000	0.000
87	0.000	0.000	0.000	0.001	0.000	0.000

Table 5.2b. (*cont.*)

Desk id	KS one-tailed	KS two-tailed	AD	RE lowest 25%	RE lowest 50%	RE two-tailed
88	0.000	0.000	0.000	0.000	0.000	0.000
89	0.000	0.000	0.000	0.003	0.003	0.000
90	0.000	0.000	0.000	0.002	0.000	0.000
91	0.000	0.000	0.000	0.002	0.002	0.002
92	0.000	0.000	0.000	0.004	0.000	0.000
93	0.002	0.003	0.000	0.002	0.004	0.005
94	0.000	0.000	0.000	0.005	0.001	0.000
95	0.000	0.000	0.000	0.047	0.001	0.001
96	0.000	0.000	0.000	0.003	0.001	0.000
97	0.000	0.000	0.000	0.002	0.000	0.006
98	0.070	0.000	0.000	0.010	0.009	0.000
99	0.010	0.000	0.000	0.012	0.004	0.004
100	0.000	0.000	0.000	0.003	0.000	0.000

Table 5.2c. *p-values (Desks 101–150).*

Desk id	KS-one tailed	KS-two tailed	AD	RE lowest 25%	RE lowest 50%	RE two-tailed
101	0.996	0.000	0.000	0.018	0.000	0.000
102	0.990	0.000	0.000	0.083	0.001	0.002
103	0.000	0.000	0.000	0.002	0.000	0.000
104	0.007	0.000	0.000	0.000	0.001	0.001
105	0.997	0.000	0.000	0.088	0.000	0.024
106	0.868	0.021	0.000	0.000	0.003	0.027
107	0.985	0.000	0.000	0.100	0.002	0.005
108	0.915	0.000	0.000	0.009	0.014	0.014
109	0.832	0.000	0.000	0.000	0.001	0.001
110	0.561	0.000	0.000	0.020	0.004	0.003
111	0.974	0.000	0.000	0.038	0.001	0.002
112	0.016	0.000	0.000	0.003	0.000	0.000
113	0.002	0.000	0.000	0.008	0.000	0.000
114	0.606	0.000	0.000	0.016	0.000	0.000
115	0.895	0.000	0.000	0.121	0.000	0.000
116	0.649	0.166	0.000	0.051	0.007	0.017
117	0.934	0.007	0.000	0.019	0.106	0.106

Table 5.2c. (*cont.*)

Desk id	KS-one tailed	KS-two tailed	AD	RE lowest 25%	RE lowest 50%	RE two-tailed
118	0.000	0.000	0.000	0.075	0.000	0.000
119	0.925	0.000	0.000	0.001	0.000	0.000
120	0.997	0.000	0.000	0.036	0.001	0.001
121	0.975	0.000	0.000	0.035	0.002	0.000
122	0.986	0.000	0.000	0.041	0.001	0.000
123	0.988	0.000	0.000	0.001	0.007	0.001
124	0.000	0.000	0.000	0.004	0.000	0.001
125	0.000	0.000	0.000	0.025	0.000	0.000
126	0.000	0.000	0.000	0.000	0.000	0.000
127	0.158	0.113	0.000	0.020	0.075	0.075
128	0.120	0.001	0.000	0.000	0.011	0.011
129	0.120	0.001	0.000	0.000	0.011	0.011
130	0.000	0.000	0.000	0.000	0.000	0.000
131	0.000	0.000	0.000	0.003	0.000	0.000
132	0.000	0.000	0.000	0.006	0.000	0.000
133	0.000	0.000	0.000	0.423	0.423	0.000
134	0.000	0.000	0.000	0.000	0.000	0.000
135	0.000	0.000	0.000	0.012	0.001	0.001
136	0.010	0.007	0.000	0.000	0.000	0.000
137	0.845	0.000	0.000	0.001	0.003	0.003
138	0.995	0.000	0.000	0.004	0.003	0.003
139	0.000	0.000	0.000	0.000	0.000	0.000
140	0.263	0.516	0.000	0.015	0.001	0.001
141	0.000	0.000	0.000	0.004	0.000	0.000
142	0.000	0.000	0.000	0.001	0.002	0.002
143	0.000	0.000	0.000	0.002	0.000	0.000
144	0.000	0.000	0.000	0.005	0.000	0.000
145	0.913	0.000	0.000	0.000	0.003	0.003
146	0.563	0.936	0.000	0.176	0.170	0.170
147	0.105	0.022	0.000	0.049	0.000	0.000
148	0.028	0.023	0.000	0.012	0.002	0.002
149	0.000	0.000	0.000	0.008	0.008	0.008
150	0.955	0.002	0.000	0.000	0.000	0.000

carry out the test. The RE test appears to strike a better balance between size and power and allows for easier tuning of attention to the tail (and width thereof) of interest. In particular, the two-tailed Kolmogorov–Smirnov and Anderson–Darling tests appear to reject very often the validity of the VaR model used by each bank/desk, whereas the relative entropy test is more discerning, especially when focussing on the left tail (which is the one of greatest interest in our setting).

5.3.1 Tests Based on the Probabilities Implied by the PITs

An alternative approach is to test the null hypothesis that the observations (the portfolio returns) occur with probabilities implied by the VaR model (henceforth, the *implied probabilities*) against the alternative that they occur with probabilities given by their empirical distribution. The implied probabilities are probabilities defined in such a way that the VaR model is correct. To this end, they are defined as the probabilities implied by the probability integral transforms (PITs) of the return observations under the distribution function that generates the VaR estimates, i.e.

$$\pi_s = \frac{(PIT_s - PIT_{s-1})}{PIT_T - PIT_1}. \tag{5.16}$$

Here, $y_1 \leq y_2 \leq y_2 \cdots \leq y_{T-1} \leq y_T$ are the portfolio returns, ranked from lowest to highest, and $PIT_s := F(y_s)$ are the corresponding probability integral transforms, where $F(y_t) := P(Y_t \leq y_t)$ is the cumulative density function of the distribution of time-t portfolio returns under the VaR model. For example, consider the VaR model that assumes a typical location-scale data-generating process (DGP). Then

$$F(y_t) = F\left(\frac{y_t - \mu_t}{\sigma_t}\right) \tag{5.17}$$

and the VaR at the confidence level $1 - \alpha$ is

$$VaR_{1-\alpha} := -y_s^* \quad : \quad P\left(Y_s \leq y_s^*\right) = 1 - \alpha \tag{5.18}$$

where

$$y_s = \mu + \epsilon_\alpha \sigma_s. \tag{5.19}$$

Here, ϵ_α is a random variable that follows some scale-location distribution, such as the normal (Gaussian).

Also, since the portfolio returns are ranked in ascending order, we have that $PIT_{s-1} \leq PIT_s$, $s = 1, 2, \ldots, \tau$.

The empirical probabilities are

$$q_s = \frac{1}{\tau}.$$

This null hypothesis can be tested using a likelihood ratio, which is distributed as a Chi-squared random variable with one degree of freedom (because there is only one estimating equation and, hence, only one moment condition, namely the one that must be satisfied by the econometric model of the DGP that underpins the VaR model):

$$= 2\frac{l(y_1, y_2, \ldots, y_\tau | p(y_s) = \pi_s)}{l(y_1, y_2, \ldots, y_\tau | p(y_s) = \frac{1}{\tau})} \tag{5.20}$$

$$= 2\frac{log\left(\Pi_{s=1}^{\tau}\frac{PIT_s - PIT_{s-1}}{PIT_\tau - PIT_1}\right)}{log\left(\frac{1}{\tau}\right)^\tau}$$

$$= 2\frac{log\left(\Pi_{s=1}^{\tau}\frac{PIT_s - PIT_{s-1}}{PIT_\tau - PIT_1}\right)}{\tau \times log\left(\frac{1}{\tau}\right)} \sim \chi_1^2.$$

5.4 Conclusions and Final Remarks

This chapter provides an alternative to exceedance or density-based evaluation of VaR models that are discussed in Chapters 2 and 4. This alternative is based on empirical likelihood. As can be seen from the application, empirical likelihood can have some advantages over more traditional tests of VaR models.

References

Anderson, T. W. and Darling, D. A. (1952). Asymptotic theory of certain "goodness of fit" criteria based on stochastic processes. *Annals of Mathematical Statistics*, 23, 193–212.

Berkowitz, Jeremy. (2001). Testing density forecasts, with applications to risk management. *Journal of Business & Economic Statistics*, 19, 465–474.

Christoffersen, Peter F. (1998). Evaluating interval forecasts. *International Economic Review*, 39, 841–862.

Diebold, Francis X., Gunther, Todd A. and Tay, Anthony S. (1998). Evaluating density forecasts with applications to financial risk management. *International Economic Review*, 39, 863–883.

Gordy, M. B. and McNeil, A. (2018). Spectral backtests of forecast distributions with application to risk management, Unpublished Manuscript,

Kitamura, Y. (2006). Empirical likelihood methods in econometrics: theory and practice. Cowles Foundation Discussion Paper, 1569.

Kolmogorov, A. N. (1933). Sulla determinazione empirica di una legge di distribuzione. *Giornale dell'Istituto Italiano degli Attuari*, 4, 83–91.

Lopez, J. A. (1998). Methods for Evaluating Value-at-Risk Estimates, *Economic Policy Review*, 4(3), 2–18.

Owen, Art B. (2001). *Empirical likelihood.* (Chapman and Hall/CRC Boca Raton).

Post, Thierry, and Potì, Valerio. (2017). Portfolio analysis using stochastic dominance, relative entropy, and empirical likelihood. *Management Science*, 63, 153–165.

Rosenblatt, Murray. (1952). Remarks on a multivariate transformation. *The Annals of Mathematical Statistics*, 23, 470–472.

Smirnov, N. (1948). Table for estimating the goodness of fit of empirical distributions. *The Annals of Mathematical Statistics*, 19, 279–281.

Wilks, S. S. (1938). The large-sample distribution of the likelihood ratio for testing composite hypotheses. *The Annals of Mathematical Statistics*, 9, 60–62.

6 *Evaluating Banks' Value-at-Risk Models during the COVID-19 Crisis*

CHRIS ANDERSON AND DENNIS MAWHIRTER*

6.1 Introduction

In March 2020, markets were in turmoil over COVID-19. Volatility spiked, fixed income spreads rose, bases diverged dramatically, and liquidity dried up. Amid this turmoil, banks faced losses larger than predicted by their Value-at-Risk (VaR) models, which triggered a string of backtesting exceptions. While large, unexpected market moves will inevitably trigger losses larger than VaR models anticipate, those models can also adapt to changing market conditions. Our key question is how well banks' VaR models performed during the COVID crisis and whether they sufficiently adapted to market conditions. We approach this question using daily desk-level data on banks' profit and loss (P&L) and regulatory VaR from regulatory metrics required by the Volcker rule. We examine data from 2019 Q1 to 2020 Q2, using 2019 as a baseline year to which we can compare the COVID-related activity in 2020.

Our main approach tests whether backtesting exceptions are predictable. Under the null hypothesis that a VaR model is specified correctly, no prior information should be able to predict a future exception. If a factor predicts exceptions, that is evidence that the VaR model excludes relevant information from that factor. We additionally investigate whether this predictability has stayed constant throughout the entire sample, or whether it only appears in 2020.

First, we find that prior backtesting exceptions predict future ones over roughly two-week horizons. Over the full sample, an extra

* Federal Reserve Board of Governors. Chris Anderson can be contacted at christopher.s.anderson@frb.gov and Dennis Mawhirter at dennis.w.mawhirter@frb.gov. We thank Alice Abboud and Alex Jiron for assistance with compiling market factor data, David McArthur for assistance with the Volcker metrics data set, and Lubomir Petrasek and Stephen Zoulalian for sharing their Volcker desk classifications. We thank David Lynch for his extremely helpful feedback. This paper reflects the views of the authors and does not reflect the views of the Federal Reserve Board.

backtesting exception within the previous week forecasts an 8.7 percentage point higher chance of a future exception. Further controlling for exceptions over the past four weeks, we find that each exception over the previous week and two weeks predicts a 7.9 and 2.5 percentage point higher chance of a future exception respectively. We also find evidence of increased predictability during 2020: Each extra backtesting exception over the previous week forecasts a 4.0 percentage point higher chance of a backtesting exception in 2020 versus 2019. This pattern qualitatively holds across desks of different asset classes as well.

Next, we find that recent market volatility predicts future backtesting exceptions. We regress backtesting exceptions on the absolute value of lagged changes in various market factors, including changes in interest rates, bond spreads, and exchange rates, as well as on the level of the VIX. We robustly find that a high level of the VIX forecasts backtesting exceptions. In 2020, a one standard deviation increase in the level of the VIX forecasts a 1.8 percentage point increase in the probability of an exception. The results also hold qualitatively across different asset classes.

We then address a secondary question of which types of market movements were most closely associated with contemporaneous backtesting exceptions. We find that no single market factor appeared to drive backtesting exceptions, but rather several different factors mattered. When broken down by asset class, backtesting exceptions often relate to large movements in related market factors, although some factors, such as changes in investment grade spreads and changes in the VIX, affect seemingly unrelated desks as well.

Taken together, these results show that backtesting exceptions are predictable from both recent exceptions and from recent market volatility, indicating that banks' VaR models did not react quickly enough to changes in market conditions. They also show that no single factor was the major determinant, but rather a range of different market movements mattered.

This chapter relates to a larger literature evaluating the performance of banks' VaR models. O'Brien and Szerszen (2014) is the most closely related paper, which evaluates the performance of banks' VaR models before and during the 2008 financial crisis. They find that banks' VaR models were overly conservative prior to the crisis, but then exhibited high exception rates and clustering of exceptions during the crisis, indicating that the models react too slowly to changes in market conditions. Berkowitz and O'Brien (2002) provide earlier empirical evidence that banks' VaR models are too conservative on average, but that backtesting exceptions are overly clustered. Berkowitz et al. (2009) analyze the performance of VaR models across four different business lines at a large bank and find evidence that exceptions are clustered. Perignon et al. (2008) find evidence that the six largest Canadian banks' VaR models are overly conservative. Perignon and Smith (2010b) provide additional evidence that VaR models are overly conservative for an international sample of banks. Perignon and Smith (2010a) further show that overall VaR estimates are overly conservative and are likely to be overstated at the risk class level as well.

6.2 Data and Summary Statistics

Our main data source is the Volcker desk metrics. As a requirement of the Volcker rule, large banks are required to report daily information about each trading desk, including P&L breakdowns and a 99th percentile regulatory VaR over a one-day holding period. The P&L is broken down by whether it is due to existing positions or due to new positions that include the results of intraday trading as well as fees, commissions and spreads. The P&L due to existing positions is further broken down by category, including P&L due to changes in risk factors.

Firms do not report a standardized clean P&L, which is the P&L that would have been realized based on their initial portfolios excluding fee income. In essence, this clean P&L measure is the best measure for comparing to VaR because it captures the realization of the kinds of probabilistic market risk factors that VaR attempts to measure. Clean P&L is collected in a separate regulatory data source known as the Market Risk Rule backtesting data, which firms subject to the Market Risk Rule (those with more than $1 billion in trading assets and liabilities) must report on a semiannual basis for all of their trading subportfolios. Subportfolios do not align perfectly with trading desk definitions and the trading positions covered under the Volcker rule may be different from those covered by the Market Risk Rule, so it is not possible to directly merge these two data sets.

In order to backtest firms' VaR models, we must construct clean P&L for each firm as a combination of the different forms of P&L in the existing positions breakdown. By comparing with the Market Risk

Rule backtesting data, which does include clean P&L, we can determine for one firm which combination is appropriate. Expert judgment based on supervisory experience with the Volcker metrics data was informative for several other firms. For the remaining metrics reporters, we used the simplest combination that led to an exceedance rate closest to the expected 1% in the pre-COVID crisis period. In most cases, clean P&L is the sum of P&L due to changes in risk factors plus the residual P&L.

We then select the sample of desks. Some desks that hedge the firm's banking book exposures report their VaR and P&L in inconsistent ways. Some report a VaR solely for the market hedges and a P&L including both the banking book exposure and the market hedges, or vice versa. We exclude these desks by restricting the sample to desks for which, in the period prior to February 15, 2020, the mean regulatory VaR is between one to five times the standard deviation of P&L. Next, we exclude the smallest trading desks since firms may not invest as many resources in developing VaR models for these desks. Among the desks remaining from the first screen, we exclude the desks in the bottom 25th percentile of mean regulatory VaR within each firm. The final sample consists of thirteen firms with a total of 541 trading desks.

For trading desk i on business day t, we construct an indicator variable for backtesting exceptions as

$$Exception_{i,t} = \begin{cases} 1 \text{ if } -P\&L_{i,t} > VaR_{i,t-1} \\ 0 \text{ otherwise} \end{cases} \tag{6.1}$$

where $P\&L_{i,t}$ is the clean P&L and $VaR_{i,t-1}$ is the corresponding 99th percentile regulatory VaR in units of losses. The time subscripts correspond to when the variables are observed.

Figure 6.1 plots the percent of desks with backtesting exceptions for each day from 2019 Q1 to 2020 Q2. Exceptions are fairly stable until the COVID crisis, when they spike dramatically over the course of approximately a month, and then return to their previous behavior.

For asset-class-specific analysis, we classify desks into one of six categories: Equity, credit, rates, foreign exchange (FX), fixed income (FI) and municipals (muni). Desk classifications are based on whether their names contain certain related key words. Broadly speaking, credit comprises corporate credit products, such as cash bonds or credit

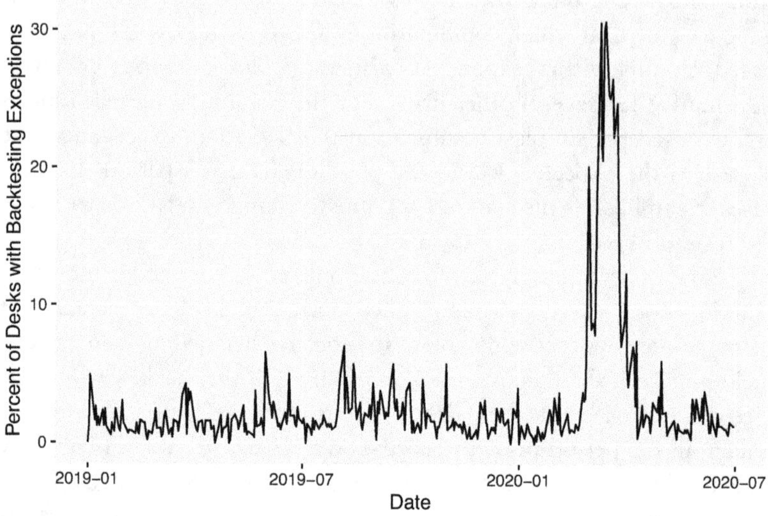

Figure 6.1 Percent of desks with backtesting exceptions over time.

default swaps, fixed income comprises cash interest-rate-heavy products, such as mortgage-backed securities or Treasuries, and rates comprise interest rate derivatives primarily.

For analysis using market factors, we assemble data on a variety of indicators. Most data are downloaded from Bloomberg.[1] These indicators include (1) the level of the VIX, (2) ten-year Treasury rates, (3) MBS Spread from the Bloomberg Barclays US MBS Fixed Rate Average Option-Adjusted Spread Index, (4) investment grade corporate bond spread from the Bloomberg Barclays USD Liquid Investment Grade

[1] The Bloomberg variable names and descriptions (when relevant) are as follows: The VIX is VIX_INDEX_PX_LAST, the 10Y Treasury rate is USGG10YR_INDEX_PX_LAST, the mortgage-backed security (MBS) spread is LUMSOAS_INDEX_PX_LAST (Bloomberg Barclays US MBS Fixed Rate Avg OAS), the investment grade (IG) corporate bond spread is BLQCOAS_INDEX_PX_LAST (Bloomberg Barclays USD Liquid Investment Grade Corp Average OAS), CDX NA IG is CDX_IG_CDSI_GEN_5Y_CORP_PX_LAST, USD FX is DXYCURNCY_PX_LAST (US Dollar Index), Oil is USCRWTIC_INDEX_PX_ LAST (US Crude Oil WTI Cushing OK Spot), the US stock market is SPX_INDEX_PX_LAST (S&P 500 Index), and the implied repo rate for the 10Y US Treasury futures is TY1_COMDTY_FUT_IMPLIED_REPO_RT.

Corporate Average Option-Adjusted Spread Index, (5) CDX NA IG, (6) a broad US dollar index, (7) WTI oil prices, (8) S&P 500 index return and (9) the implied repo rate for ten-year Treasury futures. CDX NA IG is the investment grade credit default swap (CDS) index. Implied repo rate is a way of measuring the divergence between the price of a Treasury future and an underlying spot Treasury bond. The CDS-bond basis reflects the median difference between CDS and bond spreads for reference entities within the CDX NA IG index. It is calculated by comparing the interpolated CDS spread and the z-spread for the primary reference obligation.

6.3 Were VaR models Missing Relevant Factors?

We begin by examining whether banks' VaR models were missing relevant factors that might have improved their performance. Our main approach is to test whether any factors predict future backtesting exceptions. If a VaR model is correctly specified, then backtesting exceptions should be unpredictable. A factor's ability to forecast backtesting exceptions is evidence that the VaR model does not incorporate relevant information from that factor (Christoffersen, 2011).

First, we examine whether prior backtesting exceptions forecast future ones. If so, this pattern would be evidence of VaR models slowly incorporating new information. For this analysis, we regress current backtesting exceptions on lagged weekly sums of prior exceptions according to

$$Exception_{i,t} = \alpha_i + \sum_{k=1}^{4} \beta_k \left(\sum_{j=1}^{5} Exception_{i,t-j-5(k-1)} \right) + \varepsilon_{i,t}, \qquad (6.2)$$

where α_i are desk-specific intercepts and we pool the regression across all desks. To correct for the correlation of backtesting exceptions across different desks at the same time, we cluster observations by time. We use the linear model for simplicity; however, Section 6.5 shows that the results are qualitatively similar to the marginal effects from a logistic model.

Table 6.1 contains the results of this regression, which shows that past backtesting exceptions forecast future ones. The first two specifications examine the extent to which prior backtesting exceptions forecast a future exception. The first shows that each backtesting exception over the previous one to five business days predicts an 8.7

Table 6.1. ***Predicting backtesting exceptions from lagged exceptions.***

	Dependent variable:		
	100 × Exception indicator		
	(1)	(2)	(3)
Exceptions over 1–5 days	8.74***	7.91***	3.97***
	(0.67)	(0.68)	(0.47)
Exceptions over 6–10 days		2.50***	1.49***
		(0.33)	(0.31)
Exceptions over 11–15 days		0.45	0.77***
		(0.28)	(0.27)
Exceptions over 16–20 days		−0.30	0.39*
		(0.22)	(0.23)
Year 2020			1.27***
			(0.42)
Year 2020 × Exceptions over 1–5 days			5.62***
			(0.88)
Year 2020 × Exceptions over 6–10 days			0.90*
			(0.54)
Year 2020 × Exceptions over 11–15 days			−0.88*
			(0.51)
Year 2020 × Exceptions over 16–20 days			−1.26***
			(0.42)
Observations	300,143	273,216	273,216
Adjusted R^2	0.11	0.12	0.13
F Statistic	71.60***	70.37***	75.03***

Note: *p < 0.1; **p < 0.05; ***p < 0.01
SEs are clustered by time.

percentage point higher probability of a current backtesting exception. The second includes further lags up to twenty business days prior, which is approximately a month, and shows that exceptions over the previous two weeks forecast exceptions. Each exception from the prior one to five and six to ten days forecasts a 7.9 and 2.5 percentage point higher probability of an upcoming exception respectively. Further lags are both statistically and economically irrelevant.

The third specification examines the extent to which the first half of 2020 differs from 2019. Are backtesting exceptions always so predictable or is the COVID crisis special? The regression shows that in 2019 backtesting exceptions were similarly predictable from previous exceptions, but to a lesser magnitude. During 2020, exceptions from one to five days prior predicted a 5.6 percentage point higher chance of future exceptions compared to 2019. The economic magnitude of other horizons is smaller. Additionally, the significant year 2020 indicator variable shows a spike in the unconditional rate of exceptions.

Table 6.2 runs the third specification separately for the following asset classes: Equity, credit, rates, foreign exchange (FX), fixed income (FI), and municipals (munis). Some of these patterns hold consistently across all desk types: Exceptions during the past week consistently predicted that future exceptions would be more likely; this pattern was stronger in 2020 compared to 2019, and the unconditional rate of exceptions was higher during 2020. There is greater heterogeneity in whether backtesting exceptions from the prior six to ten days forecasted exceptions. Equity and credit desks saw forecastability over a two-week period that was similar between 2019 and 2020 whereas FX and Muni desks saw forecastability over a two-week period only for 2020.

Broadly, these regressions indicate that banks' VaR models are slow to respond to changing market conditions through the COVID crisis, even over a two-week period, consistent with other work such as O'Brien and Szerszen (2014).

The sample period is from the beginning of 2019 Q1 to the end of 2020 Q2. Section 6.2 contains more details about the asset classes.

Next, we investigate the extent to which recent lagged market factors can forecast backtesting exceptions. We run a regression of the form

$$Exception_{i,t} = \alpha_i + \sum_k \beta_k F_{k,t-1} + \varepsilon_{i,t} \tag{6.3}$$

where α_i are desk-specific intercepts and $F_{k,t-1}$ are lagged market risk factors. Since volatility is a major driver of Value-at-Risk, we include the absolute value of movements in a wide range of market factors as

Table 6.2. *Predicting backtesting exceptions from lagged exceptions by asset class.*

	Dependent variable:					
	100 × Exception indicator					
	Equity (1)	Credit (2)	Rates (3)	FX (4)	FI (5)	Muni (6)
1–5d Except.	3.09*** (0.69)	3.63*** (0.63)	3.05*** (0.81)	2.09** (0.98)	5.81*** (1.63)	2.45** (1.12)
6–10d Except.	1.99*** (0.68)	2.01*** (0.53)	0.67 (0.55)	−1.04* (0.62)	1.07 (1.28)	−0.19 (0.61)
11–15d Except.	0.23 (0.54)	0.60 (0.43)	1.27** (0.59)	0.14 (0.98)	0.08 (0.72)	0.22 (0.73)
16–20d Except.	1.09* (0.56)	0.12 (0.39)	−0.55 (0.35)	−0.66 (0.62)	0.60 (0.89)	0.72 (0.90)
2020	1.84*** (0.46)	1.38*** (0.48)	0.87** (0.44)	0.35 (0.57)	1.08** (0.55)	1.68** (0.71)
2020 × 1–5d Except.	6.34*** (1.44)	6.32*** (1.10)	6.68*** (1.60)	6.94*** (1.66)	4.31** (2.06)	5.97** (2.50)

2020 × 6–10d Except.	−1.01	1.24	0.41	3.47**	0.51	7.38***
	(1.11)	(1.06)	(0.91)	(1.36)	(1.60)	(2.13)
2020 × 11–15d Except.	0.33	−1.98***	−1.24	2.81*	−0.98	−2.49
	(0.85)	(0.75)	(0.86)	(1.57)	(1.06)	(1.67)
2020 × 16–20d Except.	−1.71**	−0.54	−0.58	0.02	−1.33	−3.43**
	(0.76)	(0.64)	(0.52)	(1.31)	(0.98)	(1.36)
Observations	51,413	83,782	43,533	20,636	27,185	18,107
Adjusted R^2	0.13	0.15	0.10	0.16	0.12	0.16
F Statistic	71.52***	84.99***	50.13***	89.38***	67.16***	90.95***

Note: *p < 0.1; **p < 0.05; ***p < 0.01
SEs are clustered by time.

dependent variables along with the level of the VIX. We divide all of these variables by their standard deviations over 2016 to 2020 to ease the interpretation of the regression coefficients.

The sample period is from the beginning of 2019 Q1 to the end of 2020 Q2. All market factors are lagged one business day. The "Level of VIX" is the level of the VIX in units of standard deviations. Other variables represent the absolute value of standardized movements of the relevant market variables. For the purposes of standardization, all standard deviations are calculated using time series of the factors beginning in 2016. Section 6.2 contains more details about the market factors.

The sample period is from the beginning of 2019 Q1 to the end of 2020 Q2. All market factors are lagged one business day. The "Level of VIX" is the level of the VIX in units of standard deviations. Other variables represent the absolute value of standardized movements of the relevant market variables. For the purposes of standardization, all standard deviations are calculated using time series of the factors beginning in 2016. Section 6.2 contains more details about the market factors and asset classes.

Table 6.3 shows that recent market factors contain predictive power. All coefficients are in units of standard deviations in order to ease in interpretation. The level of the VIX has the strongest impact. Across the full sample, a one standard deviation increase in the level of the VIX forecasts a 1.8 percentage point increase in the probability of a backtesting exception. This forecastability exists in both 2019 and 2020, although with a larger magnitude in the latter year, indicating that VaR models are excluding relevant information contained in the VIX. The only other factor that is both statistically significant and stable between 2019 and 2020 is movements in the 10Y Treasury yield.

Table 6.4 shows similar regressions broken down by asset class. We limit each regression to a set of variables we expect to be most relevant for that market, partially to address collinearity in these variables. Interestingly, a high level of the VIX positively forecasts exceptions across all of the asset classes (although the effect is statistically insignificant for rates desks). In some cases, recent volatility in risk factors relevant to that asset class forecast future exceptions – for example, movement in the 10Y Treasury yield increases exceptions

Table 6.3. ***Predicting backtesting exceptions from lagged market factors.***

	Dependent variable:		
	100 × Exception indicator		
	Full sample (1)	2019 (2)	2020 (3)
Level of VIX	1.79***	1.20***	1.80***
	(0.47)	(0.42)	(0.65)
10Y Treasury Vol	0.79**	0.36**	1.39**
	(0.38)	(0.17)	(0.56)
MBS Vol	−0.10	0.01	−0.23
	(0.32)	(0.27)	(0.33)
IG Corp Vol	0.12	−0.57*	0.33
	(0.43)	(0.33)	(0.63)
CDX NA IG Vol	0.11	−0.11	−0.26
	(0.43)	(0.27)	(0.58)
USD FX Vol	0.47	0.45*	−0.43
	(0.53)	(0.26)	(1.48)
Oil Vol	−0.33***	0.78***	−0.29*
	(0.12)	(0.27)	(0.15)
US Stock Vol	0.65	−0.01	1.27*
	(0.48)	(0.32)	(0.70)
CDS-Bond Basis Vol	−0.02	0.05	−0.32
	(0.38)	(0.30)	(0.47)
10Y Treasury Basis Vol	0.24	0.03	1.36*
	(0.21)	(0.16)	(0.76)
Observations	217,071	164,366	52,705
Adjusted R^2	0.11	0.05	0.18
F Statistic	47.94***	17.13***	24.91***

Note: *p < 0.1; **p < 0.05; ***p < 0.01
SEs are clustered by time.

for both rates, fixed income, and muni desks – but this is not universally true.

In summary, we find substantial evidence that VaR models were missing relevant factors. Prior backtesting exceptions over

Table 6.4. *Predicting backtesting exceptions from lagged market factors by asset class in 2020.*

	Dependent variable:					
	100 × Exception indicator					
	Equity (1)	Credit (2)	Rates (3)	FX (4)	FI (5)	Muni (6)
Level of VIX	1.73***	1.65***	1.25	1.85***	1.55***	3.70***
	(0.46)	(0.50)	(0.83)	(0.50)	(0.45)	(1.07)
10Y Treasury Vol	0.34	1.18*	2.47***	0.72	2.43***	2.37**
	(0.48)	(0.68)	(0.84)	(0.92)	(0.48)	(1.20)
MBS Vol					−0.04	
					(0.32)	
IG Corp Vol	−0.11	0.68		−0.35	1.63***	−0.26
	(0.36)	(0.61)		(0.53)	(0.56)	(1.07)
CDX NA IG Vol		0.001			−1.91***	
		(0.63)			(0.52)	
USD FX Vol			1.11	−0.08		
			(1.49)	(1.24)		

Oil Vol				−0.09		
				(0.11)		
US Stock Vol	0.93	1.03		2.13**	0.81	
	(0.61)	(0.83)		(1.02)	(0.50)	
CDS-Bond Basis Vol		0.02			−0.33	−1.08*
		(0.30)			(0.33)	(0.58)
10Y Treasury Basis Vol			1.61		0.29	2.58
			(1.29)		(0.66)	(1.80)
Observations	10,455	15,776	8,580	3,618	5,470	3,385
Adjusted R^2	0.17	0.20	0.17	0.20	0.18	0.22
F Statistic	22.47***	28.12***	22.51***	24.89***	24.77***	31.85***

Note: $^{*}p < 0.1$; $^{**}p < 0.05$; $^{***}p < 0.01$
SEs are clustered by time.

the previous two weeks help to forecast future exceptions, indicating that VaR models are likely slow to respond to changes in market conditions. And market factors, particularly the level of VIX, forecast backtesting exceptions as well, indicating that VaR models could be improved by incorporating some of this information.

6.4 Which Factors Were Associated with Contemporaneous Backtesting Exceptions?

In this section, we examine which market movements were most associated with contemporaneous backtesting exceptions. We run a regression of the form

$$Exception_{i,t} = \alpha_i + \sum_k \beta_k F_{k,t} + \varepsilon_{i,t}, \tag{6.4}$$

where α_i are desk-specific intercepts and $F_{k,t}$ are contemporaneous market risk factors. As before, we standardize these variables to aid in interpreting the regression coefficient. In these regressions, all volatility factors represent the absolute value of changes in the relevant factor. Notably, VIX Vol now indicates contemporaneous changes in the VIX – the regressions do not include the level of the VIX. Since these regressions use contemporaneous variables, they do not evaluate the banks' VaR models. Instead, they indicate the types of market movements that occurred around exceptions.

The sample period is from the beginning of 2019 Q1 to the end of 2020 Q2. All market factors are contemporaneous. The variables represent the absolute value of standardized movements of the relevant market variables. For the purposes of standardization, all standard deviations are calculated using time series of the factors beginning in 2016. Section 6.2 contains more details about the market factors and asset classes.

Table 6.5 shows the results of the full-sample regression. No clear picture emerges. Across the full sample, movements in investment grade (IG) corporate bond spreads, the US stock market, and the VIX relate to more frequent backtesting exceptions, but the pattern differs for individual years. During the COVID crisis in 2020, large movements in the Treasury futures basis, the VIX, and MBS spreads were most associated with contemporaneous backtesting exceptions

Table 6.5. ***Associating backtesting exceptions with contemporaneous market movements.***

	Dependent variable:		
	100 × Exception indicator		
	Full sample (1)	2019 (2)	2020 (3)
VIX Vol	0.79**	0.62**	0.98**
	(0.39)	(0.31)	(0.43)
10Y Treasury Vol	0.71*	0.55***	0.77
	(0.39)	(0.18)	(0.48)
MBS Vol	0.42	0.02	0.60**
	(0.27)	(0.24)	(0.29)
IG Corp Vol	1.22***	0.48	0.62
	(0.27)	(0.38)	(0.43)
CDX NA IG Vol	−0.21	−0.45	−0.16
	(0.30)	(0.30)	(0.33)
USD FX Vol	0.84*	0.20	1.64*
	(0.47)	(0.18)	(0.98)
Oil Vol	−0.11*	0.96***	−0.12**
	(0.06)	(0.28)	(0.05)
US Stock Vol	0.73**	0.33	0.84*
	(0.33)	(0.46)	(0.45)
CDS-Bond Basis Vol	0.20	−0.08	−0.02
	(0.32)	(0.30)	(0.35)
10Y Treasury Basis Vol	0.31	−0.10	1.97***
	(0.22)	(0.08)	(0.71)
Observations	216,943	164,973	51,970
Adjusted R^2	0.12	0.05	0.20
F Statistic	52.90***	18.01***	27.50***

Note: *$p < 0.1$; **$p < 0.05$; ***$p < 0.01$
SEs are clustered by time.

(controlling for other market movements). Movements in the value of the dollar and global stock indices also have large estimated coefficients, but are not individually statistically significant, likely due to common movement across these factors.

Table 6.6. ***Associating backtesting exceptions with contemporaneous market movements by asset class in 2020.***

	Dependent variable:					
	100 × Exception indicator					
	Equity (1)	Credit (2)	Rates (3)	FX (4)	FI (5)	Muni (6)
VIX Vol	1.67** (0.74)	0.48 (0.32)	1.64** (0.74)	0.66 (0.54)	-0.27 (0.55)	2.25** (1.00)
10Y Treasury Vol	0.65 (0.85)	1.40** (0.62)	1.49*** (0.57)	0.64 (0.59)	1.19*** (0.39)	1.51 (1.03)
MBS Vol					0.48 (0.33)	
IG Corp Vol	1.29*** (0.36)	2.17*** (0.40)		1.58*** (0.50)	1.52*** (0.29)	2.88*** (0.80)
CDX NA IG Vol		-0.71 (0.47)			-0.10 (0.34)	
USD FX Vol			3.04*** (0.92)	−0.41 (1.15)		
Oil Vol				−0.14** (0.06)		

US Stock Vol	0.44	1.35***		1.76**	1.29***	
	(0.35)	(0.42)		(0.84)	(0.48)	
CDS-Bond Basis Vol		0.14			−0.12	−0.59*
		(0.29)			(0.32)	(0.35)
10Y Treasury Basis Vol			2.35***		1.68*	0.88
			(0.65)		(0.86)	(1.33)
Observations	10,311	15,560	8,459	3,566	5,391	3,337
Adjusted R^2	0.19	0.22	0.18	0.22	0.19	0.26
F Statistic	26.18***	30.30***	24.22***	26.19***	26.96***	38.84***

Note: *p < 0.1; **p < 0.05; ***p < 0.01
SEs are clustered by time.

Table 6.7. *Linear regression coefficients compared to logit marginal effects.*

	Linear regression	Logit marginal effects
Exceptions over 1–5 days	7.91	2.19
Exceptions over 6–10 days	2.50	0.76
Exceptions over 11–15 days	0.45	0.13
Exceptions over 16–20 days	−0.30	−0.24

Table 6.8. *Linear regression coefficients compared to logit marginal effects.*

	Linear regression	Logit marginal effects
Exceptions over 1–5 days	3.97	1.70
Exceptions over 6–10 days	1.49	0.68
Exceptions over 11–15 days	0.77	0.38
Exceptions over 16–20 days	0.39	0.17
Year 2020	1.27	2.29
Year 2020 × Exceptions over 1–5 days	5.62	0.32
Year 2020 × Exceptions over 6–10 days	0.90	-0.09
Year 2020 × Exceptions over 11–15 days	−0.88	-0.48
Year 2020 × Exceptions over 16–20 days	−1.26	-0.70

Table 6.6 breaks down these regressions by asset class for 2020 specifically. Each regression limits the factors to those that are more relevant for that asset class, which helps to address multicollinearity in the factors. In many cases, desks face exceptions in response to increased movement in relevant market factors – for example, credit desks respond to changes in IG spreads and rates desks respond to changes in Treasury yields and the Treasury basis – but this does not hold across all factors. For example, large movements in the level of the stock market were not strongly associated with more backtesting exceptions. A common pattern is that large movements in IG corporate spreads were associated with backtesting exceptions across all desks except for rates desks.

Overall, no single market factor seems to have been associated with backtesting exceptions, but rather many different factors moving at the same time.

6.5 Comparing Linear and Logistic Regressions

Tables 6.7 and 6.8 show the coefficients for the linear regressions from the second and third specifications of Table 6.3 compared to the average marginal effects from a corresponding logistic regression (multiplied by 100 to put them in percentage point units). The same qualitative pattern holds, whereby more recent backtesting exceptions have a stronger ability to predict future exceptions, although the magnitudes of the coefficients are larger for the linear regressions.

References

Berkowitz, J., Christoffersen, P. and Pelletier, D. (2009). Evaluating Value-at-Risk models with desk-level data. *Management Science*, 57(12), 2213–2227.

Berkowitz, J. and O'Brien, J. (2002). How accurate Are Value-at-Risk models at commercial banks? *The Journal of Finance*, 57(3), 1093–1111.

Christoffersen, P. (2011). *Elements of Financial Risk Management. Academic Press*. Google-Books-ID: YkcMBGYbRasC.

O'Brien, J. and Szerszen, P. J. (2014). An evaluation of bank VaR measures for market risk during and before the financial crisis. *Finance and Economics Discussion Series (FEDS)*.

Perignon, C., Deng, Z. Y. and Wang, Z. J. (2008). Do banks overstate their value-at-risk? *Journal of Banking & Finance*, 32(5), 783–794.

Perignon, C. and Smith, D. R. (2010a). Diversification and value-at-risk. *Journal of Banking & Finance*, 34(1):55–66.

(2010b). The level and quality of value-at-risk disclosure by commercial banks. *Journal of Banking & Finance*, 34(2), 362–377.

7 *Performance Monitoring for Supervisory Stress-Testing Models*

NICK KLAGGE AND JOSE A. LOPEZ*

7.1 Introduction

Most models built for risk management purposes are used to generate forecasts of potential future outcomes that assist in taking potentially risk mitigating actions today. Risk managers must have in place a performance monitoring framework to ensure that their models are operating effectively and as intended. Fortunately, many standard statistical measures and tools are available with which to do so; for example, the use of statistical tests for monitoring Value-at-Risk models as per Acerbi and Szekely (2019).

However, stress-testing models pose a unique set of challenges with respect to performance monitoring. In particular, unlike standard forecasting models that generate unconditional forecasts, stress-testing models generate conditional forecasts based on stress scenarios that are unlikely to occur. This critical difference greatly limits one's ability to assess model projections with observed outcomes. Nonetheless, performance monitoring remains a necessary component of model development and evaluation, even for stress-testing models.

In this chapter, we discuss the challenges surrounding the performance monitoring of stress-test models and propose a set of tools and approaches for that purpose. These tools are relevant for the stress tests as embodied in the Federal Reserve's annual Comprehensive Capital Analysis and Review (CCAR) stress-testing program as mandated

* Federal Reserve Bank of New York and Federal Reserve Bank of San Francisco.
The views expressed here are those of the authors and not necessarily those of the Board of Governors of the Federal Reserve System, the Federal Reserve Bank of New York or the Federal Reserve Bank of San Francisco. We acknowledge helpful comments and suggestions from David Lynch, Akhtarur Siddique, and other colleagues and conference participants. We thank Zach Modig for his research assistance.

under the Dodd–Frank Act (DFA), as well as other firm-conducted and supervisory stress testing exercises.

Given the critical role of models in bank operations, the Federal Reserve and the Office of the Comptroller of the Currency have set guidelines for the establishment of model risk management programs, which ensure that the models in question are functioning appropriately and performing to expectations. These guidelines are described in Supervision and Regulation Letter 11-7 "Supervisory Guidance on Model Risk Management," which is more commonly known as SR 11-7. In particular, an element of the model risk management program, which this chapter seeks to further develop, is a framework for performance monitoring. This term encompasses activities defined in SR 11-7 under the headings "Ongoing Monitoring" and "Outcomes Analysis," which include benchmarking, sensitivity testing, and backtesting. Although performance monitoring is undertaken at the individual model level as part of the conceptual validation process, we outline a comprehensive program for performance monitoring of the aggregated outcomes from stress test models.

We characterize this approach to model risk management by borrowing a pair of terms from the software development literature. "White-box testing" encompasses any review activity that requires some access to the inner workings of a model, either conceptually or concretely. This category includes activities such as conceptual validation or code review. By contrast, "black-box testing" encompasses any review activity that does not require access to the inner workings of a model and in which the focus is mostly on modeling results. This category includes activities such as benchmarking, sensitivity testing, and backtesting.[1]

In some cases, such as certain vendor models, black-box testing may be the only tool available; in other cases, it would serve as a complement to white-box testing activities. Since black-box testing tends to be more easily automated than white-box testing, it can be performed at higher frequency and with lower investment of human resources. Black-box testing is valuable for its ability to raise important questions rather than to answer them conclusively. For example, a black-box

[1] For further discussion of these techniques, see Jan et al. (2013) as well as Khan and Khan (2012).

benchmark test may indicate that two models give very different answers under certain conditions, but it would need to be followed by a white-box test to understand the causes of the observed discrepancy. In this way, the two types of test are complementary, with low-resource black-box tests helping reviewers to focus high-resource white-box tests more effectively.

Black-box testing faces some significant challenges in a stress-testing context. Most prominently, the models are designed to produce outputs that are conditioned on the input scenario variables. In contrast to unconditional models, it is not necessarily appropriate to assess the performance of these conditional models by direct comparison of outputs to realized outcomes, since the realizations of macroeconomic conditions will almost certainly differ from those specified in any given stress scenario. Indeed, the model outputs under the most severe scenarios are of the most interest in a stress-testing context, but by definition, realized conditions will likely be dissimilar to the conditions postulated in these scenarios. We propose sets of model diagnostics that help to address this concern directly.

The chapter is structured as follows. Section 7.2 provides a short review of relevant literature on performance monitoring. Section 7.3 provides a general discussion on various possible approaches to the performance monitoring of bank stress-testing models and introduces useful heuristic notation. Section 7.4 presents our proposed set of diagnostic tools and approaches for conducting such performance monitoring. We also discuss a simple example of stock return modeling to illustrate some of the proposed tools. Section 7.5 presents actual examples of performance monitoring done using data derived from the DFAST supervisory modeling framework, and Section 7.6 concludes.

7.2 Literature Review

At the start of our discussion, we highlight that our preferred term for the diagnostic tools and approaches discussed below is “performance monitoring,” although the term “performance testing” is also commonly used. We make this subtle, but important, distinction because performance testing tends to imply the application of statistical tests that “accept” or “reject” a given hypothesis with some degree of statistical accuracy.[2] Our purpose here is broader than that, especially since stress test projections are purposefully constructed for unlikely outcomes. Instead, we propose the term "monitoring," which can include hypothesis testing but also allows for other criteria to be used in ascertaining a model's performance. An example of such could be model consistency, which is defined by Pesaran and Smith (1985) as "in the sense that [a model] does not generate self-contradictory answers to the questions posed."

A key challenge in performance monitoring for stress-testing models is that their main objectives are to describe events that are unlikely to occur.[3] Most prominently, stress test projections are conditional in nature since they project outcomes given hypothetical future values of scenario variables. Conditional forecasting is outside of the mainstream literature on forecast evaluation, which focuses on either unconditional forecasts or quantile forecasts (as in literature on Value-at-Risk modeling). Furthermore, the conditional scenarios of greatest interest (i.e., extreme stress scenarios) are by definition rarely similar to observed events. Most of the plausible performance tests explored in the literature involve either focusing on projections using baseline scenarios, so that forecasts may be considered to be "close" to unconditional, or they develop additional stress-testing models that produce density or quantile forecasts.

Thus, performance monitoring of stress-testing models presents several challenges from both theoretical and operational perspectives. However, not engaging in performance monitoring of some type is costly as well. A clear example of this is provided by Frame et al. (2015) in their case study of the failure of the stress-testing model used to generate supervisory risk-based capital stress tests for Fannie Mae and Freddie Mac, the former government-sponsored mortgage funders. The Office of Federal Housing Enterprise Oversight (OFHEO) was the supervisor of these two government-sponsored enterprises (GSEs) from 1992 to 2008 and was tasked by law to develop risk-based capital regulation based on a stress test. The stress-test model used to generate these capital regulations was set in

2 As noted by Pesaran and Smith (1985), "[w]hereas [model] selection procedures treat all the models symmetrically, testing procedures give one particular model, the null hypothesis, a privileged status."

3 Hughes (2012) forcefully claims that "[i]n building models for stress-testing, validation against standard forecast criteria is not appropriate."

place and frozen as of 2002, and the GSEs met their model-implied capital requirements over the subsequent seven years before they were placed in federal conservatorship in 2008. Frame et al. (2015) highlight that an important component of the failure of the capital regulations was that "the supervisor neither re-estimated (recalibrated) the model nor introduced new variables despite well-documented changes in mortgage underwriting practices" over the period. The lack of performance monitoring clearly contributed to the failure since careful monitoring would likely have highlighted the staleness of the data and assumptions embedded in the model. Similar motivation for performance monitoring can be found in Rajan et al. (2015). This chapter shows how the rise of mortgage securitization changed the relationship between observable loan characteristics and default probability, resulting in the deterioration of formerly reliable statistical forecasting models.

A few studies have addressed certain aspects of conditional forecasting. Faust and Wright (2008) focus specifically on the issue of evaluating conditional forecasts in the context of central bank projections of output and inflation. By imposing an assumed structure on the relationship between conditional and unconditional forecasts, the authors are able to modify traditional unconditional forecast efficiency tests for use with conditional forecasts. They find some evidence of forecast inefficiency in the macroeconomic conditional projections they examine. This approach could have applicability for CCAR stress-testing as well, although the DFAST scenarios are multivariate in nature and typically do not consist of simple differences between the unconditional and conditional forecast paths. Clark and McCracken (2016) extend this work in the context of assessing conditional forecasts from vector autoregression models. Specifically, they develop tests of forecast bias, efficiency, and comparative accuracy of conditional versus unconditional forecasts from VAR models.

A second type of conditional model evaluation is described by Giacomini and White (2006). The authors describe methods to compare the predictive ability of two models, conditioning on potentially relevant information such as the state of the business cycle or past relative performance. While this method does not evaluate the counterfactual conditional forecasts used for CCAR stress testing, it is useful in expanding the concepts of model performance monitoring beyond pure unconditional forecasting performance.

Some econometric frameworks may be useful in evaluating different conditional model forecasts for consistency. For example, Patton and Timmermann (2010) present a general framework for statistical testing of monotonicity relations. Many sensitivity analyses may have natural interpretations as statements about monotonicity, though the limited available data may result in tests with low power.

While not directly addressing the conditional forecasting issue, Pesaran and Timmermann (2005) provide a useful discussion of the role of real-time model performance monitoring in the selection and modification of forecasting models. For example, with respect to model selection, they highlight the value of cross-validation exercises as well as performance monitoring exercises, such as monitoring the properties of the model's forecast errors.[4] They also clearly suggest that "the process of monitoring and modifying the econometric model in real time should be set out in advance prior to the beginning of the experiment." Setting such evaluation criteria *ex ante* is a very prudent step and likely to be an important component of a performance monitoring program.

Finally, some authors have begun to develop heuristic approaches that may help assess the reasonableness or stability of stress-testing models in a performance monitoring context. Hardy and Schmieder (2013) use international cross-sectional information on banking crises to estimate rules of thumb for various components of bank capital ratios under crisis conditions, which may serve as a benchmark for certain stress-testing models. Taleb et al. (2012) develop a simple metric to summarize the convexity of a model's output with respect to its inputs, which may be used to gauge sensitivity to tail outcomes. However, these approaches have not been applied to stress-testing models as of yet.

As the Federal Reserve stress-testing program has been in place since 2011, several studies have reviewed the results directly. We summarize these studies in Section 7.5 after providing greater detail on the specific nature of the stress test output.

[4] See also Granger and Huang (1997) regarding cross-validation techniques and Hughes (2012) for a particular discussion of these techniques in a stress-testing context.

7.3 Performance Monitoring

The Federal Reserve's annual CCAR stress-testing program has become a key tool for both microprudential bank supervision and macroprudential policy; see Williams (2015) for further discussion and discussion of these policy objectives. The effective model risk management of the various data inputs, models, and model outputs is quite important and falls under the supervisory expectations detailed in SR 11–7. While the guidance covers various aspects of model risk management, this chapter focuses just on performance monitoring. This term encompasses activities defined in guidance under the headings of "Ongoing Monitoring" and "Outcomes Analysis," which include sensitivity testing, benchmarking, and backtesting.

While the tools and approaches discussed here are applicable for both black- and white-box testing as defined above, we will mainly discuss the perspective of black-box testing, since it more closely reflects the current needs of model validation and supervisory review of DFAST stress-testing models. We will also focus here on the macroeconomic scenario of DFAST that must be examined by all covered firms.

We now introduce some notation that will be useful in describing various aspects of performance monitoring. This heuristic notation scheme is specifically geared toward stress-testing models. Furthermore, it is also geared toward deterministic models. Although it could easily be generalized to stochastic models such as Monte Carlo simulations, we focus on deterministic models for simplicity of notation.

Consider a stress-test modeling effort by modeler m, which for our purposes could be an internal model developer with full access to the modeling details or an internal modeler implementing an external modeling solution. A model f_m is a function that maps a vector (or set) of inputs X to a vector of outputs Y:

$$f_m(\mathrm{X}) = Y. \tag{7.1}$$

Using the terminology introduced above, white-box tests require knowledge of the functional form of f_m, whereas black-box tests do not. This distinction may be an appealing feature of black-box tests when, for example, comparing models with very different functional forms or with functional forms that are not completely transparent.

In stress-testing models, the input vector X consists of several distinct types of information, for which we use the following notation:

$$f_m(P, S, t; \theta) = Y. \tag{7.2}$$

The vector P in Equation 7.2 represents information on the portfolio or item being stress-tested.[5] This will generally consist of a set of positions, along with a finite set of model-relevant characteristics for each position (e.g., duration or credit rating). For some models, such as those estimated at the portfolio level, P would be considerably simpler, containing a set of aggregate statistics. However, it can be quite large with respect to loan-level data, such as provided in the regulatory Y-14 reporting forms.[6]

The vector S in Equation 7.2 represents information on the stress-test scenario in question. This vector will generally consist of several time-indexed paths of macroeconomic and financial variables; for example, quarterly paths of GDP, Treasury yields, and stock prices. Although specific models may only use subsets of the full set of scenario variables, it is easier to consider the S vector as representing the complete set of available variables in a given scenario, regardless of the model under consideration.

The scalar t in Equation 7.2 represents the valuation date or "starting point" of the stress test. This is generally relevant because it defines the starting state of "the economy," including both macroeconomic conditions and time-varying characteristics of portfolio exposures. For example, the starting valuation of a stock portfolio will be different depending on the valuation date t.

The vector θ in Equation 7.2 represents the set of numerical parameters of the model f_m. A single model may retain the same functional form over time but use changing parameter values. This may occur, for example, if a model is specified as a linear regression, but is re-estimated as new data become available, so that coefficient estimates change over time. The functional form of the regression would be an

[5] An example of a non-portfolio item subject to stress testing would be a component of a firm's pre-provision net revenue, risk-weighted assets, or capital levels. Relevant information for such objects could include current asset balances or historical values of the component.

[6] The Federal Reserve's Y-14 reporting forms are summarized at www.federalreserve.gov/apps/reportforms/categoryindex.aspx?KZ9MpP8mEQY=.

inherent aspect of the model f_m, but specific coefficient estimates would be included in the parameter vector θ.

In stress-testing models, the output vector Y will generally consist of a time-indexed vector of ratios or dollar values over the scenario horizon; for example, quarterly write-downs on a credit portfolio or quarterly revenues from loan origination fees conditional on stress scenario S. If the model produces output at a higher level of granularity, then the vector Y will also reflect this disaggregation; for example, some models may generate loss estimates at the loan level, while others might do so at the portfolio level.

For diagnostic purposes, it may sometimes be desirable to summarize the vector-valued model output Y with a single scalar y. This value will often be a sum or average across time and/or components, possibly normalized by a measure of portfolio size. For example, for a model forecasting write-downs on a loan-level portfolio over the nine quarters of the DFAST horizon, y may be the total write down; alternatively, it may be the total write-down per dollar of exposure. The exact definition should be suited to the purpose at hand; some examples will be mentioned below. For convenience, we can compress our notation from Equation 7.2 to reflect this summary output in place of the vector-valued output:

$$f_m(P, S, t; \theta) = y. \tag{7.3}$$

In many cases, it may be sensible to begin by looking at the summary output, then drill down to the individual elements of the vector-valued output (e.g., values for different forecast quarters).

One additional piece of notation will assist in the exposition, i.e.,

$$f_{actual}(P, S_{actual}, t) = y_{actual}. \tag{7.4}$$

In Equation 7.4, the function f_{actual} represents a specific "model": the real world. The vector S_{actual} represents the paths that macroeconomic and financial variables actually took, starting at the valuation date t, over the relevant time horizon. Given a portfolio P, the function f_{actual} returns y_{actual}, the actual realization of the modeled quantity, such as credit losses or revenues from loan fees.

It may seem somewhat artificial to describe the real world in the terms of Equation 7.4. However, this notation highlights the underlying similarity between the real world and models thereof from a black-box-testing perspective: both are treated as hidden processes that translate a set of observable inputs into a set of observable outputs.

Note that the function f_{actual} has a very restricted domain. It can only return output if t is an actual historical date, P is a set of assets that actually existed on that date, and S_{actual} is the actual set of paths of macroeconomic and financial variables that were realized following that date. Despite these restrictions, f_{actual} can play an important role in black-box testing, for obvious reasons. The next section will define a variety of black-box model diagnostics using the framework just described.

7.4 Performance Monitoring Tools

In this section, we define a basic set of black-box diagnostic tools for performance monitoring. Although we hope that they have broader applicability as illustrated in our stock return modeling example, we focus specifically on diagnostics that will be useful and feasible in the context of bank stress testing models.

First, we seek to develop a framework that will be applicable across a wide variety of stress-testing models, including credit risk, market risk, operational risk, and other related models. Black-box testing is appealing in this context, given that it does not depend on any specific functional form of the underlying model (such as, for example, tests that are specific to least-squares regressions).

Second, we take as given the conditional approach to stress-testing. Specifically, we assume that the models being monitored that are designed to produce conditional expectations of outputs given a specified scenario. They do not produce unconditional forecasts or probability distributions of outputs, and the scenarios themselves are not identified with a percentile of any probability distribution of inputs. While forccasts of these kinds might provide additional avenues for performance monitoring, they are not widely used in stress testing as it is currently practiced.

Third, we respect the fact that additional model runs are costly and, at times, just not available. The stress-testing process is highly complex, data-intensive, time-intensive, resource-intensive, and highly controlled. Thus, our basic framework relies only on model runs that are already likely to be required in the course of a normal stress-test process. We indicate a few places where supplementary runs could be informative, but clearly flag these as such.

Finally, we recognize that actual outcome data, where available, are only moderately informative for stress-testing models. By definition, actual data will not correspond to the types of severe scenarios that are the primary focus of stress-testing exercises. Thus, while a model's performance in more stable conditions is of interest, it is not an overriding concern. For this reason, we discuss outcomes analysis in this framework, but present it on an equal footing with several other measures.

We consider these diagnostic tools to be "semi-automatic." They are more automated than a white-box conceptual review, but the data environment is too sparse to allow for fully automated statistical tests, where performance is assessed by rule, as in Pesaran and Timmermann (2005). Instead, these diagnostics will generate information that is useful only when interpreted through human judgment. For example, visual analysis supplemented with summary statistics will likely play an important role. The results of the black-box diagnostics may not be dispositive, but rather provide a jumping-off point for further white-box analysis. For example, two models may provide different risk rankings over two portfolios. To understand the implications of this result, analysts may need to make reference to the specifics of the two models to explain "why" it occurred. The ensuing explanation may be satisfactory, or it may indicate problems with one of the models that require further model development.

We divide the section into the three general categories of output sensitivity analysis, output benchmarking and output backtesting.

7.4.1 Output Sensitivity Analysis

Sensitivity testing encompasses a wide variety of diagnostics focusing on a single model. Sensitivity tests may be conducted without reference to a second model or to results from the real world. However, they are likely to be the most informative when compared with analogous results from other models or from actual outcomes from the real world.[7]

[7] See Board of Governors (2013) for further discussion of this topic with regard to supervisory expectations.

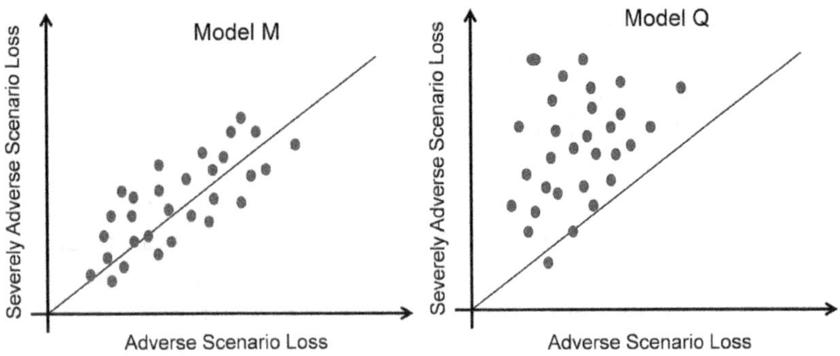

Figure 7.1 Scenario sensitivity testing using scatterplots.

7.4.1.1 Scenario Sensitivity Analysis

This class of diagnostics measures the response of a model's output to a change in the input scenario paths S. For stress test models, this is one of the most important diagnostic measures, as it can tell us how model outcomes change as the underlying macroeconomic scenario drivers change.

Scenario sensitivity testing consists of comparing the following output values from the same model m across two scenarios k and l:[8]

A: $f_m(P, S_k, t; \theta_m)$

B: $f_m(P, S_l, t; \theta_m)$

Possible ways of analyzing the data include:

- Scatterplots of the outputs across scenarios. The 45° line provides a clear reference to judge whether outputs change as expected across the scenarios. Figure 7.1 shows two scatterplots comparing hypothetical model outputs for various portfolios under an adverse scenario and a severely adverse scenario. This type of analysis would be useful for comparing a champion and a benchmark model across various portfolio segments.

[8] Note that, because model output may be vector-valued, all diagnostics are also potentially vector-valued. Thus, while two models generating output at a portfolio level can only be compared at the portfolio level, more granular models may be capable of producing diagnostics at disaggregated segment or position levels.

  - A graph with most points above the 45° line, as on the left-hand side of Figure 7.1, indicates a model that generally captures the intuition that losses should be greater under more severe scenarios – though particular attention could be paid to points below the 45° line.
  - A graph with points more evenly distributed above and below the 45° line, as on the right-hand side of Figure 7.1, indicates a model with much less scenario sensitivity, which could be appropriate but likely requires further analysis and understanding.
- Regression of more stressed outputs against less stressed or baseline outputs, which is a formalization of the scatterplot diagram. We should expect a slope coefficient greater than one, though statistical significance may be limited in a small sample.
- Spearman rank correlation of a single model's outputs across two different scenarios.
  - Imagine the (possibly unlikely) case where the ranking of model projection values are identical across two scenarios. The corresponding rank correlation statistic of one suggests that the model has a methodology that scales up portfolio segment losses across scenarios in a relatively consistent way.
  - Consider the case in which the rank correlation is zero. This result does not give much of a sense of the performance of the model's approach across the scenarios. The result just notes that the methodology may be handling the firm projections quite differently across the scenarios.
  - Consider the possible cases in which the rank correlation is significantly negative. In these cases, the portfolio segments with the higher losses in the baseline scenario are having their losses scaled up in the adverse scenario by much less than the segments that had the lower losses in the baseline scenario. While this does not constitute evidence of poor model performance, it is an anomalous outcome that would require a better understanding of its drivers.
- Comparison of rank correlations across the two models for the same two scenarios.
  - Consider the case in which the rank correlation statistics for two models of interest are very similar. Such a result would suggest similar degrees of implied macroeconomic sensitivity by the two models, which could be affirming of their relative status to each other or problematic if they were designed to be different.

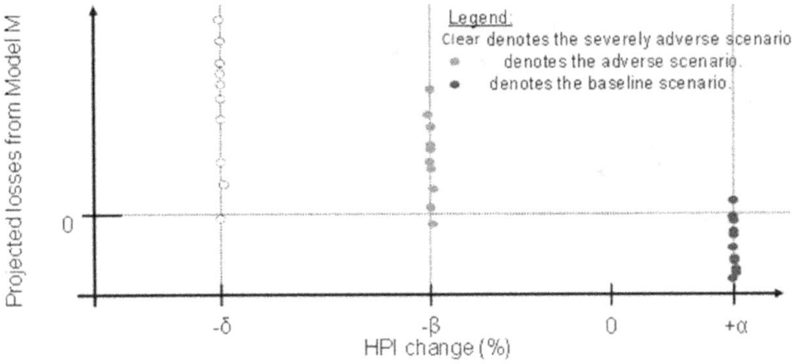

Figure 7.2 A model's scenario sensitivity with reference to a macroeconomic variable.

  - A similar line of conclusions and further analysis would arise if the rank correlations were markedly different.
- If a particular macroeconomic variable is salient for a given model (e.g., change in house price index (HPI) for a mortgage loss model), summary measures of this variable can be used to assess the model output:
  - Consider a scatterplot of model output against such a summary macroeconomic variable. Figure 7.2 shows a hypothetical example of such a plot for a mortgage model applied to several different mortgage portfolios, where the summary macroeconomic variable is the degree of HPI change across the scenarios; that is, the baseline scenario posits a slight +α% increase in the HPI while the severely adverse scenario has a sharp –δ% decrease.[9]
    - A rough empirical estimate of the model's sensitivity would be the slope of the fitted line through the clusters of datapoints.
    - If the graphed relationship is linear and downward-sloping, this suggests that the model's implied sensitivity to this variable is negative, which is a reasonable expectation for losses.
    - If the relationship is linear but flat or upward-sloping, this would suggest a lack of macroeconomic sensitivity that would require more analysis and understanding.

[9] We recognize that other scenario variables are most likely varying across scenarios as well, but we are highlighting sensitivity analysis with respect to a single variable. Multivariate extensions could be constructed; for example, by using only directional changes or binned magnitudes of these changes.

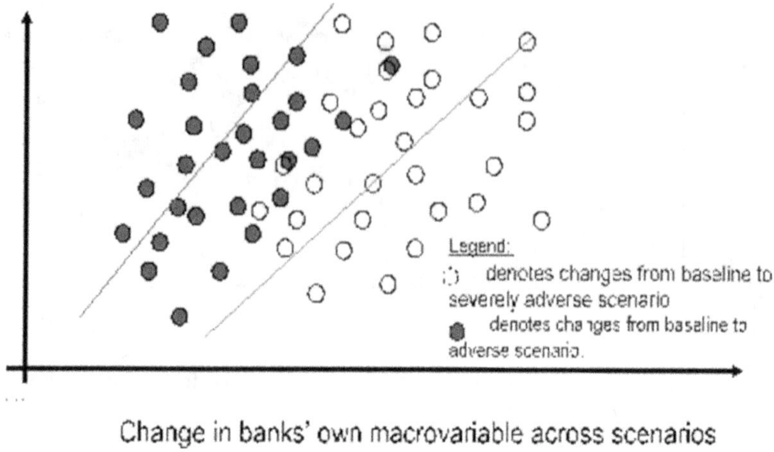

Figure 7.3 Scenario sensitivity across multiple portfolio segments and a macroeconomic variable.
(Note: plotted datapoints represent different portfolio segments)

- Graph with scenario differences in a macroeconomic variable on the x-axis and the differences in scenario projections on the y-axis. In Figure 7.3, each datapoint represents a single bank's changes in the macroeconomic variable and projections in question across the two scenarios; the blue series representing changes from its own baseline to its own adverse scenario, and the red series representing changes from its own baseline to its own severely adverse scenario. Note that since the graph is displaying results from the banks' own scenarios, the changes in macroeconomic variables will differ. This type of analysis would be useful for an RET trying to assess banks' relative model sensitivity.
  - Regression analysis provides a summary view on these sensitivity estimates. Any datapoints (i.e., bank model sensitivities) falling far from the trend may warrant further attention.
- Calculate scenario "deltas" or "sensitivities," defined as the change in model output between two scenarios divided by the difference in the macroeconomic variable between the scenarios. These ratios can be used to examine the relative magnitudes of these ratios or sensitivities across portfolio segments over the scenario horizon.
  - This analysis could be conducted with changes in cumulative model output or with changes in quarter-specific model outputs to assess differences across forecast horizons.

    - That is, graphing these sensitivity ratios at each of the nine forecast quarters could provide additional insights on the model's forecasting implications.

- For example, roughly straight lines for these sensitivities across the nine quarters would suggest a constant macroeconomic sensitivity over the forecast horizon, which might be reasonable or not depending on a variety of factors, such as the scenario variable paths.
- Analysis of these sensitivity time profiles across portfolio segments would provide evidence on whether the observed variation is reasonable given the known variation across the segments.

We will usually be interested in testing how the model responds when moving from the baseline scenario to the adverse scenario and to the severely adverse scenario. At a minimum, we should investigate whether the model outputs move monotonically in the expected direction with the declared severity of the scenario; for example, that losses increase or that revenues decline in more adverse scenarios. A violation of this expectation is not necessarily prima facie evidence of a problem with a model, but a model owner should be able to furnish a clear explanation when such a violation of intuition is observed, such as specific portfolio characteristics that interact with a variable's scenario path.

In some cases, it may be possible and desirable to generate supplemental model runs to calculate additional diagnostics. Changing between the pre-specified supervisory scenarios entails changing virtually every forecast variable, but at times, we may have a special interest in the response of model output to a change in a single variable. In such cases, we can generate supplemental runs in which only one variable among the supervisory inputs is changed.

To help illustrate these scenario sensitivity techniques, we constructed a simple example based on stress testing stock return models. Based on our notation, consider the stress-testing model

$$f_i(P_j, S_k, t; \theta_i),$$

where

- P_j represents an equity portfolio, which for this exercise is a market-weighted portfolio based on S&P 500 firms from a specific industry.
- f_i represents a model. For this exercise, we use two simple models. The first is a classic "CAPM beta" model, where individual stock

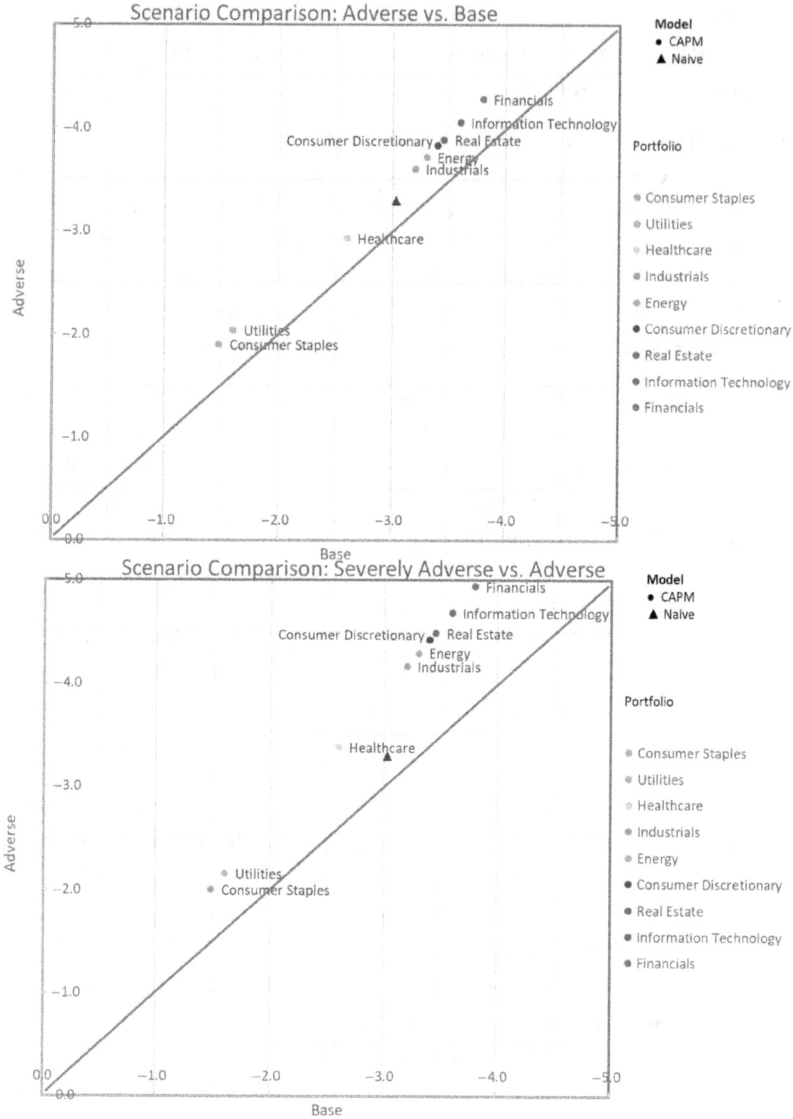

Figure 7.4 Scenario sensitivity testing using scatterplots of stock return projections.

Panel A. Baseline vs adverse scenario projections

Panel B. Adverse vs severely adverse scenario projections Figure 7.5 collects all of the scenario projections for the CAPM model and provides the sensitivity analysis discussed above with regard to Figure 7.2. By collecting

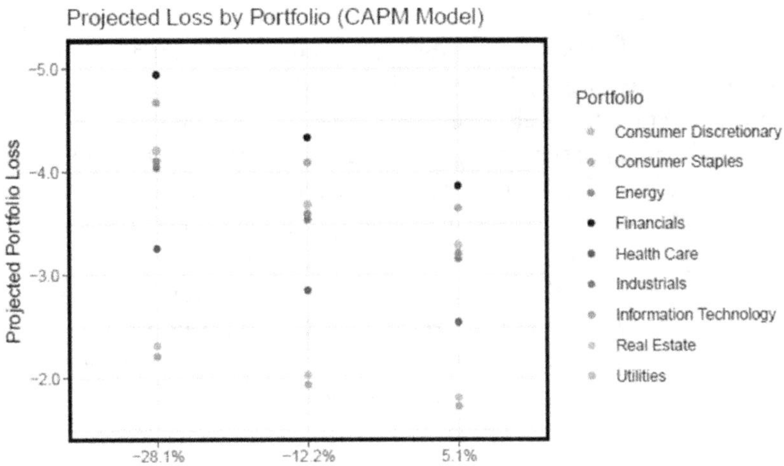

Figure 7.5 Scenario sensitivity across industry sectors and scenario index returns.

returns are regressed against market returns (in this case, the S&P 500 index), and the estimated "beta" coefficients are used to represent the sensitivity of each stock's price to movements in the broad index. The second is a "naïve" model in which each stock's return is simply assumed to equal the market return; i.e., the beta coefficients are set to one.

- S_k represents a stress scenario. For this exercise, we use the US equity market spot price shocks from the Federal Reserve's adverse and severely adverse global market shock scenarios in 2018. The price shocks were +5.1% in the baseline scenario, –12.2% in the adverse and –28.1% in the severely adverse scenario.
- We do not use the time index t in this exercise, as neither of the models being used conditions on any time-based market characteristics.

Figure 7.4 (*cont.*) all the projections in this format, the relative magnitudes of the loss projections with respect to the scenario index loss, which is reported on the x-axis, are clearly visible and could be used to examine the model's relative sensitivity. Of course, the CAPM is a linear model, so this information is already reflected in the industry betas used to generate the projections. However, with more complicated models, this diagnostic would be very helpful, especially if a significant amount of dispersion among the sensitivity measures was observed.

We also do not vary θ_i, the set of parameter estimates for each model f_i, in this example. As an extension, for example, this could be used to assess the CAPM model for sensitivity to the time period over which the beta parameters were estimated.

Our first diagnostic analysis is to consider scatterplots of the two models' scenario projections. Figure 7.4 presents a comparison of the two models' projections for the baseline and the adverse scenarios in the first panel and for the adverse and severely adverse scenarios in the second panel. In both panels, the projected stock returns for the nine industry sectors we consider are represented, and they can be clearly seen as labeled as different symbols. However, since the naïve model sets the beta coefficient equal to one in for all sectors, all nine points lie exactly on top of each other and can only be seen as the labeled triangle. Clearly, the first – if obvious – diagnostic outcome here is that the naïve model misses an important degree of heterogeneity observed across the projected industry returns.

The second diagnostic outcome is that all the projected returns are below the 45° line, indicating that all of the models' projected returns are lower in the worse scenarios graphed on the y-axes. This outcome is what we expected, and the scatterplot confirms that outcome. The third outcome visible from the scatterplots is the rank-ordering of industries based on the CAPM model's projected returns, which are entirely dependent on the industry-level beta estimates. When considering different scenarios at a future point in time, this rank-ordering provides another diagnostic tool for monitoring the model's performance.

7.4.1.2 Portfolio Sensitivity Analysis

This class of diagnostics measures the response of a model's output to a change in the underlying portfolio or sub-portfolio to which it is being applied while keeping the scenario fixed. This sort of analysis is valuable in a stress-testing context because we would expect stress-testing models to be responsive to changes in the input portfolio.[10] Note that in this case especially, it is probably preferable that the output y (or Y)

[10] Another possible interpretation of portfolio sensitivity analysis would be as a cross-validation exercise. That is, if random subsegments or loans are defined as separate test portfolios, we would expect the model outputs to be very similar aside from standard random variation. However, the usefulness of this approach may be limited since a departure from this expected outcome might just be due to an input portfolio that was formed with a random bias of some sort.

be scaled by portfolio size to facilitate comparability between portfolios. For example, for a credit loss model, the summary variable would be total write-downs per dollar of exposure, rather than total write-downs.

Notationally, portfolio sensitivity analysis consists of comparing output values from the same model m for two portfolios p and q:

A: $f_m(P_p, S, t; \theta_m)$

B: $f_m(P_q, S, t; \theta_m)$

Possible ways of analyzing the data include:

- Graphical comparisons of outputs across portfolios (e.g., bar charts)
- If salient summary measures of portfolio characteristics are available (e.g., weighted average FICO score), these can be used to assess the model output using a scatterplot or regression of the model output on the portfolio characteristic measure.

This comparison may not always have an immediate interpretation, given the diversity of portfolio segments considered. However, in many cases, subject matter experts may have an intuitive sense of the risk-ranking of at least certain segments, and the diagnostic data can be compared to that intuition.

In cases where the model f_m generates results at a disaggregated level, it may be possible to calculate these diagnostics using subcomponents of a single portfolio. For example, with a mortgage credit loss estimation model, a given portfolio could be subdivided between prime and subprime borrowers, and the estimated losses on the subportfolios compared to verify that they are intuitively ranked. With respect to stock returns as in our numerical example, this exercise is done with respect to the industry-level portfolios and could be extended to consider sub-industry portfolios. This type of comparison is likely to employ highly domain-specific subdivision rules. In the presence of a benchmarking model, the two sets of results could be compared using the aforementioned scatterplots as well as standard and rank correlation coefficients.

7.4.1.3 Parameter Sensitivity Analysis

This class of diagnostic tools measures the response of a model's output to a change in one or more of the model parameters, θ_m. Such diagnostics are a way of quantifying and analyzing parameter uncertainty risk. For example, in a statistical model, estimated parameters can only be determined to a given degree of precision, and we should understand the implications for model output of this uncertainty. In other cases, models may rely on parameters that are calibrated or even set using expert judgment, and in these cases, we should also understand how the model responds to changes within a reasonable range.

Parameter sensitivity analysis consists of comparing the following output values from the same model m and scenario s over two sets of parameters θ_{m1} and θ_{m2}. Notably, this class of diagnostics requires supplemental model runs using another set of model parameters. Notationally,

A: $f_m(P, S, t; \theta_{m1})$

B: $f_m(P, S, t; \theta_{m2})$

Similar to the tools discussed above, possible ways of analyzing these sets of differing model output include:

- Scatterplots of output under one parameter set vs the other.
- Statistical tests to determine whether the differences in output across the different parameter sets have a zero mean and other related regression analysis.

Parameter sensitivity analysis may be especially useful in cases where a given model is being re-estimated; for example, to incorporate more recent data. In this case, the model structure will stay the same, but coefficients will change, and it is useful to have a holistic picture of how the aggregate change will affect output, holding other things constant. In other cases, it may be desirable to examine the sensitivity of a model's output to a change in a single parameter; for example, when a parameter is unobservable and set judgmentally.

In the case of a model re-estimation mentioned above, the size of the change to parameter values will be determined naturally by the observed data. In other cases, however, the size of a parameter shock will have to be determined judgmentally. In these situations, the ideal is to use a data-driven approach to set the size of the parameter shock. For example, in a regression framework, it may be appropriate to shock an estimated parameter by one standard error of the estimate. Or, in a loss model using a segment-level historical average LGD, it may be appropriate to shock the average by the standard deviation of observed historical LGDs. Grounding the analysis in the data in this fashion helps to ensure that the parameter sensitivity is reasonable and directly applicable; by contrast, a naïve parameter change, such as a flat 20% shock, may be unrealistically large for some parameters, but negligibly small for others. Similarly, with respect to calibrated or judgmental parameters, care should be taken to vary them sufficiently to adequately test the established choice, but not to introduce an excessive and likely useless degree of variation into the analysis.

7.4.1.4 Date Sensitivity Analysis

This class of diagnostics measures the response of a model's output to a change in the valuation date used to run the model. This type of sensitivity analysis is somewhat more abstract than the others outlined above, but may still provide valuable information about a model. Date sensitivity analysis may be useful by measuring the response of a model's output to changes in the starting environment. For example, expected losses on a portfolio containing Greek sovereign bonds would be different depending on whether the valuation date used was in 2009 or 2012. Such analysis could also provide insight on the cyclical sensitivity of a model. A "through-the-cycle" model should return similar results regardless of the starting date, while a "point-in-time" model should return results that are sensitive to the starting date.

Date sensitivity analysis consists of comparing the output values from the same model m for two valuation dates t_1 and t_2:

A: $f_m(P, S, t_1; \theta)$

B: $f_m(P, S, t_2; \theta)$

As before, possible ways of analyzing the data include scatterplots of outputs using the two valuation dates and regression analytics, such as the use of statistical tests to determine whether the differences in output across the different valuation dates have a zero mean.

Because of the complexity inherent in interpreting the results of date sensitivity analysis, and because this class of diagnostics requires conducting additional model runs, it is probably best used in specific cases where there is a concern about model sensitivity to some date-related piece of information.

7.4.2 *Output Benchmarking*

Output benchmarking compares the outputs of two models given the same inputs in order to directly understand the role of modeling choices while holding other inputs constant. This type of analysis is also important to cases in which benchmarking models are maintained for comparison with the chosen production model. Output benchmarking consists of comparing the following output values for two models *i* and *j*:

$$\text{A: } f_i(P, S^*, t; \theta_i)$$

$$\text{B: } f_j(P, S^*, t; \theta_j),$$

where S* denotes the union of the scenario variables used by the two models. While it is not necessary for the two models to use the same set of macroeconomic variables, it is necessary that the two sets of variables are constructed under the same scenario logic.

Possible ways of analyzing the data include:

- Graphs to provide visual comparisons.
- Scatterplots of outputs from models *i* and *j* across portfolios. Visual investigation of pattern relative to a 45° line, identification of outliers, and simple regression analysis would provide useful insights into relative performance.
- Calculation of Pearson correlation coefficients or Spearman rank correlation coefficients between the outputs of models *i* and *j*.
- Use of statistical tests to determine whether the differences in output across the different models have a zero mean, suggesting agreement in their projections.

As an illustrative example of output benchmarking, Figure 7.6 presents output bar charts of the industry stock return projections from our earlier example for all three scenarios. As before, this analysis highlights the heterogeneity of projected returns from the CAPM model relative to the naïve model and should suggest to the analyst that the latter model is likely insufficient for stress-testing purposes. The analysis could also be framed in terms of the naïve model serving as a benchmark for the CAPM model; that is, if the results of the naïve model do not seem to represent an average of the CAPM model results, something may be incorrect in the production of the CAPM model.

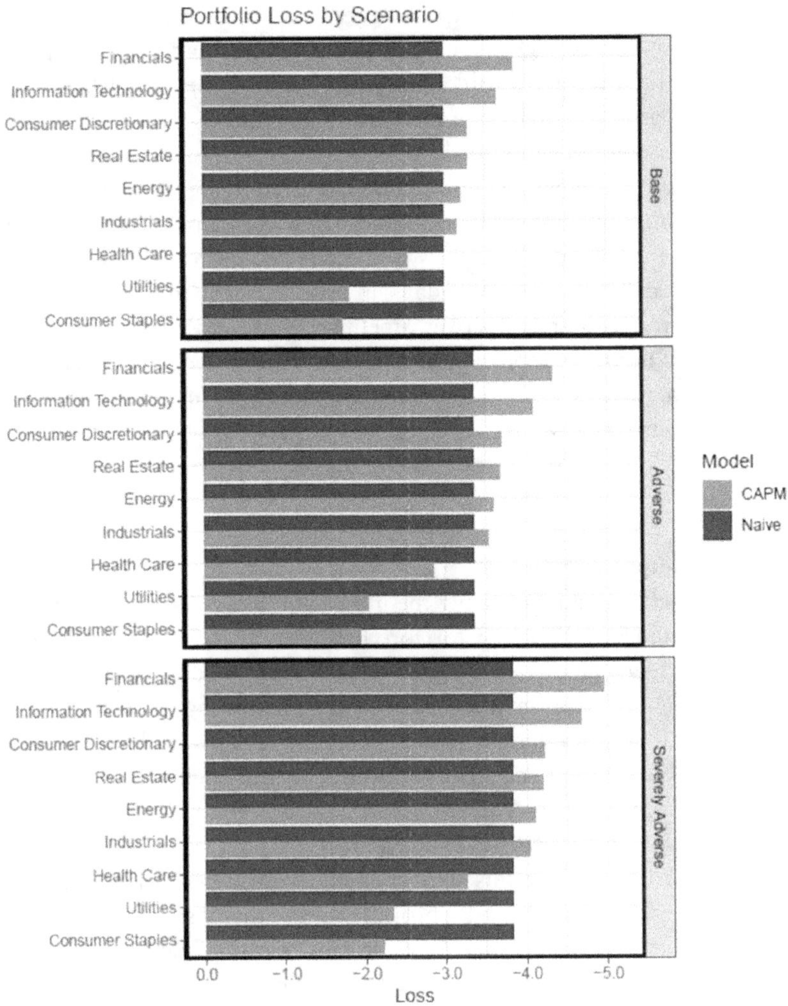

Figure 7.6 Benchmarking analysis of the CAPM and naïve models across scenarios.

Again, this battery of diagnostics does not provide an answer as to whether the model in question or the benchmark model is "better." Instead, the diagnostics provide users with insights on relative model performance at a point in time and allow performance monitoring over time. For example, large outliers or a significant positive difference between the two models' output suggest additional topics of inquiry and analysis for assessing the main model's performance. Similarly, a meaningful change in the rank correlation between the models' relative performance or the quality of the benchmark model could raise questions that should be addressed.

If the main and benchmark models have been in place for some time (such as, multiple annual DFAST runs), these comparisons can also be made across time. For a relatively new model, supplementary runs may be generated as of past DFAST dates in order to make this comparison. Trends in relative estimates over time may also be assessed.

If a new model is replacing an existing model, the old model may serve as a benchmark. This comparison requires either generating output from the new model at an old date with old portfolios, or generating output from the old model at a new date with new portfolios.

7.4.2.1 Output Backtesting

Output backtesting is probably the most commonly discussed method of performance monitoring for forecasting models; i.e., how similar was the model's prediction to what actually happened? Unfortunately, for the reasons mentioned in Section 7.2, backtesting is only moderately useful as a monitoring tool for stress-testing models that are based on conditional scenario paths that will explicitly not happen. Nonetheless, we discuss such diagnostic tools here due to their prominence in the model evaluation literature.

Output backtesting in this context can be done in two ways. The first approach is comparing model projections for the baseline scenario – both the supervisory one and the firm's own within the DFAST context – and with the actually observed outcomes; however, please recall that this approach is a joint analysis of the model and the proximity of the baseline scenario to the actual outcomes. To focus just on the model, we suggest comparing the following output values:

A: $f_m(P, S_{actual}, t; \theta_m)$

B: $f_{actual}(P, S_{actual}, t)$

In this form, backtesting can be seen as a special case of benchmarking. Possible ways of analyzing the data include:

- Graphs and scatterplots of modeled vs actual values,
- Model fit metrics, such as R-squared and hypothesis tests.
- Residual analysis, including graphs and more formal tests, such as Wooldridge moment tests.

This class of diagnostics requires a supplemental model since the supervisory scenarios will never coincide precisely with the true realization of S_{actual}. Thus, to conduct this exercise, supplemental model runs must be generated using S_{actual} as an input. Additionally, these diagnostics require the collection of y_{actual} for the quantity of interest. This information may or may not be readily available or may only be available with a lag.

Model testing often includes both "in-sample" and "out-of-sample" backtesting. In-sample backtesting evaluates the model's ability to fit outcomes over the sample chosen for model estimation; out-of-sample backtesting evaluates the model's ability to fit outcomes outside of that sample, whether from the same time period but not included in the sample or from a different time period. Out-of-sample backtesting helps to ensure that the model is not over-fit to the estimation data. The latter type of out-of-sample backtesting, called out-of-time backtesting, evaluates the model's ability to fit outcomes outside of (most commonly after) the historical period from which the estimation sample was drawn. Out-of-time backtesting helps to assess a model's stability over time. Since stress test models are intended to be used for out-of-sample forecasts, out-of-sample backtesting, and in particular out-of-time backtesting, is an important diagnostic. At the same time, stress test models are intended to be used for stressed conditions, but out-of-time periods may not contain stressed conditions. For this reason, in-sample backtesting may also play an important diagnostic role and should be present in a model risk management framework.

7.5 Extant Performance Monitoring of DFAST Stress-Testing Output

Stress testing has become a key component of the Federal Reserve's supervisory monitoring of bank holding companies with greater than $50 billion in assets since the passage of the DFA in 2010. In broad terms, the Federal Reserve constructs its own models for bank losses, revenues, risk-weighted assets and capital levels under the three supervisory macroeconomic scenarios – the aforementioned supervisory baseline, adverse and severely adverse scenarios. These projections are used to determine whether the affected firms will have sufficient capital over the nine-quarter scenario horizon. If a firm does not meet all of the capital thresholds throughout the entire nine quarters for all scenarios, remedial capital actions must be enacted and planned for.

In an effort to make this important policy exercise transparent to the public, the Federal Reserve publishes select firm-level projections from its own models. Using our earlier notation, we have

$$f_{FED}(P_j, S_q, t; \theta_{FED}) = Y_{FED},$$

where j = {1,. . .,N}, N is the number of CCAR firms for which DFAST projections are available in year t, and q = {supervisory baseline, adverse, and severely adverse}.[11] Full sets of such projections are now available for 2013 through 2016.[12] These projections allow for useful examples of the performance monitoring of stress-testing models, particularly across firms and starting dates.

The first study we highlight on this topic by Glasserman and Tangirala (2016), who conduct an in-depth analysis of the DFAST loan loss projections generated in 2013 and in 2015, although they also examine projections published in 2009 and 2012. For example, they examine histograms of loss rates across firms and portfolios for all four of these data years; that is they compare $G_t(f_{FED}(P_{jk}, S, t; \theta))$ – the probability distribution function (pdf) of loss rates across firms and portfolios for the supervisory severely adverse scenarios – for each of the four years. The authors fit a parametric pdf to the pooled data from 2012 through 2014 for reference and use a two-sidedKolmogorov–Smirnov test for the equality of the empirical G_t functions. They find that there is no statistical difference in the functions across the years. This result supports their overall argument that the DFAST projections are becoming less informative over time since they are quite similar in nature.

They also conduct scenario sensitivity analysis as discussed in Section 7.4.1.1 using the DFAST 2014 projections for the thirty

[11] Please be aware that the DFAST requirement for analysis of an adverse scenario was removed by recent legislation and will be eliminated from future exercises, pending further rulemaking.

[12] See Glasserman and Tangirala (2016) for discussion of the Federal Reserve stress-testing data releases prior to 2013.

covered firms in that year. Specifically, they examine $f_{FED}(P_{jk}, S_q, 2014; \theta)$ for $j = \{1,\ldots,30\}$, $q = \{$supervisory adverse, supervisory severely adverse$\}$, and $k = \{1,\ldots,7\}$ representing the seven aggregate loss rates that were projected and publicly reported. They provide a firm-level scatterplot across the two scenarios as well as accompanying regression analysis. Even though regression coefficients do exhibit significant variation, they conclude that the nearly perfect linear relationship observed suggests that the scenario sensitivity is too low and insufficiently informative at the firm-level perspective.

They also examine the scenario sensitivity across the seven loss rate categories by presenting scatterplots for each category with the thirty firm-specific points. Once again, even though the regression coefficients across the categories vary notably, they present evidence of strong linear relationships that they argue provide insufficient variation to be useful for a public assessment of the Federal Reserve's DFAST models.

The authors also examine a form of date sensitivity analysis as discussed in Section 7.4.1.4; that is, they examine $f_{FED}(P_{jk}, S_{SA}, t; \theta)$ for $t = \{2012, 2013, 2014\}$. They conduct their analysis at the firm-portfolio level in units of loss dollars; i.e., Y_{jkt} is firm *j*'s cumulative projected losses on portfolio *k* for the specified DFAST starting date in year *t*. They examine Y_{jt} as the weighted average loss rate across the *k* portfolios. They conclude that there is a high degree of predictability across time, which in their approach again limits the usefulness of public information being generated by the Federal Reserve's DFAST stress tests.

The second set of studies we highlight are a series of short articles that address several topical questions related to the DFAST stress tests by examining the DFAST projections generated by both the Federal Reserve and the covered firms themselves. Hirtle et al. (2014) explore the question of whether banks attempt to mimic the Federal Reserve's projections. The authors compare the two sets of projections reported in 2013 and 2014 to see if there was convergence within this time period. Using our notation, the authors compare

$$A: \sum_{j=1}^{18} f_{Fed}\left(P_j, S_{SA}, t; \theta\right)$$

$$B: \sum_{j=1}^{18} f_j\left(P_j, S_{SA}, t; \theta_j\right),$$

where the objects of interest are the covered CCAR firms' projected cumulative net income, PPNR, total net charge-offs, and net charge-offs in seven reported loan portfolios in dollars under the supervisory adverse scenario; and the summation is across the eighteen firms for which projections were available in both years $t = \{2013, 2014\}$. Their analysis found some evidence that the aggregate net income projections made by the firms did get closer to the Federal Reserve projections, but that there was some diversity of results across the subcomponents that make up net income, particularly the projections of loan portfolio net charge-offs. Hirtle and McKay (2015) extend the analysis to include the 2015 DFAST projections, which provides further mixed evidence regarding the question of whether the bank and Federal Reserve projections are converging. This study found that aggregate net income and PPNR projections did seem to converge, but that projected loan losses did not. That the gaps between the projections are of different magnitudes for different loan types suggests that a variety of factors are at play and likely do not represent an unhealthy development of a modeling "monoculture" within the supervisory DFAST stress-testing program.

Deng et al. (2015) continue to examine the question of whether firm projections are converging to the Federal Reserve projections by using a regression analysis that mixes firms' projections across years. That is, they conduct regression analysis on both the levels and changes in the firms' projections for various stress-testing items across the years 2013, 2014 and 2015. The explanatory variables were lagged values of the firm and Federal Reserve projections. Their analysis again provides mixed evidence that the firms' stress test projections are converging with those from the Federal Reserve.

Finally, Hirtle et al. (2015) compare their own top-down CLASS model projections under the 2014 severely adverse scenario with the Federal Reserve's DFAST results. In our notation, they compare:

$$A: f_{Fed}\left(P_j, S_{SA}, 2014; \theta_{Fed}\right)$$

$$B: f_{CLASS}\left(P_j, S_{SA}, t; \theta_{CLASS}\right),$$

for $j = [1,30]$. The specific model output that they examine are several income statements as well as the change in the ratio of common equity to risk-weighted assets. They found reasonably high correlations between several sets of projections, although the regression R-squared values were lower due to differences in the means across the model projections.

7.6 Conclusion

Monitoring the performance of a model whose outputs are fed into a decision-making process is a critical component of ensuring continued adherence to the modelers' underlying goals. An extensive econometric literature exists on how to perform such monitoring, both in general and for specific fields of interest. For example, for macroeconomic policy, several studies have investigated the relative value of such model outputs to the underlying policy objectives; see Romer and Romer (2008) for this type of analysis.

In contrast, in the area of bank stress-testing models for internal capital allocation purposes and for supervisory purposes such as DFAST stress testing, the literature on model performance monitoring has been sparse for two reasons. First, the active use of stress testing by banks and supervisors is a relatively recent phenomena, which can be dated most clearly to the Federal Reserve's S-CAP exercise in early 2009, although it had been widely discussed prior to that. Second, as mentioned before, these models generate conditional forecasts based on stress scenarios that are unlikely to occur as opposed to actually observed outcomes. The goal of our chapter was to highlight these challenges, but more importantly, contribute to the development of a diagnostic framework with specific recommendations that should facilitate current monitoring efforts and hopefully spark further work in this area.

References

Acerbi, C. and Szekely, B. (2019). The Minimally Biased Backtest for Expected Shortfall. *Risk*, 29, September, 1–6.

Board of Governors of the Federal Reserve System (2011). Supervisory Guidance on Model Risk Management. *SR Letter* 11-7, 4/4/2011.

(2013). Capital Planning at Large Bank Holding Companies: Supervisory Expectations and Range of Current Practice.

(2016). Dodd–Frank Stress Testing 2016: Supervisory Stress Test Methodology and Results.

Clark, T. and McCracken, M. (2016). Tests of Predictive Ability for Vector Autoregressions Used for Conditional Forecasting. *Journal of Applied Econometrics*, 32, 533–553.

Deng, A., Hirtle, B. and Kovner, A. (2015). Are BHCs Mimicking the Fed's Stress Test Results? *Federal Reserve Bank of New York Liberty Street Economics*, September 21.

Faust, J. and Wright, J. (2008). Efficient Forecast Tests for Conditional Policy Forecasts. *Journal of Econometrics*, 146, 293–303.

Frame, W. S., Gerardi, K. and Willen, P. S. (2015). The Failure of Supervisory Stress Testing: Fannie Mae, Freddie Mac, and OFHEO. Manuscript, Federal Reserve Bank of Atlanta.

Giacomini, R. and White, H. (2006). Tests of Conditional Predictive Ability. *Econometrica*, 74, 1545–1578.

Glasserman, P. and Tangirala, G. (2016). Are the Federal Reserve's Stress Test Results Predictable? *Journal of Alternative Investments*, 18, 82–97.

Granger, C. W. J. and Huang, L. L. (1997). Evaluation of Panel Data Models: Some Suggestions from Time Series. UCSD Working Paper #97-10.

Hardy, D. C. and Schmieder, C. (2013). Rules of Thumb for Bank Solvency Stress Testing. *IMF Working Paper* WP/13/232.

Hirtle, B., Kovner, A. and McKay, E. (2014). Becoming More Alike? Comparing Bank and Federal Reserve Stress Test Results. *Federal Reserve Bank of New York Liberty Street Economics*, July 21.

(2015). Are BHC and Federal Reserve Stress Test Results Converging? What Do We Learn from 2015? *Federal Reserve Bank of New York Liberty Street Economics*, April 15.

Hughes, T. (2012). Validating Stress-Testing Models. Moody's Analytics whitepaper, June.

Jan, S. R., Shah, S. T. U., Johar, Z. U., Shah, Y. and Khan. F. (2016). An Innovative Approach to Investigate Various Software Testing Techniques and Strategies. *International Journal of Scientific Research in Science, Engineering and Technology*, 2, 682–689.

Khan, M. E. and Khan, F. (2012). A Comparative Study of White Box, Black Box and Grey Box Testing Techniques. *International Journal of Advanced Computer Science and Applications*, 3, 12–15.

Patton, A. J. and Timmermann, A. (2010). Monotonicity in Asset Returns: New Tests with Applications to the Term Structure, the CAPM, and Portfolio Sorts. *Journal of Financial Economics*, 98, 605–625.

Pesaran, M. H. and Smith, R. P. (1985). Evaluation of Macroeconometric Models. *Economic Modelling*, April, 125–134.

Pesaran, M. H. and Timmermann, A. (2005). Real-Time Econometrics. *Econometric Theory*, 21, 212–231.

Rajan, U., Seru, A. and Vig, V. (2015). The Failure of Models that Predict Failure: Distance, Incentives, and Defaults. *Journal of Financial Economics*, 115, 237–260.

Romer, C. and Romer, D. (2008). The FOMC versus the Staff: Where Can Monetary Policymakers Add Value? *American Economic Review*, 98, 230–235.

Taleb, N., Canetti, E., Kinda, T., Loukoianova, E. and Schmieder, C. (2012). A New Heuristic Measure of Fragility and Tail Risks: Application to Stress Testing. *IMF Working Paper* WP/12/216.

Williams, J. C. (2015). Macroprudential Policy in a Microprudential World, *Federal Reserve Bank of San Francisco Economic Letter*, June 1.

8 Counterparty Credit Risk

EDUARDO CANABARRO

8.1 Introduction

Counterparty credit risk (CCR) is the risk of incurring a loss when your derivatives counterparty defaults. The loss includes the amounts owed by the defaulted counterparty as well as the cost incurred to replace the derivatives or unwind their hedges.

Many derivatives (e.g., interest swaps, cross-currency swaps and forwards) start with a value of or near zero, which means that there is no credit exposure to either of the counterparties at the inception of the contracts. But, as time goes by and the markets move away, the present values of the derivatives change and one counterparty may find itself exposed to loss in the event of the default of the other. This is most common in over-the-counter (OTC) derivatives that are not subject to margin (collateralization) agreements.

Large derivatives dealers started to focus on their CCRs in the early 1990s. At that time, many of the long-dated OTC derivatives (mainly interest and cross-currency swaps) that were initiated in the 1980s had accumulated substantial values due to the markets' moves since their inception. The dealers were concerned with the size of their derivatives credit exposures and with the potential for these exposures to grow even larger in the future, especially with counterparties whose credit qualities were worsening.

The tax court case of Bank One *v* Internal Revenue Service was a landmark case where CCR was explicitly recognized.[1] Stanford University's Professor Darrell Duffie was an expert witness in the case

[1] See 120 T.C. 174 (U.S.T.C. 2003): "As matters of first impression, the Tax Court, Laro, J., held that: (1) mark-to-market rule and valuation requirement for swaps and financial derivatives was method of accounting, subject to clear reflection of income standard; (2) taxpayer's method of accounting for swaps income did not clearly reflect income; (3) IRS' method of accounting for swaps income did not clearly reflect income; (4) valuing each swap at its midmarket value, adjusted on dynamic basis for credit risk and administrative costs was acceptable; (5) proper

and he wrote an influential report explaining how the CCRs (bilateral, faced by both counterparties) should be incorporated in the valuation of a portfolio of OTC derivatives.[2]

The first quantitative models to quantify OTC derivatives' current and potential exposures as well as to price CCR were developed in the early 1990s. The models were complex and computationally intensive in platforms that were very primitive under today's standards. Only the largest and most sophisticated derivatives dealers (large banks) had access to them.[3]

Fast-forward, three decades have passed, important market events have occurred, much experience has been gained in the management of CCR. The events of 1998 (Russia's default and the Long-Term Capital Management's debacle) and 2008 (the Great Financial Crisis) have set important marks for the progress of CCR management.

In this chapter, I intend to describe the current state of CCR management, modeling and validation as of the early 2020s.

8.2 Definitions and Terminology

In this section we define the fundamental measures and terminology that are used in the CCR management.

The setting is: there is a portfolio of OTC derivatives between two counterparties which we designate as A and B (Figures 8.1). We look at the trades and CCR from the perspective of counterparty A. A similar view, not generally symmetric, can be constructed from the perspective of counterparty B.

Netting is the legally enforceable right of A to claim the net value of its portfolio of derivatives with B upon B's default. If there were no legally enforceable netting, A would have to: 1) pay the full values of the derivatives that had negative values for A and 2) claim the values of the derivatives with positive values for A against the estate of the

credit risk adjustment would reflect creditworthiness of both parties and (6) proper administrative costs adjustment was limited to incremental costs."

[2] See Duffie, Darrell; Expert Witness Report, 2001. Available at http://web.stanford.edu/~duffie/bankone.pdf

[3] See Canabarro, E. and D. Duffie, "Measuring and marking counterparty risk," chapter 9 in Leo Tilman, *Asset/Liability Management in Financial Institutions*, Euromoney Books, 2003. Available at https://web.stanford.edu/~duffie/Chapter_09.pdf

time	*0*	*1*	*2*	*3*	*4*	*5*
Trade 1	1.26	−0.03	1.32			
Trade 2	0.63	0.18	0.89	1.14		
Trade 3	0.62	1.24	1.01	−1.47	−0.04	
Trade 4	−1.53	−1.57	−1.59	−1.08	0.52	1.06
Trade 5	−0.98	−0.64	−0.06	−0.62	−0.65	−0.30
Market Value	0.00	−0.80	1.57	−2.04	−0.17	0.77
Netted Exposure to B	**0.00**	**0.00**	**1.57**	**0.00**	**0.00**	**0.77**
Non-netted Exposure to B	**1.25**	**1.43**	**3.22**	**1.14**	**0.52**	**1.06**

Figure 8.1 Market values and credit exposures, netted and non-netted, created by the portfolio of trades between counterparties A and B. Valuations and exposures as seen by counterparty A. The trades have different maturities and they do not contribute to exposures beyond their maturities.

defaulted counterparty B. This would make A's exposure to B's default larger than it would be in the netted case. Netting is established via legally enforceable contracts between the two counterparties in jurisdictions that allow it to be enforced. Netting is a fundamental mechanism to reduce CCR.

Margining (collateralization) is another key CCR reduction mechanism. The margin agreement between the two counterparties establishes that the portfolio of derivatives is marked to market daily and that the counterparty that owes money to the other has to post collateral to cover its liability that exceeds a small threshold. Margin agreements usually come together with netting agreements and they can reduce CCR drastically. Collateral is usually in the form of cash but could also be in the form of liquid securities.

Current exposure (CE) is the amount that A could lose if B were to default today. In the presence of enforceable netting and margin agreements, the CE is the positive value of the sum of the values V_i of the $i = 1,\ldots,n$ derivatives in the portfolio, net of the collected collateral:

$$CE = \max\left(\sum_{i=1}^{n} V_i - Collateral, 0\right)$$

The value of each trade is its marked-to-market value.

Expected exposure at a future time t (EE_t) is the expected amount that A could lose if B were to default at time t. We do not know with certainty what will be the value of the portfolio of derivatives at any future time. Thus, EE_t has to be estimated probabilistically. The assessment of EE_t depends on the market factor models used to estimate it. Different models with their different assumptions can generate different future market scenarios and different EE_t. We will discuss these models in the next section. The *expected exposure curve* is the graph of the EE_t over time.

Potential exposure at future time t (PE_t) is an estimate of the tail of the estimated probability distribution of the amount that A could lose if B were to default at a specified time in the future. PE_t has to be assessed probabilistically with a certain degree of confidence. For example, it is common to estimate PE_t at 95% or 99% confidence levels, meaning that these *PE*s are not expected to be exceeded in more than 5% or 1% of the contemplated future market scenarios, respectively. The estimates of PE_t are heavily dependent on the models used to calculate them. More so than the estimates of EE_t because they are estimates of the tail of the estimated probability distribution. *Potential exposure curve* is the graph of the $\mathrm{PE_t}$ over time.

The different profiles of Figures 8.2 and 8.3 are important to build intuition on CCR. Derivatives whose main payments settle through time have exposure curves that peak and then decline. Derivatives whose main payments are at or near their maturities have exposure curves that increase all the way to the end. They generate large future exposures if their maturities are long.

The graphs in Figures 8.2–8.5 are for portfolios comprised of one single derivative. In all these cases the starting value of the derivative is zero. Similar graphs can be constructed for portfolios of multiple, sometimes thousands of derivatives with a counterparty. The *EE* and *PE* curves will then reflect the sum of the values of the derivatives and their different maturities. The starting value of the portfolio is likely to be different from zero since many trades may be off market now, having been initiated some time ago.

CCR managers set limits on *CE*, EE_t and PE_t for each individual counterparty. The limits reflect the credit quality of the counterparty and they are a function of time. Usually the exposures that occur further into the future are subject to lower limits reflecting the higher uncertainty of the market scenarios as well as of the credit quality of

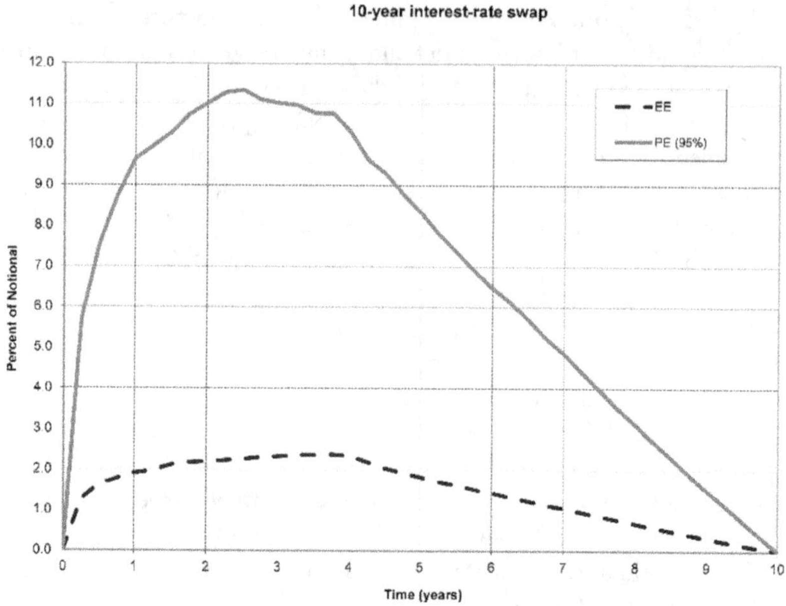

Figure 8.2 EE_t and PE_t for a 10-year interest rate swap without margin agreement. PE_t peaks at 11% of the notional amount of the swap, around 2.5 years into the future. EE_t peaks at 2.5% of the notional amount, around 4 years into the future. The explanation for the shape of the profile is that the cash flows of the swap occur gradually over time and after they get settled they do not create further exposure. The curve rises initially as the cumulative market volatility dominates over the settlements of the swap's cash flows. Later, the settlement of cash flows dominates over the accumulation of volatility.

the counterparty in the future. The sizes and types of trades allowed with the counterparty produce exposures that conform to the limits established by the CCR managers.

It is possible that certain new trades with a counterparty would reduce existing CE, EE_t and PE_t in the presence of netting agreements. Those trades are highly valued by CCR managers. They are called offsetting trades.

8.2.1 Expected Credit Loss

Based on the expected exposure profile of Figure 8.6, we can calculate the expected credit loss using the profile of marginal loss rates.

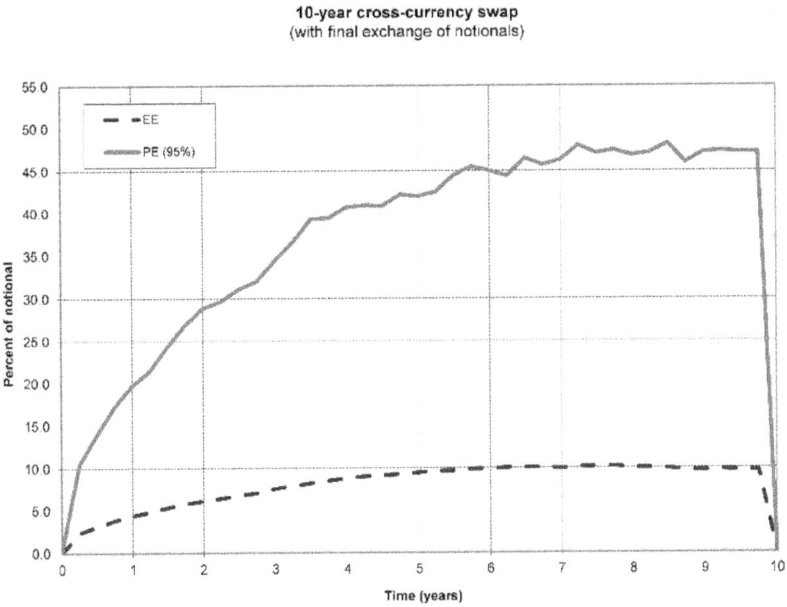

Figure 8.3 EE_t and PE_t for a 10-year cross-currency swap with final exchange of notional amounts and without margin agreement. PE_t peaks at 47% of the notional amount of the swap, near its maturity. EE_t peaks at 10% of notional amount of the swap, near its maturity. The exposures created by cross-currency swaps are much larger than the ones created by the interest rate swaps. This is because the biggest cash flow (the exchange of notional amounts denominated in the different currencies) occurs at maturity. Thus, the fluctuations of the values of the currencies and their respective notional amounts accumulate all the way to the end.

The marginal loss rate is the product of the marginal probability of default by one minus the expected recovery rate. Figure 8.7 shows the two curves. EE_t should be calculated conditional on default of the counterparty in order to capture any correlation between the exposure and the credit quality of the counterparty (right- or wrong-way risk). In most cases the correlation is not materially different from zero. But there could be cases where it is materially positive or negative.

Example: counterparty B is a producer of oil who sells its future oil production to counterparty A via a strip of forward contracts. B will owe money to A in the case that the oil price goes up. Higher oil prices

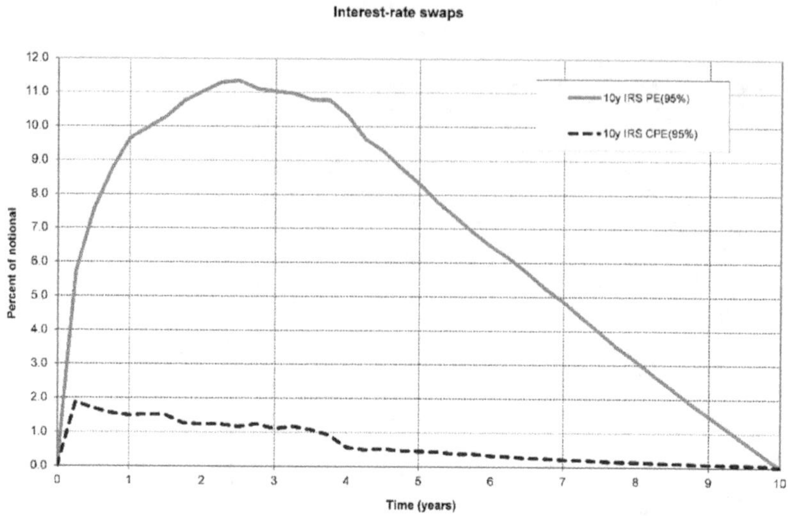

Figure 8.4 PE_t for a 10-year interest rate swap with and without margin agreement. The daily marking-to-market and exchange of collateral reduce exposures massively: the peak of PE_t decreases from 11% to 2% of notional, a reduction factor of 5 times.

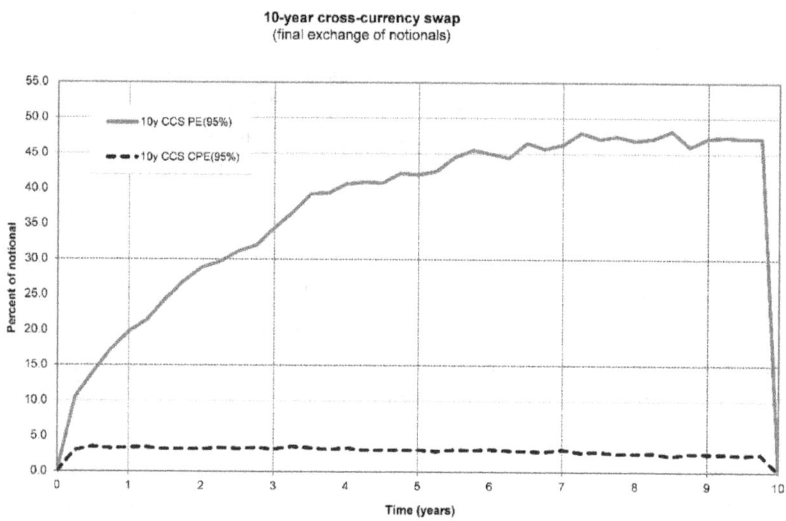

Figure 8.5 PE_t for a 10-year cross-currency swap with final exchange of notional amounts, with and without margin agreement. Daily marking-to-market and exchange of collateral reduce exposures massively. The peak of PE_t declines from 47% to 3% of notional.

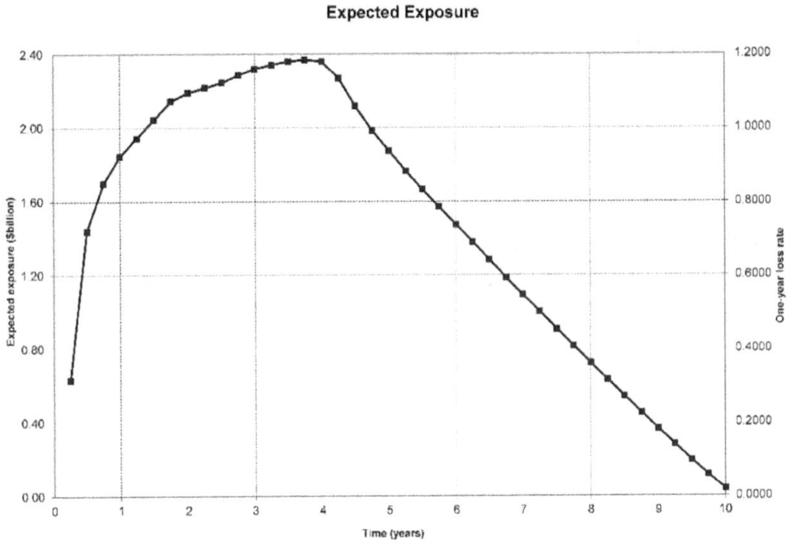

Figure 8.6 Expected Exposure created by the portfolio of derivatives with counterparty B.

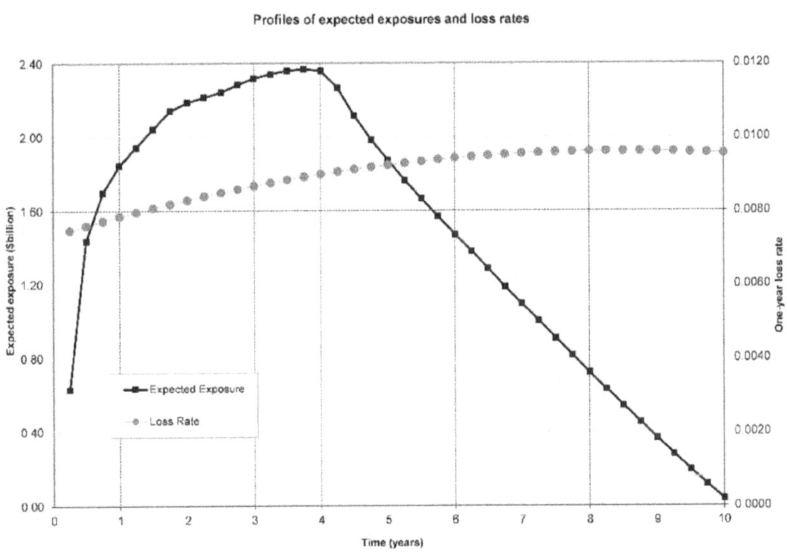

Figure 8.7 Conditional expected exposure and marginal loss rates for the portfolio of derivatives with counterparty B.

are favorable to B to the extent that B hedges only partially its future production. This is right-way risk.

$$Expected\ Credit\ Loss = EE' \cdot p \cdot \Delta t$$

Where:

- EE' is the row vector representing EE_t;
- p is the column vector of annualized loss rates;
- Δt is a scalar, the time interval for which EE_t and p_t apply. In the graph, $\Delta t = 0.25$ years.

EE_t has to be conditioned on p_t in order to capture the correlation between the exposure and the probability of default.

Credit Valuation Adjustment (CVA)

The CVA is an adjustment to the default-free value of the portfolio of derivatives between counterparties A and B to mark to market the credit risk faced by both counterparties. Counterparty A faces the risk that counterparty B defaults. Counterparty B faces the risk that counterparty A defaults. So the adjustment is the net valuation of the credit risk faced by both.

$$CVA = EE'_B \cdot p_B \cdot \Delta t - EE'_A \cdot p_A \cdot \Delta t$$

Where:

EE'_B is the column vector of the conditional expected exposures faced by counterparty A with respect to counterparty B;
p_B is the column vector of annualized credit loss rates of counterparty B, implied from its credit spread curve;
EE'_A is the column vector of the conditional expected exposures faced by counterparty B with respect to counterparty A;
p_A is the column vector of annualized credit loss rates of counterparty A, implied from its credit spread curve;
Δt is a scalar, the time interval for which the EE_t and p_t apply.

All quantities are derived from market prices and their dynamics. CVA is a market valuation and as such it is calculated under the risk-neutral probability measure (as opposed to the real probability measure under which expected loss is calculated).

8.3 Measurement, Pricing and Stress Testing

In this section we describe the general methodologies used to calculate potential exposures, expected credit losses and prices of CCR.

Let's establish from the start that all these methodologies involve substantial model risk and uncertainties. Projecting future market scenarios, future market prices, future credit qualities of the counterparties and future credit exposures is inherently subject to irreducible uncertainty. Thus, all the numbers produced need to be understood as probabilistic estimates subject to substantial uncertainty.

Calculation of EE_t and PE_t of the portfolio of trades between A and B

(1) Simulate all the market prices (i.e., the joint market scenarios) that are required to price the trades of the portfolio of trades between A and B at each future date t. The length of the simulations has to be as long as required to value all the trades in the portfolio all the way to their maturities.
(2) Calculate the values of the trades at each date t.
(3) Apply netting if applicable.
(4) Apply the collateral rules if applicable.
(5) Calculate EE_t as the average exposure across all market scenarios simulated at t.
(6) Calculate PE_t as the 95- or 99-percentile of the exposure distribution across all market scenarios simulated at t.

These calculations can be computationally intensive especially when (a) the number of trades is large, (b) the maturities of the trades are long and (c) the pricing of the trades is complex and computationally intensive. Shortcuts and approximations may need to be used in order to save time and computational effort especially when the values of the trades themselves have to be calculated via Monte Carlo simulations.

The application of collateral rules usually assume that collateral cannot be exchanged until a certain conservative delay. Usually, this delay is one or two weeks. The delay in exchange can be due to disputes on the marked-to- market values of the trades or delays in the transfer of funds.

The correlations between credit loss rates and exposures are automatically captured in the joint simulations of all market prices, including the credit spreads.

8.3.1 Calculation of CVA

(1) Simulate all the market prices (i.e. the joint market scenarios) that are required to price the trades of the portfolio of trades between counterparties A and B at each future date *t*. The length of the simulations has to be as long as required to value the trades in the portfolio to their maturities.
(2) Simulate the risk-neutral probabilities of default and credit loss rates of both counterparties at each future time *t*. They are correlated with all other market prices in the joint market scenarios.
(3) Calculate the values of all the trades at each date *t*.
(4) Apply netting if applicable.
5) Apply the collateral rules if applicable.
(6) Calculate $EE_{A,t}$ and $EE_{B,t}$ as the average exposure across all market scenarios simulated at *t*.
(7) Multiply -$EE_{A,t}$ and $EE_{B,t}$ by the respective credit loss rates $\Delta t.p_{A,t}$ and $\Delta t.p_{B,t}$ for each time *t*.
(8) Calculate the CVA as the sum of the products in (7).

Notice that all the simulations for CVA are under the *risk-neutral probability measure* as implied from market prices. Again, the correlations between credit loss rates and exposures are automatically captured in the joint simulations of all market prices, including the credit spreads.

8.3.2 Stress Testing

The stress testing of CCR involves the stress testing of the exposures, default events as well as changes in CVAs and its attached hedging costs. In situations of stressed markets, the price changes (volatility) can be large causing increases in exposures, collateral collection may be impaired, multiple and correlated default events may occur, CVA hedging may be difficult and costly. It is important to account for all these CCR components. The precise estimation may be impossible but conservative proxies should be applied wherever required.

8.4 The Experiences of 1998 and 2008

The episodes of 1998 (i.e., Russia's default and the LTCM's debacle) and 2008 (the Great Financial Crisis) taught us important lessons about CCR and its management. In this section we comment on our key learnings.

First, when a large and active counterparty (like LTCM in 1998 and Lehman Brothers in 2008) has large trading losses it loses the confidence of market participants, it cannot trade anymore, it cannot hedge its open positions and its trading losses increase. Margin agreements become ineffective and the counterparties of the distressed entity may face large losses too. These extreme distress situations are not generally captured well by the potential exposure models despite the conservative elements and assumptions that many of them contain.

Second, wrong-way risks and market illiquidity can preclude the dynamic hedging of the CVA of a counterparty. The case of the monoline insurers (e.g. MBIA) in 2008 is an example. The monolines sold credit protection on pools of mortgages. When the mortgages went sour, the value of the protection rose and the credit quality of the insurers declined simultaneously. The banks that had bought credit protection from the insurers saw their CVAs of the monolines skyrocket and they were not able to hedge them dynamically because the markets for the mortgage pools and for the credit protection on the monolines dried up. Thus, continuous hedging of CVA is not the proper assumption for all cases and assessments of the situations where it may not be possible have to be made.

Third, the estimates of counterparty future exposures can be very wrong and imprecise. Especially when markets are in distress. The very existence of such large counterparty exposures may influence and tilt the markets which then move further against the holders of these exposures.

Fourth, marking-to-market or marking-to-model of illiquid risks can cause large losses when fire sales occur. The depressed prices cause losses, which then cause further liquidations, more fire sales and lower market prices. This happened in 2008 and it created contagion effects across financial institutions.

All the above imply that we need a fair amount of caution in dealing with CCR. Large CCR is very difficult to manage and hedge, especially in distressed market conditions. Stress tests and conservative estimates of potential exposures are important metrics to size counterparty risk. One should not count on the ability to hedge CVAs dynamically in extreme and distressed market conditions.

8.5 The Capitalization of CCR

The capitalization of CCR has to combine measures of aggregate CCR at the level of the portfolio of counterparties with the specific results of stress tests. The Basel Committee's standard provides a reasonable measure of the total portfolio's CCR.[4] Stress tests tend to focus on the largest and riskiest counterparties and assume that they default under adverse market (exposure) conditions. They also include contagion effects where the default of a large counterparty could lead to the defaults of others. These measures are proxies for the real risks that could be faced and, as such, they should be conservative measures of the overall portfolio risk as well as of the concentrations on industries and counterparties.

8.6 Validation of CCR Models

Models to calculate credit exposures, credit losses and CVAs are the largest, most complex and most computationally intensive models used by large OTC derivatives dealers. They have to link and process data coming from many different sources including from the trading desks, legal departments, collateral management systems, etc.

The fundamental model components of the CCR management system are:

(a) the generator of future market scenarios;
(b) the pricing models for all derivatives types;
(c) the credit exposure calculators that apply netting and margining rules;
(d) the CVA calculators;
(e) the economic and regulatory capital calculators.

8.6.1 Generator of Future Market Scenarios

Market scenarios have to be generated for all future times and for all intervening market risk factors to allow for the calculation of the future credit exposures. Hundreds (maybe thousands) of market risk factors have to be simulated jointly: interest rates, credit spreads, foreign exchange rates, commodities prices, equities prices, etc.

4 See Canabarro, E, E. Picoult and T. Wilde, "Analyzing counterparty risk," Risk, September 2003.

The probability distributions of the market risk factors at each future date as well as their correlations are important features of the simulations. They can have substantial impact on the credit exposures calculated. For dates that are deep into the future, the drift (i.e. the trend) of the risk factors is very important. That is, the first moment may be as relevant as or more relevant than the higher moments of the distribution of the risk factors. There are no right or wrong choices for the joint dynamics of the market risk factors. All have to be grounded in common sense. It is hard to say a priori what is the direction of conservatism for drifts and correlations since the resulting credit exposures will depend on the direction of the trades held with each counterparty.

8.6.2 *Pricing Models*

The trades of each counterparty's portfolio have to be simulated along the simulated market risk factors' paths. The computational effort is large and usually the pricing models need to be simplified and approximated for speed. Some accuracy may be lost in exchange for reduced computational effort. This is typically the case when the pricing models themselves rely on Monte Carlo simulations or time-consuming numerical algorithms. The approximations made and the shortcuts taken need to be verified to cover correctly the breadth of the market scenarios simulated.

8.6.3 *Credit Exposure Calculator*

The correct application of netting and collateral rules is crucial for the calculation of credit exposures. These rules can be complicated at times and their sourcing, representation and storage needs to be validated thoroughly.

8.6.4 *CVA Calculator*

The CVA calculator integrates the exposure calculations with the risk-neutral probabilities of default of the counterparties along the simulated market risk factors' paths. These probabilities are extracted (implied) from the simulated credit spread curves. The calculator also has to provide the sensitivities of the CVAs to market risk factors, including the credit spreads. These sensitivities are used for hedging the CVAs. The numerical calculation of the sensitivities can involve computational effort that is an order of magnitude larger than the calculation of the CVA itself.

8.6.5 *Economic and Regulatory Capital Calculators*

These calculators combine the simulated credit exposures with the simulated probabilities of default of the counterparties to estimate the tail loss of the total portfolio of counterparties. Ideally the tail estimate would come from the joint simulation of exposures and probabilities of default. In practice approximations are made to simplify the calculations and to use pre-computed exposures at the level of each counterparty. For example, the Basel Committee's regulatory capital estimate is based on the expected exposures, grossed up by a scaling factor (called alpha),[5] and the stressed probabilities of default. More sophisticated economic capital models may use the entire set of simulated market scenarios (hundreds or thousands of them) in order to capture the relevant correlations among all exposures and all probabilities of default jointly. Stress test's measures like the losses due to default of the largest and riskiest counterparties may also be added to portfolio-based estimates of losses.

All models and calculators used in CCR management should be registered in the model inventory and documented well. Documentation should be concise and clear identifying the most substantive assumptions, choices and tests made in the construction of the models. The documentation should allow for the validation and assessment of the models by independent parties.

Model validators should focus on the model components (a)–(e) above. Weaknesses in any of the components could compromise the entire CCR management system.

8.7 The Cost of Hedging the CVA

The cost of hedging the CVA of certain large counterparties can grow very large at times of market stress. During these periods, the volatility is elevated and potentially adverse correlations between exposure and the

[5] See *ibid.*

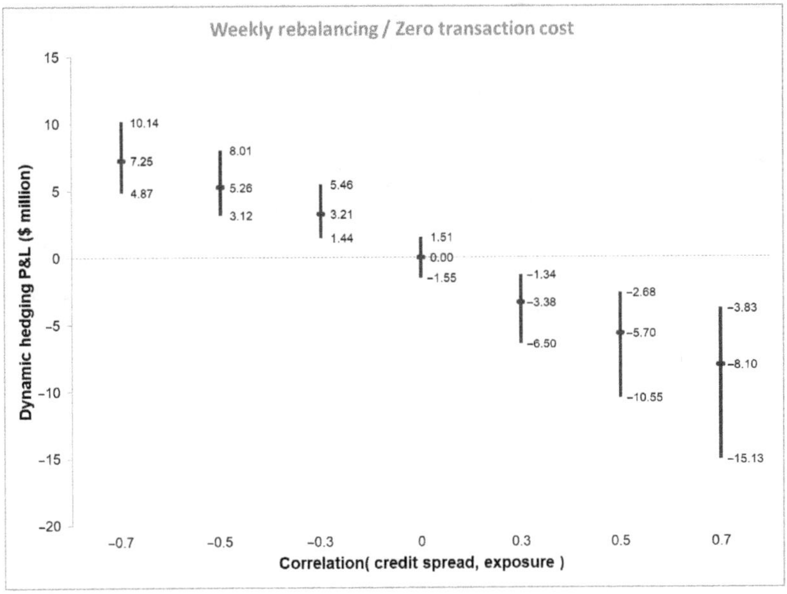

Figure 8.8 CVA hedging profit and loss (P&L) under normal market conditions and zero transaction costs. The hedging errors are small and symmetric in the absence of wrong- or right-way risks. Wrong-way (right-way) risk induces expected losses (gains) in the hedging program. Each bar contains the 5- and 95-percentiles of the simulations and the average across all 30,000 simulated hedging paths.

counterparty credit quality may emerge. This was the case of the mono-line insurers in 2008. Figures 8.8–8.10 illustrate simulations of hedging costs under normal and stressed market conditions. These graphs were obtained by the simulations of the hedging error and cost of the CVA of a counterparty whose portfolio was a strip of natural gas forwards with maturity of five years. The initial value of the CVA was –$68 million.[6]

Simulation exercises similar to the one above should be considered as part of comprehensive stress testing and validation programs of CCR. A typical large dealer will have a relatively small number, maybe a handful, of counterparties that will be large enough to command this type of analysis. Thus, performing simulations and stress tests for the

[6] For a full description of the models and simulations of the hedging costs see Canabarro, E., "Stress test of counterparty credit risk and dynamic hedging of the CVA," chapter 12 in Canabarro, E. and M. Pykhtin, *Counterparty Risk Management*, Incisive Media, 2014.

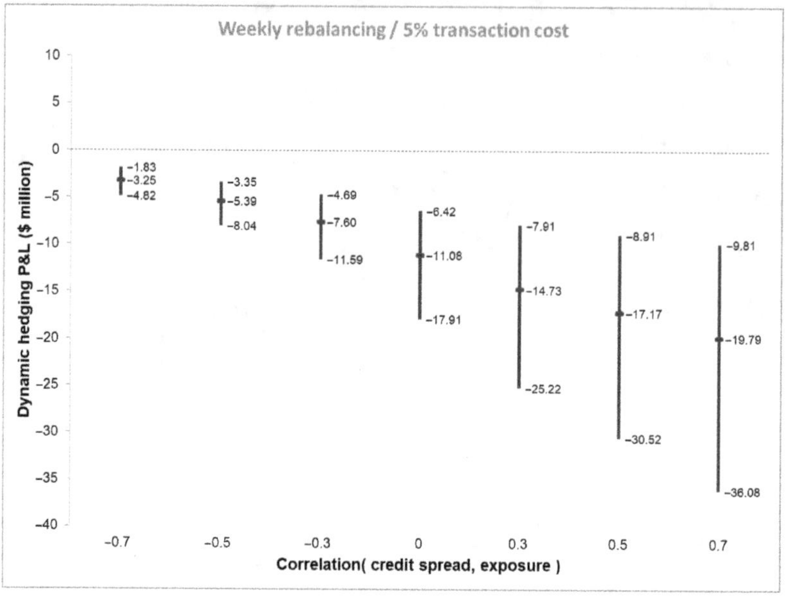

Figure 8.9 CVA hedging profit and loss (P&L) under normal market conditions and 5% transaction costs. The hedging errors are not symmetric. Wrong-way (right-way) risk induces larger (lower) expected losses in the hedging program. Each bar contains the 5- and 95-percentiles of the simulations and the average across all 30,000 simulated hedging paths.

dynamic hedging costs of the CVA of the largest counterparties should not be a prohibitively expensive task and it would increase substantially the dealers' insights into the risk profiles of their overall counterparty credit risk.

The key for the successful implementation of the simulation exercise is the simplification of the problem to a tractable and implementable form. The decisions on what and how to simplify the problem require knowledge of the major features of the problem at hand, financial engineering expertise and good judgment to determine what is fundamental to retain in order to preserve the economic essence of the problem. Unfortunately, there is no off-the-shelf recipe to apply. The nature, shape and dynamics of the underlying exposures and credit spreads need to be fully understood and considered to determine how the simulation model should be specified. Thus, this type of stress test is most suitable to be applied by the dealers individually as part of their own stress testing and validation

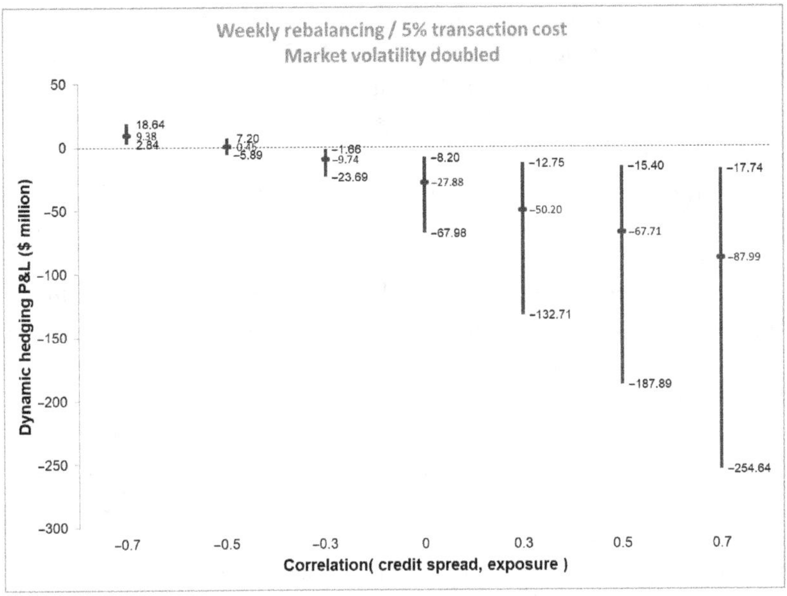

Figure 8.10 CVA hedging profit and loss (P&L) under stressed market conditions and 5% transaction costs. The hedging errors are not symmetric. Extreme right-way risk can induce small gains. Extreme wrong-way risk induces very large losses. Each bar contains the 5- and 95-percentiles of the simulations and the average across all 30,000 simulated hedging paths.

exercises. It is difficult to imagine that it could be standardized under a supervisor's prescription as part of a supervisor-specified scenario.

8.8 A Few Words on Backtesting and Stress Testing

Backtesting and stress testing are valuable tools to validate the CCR models. In backtesting we assess how the models would have performed in the past if they had been applied then. In stress testing we assess how the models would perform under stressed and extreme market situations. The results of the tests can support our confidence in the models.

8.9 Summary and Conclusions

In this chapter we explained the fundamentals of the measurement and pricing of CCR as well as important aspects of the validation of CCR models.

Much progress has been made since the early 1990s. Today, most active derivatives dealers have well-developed technology to measure and manage counterparty risks. But counterparty credit losses will continue to occur, especially in large and concentrated CCRs, once in a while. Caution and conservatism are the fundamental rules for successful CCR management. The key is the management of the size of the exposures and the diversification of CCRs across counterparties and market risk factors.

Our illustrations and examples should help the reader to build his intuition about the key elements of CCR models. Usually the texts on CCR models are much more complex than ours. This does not make them more correct, more accurate or more helpful. CCR measurement is quite simple and intuitive. Higher complexity and mathematics cannot reduce the inherent uncertainties of the CCR estimations. There are many embedded assumptions and predictions that extend for long periods of time.

Validation is a fundamental part of the model risk management process. CCR models because of their sheer scale, scope and complexity entail great challenges for validation. We highlighted the model components to be validated and some of the criteria and tests to be applied.

References

Canabarro, E. (2014). Stress test of counterparty credit risk and dynamic hedging of the CVA, in Canabarro, E. and M. Pykhtin, *Counterparty Risk Management*, Incisive Media, 2014.

Canabarro, E., E. Picoult and T. Wilde. (2003). Analyzing counterparty risk, *Risk*, September 2003, 117–122.

Canabarro, E. and D. Duffie. (2003). Measuring and marking counterparty risk, in Leo Tilman, *Asset/Liability Management in Financial Institutions*, Euromoney Books, 2003.

Duffie, D. (2001). Expert Witness Report. Available at http://web.stanford.edu/~duffie/bankone.pdf

9 Validation of Retail Credit Risk Models

SANG-SUB LEE AND FENG LI*

9.1 Introduction

Retail lending includes all types of loans targeted at consumers, including mortgages, Home Equity Loans and Lines of Credit (HELOAN and HELOC), credit cards, auto loans and other personal loans and lines of credit. Just considering the US banking industry, retail loans make up approximately one third of total US debt. In many countries, the relative size of household debt is far greater than that of the United States (Figure 9.1).

Financial institutions offering retail products need to decide not only to whom to make these loans, but also how to price loan products, manage existing accounts, and maintain adequate reserves and capital against future losses. In order to maximize profit while controlling credit risk, retail lenders need to be able to quantify the risks and rewards involved with retail credit accurately. Use of statistical models to estimate the risks and rewards for retail lending is becoming a common practice for lenders. These credit risk models are widely used in assisting decision making in various business areas, including credit approval, portfolio management, capital management and loan loss provisioning.

The advances of big data and internet technology have provided a significant boost to the expansion of FinTech credit markets, especially in the consumer loan markets (Buchak et al. 2018; Committee on the Global Financial System and the Financial Stability Board 2017). One of the important premises for the rise and success of the FinTech-based lending model is the ability of FinTech credit platforms to evaluate credit risk more effectively utilizing big data analytics, and thus deliver

* The views expressed in this chapter (and other chapters in the book) are those of the authors alone and do not establish supervisory policy, requirements or expectations. They also do not represent those of the Comptroller of the Currency.

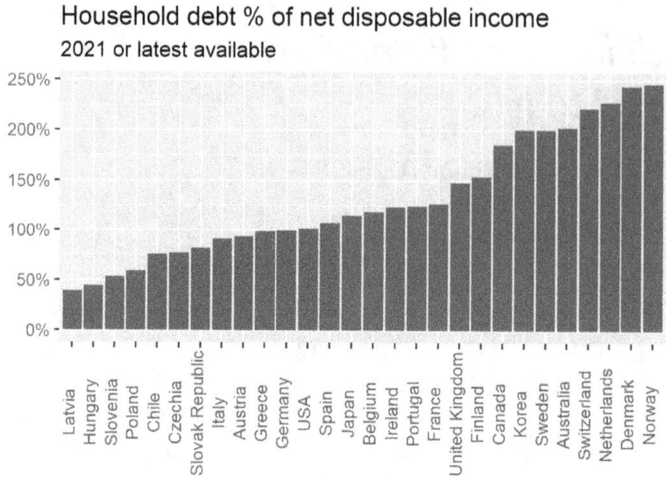

Figure 9.1 Household debt to net disposable income by country 2021.
Source: OECD

better risk-adjusted returns. Accurate and reliable credit risk models have become more and more critical to maintaining successful and profitable retail lending operations. Relying on poorly specified models can result in lost revenue, and eventually may threaten the solvency of financial institutions as we witnessed during the Great Recession.

Given the importance of models' accuracy and performance, sound model validation is obviously an important issue to financial institutions as well as to regulators. With recent developments in the regulatory environment (e.g., CCAR/Dodd–Frank Stress Testing) and renewed elucidation of regulatory expectations with regard to model risk management (FRB & OCC, 2011), the last 10 years have seen a significant improvement in retail model validation. In this chapter, we review several popular retail credit risk model frameworks used in the industry, and discuss some key issues related to retail credit risk model validation as well as areas for improvement. The emerging trend of utilizing machine learning (ML) techniques in retail credit risk modeling, and the potential benefits and challenges it poses, are also discussed.

Given the growing importance of macro stress testing in financial institutions' risk management practices and the implementation of the Current Expected Credit Loss (CECL) standard for bank loan loss reserve accounting, this review focuses mostly on validation of retail loss forecasting models. Although there are a variety of different retail credit products targeted at different types of borrowers notwithstanding, models used for different retail products are fairly similar. As such, our discussion will proceed focusing on general validation issues around the common model framework used across different products. However, where relevant, we will also make note of important issues that are unique to individual products.

9.2 Importance of Retail Credit and Retail Credit Risk

Household debt has grown significantly over the post-war period, overtaking that of the business sector. As of the fourth quarter of 2021, the total domestic nonfinancial debt outstanding in the USA was $65 trillion,[1] of which about $18 trillion was retail household debt, whereas nonfinancial business debt was $18.6 trillion (Flow of Funds, 2022 Q1). In many countries, the relative size of household debt is far greater than that of the United States.

In most industrialized countries, the biggest and most important component of retail credit is residential mortgages. In the USA, two thirds of total outstanding retail debt is accounted for by home mortgages with a total amount of $11.7 trillion as of 2021 Q4. Of this sum, $4.4 trillion consists of consumer credit, which is distributed among various forms of credit including automobile loans, student loans, and revolving credit card debt (Figure 9.2).

The size and composition of household consumer debt has significant implications for macroeconomic performance and financial stability (IMF 2017; Zabai, 2017). A high level of household debt makes an economy more vulnerable to adverse economic shocks. Both the Great Recession and the Great Depression in the USA were preceded by a dramatic increase in household debt. In particular, excessive household leverage fueled by easy credit and a housing boom is widely believed to be the main cause of the Great Recession (Mian and Sufi, 2014). In fact, this pattern of huge run-ups in household debt and real estate prices, followed by subsequent asset price collapses, seem to be the hallmark of the major post-war banking and financial crises (IMF 2012; Jorda

[1] Table D.3: Debt Outstanding by Sector, Flow of Funds, Board of Governors of the Federal Reserve System (www.federalreserve.gov/apps/fof/DisplayTable.aspx?t=d.3).

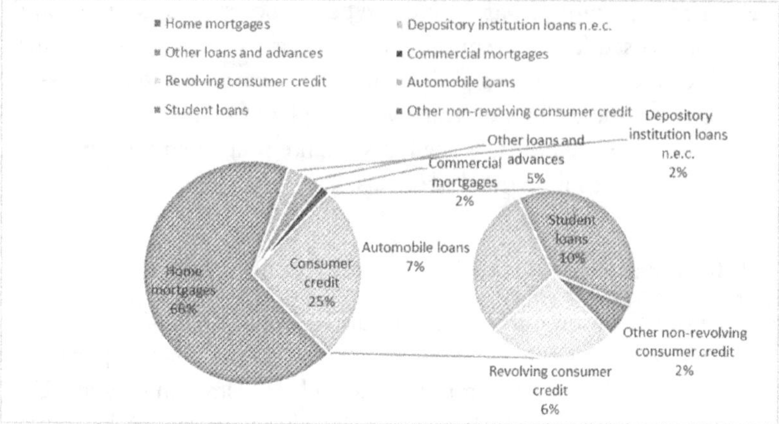

Figure 9.2 Loans and liabilities of US household and nonprofits.
(Source: Flow of Funds, 2022 Q1, Board of Governors of the Federal Reserve System)

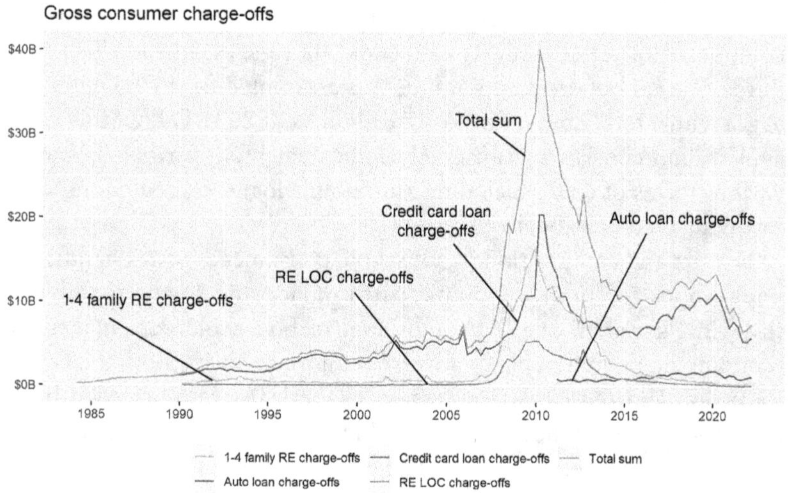

Figure 9.3 US Commercial banks consumer credit charge-offs.
Source: Call Report

et al. 2016), and a growing body of literature documents a similar boom-bust pattern between household debt and economic activity across different countries and time periods (Mian and Sufi 2017) (Figure 9.3).

Financial institutions offering retail credit need to make various decisions, including to whom to make these loans, how to price loan products, manage existing accounts and maintain adequate reserve and capital against future losses. It has become a standard practice that retail lenders utilize statistical models to manage credit risks related to retail lending. Accurate and reliable credit risk models are critical not only in maintaining successful and profitable retail lending operations, but also in ensuring the financial health of financial institutions. Poorly specified credit risk models adversely affect the performance of the individual financial institutions, and as a result, may amplify the boom-bust cycle by underestimating credit risk during the boom and being overly conservative during the downturn.

9.3 Evolution of the Retail Credit Risk Model Framework

Despite its enormous size and importance of consumer credit and lending, risk associated with the lending had not received much attention until the mortgage crisis in the USA in the late 2000s. For this reason, pre-crisis retail credit risk modeling activity was largely focused on credit scoring models applied to approval of loan applications.

There is a wealth of information available regarding retail borrowers and their creditworthiness. Typical application packets for mortgages include rich demographic and financial information about the applicants. Massive amounts of application and performance data from past accounts are collected and analyzed by banks and other retail lenders for credit granting and other business decision making. The emergence of credit bureaus, which aggregate performance information of various accounts held by individual borrowers at different financial institutions on a real time basis, has enormously expanded retail lenders' available information set. Availability of massive, highly granular, and standardized data is one of the key distinguishing factors of retail credit. Large volumes of account-/borrower-level origination and performance data accumulated over time are then put to use to build an expert system that can be used to efficiently guide and process critical decision making with a large volume of business. Most large financial institutions extended their use of retail credit statistical models, either built internally or developed by third-party vendors, to evaluate and quantify the credit and other risks associated with retail credit. The statistically developed credit risk models are used in decision making in various business areas, including credit approval, portfolio management, capital management, and loss provisioning.

Two types of credit risk models are widely used in retail lending: credit scoring models are used to measure relative performance to support business decisions, such as whether or not to grant credit to new applicants or setting credit limits, whereas loss forecasting models are used to predict losses over a certain period of time. The main focus of a credit scoring model is the ordinal risk profile or risk ranking, and the model is not designed to estimate the level estimate of probability of default per se, but to provide a relative measure of credit risk.[2] On the other hand, for a loss forecasting model, accuracy of default probabilities is of first-order importance. The difference in emphasis on relative (ordinal) versus absolute (cardinal) measures of default probability is, however, not a fundamental difference, but a difference due to business practices.

A more fundamental difference between the two types of model is the general model framework used: traditional credit scoring models use essentially a static model framework where static borrower information is used to predict the performance outcome over a fixed time interval. Loss forecasting models, on the other hand, attempt to predict dollar losses over time at a portfolio or sub-portfolio level. As such, the statistical model frameworks used by loss forecasting models are generally dynamic and equipped to address the dynamic nature of credit risk.

9.3.1 Static Credit and Behavioral Scoring Model

Credit and behavioral scoring models for consumer products have been used by many lending institutions for a relatively long period of time. The main objective of credit scoring is to discriminate between different groups based on creditworthiness in a pool of applicants for credit granting to inform decision making. Credit scoring models are developed to evaluate credit granting decisions in an automated and consistent manner so that a high volume of applications can be processed relatively efficiently.

[2] Credit scores are designed to be a measure of relative credit quality over a specified time horizon, and are not meant to be measures of PD. These models are typically calibrated to actual default behavior at a specific point in time, and the relationship between their PD estimates and actual bad rates may not be robust over time.

The traditional application scorecard has been used since the 1950s, when it was first realized that Fisher's earlier work on discriminatory analysis and classification could be applied to lending decisions. Different retail scoring models have been developed and are currently used in a variety of different areas. Credit scoring and behavioral scoring models are numerical models that help financial institutions make business decisions such as extending credit to potential borrowers who apply for credit. Assuming the underlying risk factors that determine creditworthiness of borrowers are stable over time, credit scoring models are built based on past applicant data from the same lenders' or on other lenders' data with their subsequent performance, and models developed as such are used to rank the credit risk of current applicants. The data available for use in credit scoring models was vastly expanded with the development of credit bureaus where detailed and high frequency information on all of the official credit lines held by consumers is available.

While the possibility of using statistically developed credit scoring models for lending decisions was recognized much earlier, the application of credit scoring models in practice did not become popular until a massive volume of credit card applications arriving on a daily basis gave rise to an urgent need for an automated lending system based on a firm statistical foundation in the late 1960s and early 1970s. The initial success of credit scoring models in credit cards led to the application of credit scoring models to different retail products such as home loans.

A behavioral scoring model is an extension of a credit scoring model where the main use of the it is to help lenders manage existing accounts rather than to help make credit granting decisions regarding potential new customers. Behavioral scoring models augment the information available from the application with recent payment/behavioral history as well as up-to-date information available from credit bureaus regarding existing customers to better forecast their performance within a fixed time horizon in the future. By doing so, behavioral models help with managing existing clients through such decisions as reassigning credit limits and drawing up loss mitigation strategies. Traditionally, behavioral models have been built using the same kind of static models that are used in application scoring.

Traditional credit/application scoring models aim to solve a classification problem where borrower information available from applications and from other sources is processed and translated into "good" and "bad" to minimize misclassification. Banks have explored a number of different statistical as well as non-statistical discriminant analysis methods (Thomas et al. 2002; Thomas 2010, 2000). The most popular approach to building credit scoring models has been regression-based discriminant analysis. A number of linear as well as nonlinear probability models have been tried, and the logistic regression model emerged as the most popular choice among them. These probability regression models formally link credit scoring to a probability of default.[3] In doing so, these models not only allow lenders to sharpen their analysis and decision making, but also broaden the use of credit scoring models to other applications such as risk pricing and regulatory capital where cardinal probability of default matters. In such applications where default probability is explicitly used rather than the score being used as a risk ranking tool, calibration quality or accuracy of default probability should be a more important focus of validation than the discriminatory power of the models.

Alternative credit scoring methods have been used as well. For example, the problem of finding the best linear discriminant between groups can be modeled as a linear programming problem. Given a linear scorecard structure and a cut-off point, the misclassification error is measured as the distance between the score and the cutoff point when the borrower is misclassified. Then, the best linear discriminant is found by minimizing the sum of misclassification errors through linear programming (Thomas et al. 2002; Thomas 2010, 2000).

Other classes of approaches that have received increasing attention recently are non-parametric and data mining approaches. Advances in computing technology and easier access to powerful computing allow such computationally intensive techniques to be more feasible and attractive. A variety of different classification and machine learning techniques (Hastie et al. 2009) such as classification trees (Breiman et al. 1984) and neural networks have been applied to credit scoring. These methods were developed and initially applied in other areas but picked up in retail credit scoring and other credit risk applications. Several recent studies have applied machine learning classification tree models to credit card portfolios (Glennon et al. 2007; Khandani et al. 2010; Butaru et al. 2015). In an interesting recent application, Sirignano et al. (2016) applied deep neural networks (Goodfellow

[3] See Footnote 2 for a caveat.

et al. 2016; Taddy 2018), neural networks with three or more hidden layers, to US mortgage data and built multi-period dynamic machine learning transition models. Machine learning methods tend to be relatively more complex and lack transparency and interpretability. While interest in machine learning methods in retail credit risk modeling is growing rapidly with the advances of more efficient techniques, faster computers, and big data, widespread use of these techniques in practice requires a better understanding and further evidence of their robustness and stability (see Section 9.4.6 for more on ML).

9.3.2 Multi-Period Loss Forecasting Models

The goal of loss forecasting models is to predict dollar losses for a portfolio or sub-portfolio over time. Thus, while predicting default incidence is still the most important component, predicting default incidence alone is not sufficient – dollar exposure at risk and loss severities should be considered as well.

Traditional retail credit scoring models used for loan applications are static and predict cumulative behavior over a fixed horizon, whereas typical loss forecasting models explicitly consider the time dimension and attempt to model dynamic loan/portfolio performance over time. Time-varying economic data can also be included to capture the impact of the economic environment on expected credit losses along with other controlling factors capturing changes in the underlying portfolio. Since loss forecasting models are used to predict expected losses, measures of predictive accuracy relative to actual outcome rather than discriminatory power are considered to be more relevant.

Loss forecasting is an integral part of managing credit risk for retail lending institutions. Accurate (expected) loss forecasts are crucial not only for efficient business and capital planning, but more importantly for financial health of financial institutions. Retail loss forecasting models are used in normal business processes such as reserving allowance for (expected) credit losses as well as in stress testing for capital adequacy.

A variety of different loss forecasting models are used in practice to forecast credit losses of a retail portfolio, each of which has its own strengths and weaknesses. Levels of granularity and complexity vary significantly over different models, and the choice of model used by institutions depends on various factors, such as resource constraints and (lack of) technical expertise, materiality of a portfolio, data availability, and transparency, to name a few. Although institutions have flexibility in selecting a specific model loss forecasting framework, the degree of complexity and sophistication of the loss forecasting model used by a lending institution is generally expected to be commensurate with the size and complexity of the retail portfolio for which the model is designed.

9.3.2.1 Aggregate or Segmented Pool-Level Modelling Approaches

Net Charge-Off Model

A net charge-off model is a top-down model where a time series of portfolio-level net losses is fitted on underlying macroeconomic or regional economic risk drivers. Lagged dependent variables are often included to better capture in-sample dynamics or soak up serial correlation in the residuals. Variables capturing portfolio characteristics are typically missing in this type of model although some loan and borrower attributes can be used as segmentation variables. Hence, the model framework cannot capture the impact of changes in portfolio characteristics and their interactions with macroeconomic risk drivers, which is important for highly material dynamic portfolios. These models, however, are simple to develop and might be considered acceptable for estimating credit losses for small portfolios that are relatively stable in underlying characteristics. Net charge-off models can be also useful for challenging and benchmarking more sophisticated loss forecasting models.

Static Roll-Rate Model

Roll-rate models are typically used for short-term (e.g., six to twelve month horizon) loss forecasting for retail portfolios. Roll-rate models estimate the transition rates at which loans with a certain initial status or segment (current, 30 DPD, 60 DPD etc.) roll into different statuses/ segments based on recent historical data. While roll rates can be calculated either in terms of counts or balance, balance-weighted roll rates are typically used in practice. After the roll rate is estimated for each segment, each respective roll-rate percentage is applied to the balance.

The main advantages of the model framework are simplicity and transparency. Roll-rate models are predicated on the presumption that transition performance in the recent past is a good predictor of future performance. However, loan performance could vary significantly across different phases of the credit cycle and in different macroeconomic environments, and roll-rate models could exhibit poor forecasting performance beyond the short-term horizon. Thus, while roll-rate models are popular for business as usual (BAU) short-term loss forecasting purposes, they may require additional sensitivity analyses (in terms of determining the look-back period) and careful judgment about potential changes in future trends.

Roll-rate models could provide more accurate predictions over short-term horizons than other more complex statistical models. In some cases, short-term predictions from roll-rate models are stitched together with longer term forecasts from more sophisticated loss forecast models. However, the benefits of such combinations and the way in which two models are combined need to be demonstrated and supported based on careful analysis.

Like net charge-off models, roll-rate models usually cannot control for loan and borrower attributes, thus it is important to segment the underlying population into homogeneous groups so that the estimated roll rates are stable over time and not affected by the change in population mix. Also note that economic variables are usually not built into simple roll-rate models, and current economic conditions are assumed over the short forecast horizon.

Vintage Loss Forecasting Model

The vintage loss forecasting model framework has a long history in retail portfolio modeling. Vintage loss forecasting models segment the retail portfolios by vintage and other credit characteristics, and estimate losses based on the age of the vintage segments and the historical performance of portfolios with similar risk characteristics. In retail lending, different vintages often exhibit quite different performances over time for various reasons, such as changes in underwriting policy, and/or the macroeconomic/credit environment, and people in the retail lending industry routinely conduct vintage analyses where performance of different vintages is tracked and analyzed. Vintage models have been popular among practitioners when modeling retail credit portfolios due to their simplicity and interpretability.

There are a number of factors that may drive performance of different vintages. The vintage loss model framework attempts to explain vintage dynamics by decomposing loss (or another modeling target of interest) into three components: (a) vintage (or cohort) effect due to time varying underwriting standards; (b) seasoning or maturation effect and (c) time based effects, which include the impact of management actions, seasonality, and the underlying economic environment. The general form of the vintage model can be expressed as:

$$LR(i,t) = f_m(a) + f_v(i) + f_p(t) + e_{i,t}$$

where $LR(i,t)$ = (transformation of) loss rate for vintage i at time t;

$f_m(a = t - i)$ = maturation (or seasoning) component;
$f_v(i)$ = vintage quality component;
$f_p(t)$ = time specific effects;
$e_{i,t}$ = error term.

These three components are well-known drivers of retail credit portfolios and are consistent with the variables typically included in most standard retail loss forecasting models. So, the basic concept is similar to standard survival and hazard models. How those three components are captured varies in practice. In some implementations, each functional component is estimated parametrically using observable factors, such as vintage average credit scores and regional/macroeconomic factors. However, observable vintage credit attributes are difficult to incorporate because the underlying composition of vintage cohorts may change due to the seasoning of the vintage cohorts over time.

Another type of model, known as age-cohort-period (ACP) or Dual time Dynamics (DtD) (Breeden 2010), are used in several vendor developed models. These models typically use a two-step process for model estimation. These models first decompose historical data into three functional components (i.e., maturation, vintage quality, and time dependent environmental components) non-parametrically by making several identification assumptions. Additional modeling steps are then taken to use the identified components for future vintage forecasts. For example, extrapolation of the maturation curve is required for highly seasoned loans, and a separate econometric model is estimated for the historical time-dependent environmental component with historical economic factors.

Identifying individual components can be challenging in practice. The validity of identifying assumptions is difficult to judge and invalid assumptions could result in poorly specified models with counter-intuitive results. Poorly identified components could attribute what is essentially due to economic factors to other components, muting the true economic sensitivity. Hence, clear understanding of the underlying assumptions and careful outcome analysis are crucial for successful implementation of this type of model. Vendor-provided models, however, can often be limited in transparency, and it may be difficult for users with limited technical expertise to fully understand the implications and limitations of the assumptions made, which can be problematic especially when the output from the model is inconsistent with expectations. Since these models assume that different cohorts exhibit similar maturation patterns and responses to economic factors, proper segmentation is crucial in capturing important risk attributes. When comparing the vintage model framework with alternatives (e.g., loan-level models), these caveats need to be evaluated carefully.

9.3.2.2 Loan-Level Model

Loan-level models can incorporate loan-level factors which can capture the impact of portfolio mix shifts. Loan-level models generally take the expected loss approach, where losses are estimated in terms of three components: probability of default (PD); exposure at default (EAD) and loss given default (LGD). In retail portfolios, the definition of default can be driven by regulatory requirements, which vary across different products. Each individual component is estimated separately based on component-specific risk drivers. Separate modeling of the underlying components rather than modeling dollar loss as a whole provides additional granularity and precision when different components are driven by different risk factors.

For any account, expected credit loss can be calculated as the product of the PD, LGD and EAD estimates for the account. The total portfolio credit loss is then the sum of the credit loss estimates for individual loans.

$$E[Loss_t] = \sum_{i=1}^{n} PD_i \times EAD_i \times LGD_i$$

The loan-level expected approach can be further classified by the models used for the individual components.

PD Model

1. Definition of Default

The definition of default depends on the portfolio and the product, as well as the type of model. In commercial portfolios, the definition of default is typically based on subjective conditions and is more complex. For example, the definition of default employed in Basel II is both subjective and objective. Under Basel II/III, one of the following two conditions are to be met for a commercial facility to be considered as default: first that "the bank considers that the obligor is unlikely to pay in full," and second, that "the obligor is past due more than ninety days on any material credit obligation." (Basel 2005).

In retail portfolios, however, an objective definition of default based on a time threshold is often used. The most popular definition of default used for retail exposures for loss forecasting purposes is the one based on the past due thresholds in the Federal Financial Institutions Examination Council's (FFIEC) Uniform Retail Credit Classification and Account Management Policy. According to the policy, open-ended retail exposures (e.g., credit card, HELOC) and residential mortgages are in default at 180 days past due and other retail exposures (e.g. Auto loan) are in default at 120 days past due. In addition, a retail exposure is in default if the bank has taken a full or partial charge-off or write-down of principal for credit-related reasons[4]. This definition of retail default is also consistent with the definition used by Basel II/III.[5] 90 days past due is an often used threshold in default modeling for score card models as well as in academic studies. It is important to note that the definition of default has direct consequences on LGD estimates (see LGD section below).

2. Hazard/Survival Model

Survival analysis was first applied with mortality data in the medical/ biostatistical field and then extended to engineering and other areas. Since the event of interest (default or closure) will not have occurred in many cases in the sample, the sample data is typically right censored

4 The typical definition of retail default used by banks is somewhat broader than this definition and includes delinquencies (60+DPD) with bankruptcy, Chapter 7 bankruptcy discharge, and delinquent loans with modification.

5 However, Basel II permits banks to use the local retail definition of default in non-U.S. jurisdictions for retail exposures held by a bank's non-U.S. subsidiary in that non-U.S. jurisdiction, subject to prior supervisory approval.

and the censored nature of the data has to be explicitly considered in the estimation. Survival analysis is concerned with estimating the likelihood of an event to occur at different points in time and correctly incorporate information from both censored and uncensored observations in estimation.

The survival function gives the probability that a subject survives longer than some specified period t. So, the focus is not only whether an event occurred, but also when it occurred. The survival function is defined by the following formula:

$$S(t) = Prob(T > t)$$

where the random variable T is a subject's survival time and t is any specific time of interest. In estimating the survival function, even if the subject is right-censored, survival analysis still incorporates the subject's survival time until it is right censored.

Another way to describe the survival function is to use the hazard function, $h(t)$ which gives the hazard rate, at time t:

$$h(t) = \lim_{\Delta t \to 0} \frac{prob(t \leq T < t + \Delta t | T \geq t)}{\Delta t} = \frac{Prob(t \leq T < t + \Delta t)}{S(t)}$$

The hazard rate at time t is the instantaneous rate of the event to occur per small unit time interval conditioned on survival until time t. Thus, the hazard function can be used to approximate the conditional probability of termination at time t just the same way that the height of the probability density can be used to approximate probability. In practice, it is very common for the survival time to be measured discretely in terms of an interval. In such cases, discrete time hazard functions are used where the hazard within the interval is constant. The discrete time hazard function provides the conditional probability of the event to occur at each time interval t:

$$h(t) = prob(T = t | T \geq t)$$

Parametric survival models make specific assumptions about the distribution of the survival time and the hazard function is accordingly specified parametrically by the distribution function of the survival time. The distributions used in parametric survival models include exponential, Weibull, lognormal, gamma, log-logistic and Gompertz distribution. Explanatory variables, x_t, can be

Model	Hazard Function	Survival Function	Type
Exponential	γ	$\exp(-\gamma t)$	PH,AFT
Weibull	$\gamma\alpha t^{\alpha-1}$	$\exp(-\gamma t^{\alpha-1})$	PH, AFT
Generalized Weibull	$\gamma\alpha t^{\alpha-1}S(t)^{-\mu}$	$(1-\mu\gamma\alpha t^{\alpha})^{1/\mu}$	PH
Gompertz	$\gamma\exp(\alpha t)$	$\exp(-(\frac{\gamma}{\alpha})(\exp(\alpha t)-1)$	PH
Log-normal	$\frac{\exp(-(lnt-\mu)^2/2\sigma^2}{t\sigma\sqrt{2\pi}(1-\Phi\left(\frac{\ln(t)-\mu}{\sigma}\right))}$	$1-\Phi((\ln(t)-\mu)/\sigma)$	AFT
Log-logistic	$\frac{\alpha(\gamma)^{\alpha}(t)^{\alpha-1}}{(1+(\gamma t^{\alpha}))}$	$\frac{1}{(1+(\gamma t^{\alpha}))}$	AFT
Gamma	$\frac{\gamma(\gamma t)^{\alpha-1}\exp(-(\gamma t))}{\Gamma(\alpha)(1-I(\alpha,\gamma t))}$	$1-I(\alpha,\gamma t)$	AFT

a. All the parameters are restricted to be positive except that $-\infty<\alpha<\infty$ for the Gompertz model.

b. Gamma function, $\Gamma(\alpha)=\int_0^{\infty}\exp(-t)t^{\alpha-1}dt$

c. Incomplete gamma function, $I(\alpha,\beta)=\int_0^{\beta}\exp(-t)t^{\alpha-1}dt/\Gamma(\alpha)$ and $0<I(\alpha,\beta)<1$.

Source: Cameron and Trivedi (Table 17.5)

Figure 9.4 Standard parametric models and their hazard and survival functions.

incorporated into the models in various ways. Two popular formulations of regression survival models are proportional hazard (PH) model and accelerated failure time (AFT) models (Figure 9.4). In a proportional hazard model, the conditional hazard rate is specified as the product of the time dependent baseline hazard component and a function of explanatory variables, x_t

$$h(t|x_t)=h_0(t)\cdot\emptyset(x_t)$$

where $h_0(t)$ is the baseline hazard and $\emptyset(x_t)$ is typically specified as $exp\,(x_t\beta)$. The accelerated failure time models specify the distribution of the log of t instead of t

$$\ln(t) = x_t\beta + e_t$$

where different distributions for e result in different models. The Weibull and exponential models are unique in that they are both proportional hazard and accelerated failure time models.

3. Cox Proportional Hazard Model

One of the most widely used survival models is the Cox proportional hazard (CPH) model. Cox's proportional hazard model incorporates independent variables in a semiparametric way and specifies the hazard function as follows:

$$h(t) = h_0(t) \cdot \exp\left(\alpha + \sum_i \beta_i x_i\right)$$

where $h_0(t)$ is the baseline hazard function which can be estimated non-parametrically.

Cox's PH model is a semiparametric model because it does not require that the distribution of survival times be known. Cox's partial likelihood method provides a method of estimating β consistently without requiring estimation of $h_0(t)$. The model estimates the impact of explanatory variables without making any strong parametric assumptions about the actual form of the baseline hazard function. The model is popular among academic studies because their main interest is the relative impact of the explanatory variables.

However, there are a couple of complications in applying the Cox model to retail loss forecasting. For loss forecasting purposes, the baseline hazard will have to be estimated. The baseline hazard can be estimated in various ways including using polynomials, spline functions and a nonparametric MLE based on the initial estimate of β (Han and Hauseman 1990). The partial likelihood method also assumes that no two events occur at the same time, which is typically violated in a discrete time observation setting. Several methods are available to address the ties.

The Cox proportional hazard model can also be applied to a competing risk framework with or without independent risks assumption (Han and Hauseman 1990).[6] In this case, proportional hazard models

[6] Deng et al. (2000) estimate a competing risk termination model for mortgages with correlated risks and unobserved heterogeneity.

for each of the risks are separately estimated assuming that if the subject fails for some other risks, it is just censored as far as the particular risk under consideration is concerned.

While still popular in academic studies, the Cox proportional hazard model is not as widely used in retail loss forecasting in industry, perhaps because of the complications mentioned above and lack of flexibility due to the proportionality assumption.

4. Panel Multinomial Logistic Model

An alternative approach that is more suitable for discrete time termination/survival data is to use panel binary or multinomial response models.[7] This is a simple extension of static binary or multinomial models to a panel setting where one estimates the conditional probability of individual event in each period by estimating stacked binary or multinomial response models.

The general specification of the model framework is

$$h^j(t) = prob^j[t \leq T < t-1 | T \geq t-1, x_t] = G(x_t \beta^j)$$

where $prob^j$ is the probability of the event j to occur and x_t is a vector of explanatory variables that could be time-varying, including age t.[8]

The most popular multinomial model used in retail credit risk modeling is the multinomial logistic model (MNL) where the time t conditional probability of alternative event j (out of k possible events) is defined as[9]

$$h^j(t) = prob^j[t \leq T < t-1 | T \geq t-1, x_t] = \frac{exp\,(x_t \beta_j)}{1 + \sum_{i=1}^{k} \exp\,(x_t \beta_i)}.$$

[7] Panel logit or probit models are equivalent to a discrete-time hazard model with a certain hazard function (see Shumway 2000).

[8] For a suitable specification of G, the above formulation also includes the discrete time version of the proportional hazard model considered by various authors. See, for example, Cameron and Trivedi (2005).

[9] The multinomial model assumes the explanatory variables do not change values across alternatives. On the other hand, in the conditional logit model, the conditioning variables vary across alternatives. In retail credit risk modeling with competing risks, the multinomial logistic model is used exclusively. However, the MNL model can be expressed as a special case of the conditional logistic model by appropriately choosing explanatory variables.

McFadden (1981) showed that the MNL model can be derived from a utility maximizing probability choice model with i.i.d., type 1 extreme value distributions for alternative events. This i.i.d. assumption, however, results in a very restrictive implication, called the *independence from irrelevant alternatives* (IIA), which implies that adding another alternative does not affect the relative odds between the two alternatives under consideration.

The IIA assumption is considered as a significant shortcoming of the model, and several alternatives have been proposed. A simple alternative to using a multinomial logistic model which is not subject to the IIA assumption is to use a series of standard binary logistic models for each of the competing risks under consideration (e.g., default, prepayment). Under this approach, performance results are recoded in a binary fashion based on the event or non-event outcome, and a separate binomial logistic regression model is estimated for the probability of each individual risk event. However, this method is inherently ad hoc in the sense that it does not constrain that only one type of risk can be observed in the estimation. As a consequence, the sum of estimated probabilities of individual risks can be greater than one. Furthermore, the approach is inefficient because it ignores information available about other competing risks in the estimation. There are other approaches to avoid the IIA assumption as well. These include the multinomial probit model, the nested logit model, and the mixed logit model (see Woodridge 2010). However, these alternatives are generally more cumbersome to estimate and used more in academic research rather than in loss forecasting modeling in practice, so the multinomial logistic model remains to be the most popular choice in practice.

In the standard maximum likelihood estimation of the MNL model, the same set of explanatory variables enters all of the probability equations for alternative events. While this might be considered natural for a competing risk framework, the selected variables may be statistically insignificant or show an unexpected sign for some of the equations. However, the standard MNL model can also be estimated by a series of binary logistic regressions which estimate conditional odds ratios between each event type and one baseline reference type (Begg and Gray 1984). The conditional probabilities estimated from each binary logistic regression are then combined to calculate unconditional probabilities.[10] The Begg and Gray (BG) approach has the benefit of allowing for different risk drivers for each termination risk. While the BG method is easier to estimate and provides additional flexibilities, it can also potentially lead to overfitting the model when used improperly.

5. Landmarking Approach

The conventional hazard models used in retail loss forecasting, whether Cox's proportional hazard model or the panel multinomial logistic model, are constructed based on origination account-level attributes such as the origination FICO score along with other time-varying environmental factors at *t*. One of the weaknesses of these origination hazard models is that they do not incorporate up-to-date account-level information, such as delinquency status and current FICO score, which is highly predictive of termination outcomes. In order to use the updated variables, their values have to be forecasted, which is not what hazard models are set out to do. Since the information content of the origination variables declines over time as the account seasons, these models based on origination characteristics only tend to perform poorly for seasoned loans.

One might still want to estimate a model using time-varying account-level variables but using the static values of the variables available at the time of projection instead of attempting to forecast these variables. However, this means that the way in which the model is implemented and used will be inconsistent with how the model is developed. This could have significant consequences for certain applications. For example, suppose stress testing hazard PD model is estimated with current delinquency status and macroeconomic variables as covariates. Since delinquent loans have much higher probabilities to transition to default, the delinquent status variable will come out to be highly predictive of the default outcome. However, (future) delinquent status, although unknown at the time of forecast, will be affected by economic conditions in the future. Thus, using the current delinquency

[10] For example, suppose that there are two competing risks, default (i = 1) and prepayment (i = 2), and that the reference state (i = 0) is active. Let the probability of the i-th risk type, conditional on the state being either the reference type or i-th type, is estimated as $p_{i,0}$. Then, the unconditional probability of i-th risk is calculated as $p_i = \frac{1}{1+\frac{p_1}{1-p_1}+\frac{p_2}{1-p_2}}$.

status at the time of forecast for the future stress period will underestimate the true impact of severe macroeconomic stress.

In order to incorporate up-to-date account-level attributes in a consistent manner, several large firms have adopted an alternative hazard modeling framework, known as the landmarking approach, in retail loss forecasting. The landmarking approach is widely used to estimate the effect of a time-varying covariate on survival data in medicine and biostatistics fields. The idea of landmarking is that at each point in time, the modeler makes use of available historical information up to that time to forecast event probabilities in the future. Such probabilities can be obtained from the data by selecting individuals at risk at that point in time and using only the information available at the point in making predictions (van Houwelingen 2007).

A discrete time landmarking hazard model can be estimated using stacked data sets. The fully stacked sample (the fully exploded panel) can be created by using each account-period record as a landmark (Figure 9.5). For example, snapshots of the entire sample can be taken each month or quarter, and the exploded panel can be constructed by stacking the snapshots together. The size of the exploded panel may become too large for some retail portfolios and various sampling techniques are employed to construct the samples. A PD model can be estimated on the stacked panel using binomial logistic regressions or the competing risk multinomial logistic model (or its variations).

A landmarking PD model can utilize various account-level variables, both at origination and at landmark or snapshot, as well as economic variables at performance period t. Several time index variables can also be used, such as age, time from landmark or snapshot, and remaining term to maturity. A typical form of the landmarking hazard model can be expressed in the following equation.

$$ln\left(\frac{h(t)}{1-h(t)}\right) = \alpha + f_1(age) + f_2(TSS) + f_3(RT) + \sum \beta_i X_i(O) + \sum \rho_i X_i(S) + \sum \gamma_j Z_j(t)$$

where

t: Forecast month, based on calendar date.

$h(t)$: probability of the event occurring in t, conditional upon having survived to t–1.

α: intercept.

Account 1	C	C	C	C	C	D30	D60	D90	Default					
Account 2	C	C	C	C	Prepay									
.	.	.	.	.	.	.	.	.	.					
.	.	.	.	.	.	.	.	.	.					
.	.	.	.	.	.	.	.	.	.					
Account N	C	C	C	C	C	C	C	C	C	.	.	.	.	Mature
	0	1	2	3	4	5	6	7	8	9	.	.	.	T
	Age													

Age at Snapshot	Age 0	1	2	3	4	5	6	7	8	Account
0	C	C	C	C	C	D30	D60	D90	Default	Account 1
1		C	C	C	C	D30	D60	D90	Default	
2			C	C	C	D30	D60	D90	Default	
3				C	C	D30	D60	D90	Default	
4					C	D30	D60	D90	Default	
5						D30	D60	D90	Default	
6							D60	D90	Default	
7								D90	Default	
8									Default	
0	C	C	C	C	P					Account 2
1		C	C	C	P					
2			C	C	P					
3				C	P					
4					P					

Figure 9.5 Illustration of exploded panel.

age: months on book, the time (in months) between origination and time t.

TSS: time since snapshot, the time (in months) between snapshot and time t.

RT: remaining term, the time (in months) until the loan reaches maturity.

$f_1(age)$: the baseline component with months on book as the time index.

$f_2(TSS)$: the baseline component with time (months) since snapshot as the time index.

$f_3(RT)$: the baseline component with remaining term as the time index.

$\sum \beta_i X_i(O)$: impact of loan-level factors X_i at origination, $t = O$.

$\sum \rho_i X_i(S)$: impact of loan-level factors X_i at snapshot, $t = S$.

$\sum \gamma_i Z_i(t)$: impact of time-varying macroeconomic factors Z_i at time t.

Since multiple landmark data sets are created from the same account, observations in the stacked sample are likely to be correlated and the maximum likelihood standard error will be underestimated. Robust standard errors for the estimated parameters can be obtained by the sandwich estimators. Generalized Estimating Equations (GEE) can be used in lieu of maximum/pseudo-likelihood estimations as well (Liang and Zeger, 1986).

6. Status Transition Model

Another widely used account-level loss forecasting model is the status transition (or migration) model. The account-level status transition model is a generalization of the pool-level roll-rate model, where transition rates are nonstationary and dependent on loan-level attributes as well as time-varying economic factors. Although pool-level transition models with non-stationary transition rates are also used in practice, their usefulness is limited because they cannot easily incorporate pool-level attributes. Thus, most status migration models are developed at the account level.

While the hazard model directly targets the probabilities of events of interest (i.e., default and prepayment) to occur at different times, the status transition model estimates a one period transition probability matrix among potential states, including terminal absorbing states, and forecasts probability of default at a different time indirectly by applying the estimated transition matrix iteratively. Once a one-step-ahead transition matrix is estimated, it can be applied iteratively to forecast over a multi-period horizon.

Statuses are typically defined by depth of delinquency and alternative terminating events such as paid-in-full and charge-off/default. However, the baseline structure of statuses can be adjusted to be more or less granular and complex depending on materiality and data availability. For example, given the high volume of modifications taken during the Great Recession, more recent status transition models for mortgages tend to incorporate modification as another status in the transition model. In some models, modification is incorporated through multiple steps: modification with principal write-down is treated as part of a broader definition of default (or troubled loans) in the first-step transition model; in the second step, a more granular breakdown of default type including traditional defaults (e.g., REOs, short sales) and modification, as well as a sub-model for modified loans, are modeled and estimated.

		t+1						
		Current	**30dpd**	**60dpd**	**90+dpd**	**Foreclosure**	**REO/FA**	**Paid in Full**
	Current	$P_{c,c}$	$P_{c,30}$	$P_{c,60}$	$P_{c,90}$	$P_{c,fcl}$	$P_{c,d}$	$P_{c,p}$
t	**30dpd**	$P_{30,c}$	$P_{30,30}$	$P_{30,60}$	$P_{30,90}$	$P_{30,fcl}$	$P_{30,c}$	$P_{30,p}$
	60dpd	$P_{60,c}$	$P_{60,30}$	$P_{60,60}$	$P_{60,90}$	$P_{60,fcl}$	$P_{60,c}$	$P_{60,p}$
	90+dpd	$P_{90,c}$	$P_{90,30}$	$P_{90,60}$	$P_{90,90}$	$P_{90,fcl}$	$P_{90,d}$	$P_{90,p}$
	Foreclosure	$P_{fcl,c}$	$P_{fcl,30}$	$P_{fcl,60}$	$P_{fcl,90}$	$P_{fcl,fcl}$	$P_{fcl,,d}$	$P_{fcl,p}$

Figure 9.6 Illustration of a retail transition matrix for mortgage loans.

For commercial loans, statuses are typically defined by credit ratings. Since credit ratings of most commercial loans tend to be stable in the short-run, the diagonal cells usually have the highest transition rates. For retail loans where transition statuses are defined by delinquency statuses, off-diagonal cells tend to have larger values (Figure 9.6).

As previously mentioned, transition probabilities can depend on account-level risk characteristics as well as economic conditions. Account-level risk characteristics may include the attributes available at origination (e.g., origination FICO score, debt to income ratio) as well as updated attributes such as current LTV and current loan balance, whose future values can be calculated or forecasted relatively easily. On the other hand, current FICO score, while being widely prescribed for account management purposes, is not widely used in the status migration model because it is difficult to forecast. Delinquency history is another piece of current account-level information that can be used in the status migration model. For example, current loans that have no delinquency history in the recent past may behave differently from current loans cured from delinquency. However, use of delinquency history makes the status transition model non-Markovian and the model could run into the curse of dimensionality over long-run forecasts even with a small number of statuses.

While a Monte Carlo simulation method could be used to overcome the curse of dimensionality, it may still take a significant amount of computational resources to process a sizable portfolio.[11]

Estimating a status transition model is relatively straightforward. Transition probabilities from any given status can be estimated using a variety of different discrete choice methods, including some of the previously mentioned approaches. The most popular models used in practice are multinomial logistic and/or binary logistic regression models.[12] The choice of modeling technique depends on the risk drivers impacting the transitions. For example, when underlying risk drivers are similar for each transition, a multinomial logistic model could be used for efficiency. A combination of binary and multinomial logistic models nested together can also be used for transitions from a given status: a standard binary logistic model is used for the transition which requires a distinct set of risk drivers, and the rest of the transitions are estimated using a multinomial logistic model. Some transition possibilities can be excluded a priori (e.g., transition from current to D60 over a month). For certain transition cells, the estimation of robust and meaningful models is not feasible due to thinly populated data, in which case estimates based on expert judgment or historical averages can be used.

One of the main advantages of the status migration model is that once successfully estimated and implemented, the model generates various forecasts including the volume of defaults and delinquencies within a single model framework. Thus, for example, a separate model is not needed to forecast D90+ volume for nonaccruals. More importantly, the model allows the business to understand how the delinquency profile will evolve and provide an early warning of deteriorating performance. This is particularly useful for account and portfolio management as well as business planning purposes.

[11] Current account characteristics can also be incorporated in status migration models using the landmarking approach, in which case no Monte Carlo simulation is required in projection.

[12] Sirignano et al. (2016) estimates a mortgage status transition model using over 120 million US prime and subprime mortgages originated between 1995 and 2014 with account-level characteristics, account-level performance history, and time-varying local economic variables. They use a deep neural network framework to capture a nonlinear relationship between explanatory variables and loan performance and they estimate the model using GPU parallel computing.

On the other hand, errors in some of the key transition matrix cells can be magnified over time and have a significant impact on multi-period loss estimates. Thus, longer horizon forecasts may not be robust to minor specification errors. This potential vulnerability to compounding errors is one of the downsides of status transition models. The structure of a status transition model also tends to be more complex. The overall model consists of a number of sub-models describing transitions in and out of various statuses. Thus, a status transition model generally takes more effort to develop, implement, execute and maintain. If performance issues arise, it would also be more difficult to diagnose the underlying sources and correct them. While a multinomial logistic model allows estimation of several transition probabilities at the same time and simplifies the development and implementation somewhat, inflexibility of the model in terms of variable selection can also result in counter-intuitive coefficient signs in some important transitions. Given the structure of the model where a number of sub-models are involved and many of the transition cells only have marginal impact, focusing on individual components of the model might not be the best approach to assessing and validating the model. Evaluation of the total output, which is based on multiple equations and models, is necessary to determine whether the framework produces accurate results for credit loss forecasts.

7. Exposure at Default (EAD) Model

Exposure at default can be thought of as the sum of two components, the current balance outstanding, and additional future drawdowns of untapped credit available. Modeling exposure at default for closed end credit is relatively straightforward. EAD for term loans can be estimated based on the amortization schedule and adjusted for the missed payments before default.[13] Revolving lines of credit, however, present additional risk exposure above and beyond the outstanding balance because as a borrower's financial condition deteriorates toward default, she will likely use up any undrawn amount remaining in the line of credit. On the other hand, most revolving lines of credit in retail (e.g., credit card, HELOC) can be either conditionally or

[13] For the Basel capital calculation, EAD is floored at current unpaid balance outstanding.

unconditionally cancellable,[14] and the issuer and lender could either freeze or reduce the available line of credit as the borrower's credit condition deteriorates.[15] Because of the strategic interaction between borrowers and lenders, EAD is difficult to forecast. An additional complication is that EAD may also depend on the time horizon to default. The longer the time to default from the estimation point, the longer the window the borrower has to draw down the untapped line of credit without being restricted.

EAD is typically measured and estimated in terms of ratio to balance or line (total or undrawn). There are three commonly used approaches to account-level EAD modeling. In the loan equivalent (LEQ) method, EAD is measured as the change in exposure from the current balance as a percentage of the remaining line amount.

$$LEQ = \frac{EAD - Current\ UPB}{Current\ Total\ Line\ Amount - Current\ UPB}$$

The LEQ measure utilizes information from both the unpaid balance and the total credit line at each point in time. LEQ could be undefined or highly unstable where the current balance is either equal or close to the total available credit line.

In the credit conversion factor method (CCF), EAD is measured relative to the current balance.

$$Credit\ Conversion\ Factor = \frac{EAD}{Current\ Balance}.$$

While the CCF measure tends to be more stable than the LEQ, it is also undefined when the current balance is zero. Furthermore, the CCF ignores information from the total line amount. The third approach, called the exposure at default factor (EADF) method, measures EAD in terms of utilization rate.

[14] Definition of "unconditionally cancellable" varies depending on the context in which the term is applied. For example, a HELOC contract which follows the regulation Z language is considered as unconditionally cancellable for regulatory capital purposes, but the same contract may be considered as conditionally cancellable for CECL reserve estimation.

[15] Under the new CECL guidelines, an allowance for unfunded commitments that are unconditionally cancellable by the issuer should not be established because credit risk on such commitments is not considered to be a liability.

$$EAD\ Factor = \frac{EAD}{Current\ Total\ Amount}$$

Selection of a particular approach can vary across different institutions, depending on various factors including data, flexibility, and model performance. While EAD is an important part of loss forecasting for open-ended revolving lines of credit, an accurate and robust EAD model is difficult to develop.

8 Loss Given Default (LGD) Model

Loss given default is typically measured and estimated as a percentage of EAD. There are several fundamental issues related to LGD quantification. The first issue is the definition of loss used in LGD measurement and modeling. Two related but different loss measurements, accounting loss and economic loss, are used to calculate LGD in credit loss forecasting. Accounting losses are losses recorded in financial reporting and total accounting loss (or accounting LGD) is defined as cumulative charge-offs net of recoveries. Under GAAP, recognition of accounting losses takes place over a period of time. When the account is first recognized as impaired, an initial charge-off is taken representing the best estimate of the ultimate loss. Additional charge-offs follow when changes in the estimated loss are recognized. A final charge-off is made when the collateral, if any, is sold and all proceeds and cost are known. Economic LGD, on the other hand, measures economic loss, which includes material discount effects and material direct and indirect costs associated with collecting exposure (BCBS, 2005). Economic LGD is used for regulatory capital calculations under Basel II (and Basel III), whereas accounting LGD is used in the models for allowance for credit losses (ACL) and stress testing. Economic LGD is generally higher because it includes both direct and indirect costs.

Second, the measurement and definition of LGD depend on the definition of default. For example, if default is defined as being ninety days delinquent or more, many defaulted loans under this definition may have been cured since the time of default, thus becoming current again. In this situation, defaulted loans ultimately may not result in any losses, which will not be known until the loans become terminated. What's important is that the LGD measurement has to be consistent with the definition of default used. A looser definition of default will, on average, give a lower LGD estimate. In retail portfolios, the definition of default is typically driven by regulatory requirements, which vary across products.

Third, liquidation of repossessed collateral (e.g., mortgage) can take a long time, especially during a stress period. If the estimation sample only includes liquidated loans, a significant amount of data could be right-censored. The right-censoring problem can be exacerbated when a loose definition of default is used. To the extent that loans with longer recovery timelines tend to have higher LGD, this could result in a biased estimate. When reasonable loss estimates are available, it may be useful to conduct an analysis on the correlation between LGD and resolution time. Recovery data are often collected and stored differently from loss data. For example, sometimes recovery data are available only at the aggregate portfolio level and cannot be attributed to specific default vintages or accounts. This can make the measurement and estimation of recovery rate and net LGD difficult.

A variety of alternative econometric models can be used for retail LGD estimation. Ordinary Least Squares is probably the simplest model, but it does not respect the boundary nature of LGD data.[16] Among the models explicitly recognizing that LGD value is bounded in [0,1], the fractional regression model proposed by Papke and Wooldridge (1996) has become a popular choice. In order to estimate the conditional mean of a fractional response variable, Papke and Wooldridge proposed a nonlinear conditional mean function.

$$E(y|x) = G(x\beta)$$

where G is a known nonlinear function satisfying $0 \leq G(\cdot) \leq 1$. A popular choice for G is the logistic function

$$E(y|x) = G(x\beta) = \frac{1}{1 + \exp(-x\beta)}$$

but any other cumulative probability distribution function can be used for $G(\cdot)$.

The model can be estimated by nonlinear least squares, or by using the Quasi Maximum Likelihood method. Papke and Woodridge

[16] LGD data are typically bounded between 0 and 1. While the actual LGD value can be negative, it is typically truncated at 0 when negative. LGD can also be greater than 1, but the lender would simply write-off the balance without pursuing any recovery when doing so would increase net loss.

(1997), proposed a QML method, based on the Bernoulli log-likelihood function given by

$$LL(\beta) = \sum_{i=1}^{n} y_i \, log\,[G(x\beta)] + (1 - y_i)\, log\,[1 - G(x\beta)].$$

Since the Bernoulli distribution is a member of the linear exponential family, the QML estimator (a form of M estimator) is consistent and asymptotically normal, provided that the conditional mean function $G(\cdot)$ is correctly specified.[17]

An alternative choice is a fully parametric approach where a specific parametric distribution, rather than just the conditional mean function, is assumed for the LGD. There are several statistical distributions that could be used for data bounded to the unit interval. For example, the beta distribution has been a popular choice because of its flexibility. However, the parametric models may not be robust to deviation from the distributional assumption.

LGD data often exhibit significant masses at the boundary values. This can be an issue if the parametric distribution assumed is not defined at the boundary points[18]. Even if the domain of the distribution covers the boundary values (i.e., 0 and 1), significant masses at the boundaries seem to suggest inconsistency with the distributional assumption. While fractional models without distributional assumptions can still be used in this case, they may not be the best modeling option when nontrivial portions of the LGD estimation sample are at the boundary values of 0 and/or 1. When a nontrivial proportion of LGD data is concentrated at the boundary values, a better approach might be to take a two-part model where the LGD is modeled as a mixture of a discrete random variable and a continuous random variable. The discrete part determines the probability mass corresponding to the boundary values and the non-boundary interval. This can be modeled as a binomial or multinomial variable and estimated using logistic regression. The non-

[17] Another related approach to confine the LGD estimate to the unit interval is an inverse function approach where $E\left(G^{-1}(y)\right) = x\beta$ is estimated by OLS and LGD is given by $\hat{y} = G\left(x\hat{\beta}\right)$. However, this transformation method generally results in a biased estimate because $G\left[E\left(G^{-1}(y)\right)\right] \neq E\left[G\left(G^{-1}(y)\right] = E(y)\right.$.

[18] One method of dealing with the boundary values when the parametric distribution is not defined at the boundary values is to add and/or subtract a small number so that the likelihood function is still defined. However, the results could be very sensitive to the number used.

boundary continuous part can be estimated by a QML fractional regression model or by a parametric model such as a beta regression model. The two-part model can be expressed as

$$Prob(y|x)\begin{cases} Prob(y=0|x) \\ Prob(y\in(0,1)\ |\ x) \\ Prob(y=1|x) \end{cases}$$

$$E(y|x, y\in(0,1)) = G(x\beta)$$

$$E(y|x) = Prob(y\epsilon(0,1)|x)\cdot G(x\beta) + Prob(y=1|x),$$

where $prob(y|x\}$ can be estimated by the ordered logistic or multinomial logistic regression and $G(x\beta)$ can be estimated by the fractional regression model or by ML with a parametric distributional assumption.

Qi and Zhao (2011) and Li et al. (2016) compared various statistical models for LGD estimation and found that OLS models perform reasonably well although some more sophisticated models have a slight edge. While the studies are based on the recovery data of corporate defaults, the various models investigated can be considered and tested in modeling retail LGD.

In case of accounting loss forecasting, the estimated total net charge-off discussed above can be distributed over the period from the time of default to the final liquidation, recognizing multi-step loss recognition practices under GAAP. The distribution curve can be constructed based on the average time profile of losses during a certain benchmark period. Time-recognized accounting LGD can be estimated directly by estimating initial and subsequent incremental loss severities over multiple forecast periods. This approach, however, requires a good historical charge-off/recovery series, which can be a significant challenge. Another variation of the accounting LGD approach is to take a non-statistical, bottom-up approach and estimate total loss by aggregating individual components, which include collateral values (general collateral value appreciation or depreciation and haircut for distressed sale) and various cost components involving collateral disposal and collection. The individual loss components are calculated based on the assumptions about the underlying cost parameters measured either relative to the loan balance or in dollar terms. These underlying assumptions, which may vary across time and/or across different segments and geographical areas, need rigorous support and are subject to validation.

9.4 Issues in Retail Credit Risk Model Validation

The widespread use of statistical models and the critical roles they play in retail lending have drawn increasing attention to managing and validating these models to ensure that they are working properly as intended. An essential element of model risk management is a sound and robust model validation process. Poorly developed models may not only lead to lost revenue but may threaten financial health of financial institutions.

As retail lenders are increasingly relying on models for decision making, and the models used in practice are becoming more and more complex, lenders have begun to recognize the importance of establishing a sound validation and model risk management framework. Recognizing the importance of model validation, OCC issued a guidance on model validation in 2000 (OCC Bulletin 2000–2016). The 2008 mortgage crisis in the USA and the heightened regulatory expectations environment following the crisis provided an important impetus for a significant change in the way validation functions are organized and performed. This change was initiated by the new interagency supervisory guidance on model risk management jointly issued by FRB (SR 11-7) and OCC (Bulletin 2011–2012).

Although regulatory expectations in relation to the guidance are somewhat different depending on the size and complexity of the banks as well as the materiality of the portfolios under consideration (SR-18, SR-19), the CCAR and DFAST banks have gradually begun to adopt effective model risk management practices and model validation has become a core component in supervisory examinations. While the new guidance calls for an enterprise-wide model risk management framework and applies to different risk areas across the board, the retail credit work stream has been one of the earliest beneficiaries of the change and retail model validation in many large banks is now on a much more sound foundation than before.

An effective validation framework has to be based on a clear understanding of the purpose and use of the model, and must include several core elements: evaluation of conceptual soundness, backtesting, benchmarking, outcome analysis, and ongoing monitoring. As with other aspects of model risk management, the guiding principle of validation is "effective challenge." Exercising effective challenge, however, is much easier said than done in practice. It requires the right balance of technical competency, business knowledge, and exercise of good judgement and common sense. Validation focusing too much on marginal technical issues can be distracting and counterproductive.

9.4.1 Model Development and Role of Independent Validation

It is often the case that some validation work may be most effectively done by model developers because of their expertise or a lack of other technical resources. In fact, a critical part of the model development process is validation testing, where various components of a model are assessed to determine whether the model is sound, properly implemented, and performing as intended.

It is certainly the case that overall model validation is expected to be aided by a good model development practice. However, the validation work performed by model developers are often reviewed by an independent party. In particular, because of the large number of account variables available and the massive volume of data involved, some retail models require relatively more time to develop. Model developers can be pigeonholed during the long process of model development. Independent and effective validation can provide an objective view with a fresh pair of eyes. An independent validation is aimed at not only conducting a critical review of the developmental evidence, but also providing additional analyses and tests as necessary.

9.4.2 Models' Purpose and Use

Model validation is for the purpose of the models' defined uses and expectations. Model validation is the set of processes and activities intended to verify that models are performing as expected, in line with their design objectives and business uses. Thus, a clear understanding of the model's purpose, use and expectation are crucial. For example, stress testing model development requires stress period data for reliable performance of the model during a stress period, which is the raison d'etre of the model. Similarly, validation of stress testing models commonly gives more weight to the performance of the model during stress periods.

Different uses and purposes of models call for different performance measures. For example, traditional credit scoring models used in credit granting decisions are developed as a classifier to separate bad borrowers from good ones. Based on that defined usage, these models are often evaluated based on measures of discriminatory power such as the K-S statistic or Receiver Operating Characteristic (ROC) curve. On the other hand, loss forecasting models are used to predict dollar losses, and predictive accuracy is considered to be much more important. A sound and accurate PD model is expected to risk rank borrowers with different credit risks well. However, a PD model with good discriminatory power in terms of measures such as K-S statistic and ROC curve does not necessarily guarantee good performance in default frequency prediction. Thus, for performance measurement of a model developed and used for the purpose of loss forecasting, goodness-of-fit, or even risk-based pricing, predictive accuracy measures would be more relevant than measures of discriminatory power.

Multiple uses of a model by different business areas for different purposes require separate validations for each use or purpose. The same model could be used with different inputs or scenarios, and/or run over different horizons. An account-level retail model is usually costly to develop and maintain. Thus, utilizing the same underlying model for different applications can be highly beneficial, especially when the goals and purposes of the different applications are deemed reasonably consistent. However, the efficiency gain from using a common model often comes at a cost: lack of specificity and/or additional complexity.

A loss forecasting model developed for a particular purpose (e.g., regulatory capital purpose) may or may not be suitable for other purposes (e.g., stress testing or ACL purposes). An existing model developed and validated for a particular purpose may not be suitable for certain other applications or may not even be consistent with the rules required by other applications, in which case some adjustment outside of the model or development of a separate model is necessary. It is a prudent policy that a retail model be tested and validated for different applications for which the model is intended, including primary as well as secondary uses. Any gaps and deficiencies resulting from the application for which the model was originally intended might be mitigated by compensating overlays or controls.

9.4.2 *Evaluation of Conceptual Soundness*

Evaluation of conceptual soundness involves assessing the quality of the model's design and construction. All of the important choices made in the model development process, including the overall statistical model framework, data sample, variable selection, and any assumptions made should be subject to a rigorous assessment. The evaluation of conceptual soundness covers documentation as well as empirical evidence supporting the method used and the model specification.

A. Statistical Modeling Framework

In many cases, several alternative modeling approaches are available for model development where each approach has its pros and cons, and choosing a particular approach can be difficult. Firms generally have more options and flexibility in terms of choosing modeling approaches for retail products. A wide range of models and methods of estimation are available and used in practice for retail credit loss forecasting and for other purposes. The choice of a particular model and methodology depends on a number of factors, including model purpose, product type, the materiality of the portfolio, data availability, resources available and management's inclination toward certain quantitative approaches and their risk tolerance. Due to availability of rich sets of retail credit data from both internal and external sources, using a relatively complex model framework that requires highly granular data is more feasible and common in retail modeling. On the other hand, a more complex model requires more resources and time not only to develop, but also to properly maintain and to control heightened model risk.

Validation needs to ensure that the chosen modeling approach has the level of sophistication that is commensurate with the product's materiality and complexity in terms of risk exposures, and that the underlying statistical model framework is theoretically sound and consistent with well-established research findings and widely accepted industry standards. Adequate model documentation is critical: documentation needs to clearly explain the underlying theoretical framework and discuss any critical assumptions, judgments, and limitations in a transparent manner. This applies regardless of whether the model is developed internally or externally by a third-party vendor.

It is important to recognize that firms need to have sufficient in-house expertise and competency to understand and be able to properly apply the methodology and manage the model. The fact that a modeling approach is sound and used by some firms does not necessarily mean that the approach is an appropriate option for every firm. Firms sometimes adopt an approach for which they do not have proper understanding and expertise and end up with a poorly developed/executed model. In this case, the issue is not the underlying modeling approach per se, but a poor execution of the approach due to lack of expertise. Similarly, firms often adopt a third-party vendor model without an adequate understanding of the model and its shortcomings, and eventually end up switching to another model. This can be very costly and time-consuming. Given several alternative modeling options available, choosing a particular approach requires a critical evaluation and comparison of different statistical model frameworks, taking into account the firm's strategic direction, resource constraints and regulatory expectations.

Firms may want to develop multiple models for comparison or benchmarking purposes. More and more firms are developing alternative models to challenge and benchmark the champion model. In large firms, in particular, developing challenger/benchmark model(s) is becoming the norm for material retail portfolios. The champion/challenger approach allows the bank to fully explore and evaluate various modeling approaches to make better modeling decisions. Challenger/benchmark models are particularly beneficial when they are based on a different approach or framework than the champion model, and more robust to the known weaknesses of the champion model. A benchmark model that is either poorly specified or highly similar to the champion model does not provide any meaningful challenge or insights about the champion model and will be a waste of resources. To the extent that the benchmark model can be used to inform overlays or alter the model outcome, it is recommended that the model be validated with the same rigor as that of the champion models to ensure the challenge is meaningful and effective.

B. Data and Sampling

The development data set used to build a model is of critical importance and also needs to be validated for accuracy, relevance and representativeness. A large volume of application and performance data from the past accounts is collected internally by financial institutions as well as externally by credit bureaus and third-party data vendors. Availability of massive and highly granular account-level data is one of the hallmarks of retail modeling compared to other areas. While a lack of reliable data with sufficient history is often singled out as the main obstacle in commercial credit modeling, there is a wealth of account-level information available for retail products.

The large volume of data involved in retail modeling, however, poses challenges of its own: it takes a considerable amount of institutional knowledge and resources to clean and prepare the data so that it can be used for model development. Various one-time historical events such as mergers and acquisitions, system changes and loan sales require some adjustments to create historical data that is consistent over time. Any adjustments made during data preparation steps, including treatment of missing values and outliers, data exclusion, and censoring and/or truncation, should be clearly documented and supported. Sensitivity testing also is typically performed to inform the magnitude and direction of the impact of the adjustments. When aggregated, loan-level data should tie out to the general ledger balances and other official historical reports available at the portfolio level. Independent validation ideally reviews all data processing steps carefully for accuracy and validity, including code review, and conduct additional analysis and independent testing when called for.

Development data, whether internal or external, needs to be checked for its relevance and representativeness for the firm's current portfolio or the product the model is intended for. Firms may have changed their business strategies and underwriting practices which can cause their current portfolios to be significantly different from the historical data. When the firm's portfolio has gone through significant changes and its internal historical data is no longer relevant, an appropriate measure has to be taken such as utilizing external data or making an appropriate adjustment to the model results to compensate for the data issue.

When dealing with external data from a third party or a new portfolio acquired through merger or purchase activity, the relevance and representativeness of the development sample for the current portfolio under consideration needs to be assessed and if necessary, appropriate adjustments may be made accordingly.[19]

Sampling is required for retail loan-level modeling to make the development sample manageable, but a poorly designed sample could create biases. A number of different sampling methods are used in practice, including simple random sampling, stratified sampling and choice-based sampling, for example. Some dynamic panel models such as the landmark hazard model involve a rather complicated exploded panel data structure, and properties of different sampling methods on the full exploded panel are difficult to understand. Validation aims at ensuring that sampled data is representative of the population and that sampling rates are sufficiently large to produce accurate estimates with reasonable precision.

Data censoring can also create selection bias. For example, a left-censored performance panel data set starting in 2009 will be missing all of the loans that defaulted in the early part of the Great Recession and the missing data cannot be said to be randomly censored. A biased sample can have far-reaching consequences on the model estimates and forecasting results. Importance of sampling design notwithstanding, a rigorous evaluation of sampling methodology is often missing both in development evidence and validation.

C. Variable Selection and Segmentation

A number of different variable selection methods are used in retail credit risk modeling in practice. Retail modelers work with a large number of variables from which they have to choose which ones will be included in the final model specification. Traditional variables used in retail models include borrower information from application/origination data, performance data from past history and credit bureaus, and other socio-economic data. With the large magnitude of personal activity and social networking data that has begun to be collected and captured on the web, the number of variables that can be potentially used in retail credit modeling for various purposes has grown significantly larger. Inclusion of too many variables, however, can

[19] Data matching is often based on several key attributes such as credit grade, FICO score, LTV, channel and GEO profile. Population Stability Index is a standard measure often used to compare the data sample that the model was developed on with a more recent data sample on which the model has been used. Propensity Score Matching can also be used to create relevant proxy data.

cause model overfit and poor out-of-sample forecasting performance. A large number of potential predictors, thus, requires variable reduction/selection methods that are not only computationally efficient but also produce good predictive performance.

Various variable reduction/selection methods are used in practice. These methods include model selections based on information criterion such as Akaike Information Criterion (AIC) or Bayesian Information Criterion (BIC); methods based on significance testing such as forward and backward stepwise regression; penalized (regularized) regression methods such as LASSO, LARs and Elastic Net;[20] dimension reduction methods such as PCA and factor models; and model averaging using a combination of models (Castle et al. 2009; Scott and Varian 2014; Ng 2013). These variable selection/reduction methods are designed with different objectives in mind. As such, their relative performance varies depending on the evaluation criteria and the true data generating process. Models and model selection methods should be evaluated based on criteria that are appropriate for each model's purpose. For example, the focus of the model search could be to obtain robust and reliable coefficient estimates or best forecast performance. Castle et al. (2011a) provides various criteria with which the successes of selection methods can be evaluated along with several performance measures.

Competing approaches to variable selection have different trade-offs between type I and type II errors (Castle et al. 2011b). That is, some variables will be incorrectly included and some risk drivers will be wrongly excluded by variable selection methods. An optimal variable selection method will find the optimal trade-off between the two types of errors for a given data environment. Unfortunately, there is no single variable selection method that will dominate in all data environments and different methods in certain environments could give rise to highly misleading results. While utilizing some form of variable selection algorithm can be valuable or even necessary for certain types of model and data environment, selecting risk drivers purely based on algorithmic or statistical model selection criteria is often discouraged (see also Section 9.4.6 on machine learning).

Key risk drivers for retail products are relatively well known and validation needs to ensure that any variables selected are consistent

[20] Although these methods are regularization methods, they can be used as variable selection methods.

with prevailing economic or behavioral theories and sound business knowledge. Well-known key risk drivers (e.g., LTV in mortgage) are excluded sometimes because coefficients are not statistically significant or the signs of the coefficients are counter-intuitive. In this situation, a follow-up investigation may be conducted to reveal the underlying reasons. This could be due to inappropriate model specification or data limitations. The fact that one cannot demonstrate statistical significance of a key risk driver with historical data does not mean that the risk factor will not be important in a different environment in the future. To the extent that this is driven by data limitations such as lack of historical experience, appropriate measures may be taken to compensate for the limitation.

Sample data is often affected by various one-time/temporary historical events such as policy initiatives, changes in corporate policies, mergers and acquisitions, and loan sales. These one-off events, if not properly controlled for, could have significant impacts and bias model estimates. On the other hand, frivolous use of dummy variables could inadvertently absorb some of the impacts due to other risk factors. Thus, careful attention should be paid to the use of time-specific dummy variables; in particular, what is their impact on other model estimates and how they are treated in forecasting.

The variable selection literature has focused mostly on selecting a set of variables from a much larger set of candidate variables. However, other aspects related to variable selection such as functional form and lag structure are also important and need to be subject to adequate validation as well. For example, a linear specification approximating what is truly a nonlinear relationship could produce significantly over/underestimated results for certain segments. Additionally, using macroeconomic factors with long lags may force results to exhibit too much smoothing and may be considered inappropriate in stress testing models.

One way to incorporate nonlinear relationships within a linear regression framework is to include higher order interaction terms. While reservations about using interaction terms on the basis of complexity or overfitting are unfounded, they may be used with care and with good justification. Ai and Norton (2003) note that in a typical nonlinear model such as a logistic regression widely used in retail modeling, the interaction effect is highly nonlinear and, in general, not equal to the coefficient of the interaction term, which is the marginal effect of the interaction term. In practice, however, an interaction term is included based on the sign and simple t-test on the coefficient of the interaction term, which could be misleading. On some occasions, interaction terms are included, but underlying factors are not all included, which makes the interpretation of the effect difficult.

Another way of capturing the effects of risk drivers is through segmentation. When different segments of a portfolio exhibit significant heterogeneity in terms of underlying risk drivers or sensitivities to risk drivers, an appropriate segmentation scheme is called for. Inadequate segmentation makes model performance susceptible to changes in portfolio characteristics. On the other hand, an overly granular segmentation scheme adds complexity and potentially unnecessary model risk.

Retail portfolios are often segmented based on multiple characteristics such as product, lien position (e.g., first and second lien real estate loans), market segment (e.g., conventional conforming, jumbo, CRA loans), collateral type (e.g., new and used car loans), credit score, and delinquency status. When a model is estimated at the account level, it may be sufficient to include a few interaction terms to account for heterogeneities across different segments. However, when numerous and complex interaction terms are required, the model becomes difficult to manage and interpret, and segmentation may be a better option. It is important to note that segmentation is model dependent: a segmentation scheme might be perfectly reasonable for certain model frameworks, but inappropriate for others. For example, delinquency status might be considered as a reasonable segmentation criterion for a standard Basel type PD model with a one-year fixed horizon or for a multi-period stress testing PD model based on the landmarking approach. However, delinquency status would be inappropriate as a segmentation criterion (or even as a variable) in the standard account or pool-level models for multi-period loss forecasting unless transition in and out of delinquency at each point over the forecasting horizon is explicitly modeled. Validation is supposed to ensure that the segmentation scheme is conceptually sound and supported by data, and that any deficiencies in segmentation due to data limitations are properly acknowledged and compensated for.

9.4.3 Outcome Analysis and BackTesting

Outcome analysis refers to an evaluation of model performance by comparing model outputs to actual outcomes. The goodness-of-fit of model predictions is evaluated based on how "close" the predictions are to the actual outcomes. This requires a metric for "closeness," often called the loss function in the forecasting literature, which quantifies the distance between forecast and actual outcome. As emphasized in the recent book by Elliott and Timmermann (2016), the loss function should be grounded in the true economic or business cost of the forecast error to the decision maker. A well-designed, economically motivated performance metric makes it easier to interpret and evaluate predictive performance. However, a careful consideration of decision theoretic foundation of the loss function is rarely given in practice, and informal summary statistics are often used for the performance measurement.

The nature of output comparison and evaluation depends on various factors, including the purpose and use of the model, materiality of the portfolio, data availability and volatility inherent in the data and management's risk appetite. A variety of different methods and metrics can be used in outcome analysis and model validation. Measurement and evaluation of a retail model's performance is typically based on the model's purpose as well as clearly stated expectations derived based on aforementioned factors. For example, a loss forecasting model, developed and validated for normal business applications, may not be suitable for stress testing purposes and its performance has to be tested and validated for stress periods.

If the main objective of a model is to separate borrowers by creditworthiness or to rank-order their credit risk, various measures of discriminatory power, such as Return Operating Characteristic (ROC) curve, Cumulative Accuracy Profile (CAP), K-S statistic, GINI coefficient, and Accuracy Ratio,[21] and concordance/discordance measures would be relevant metrics for outcome analysis. On the other

[21] The ROC curve is constructed by plotting the cumulative distribution of the scores of the "goods" and the "bads" against each other on the X-Y axis, respectively. The closer the curve is to the point (0,1), the better discrimination power the scorecard is considered to have. On the other hand, the ROC curve for a pure random 50–50 chance discriminator will be the straight line connecting (0,0) and (1,1). The GINI coefficient is a measure of discrimination power and is defined as (2×area under the ROC curve −1). The CAP curve is similar to the ROC curve with the following difference: the cumulative distribution of the bads is plotted not against the cumulative distribution of all the scores, not the scores of the goods. The Accuracy Ratio is a measure of discrimination power similar to the GINI coefficient, but is defined in terms of the CAP curve.

hand, if the main purpose of the model is to predict the level of outcome accurately, which is required for a good loss forecasting or pricing model, the unbiasedness and accuracy of model predictions are important, and measures of predictive accuracy and goodness-of-fit are more appropriate for model validation.

Various forms of tests, formal as well as informal, are available to test the unbiasedness of model predictions. Scatter plots and other informal graphical methods can provide good insights about where the model fails. The Mincer-Zarnowitz (1969) type of regression can be used to test unbiasedness of model predictions in time series as well as cross-sectional settings. Goodness-of-fit tests such as the Hosmer-Lemeshow chi-squared test are often used in validating the calibration of the internal rating-based approach to commercial credit and scorecard models for retail products. Similarly, actual outcomes can also be compared against a confidence interval around the predictions. While these tests can be used as a check against certain minimum standards, they provide little information regarding how accurate the model predictions are relative to the actual outcomes.

Predictive accuracy of retail loss forecasting models is typically evaluated based on accuracy measures such as (Root) Mean Squared Error (MSE), Mean (Absolute) Error (M(A)E), and Mean (Absolute) Percent Error (M(A)PE). Absolute measures such as MSE and M(A)E are scale-dependent and they can be difficult to compare across time and different segments. On the other hand, relative measures such as M(A)PE weigh forecast errors more heavily when the actual outcome is closer to zero, which is hard to justify. Relative performance measures also tend to be unstable when the level of outcome is very low. Since neither type of metric alone might be sufficient, it would be prudent to use several alternative metrics to get a comprehensive perspective of model performance. As briefly discussed earlier in this section, these metrics are not measures of the (expected) loss function derived based on true economic costs of prediction errors. Rather, they are used as simple summary statistics of predictive accuracy.

A best practice employed in conjunction with various performance criteria is the establishment of performance thresholds for various metrics. Acceptable thresholds may be determined internally based on the model's purpose, volatility inherent in the data, and management's risk tolerance. Performance thresholds that are too loose do not provide any meaningful validation tests and will cause meaningful deterioration to be missed. Using too tight a threshold based on unrealistic expectations can draw unnecessary scrutiny, which is also counterproductive.

Quantitative performance metrics and thresholds are not necessarily intended to serve as strict "Pass" or "Fail" testing tools. Special circumstances will always occur that will cause the model to violate the established thresholds. Rather, they can be interpreted as guideposts to inform stakeholders when a model's performance should be reevaluated against expectations in a more transparent and disciplined manner. As such, quantitative metrics are most useful and informative when they are used with adequate narratives and explanations. Deteriorating performance or violating the threshold typically triggers an in-depth analysis of the underlying causes and diagnosis from the model owner, which should help senior management make an informed decision about a remediation action plan. Economically motivated performance metrics and thresholds make it easier to explain the performance results to various stakeholders, and to facilitate better decision making.

In-sample performance evaluation against the full sample of the data used to estimate the model tends to be biased (i.e., performance is overestimated) because the parameters are estimated to minimize the prediction errors. Thus, an unbiased evaluation of model performance calls for out-of-sample validation, where the estimated model is tested with a new set of data that was not used in estimation and thereby provides an unbiased estimate of the likely performance of the model in the future.

For top-down time series models, out-of-sample validation requires some data to be held out from the model development. Loan-level retail models are typically validated using holdout samples because, given a large volume of loans available for retail products, holdout samples usually do not impose extra burden in terms of data availability. However, with macroeconomic and other time-varying factors affecting retail credit performance, the temporal aspect of model performance is important and out-of-sample testing alone can miss important weaknesses of a model. If sufficient performance data were available, backtesting using a separate out-of-time sample would be ideal. However, that is often not feasible due to data constraints, and even if it is feasible, it might require a significant loss of efficiency. When true out-of-time backtesting is not feasible, a practical second-best alternative, known as pseudo (out-of-time) backtesting or as the walk (or roll) forward approach, might be used where (a) the best final model is selected and estimated based on the full sample period; (b) the same model specification is estimated using a shorter sub-sample through a particular period, allowing for backtesting on an out-of-time period; (c) repeat the step (b) by moving forward, for example, one year at a time. Robustness of model performance across different economic environments may also be assessed by performing (multi-period) in-sample performance testing using different periods as the forecast starting points.

9.4.4 *Sensitivity Analysis and Benchmarking*

Sensitivity analysis can be a useful validation tool for uncovering model weaknesses that are not obvious, and for testing reasonability and robustness of a model under a wide range of input values. In particular, when a model is highly complex, nonlinear and hard to analyze analytically, sensitivity analysis with respect to key input variables over a wide range of values, including extreme and boundary values, is crucial in making sure that the model is working as intended over a wide range of circumstances under which the model is expected to be applied. Output sensitivity to simultaneous changes in several inputs can provide the model's sensitivity to risk layering or evidence of unexpected interactions when the interactions are complex. Analysis of macroeconomic sensitivity is a key part of macro stress testing model validation. Sensitivity analysis is also helpful in validating a vendor model when detailed information on the vendor model is lacking. Sensitivity analysis can also identify unintended consequences of seemingly innocuous variable transformations. Sensitivity can be measured in a number of ways: in terms of change or percentage change, static effect or cumulative dynamic effect. In the validation of a pricing model (e.g., mortgage-backed security pricing model), sensitivity analysis of various risk metrics (e.g., duration, convexity) is an important part of validation. A firm can benefit from a well-designed sensitivity analysis and learn a great deal about the inner workings of a model.

Benchmarking is also an important part of validation, especially when comprehensive backtesting is either infeasible or impractical. Benchmarking compares a model's outputs to data or outputs of alternative approaches. There are several ways to perform benchmark analysis. Models developed internally using alternative methods can be used for benchmarking. Firms typically utilize models that are either simpler or easier to estimate and maintain. Smaller firms sometimes use previous versions of updated models as benchmarks. However, this type of benchmarking practice is not meaningful and adds little value because the reason for the development of a newer version of model is to improve on weaknesses of the old model. Benchmarking is especially effective when the benchmark model is based on a sufficiently different methodology and targeted at known weaknesses of the champion model (e.g., simpler, but more robust). More recently, some big firms have begun experimenting with ML models for benchmarking. These models are relatively easy to develop and provide additional insight in terms of missing risk drivers and nonlinearities (also see Section 9.4.6). To the extent that a benchmark model can impact the outcome of a champion model (in the form of an overlay or model adjustment), it may make sense subjecting the benchmark model to the same validation standards as the champion model. When external or vendor models are used for benchmarking, firms should be careful about the underlying sample used to develop the model because differences in samples can cause significant differences between the results of the bank's internal models and the benchmark models. It is preferable to use out-of-sample performance to compare champion and challenger models because out-of-sample performance is a better indicator for robustness of the model.

Benchmarking can also be performed against market prices when available (e.g., mortgage-backed security) and/or against a bank's own historical experience as well as that of its peers. For example, historical benchmarking against peak losses and/or the peak to trough difference in losses during the Great Recession is often conducted to assess the adequacy of stress results.

9.4.5 *Ongoing Monitoring*

Ongoing monitoring is another core element of model risk management. The goal of a credit risk model is to recognize and capture the risk patterns observed in the past under the assumption that the patterns will continue into the future. However, over time, various factors that are not built into the model can come into play and affect the performance of the model, including new products, changes in underwriting practices, changes in the firm's strategic direction and changes in the economic and regulatory environments. Model limitations unrecognized at the time of a model's development may also become relevant over time as more data are gathered. Thus, it is important to perform ongoing monitoring to ensure the model continues to perform as expected.

Regular testing for data consistency is also suggested as part of the ongoing monitoring process because the model development data may not be representative of the population on which the model is being used. Population Stability Index (PSI) analysis and characteristics analysis of the key risk drivers are generally performed to test whether changes in the population merit concern. Although a population shift may not always cause performance issues for a model, PSI can provide some insight when a deterioration in model performance occurs.

Backtests that have been performed during the model's development are also expected to be performed during ongoing model monitoring. Many of these tests have been discussed in the previous section. Results from ongoing monitoring backtests can be compared back to those from the development sample to assess the model's stability and robustness. Furthermore, ongoing monitoring results can be gathered and compared over time to provide a trended view of model performance, which is very helpful in detecting systematic, as opposed to temporary, model performance changes. Systematic performance changes can indicate model deterioration that requires follow-up action. Additionally, specific to credit scoring models, early read analysis can be performed to help identify model deterioration with early warning. With early read analysis, rank-ordering and accuracy tests are performed in advance of the full development-defined backtesting window and are compared to the corresponding results using the same shortened window on the development sample.[22] Sensitivity analyses, other checks for robustness and stability, and benchmark analyses may likewise be repeated. Unless there is a good reason otherwise, the same

[22] For example, many credit scoring models are designed to predict the likelihood of a newly opened account going bad within the first 24 months on book. Rather than waiting to back-test model performance for 24 months after the model is implemented, the same tests can be performed at 6-, 12- or 18-months on book and compared to development sample results at the same time on book. This practice provides early warning of model deterioration and can enable a firm to take mitigation actions prior to booking a full 24 months of accounts using a flawed model.

thresholds used in validation backtesting can be used to assess ongoing monitoring results. Firms can also set threshold limits for differences between development sample and ongoing monitoring results.

In practice, many firms adopt a "traffic light" approach. The green, yellow, and red lights are given when the model performance falls within, at the border, or outside of the thresholds. When model monitoring results fall outside of the thresholds, a more in-depth analysis for the cause is called for. The modelers need to look into the issue and provide explanations of the results. Poor performance may be due to one-time exogenous events (e.g., system conversion) or data issues, and may not necessarily be caused by model issue per se. Benchmarking, in this situation, may help identify whether the results are due to model failure. If the investigation shows the model is at fault, a recalibration, revision, or redevelopment of the model may take place depending on the nature of the issues.

The granularity of the ongoing monitoring is expected to be at least the same as it was in development. For example, if a model is developed with multiple segments, the performance of each segment is ideally monitored separately. In some cases, monitoring can be conducted at an even more granular level by key risk factors. Monitoring at the aggregate level may not be sufficient because the forecasting errors of various segments may offset each other and give the modelers a false sense that the model performance is acceptable, causing the model risk to be overlooked. Thus, ongoing monitoring may include performance of major individual components as well as the overall model performance. For example, in an expected loss framework, the PD, LGD and EAD parameters are monitored separately in addition to the monitoring of the dollar losses.

The frequency of ongoing monitoring depends on the nature of the model, the availability of new data or modeling approaches, the materiality of the risk, and regulatory requirements. Besides scheduled periodic monitoring, banks may also verify and monitor models in some special circumstances where the models are susceptible to failure. For example, unexpected changes in the market and regulation may trigger additional model monitoring.

Finally, the overall model framework, including conceptual framework, assumptions and applications, requires that there be periodic comprehensive model validation regardless of the performance of the model in ongoing monitoring. Ongoing validation may also be triggered by and based on periodic model monitoring results. It is important to note that ongoing monitoring cannot replace periodic model revalidation because ongoing monitoring usually does not evaluate the model framework and assumptions.

9.4.6 *Future Challenges: Machine Learning and Validation*

The advances of machine learning (ML) technology and "Big Data" are fundamentally changing the way data is being collected, processed and utilized for various business purposes. Machine learning algorithms are the backbone of artificial intelligence (AI) which is getting increasingly smarter at being able to solve complex problems with little human intervention. The rapid spread of AI in various areas is due to the use of more efficient algorithms and hardware (Taddy 2018).[23]

Machine learning is a field that studies and develops algorithms to learn from complex data and produce reliable predictions in an automatic fashion. ML is divided into supervised ML (SML) and unsupervised ML (UML).[24] UML is typically used for clustering and dimension reduction. SML, on the other hand, is classical prediction modeling: predict y, given covariates (or features) x. Popular SML techniques and models include LASSO, LARs, classification/regression trees (CART) and their variants, variations of trees based on ensemble methods such as bagging and boosting (e.g., random forest and gradient boosting tree), artificial neural network (ANN), and support vector machine (SVM) (see Hastie et al. (2009)for more details of these techniques and models). While ML is considered as a subfield of computer science (Wikipedia), it is also closely related to statistics, and many of the popular ideas in ML (LASSO, Cross Validation, Trees, Random Forests, etc.) have been developed by statisticians. Whereas statisticians traditionally have focused on parameter estimation and inference based on probabilistic models, the goal of ML is to optimize (out-of-sample) predictive

[23] Taddy (2018) discusses the new class of general purpose machine learning based on deep neural networks (DNN), and the new technologies which make fitting of DNN models on big data sets feasible, namely, stochastic gradient descent (SGD) for parameter optimization, and GPUs and other computer hardware for massive parallel optimization. Also, see Goodfellow et al. (2016) for various deep learning techniques.

[24] The distinction depends on the existence of a target (outcome) variable (Hastie et al. 2009).

performance based on algorithmic models (Breiman 2001; Mullainathan and Spiess 2017; Taddy 2018; Athey 2017, 2018; Varian 2014).

The two key concepts in SML are regularization and calibration.[25] Regularization is any method that tames down statistical variability in high-dimensional estimation or prediction problems (Hastie et al. 2009; Efron and Hastie 2016). It reflects our prior belief that the type of functions we seek exhibit certain types of smooth behavior. ML algorithms are based on flexible functional forms and characterized by high dimensionality. This flexibility makes the ML model based on the best in-sample fit prone to overfitting and poor out-of-sample prediction performance (Hastie et al. 2009; Mullainathan and Spiess 2017). This problem is solved by regularization, for example, by imposing certain maximum tree depth. The optimal degree of regularization or model complexity is determined by calibrating (tuning) the regularization hyper-parameter(s) (e.g., depth of tree) through k-fold cross-validation.[26] While the algorithms embedded in ML require little human intervention, ML still requires many critical decisions such as function classes, regularizer, feature representation and tuning procedures. These choices should be determined based on expert domain knowledge. "Simply throwing it all in" is an unreasonable way of using ML algorithms (Mullainathan and Spiess 2017).

ML algorithms have been mostly applied in computer science, engineering, and biostatistics/informatics, such as search engines, image processing, and gene coding. More recently, however, the application of ML has been expanding rapidly to solve various business, socio-economic, as well as policy problems outside of these areas. For example, Athey (2017, 2018) discusses various applications of ML in economics, especially "policy prediction problems," and there is an emerging literature on applying ML tools to causal inference on

[25] The calibration step is also known as "(empirical) tuning" in the literature. Some literature also uses the term "validation" (Chakraborty and Joseph 2017), but "model validation" (as used in this book) is typically referred to the set of processes and activities designed to verify that models are performing as expected.

[26] K-fold cross-validation randomly splits the training sample into k equally sized subsamples. Then, for each value from a range of hyper-parameter values, fit the model on k-1 subsamples and evaluate the predictive performance on the remaining k-th subsample successively and get the average predictive performance. Finally, choose the value for the tuning parameter with the best average predictive performance.

treatment effects (see also Belloni et al. 2014; Mullainathan and Spiess 2017; Chakraborty and Joseph 2017).

Application of ML techniques to retail credit risk modeling has a relatively long history. With a large amount of account-level information available in the consumer lending business, data driven, automated algorithm-based ML models were thought to have, at least in theory, the potential to compete against statistical credit scoring models. Several ML credit scoring models have been developed and tested since the 1990s, but they have not been widely used in practice due to a lack of robustness and transparency until recently (Thomas 2009). Following the advances of more efficient algorithms and richer data sets along with the broad digital transformations currently under way across banks' risk management functions, there is a growing interest in ML more recently from business as well as regulators (IIF 2018). Several recent studies have applied machine learning classification tree models to credit card portfolios (Glennon et al. 2007; Khandani et al. 2010; Butaru et al. 2015). In an interesting recent application, Sirignano et al. (2016) applied deep neural networks to US mortgage data and built multi-period dynamic machine learning transition models. According to IIF's recent survey conducted in 2017, almost 40% of firms are already using ML in some capacity and a further 50% have either initiated some ML pilot project during 2017 or are planning to launch their first pilot within the next few months.

According to the same survey (IIF, 2018), two primary motivations for firms' pursuit of ML are (1) enhancement of risk management capacity in terms of better data analytics to help better understand the risks to which the firm is exposed, and establishment of a more efficient model development environment and (2) better support for consumer needs on a "real time" basis. The most prevalent area of application is in model development, especially in credit scoring and decisions. While the interest in ML in credit risk modeling has been rising rapidly in recent years, most firms seem to be adopting ML in a cautious manner. In most cases, ML techniques are being used in a complementary fashion to improve the existing production models rather than to replace them. Popular usages of ML techniques in retail credit risk model development process mentioned include data cleaning (e.g., missing data imputation, outlier detection), segmentation, and feature (variable) selection and engineering. ML is also used to develop challenger models for benchmarking purposes because it is thought that challenger models are more experimental in nature and do not require the same degree of transparency and maturity.

The cautious approach many firms are taking reflects some of the inherent limitations ML has. While ML offers many potential benefits, it presents several challenges as well. First of all, many of the sophisticated ML models are highly opaque in nature and difficult to interpret. ML adopts a flexible and complex model structure so that the model does a good job of predicting in a new test data set. The goal of the ML model is to predict, not to estimate structural parameters. While interpretability is not an explicit goal of ML modeling, it is nevertheless an important part of ML application in practice. Why should a business line sponsor – or senior management believe – the prediction coming out of the black box? This is especially relevant because uncertainty of predictions from many complex ML models are not well understood.[27] While there are several visualization tools such as partial dependency plots and variable importance plots (see Hastie et al. 2009) that provide some insights into the input-output relationship (also see Chakraborty and Joseph, 2017),[28] they have limitations and do not provide a comprehensive picture. While model complexity can be tamped down in exchange for a gain in transparency, more transparent models can be misleading and one may question whether this strategy defeats the purpose of using ML to begin with (Athey 2018).[29]

Stability and robustness of ML models is another concern. Although one of the attractive features of an ML approach is the efficiency and relative ease of model development, frequent refreshing of the model could be costly and counterproductive. ML based credit risk models are cross-sectional in nature in the sense that a typical data set includes a

[27] There is a growing interest in uncertainty quantification in ML. See, Efron and Hastie (2016) for confidence intervals for bagging and random forest predictors. For the application of variational inference (VI) to deep learning, see Goodfellow et al. (2016).

[28] For interpretation of DNN, Sirignano et al. (2016), proposes two measures: neural network's sensitivity of covariates, which is the derivative of neural network's output with respect to each covariate averaged over the sample, and marginal contribution to (negative) log-likelihood.

[29] Another concern banks have to overcome related to lack of transparency is that if ML models are used in lending, the model results should be mapped to reasonable adverse action codes which tell consumers why they were declined, which can be difficult with ML models.

large cross section of accounts with a short time dimension. The data may be too short to calibrate complex temporal structures, especially for a model designed to be used over a relatively long forecasting horizon.[30]

Finally, there is a question about suitability of the existing model risk management framework for ML models. While there seem to be diverging experiences and views on this, the most critical aspect of model risk management is proper training and procurement of the skills required to keep up with these new techniques. Development of an ML model involves many critical decision choices including proper domain structure, function classes, feature representations, regularization and tuning. These choices require staff with appropriate knowledge and experience.[31]

9.5 Conclusions

Consumer debt is an important part of a household's financial management. The size and composition of household consumer debt has significant implications for macroeconomic performance and financial stability as well. Accurate and reliable credit risk models have become more and more critical to maintaining successful and profitable retail lending operations. Relying on poorly specified models results in lost revenue, and eventually may threaten the healthiness of financial institutions as we witnessed during the Great Recession.

Financial institutions offering consumer loans rely on models not only to decide to whom to make these loans, but also how to price loan products, manage existing accounts, and maintain adequate reserve and capital against future losses. Given the importance of a models' accuracy and performance, sound model validation is an important issue to financial institutions as well as to regulators. The mortgage crisis in the USA and the heightened regulatory expectations environment following the crisis provided an important impetus for a significant change in the way validation functions are organized and performed.

[30] A good example of ML model failure is the "Google Flu Trends" experiment (Efron and Hastie 2016).

[31] FSB (2017) discusses the possibility of increasing dependencies on a small number of technologically advanced third-party vendors. The study also discusses various micro, macro, and systemic issues related to the increasing use of ML and the impacts on various stakeholders.

Meanwhile, the advances of big data and more efficient ML algorithms are fundamentally changing the way data is being collected, processed and analyzed for various business purposes including consumer lending. The growing interest in ML technologies presents several validation challenges to firms as well as regulators.

References

Ai, Chunrong and Norton, Edward C. (2003). Interaction terms in logit and probit models. *Economic Letters*, 80, 123–129.

Athey, Susan. (2017). Beyond prediction: Using big data for policy problems. *Science*, 355, 483–485.

(2018). The Impact of Machine Learning on Economics. *The economics of artificial intelligence: An agenda,* 507–547. University of Chicago Press.

Anderson, J. R., Cain, J. R., and Gelber R. D. (1983). Analysis of survival by tumor response. *Journal of Clinical Oncology*, November, 1(11), 710–719.

Basel Committee on Banking Supervision, 2005, Studies on the Validation of Internal Rating Systems, Working Paper No. 14, May.

2004, International Convergence of Capital Measurement and Capital Standards, A Revised Framework, June.

Begg, Colin and Gray, Robert. (1984). Calculation of polychotomous logistic regression parameters using individualized *regressions*. 71(1), 11–18.

Belloni, Alexander, Chernozhukov, Victor and Hansen, Christian. (2014). High dimensional methods and inference on structural and treatment effects. *Journal of Economic Perspectives*, 28(2), 1–23.

Board of Governors of the Federal Reserve System. (2015), Federal Reserve Guidance on Supervisory Assessment of Capital Planning and Positions for LISCC Firms and Large and Complex Firms (SR-15–18), December.

(2015). Federal Reserve Guidance on Supervisory Assessment of Capital Planning and Positions for Large and Noncomplex Firms (SR-15–19), December.

(2013). Capital Planning at Large Bank Holding Companies: Supervisory Expectations and Range of Current Practice, August.

Board of Governors of the Federal Reserve System and Office of the Comptroller of the Currency, 2011, Supervisory Guidance on Model Risk Management, April 4.

Breeden, Joseph L. (2010). *Reinventing Retail Lending Analytics.* Risk Books.

Breiman, Leo. (2001). Statistical modeling: The two cultures. *Statistical Science*, 16(3), 199–215.

Breiman, Leo, Friedman, Jerome, Stone, Charles J. and Olshen, R. A. (1984). *Classification and Regression Trees*. Taylor & Francis.

Buchak, Greg, Matvos, Gregor, Piskorski, Tomasz, and Seru, Amit. (2018). Fintech, regulatory arbitrage, and the rise of shadow banks. *Journal of Financial Economics*, 130(3), 453–483.

Cameron, Colin A. and Trivedi, Pravin K. (2005). *Microeconometrics: Methods and Applications*. Cambridge University Press.

Castle, Jennifer, Doornik, Jurgen and Hendry, David. (2011a). Evaluating automatic model selection. *Journal of Time Series Econometrics*, 3(1), 1941–1928.

Castle, Jennifer, Qin, X. and Reed, Robert. (2009). How to Pick the Best Regression Equation: A Review and Comparison of Model Selection Algorithms, WP. 13/2009, Dept. of Economics, University of Canterbury.

(2011b). Using Model Selection Algorithms to Obtain Reliable Coefficient Estimates, WP. 03/2011, Dept of Economics, University of Canterbury.

Committee on the Global Financial System, BIS, and the Financial Stability Board, 2017, FinTech Credit, Market Structure, Business Models and Financial Stability Implications, May 2017.

Cox, David. (1972). Regression models and life-tables. *Journal of the Royal Statistical Society, Series B*, 34(2), 187–220.

Deng, Yongheng, Quigley, John and Van Order, Robert. (2000). Mortgage terminations, heterogeneity, and the exercise of mortgage options. *Econometrica*, 68(2), 275–307.

Efron, Bradley and Hastie, Trevor. (2016). *Computer Age Statistical Inference, Algorithms, Evidence, and Data Science*. Cambridge University Press.

Elliott, G. and Timmermann, A. (2016). *Economic Forecasting*. Princeton University Press.

Financial Stability Board (2017). Artificial Intelligence and Machine Learning in Financial Services: Market Developments and Financial Stability Implications, November 2017.

Glennon, Dennis, Kiefer, Nicholas M., Larson, C. Erik and Choi, Hwan-Sik. (2007). Development and Validation of Credit-Scoring Models, Working Papers 07-12, Cornell University, Center for Analytic Economics.

Han, Aaron and Hausman, Jerry. (1990). Flexible parametric estimation of duration and competing risk models. *Journal of Econometrics*, 5(1), 1–28.

Hastie, Trevor, Tibshirani, Robert and Friedman, Jerome. (2009). *The Elements of Statistical Learning, Data Mining, Inference, and Prediction*, 2nd edition. Springer.

Institute of International Finance (2018). Machine Learning in Credit Risk: Detailed Survey Report, March.

International Monetary Fund (2017). Household Debt and Financial Stability, Chapter 2 of Global Financial Stability Report October 2017: Is Growth at Risk?

(2012). Dealing With Household Debt, Chapter 3 of World Economic Outlook.

Jorda, O., Schularick, M. and Taylor, A. (2016). The great mortgaging: Housing finance, crises and business cycles. *Economic Policy*, 31(85), 107–52.

Lewis, E. M. (1992). *An Introduction to Credit Scoring*. Athena Press.

Li, Phillip, Qi, Min, Zhang Xiaofei and Zhao, Xinlei. (2016). Further investigation of parametric loss given default modeling. *Journal of Credit Risk*, 12(4), 17–47.

Liang, Kung-Yee and Zeger, Scott L. (1986). Longitudinal data analysis using generalized linear models. *Biometrika*, 73(1), (April), 13–22.

McFadden, Daniel. (1981). Econometric models of probability choice, in *Structural Analysis of Discrete Data with Economic Applications*. ed. C. F. Manski and D. McFadden. Cambridge, MA: MIT Press, 198–272.

Mian, Atif, and Amir Sufi. (2014). *House of Debt*. Chicago: University of Chicago Press.

Mian, A., Sufi A. and Verner, E. (2017). Household debt and business cycles worldwide. *Quarterly Journal of Economics*, 132(4), 1755–1817.

Mincer, J. A. and Zarnowitz, V. (1969). The evaluation of economic forecasts. In *Economic Forecasts and Expectations: Analysis of Forecasting Behavior and Performance*, 1–46. NBER.

Mullainathan, Sendhil and Spiess, Jann. (2017). Machine learning: An applied econometric approach. *Journal of Economic Perspectives*, 31(2), 87–106.

Ng, Serena. (2013). Variable selection predictive regressions. *Handbook of Forecasting*, Vol2B, 753–786.

Papke, Leslie E. and Wooldridge, Jeffrey M. (1996). Econometric methods for fractional response variables with an application to 401(k) plan. *Journal of Applied Econometrics*, 11, 619–632.

Philippon, Thomas. (2015). Has the US finance industry become less efficient? *American Economic Review*, 105(4), 1408–38.

Qi, Min, and Zhao, Xinlei. (2011). Comparison of modeling methods for loss given default. *Journal of Banking & Finance*, 35(11), 2842–2855.

Rajan, Uday, Seru, Amit and Vig, Vikrant. (2015). The failure of models that predict failure: Distance, incentives, and defaults. *Journal of Financial Economics*, 115(2015), 237–260.

Scott, Steven and Varian, Hal. (2015). Bayesian variable selection for nowcasting economic time series. In Avi Goldfarb, Shane Greenstein, and

Catherine Tucker, editors, *Economic Analysis of the Digital Economy*: University of Chicago Press.

Shumway, Tyler. (1999). Forecasting bankruptcy more accurately: A simple hazard model. *Journal of Business*, January 2001, 101–124.

Sirignano, Justin A., Sadhwani, Apaar and Giesecke, Kay. (2016). Deep Learning for Mortgage Risk *arXiv preprint arXiv:1607.02470*.

Taddy, Matt. (2019). The technological elements of artificial intelligence. In Ajay K. Agarwal, Joshua Gans, and Avi Goldfarb, editors, *The Economics of Artificial Intelligence: An Agenda*. University of Chicago Press.

Thomas, Lyn C. (2009). *Consumer Credit Models: Pricing, Profit, and Portfolios*. Oxford University Press.

(2000). A survey of credit and behavioral scoring: Forecasting financial risk of lending to consumers. *International Journal of Forecasting*, 16, 149–172.

van Houwelingen, Hans C. (2007). Dynamic prediction by landmarking in event history analysis. *Scandinavian Journal of Statistics*, 70–85, 2007.

Varian, Hal. (2014). Big data: New tricks for econometrics. *Journal of Economic Perspectives*, 28(2), 3–28.

Wikipedia, https://en.m.wikipedia.org/wiki/Machine_learning.

Wooldridge, Jeffrey. (2010). *Econometrics of Cross Section and Panel Data*, 2nd edition. MIT Press.

Zabai, Anna. (2017). Household debt: Recent developments and challenges. *BIS Quarterly Review*, December, 39–54.

10 Issues in the Validation of Wholesale Credit Risk Models

JONATHAN JONES AND DEBASHISH SARKAR*

10.1 Introduction

In this chapter, we examine wholesale credit risk models and their validation at US banking institutions (including both bank holding companies (BHCs) and national banks). Banking institutions use these credit risk models for decision making in the areas of credit approval, portfolio management, capital management, pricing, loan loss estimation, and loan loss provisioning for wholesale loan portfolios. While differing methodological approaches have been used in the past, the most common practice in wholesale credit risk modeling for loss estimation among large US banking institutions today is to use expected loss models, typically at the loan level. Given this, our focus here will be on these models and the quantification of the three key risk parameters in this modeling approach, namely, probability of default (PD), loss given default (LGD), and exposure at default (EAD).

We address model validation issues for wholesale credit risk models in the context of different regulatory requirements and supervisory expectations. More specifically, we look at validation practices for the advanced internal ratings-based (AIRB) approach of the Basel II and Basel III framework for regulatory capital and for the stress testing framework of the Comprehensive Capital Analysis and Review (CCAR) and Dodd–Frank Act Stress Test (DFAST) for assessing enterprise-wide capital adequacy. Given that the largest banking institutions use their obligor and facility internal risk ratings in PD and LGD quantification for Basel and also for quantification of stressed PD and LGD for CCAR and DFAST, we also address issues that arise in

* The views expressed in this chapter are those of the authors alone and do not establish supervisory policy, requirements or expectations. They also do not represent those of the Comptroller of the Currency, Federal Reserve Bank of New York or the Federal Reserve System.

the validation of internal ratings systems used by banking institutions for grading wholesale loans.

According to the first validation principle put forth by the Basel Committee on Banking Supervision (BCBS) (2005), "Validation is fundamentally about assessing the predictive ability of a bank's risk estimates and the use of ratings in the credit process." Broadly speaking, model validation covers all processes, both qualitative and quantitative, that provide an evidence-based assessment of a model's fitness for purpose (see, e.g., BCBS (2009)). As noted by Scandizzo (2016), the basic objective of model validation is to manage and, if possible, to minimize model risk. Model risk can arise due to the failure of a model in the areas of design, implementation, data, processes, and use – see, e.g., Quell and Meyer (2013). Therefore, it is important to have a robust model validation framework that addresses each of these areas for the quantification of PD, LGD, and EAD.

The detail and scope of a wholesale credit risk model validation depends on the use, complexity, and associated risks of the model being reviewed. A more complex model generally requires a larger scope for the validation to test the interdependencies of different parameters or validity of assumptions under stress situations. Similarly, a greater reliance on the model by an institution, either through strategic planning or use in financial statements, should require a large scope for the validation, because of the potential risks involved in relying on the models. Accordingly, as mentioned in the preceding paragraph, a complete model validation would address each of the following areas: (1) purpose and use; (2) data; (3) assumptions and methodological approach; (4) model performance including stability and sensitivity analysis; and (5) outcomes analysis including backtesting and benchmarking.

In contrast to retail credit risk models and their validation, wholesale credit risk models pose unique validation challenges for several reasons. First, there are far fewer default events. Wholesale portfolios typically have fewer loss events, which presents challenges for risk quantification and validation. Given this limitation, a straightforward calculation based on historical losses for a given wholesale rating would not be sufficiently reliable to form the basis of a PD estimate, let alone an estimate of LGD or EAD. Second, there is greater heterogeneity and fewer observations in the data, which poses modeling challenges for portfolios with fewer default observations. For retail models, in contrast, there is a huge amount of highly granular and standardized data available. And third, there are significant data challenges stemming from merger and acquisitions in the banking industry. These challenges arise due to different internal obligor and facility rating methodologies or business practices that produce inconsistent default definitions.[1]

This chapter is organized as follows. Section 2 presents background material on the types of wholesale loan exposures for US banking institutions. In addition, this section also describes the recent range of practice in wholesale credit risk modeling with a focus on forecasting losses on loans held in the accrual portfolio and Fair Value Option loans, for which fair value accounting practices are applied. Section 3 presents an overview of the key components of an effective model validation framework. Finally, Section 4 offers a summary and concludes.

10.2 Wholesale Credit Risk Models

10.2.1 Wholesale Lending

Wholesale lending consists of two major types of loans: corporate loans and commercial real estate (CRE) loans. Corporate loans consist of a number of different categories of loans, although the largest group of these loans are Commercial & Industrial (C&I) loans. Commercial & Industrial loans are generally defined as loans to corporate or commercial borrowers with more than $1 million in committed balances that are "graded" using a banking institution's corporate loan rating process. Small business loans with less than $1 million in committed balances are typically "scored" like retail loans and are modeled separately. There are two categories of CRE loans: permanent or income-producing (IPCRE) loans and construction and land development (C&LDCRE) loans. The IPCRE loans are collateralized by the income produced by domestic or international non-owner occupied multifamily or nonfarm, nonresidential properties. For C&LDCRE loans, outstanding balances and default risk increase over the life of the loan as the property moves through various stages of construction.

[1] See, e.g., Yang and Chen (2013) for further discussion of the data challenges in the development of wholesale credit risk models with specific regard to Commercial & Industrial (C&I) modeling.

As of Q2 2017, all national banks in the United States had $1,347.6 billion in C&I loans and $1,293.8 billion in CRE loans and unfunded commitments.[2]

10.2.2 Internal Risk Rating Systems

A typical dual internal risk rating system used by banks for wholesale lending assigns both an obligor risk rating (ORR) to each borrower (or group of borrowers), and a facility risk rating (FRR) to each available facility. These ratings are used to indicate the risk of loss in a credit facility. If internal risk ratings are accurately and consistently applied, they can provide a common understanding of risk levels and allow for active portfolio management. In the dual risk rating system, the ORR represents the probability of default by a borrower in repaying its obligation in the normal course of business, whereas the FRR represents the expected loss of principal and/or interest on any business credit facility. (See Crouhy, Galai, and Mark (2001) for more details.)

Risk ratings have evolved substantially under the Basel framework, which required a relative measure of credit risk and emphasized a long-run average view of credit risk. Almost all banking institutions use the output of their business-as-usual (BAU) internal risk rating tools primarily with regard to the ORR as an input into their stress testing models for CCAR and DFAST purposes. There are three areas of concern when the internal ORR risk ratings are used for stress testing: (1) consistency of ratings across scorecards; (2) continuity of ratings over time; and (3) responsiveness of ratings to the credit cycle.

In general, issues that typically arise in the validation of internal risk ratings include:

- Discriminatory power of rating tools
- Responsiveness of ratings migrations to the business cycle
- Consistency of ratings across models and scorecards
- Stability of all components of the rating process over time, and
- Effectiveness of processes and controls around the rating assignment.

[2] These exposure amounts are taken from *Commercial Credit MIS*, Second Quarter 2017, August 31, 2017, Office of the Comptroller of the Currency.

For the purposes of PD estimation, there is an important difference between PDs used in the AIRB approach versus those used for CCAR and DFAST. For AIRB, PD is an empirically derived unconditional estimate of credit quality based on realized default rates with a horizon of one year. Unconditional PD under a point-in-time (PIT) internal obligor ratings philosophy is an estimate of default probabilities over a year, whereas under a through-the-cycle (TTC) internal obligor ratings philosophy, the unconditional PD is an estimate of the long-run average of default probabilities over a mix of economic conditions that spans a full business cycle.

In contrast, the stressed PDs used for CCAR/DFAST are PDs conditional on a given specific set of macroeconomic conditions for the adverse and severely adverse stress scenarios. Internal borrower ratings play an important role as predictor variables in the stressed PD and migration models.

10.2.3 Wholesale Loss Modeling Overview

In this section, we present an overview of the modeling framework used to estimate expected losses for loans held in the accrual wholesale loan portfolio and losses for Fair Value Option (FVO) wholesale loans. Loans held in the accrual portfolio are those measured under accrual accounting rather than fair-value accounting. Fair Value Option (FVO) loans are loans to which the bank has elected to apply fair-value accounting practices. FVO loans and commitments are held for sale (HFS) or held for investment (HFI), and they are driven by fair value accounting. Losses on fair value loans and commitments reflect both expected changes in fair value of the loan, and any losses that may result from an obligor default under a given scenario.

The quantitative models for measuring credit risk have evolved in response to a number of macroeconomic, financial, and regulatory factors (See, e.g., Altman and Saunders (1998), Alam and Carling (2010), and Carhill and Jones (2013)). First, in order to comply with the regulatory capital requirements of Basel II for the Advanced Internal Ratings Based Approach, the largest US banks developed models for producing estimates of PD, LGD, and EAD that could be plugged into the supervisory formula to compute the Pillar 1 minimum capital requirement for credit risk. With respect to PD estimation, average PDs estimated by banks' internal models were mapped through a supervisory formula in order to obtain conditional PDs required within the Asymptotic Single Risk Factor (ASRF) framework of Basel II and Basel III for credit risk.

Second, the financial crisis and Global Recession of 2007–09 motivated banks to develop quantitative models for credit risk that could be used for stress testing and which incorporated macroeconomic risk drivers. The enterprise-wide stress tests associated with CCAR/DFAST are a regulatory requirement that has had an important impact on the development of credit risk models. Finally, as noted by Scandizzo (2016), the refinement of credit scoring systems, the incorporation of more accurate measures of credit risk derivative valuation, and the increasing focus on measuring risk at the portfolio level have also had an impact on the development of credit risk models.

10.2.3.1 Accrual Loans

For purposes of our discussion here, we focus on the expected loss approach used by banks in CCAR and DFAST to forecast losses on wholesale loans over a stress horizon. For the accrual wholesale loan portfolio, the expected loss (EL) on a given loan at time *t* is given by the product of the probability of default (PD), loss given default (LGD), and exposure at default (EAD) at time *t*, that is,

$$\mathrm{EL_t} = \mathrm{PD_t} \times \mathrm{LGD_t} \times \mathrm{EAD_t}.$$

With this approach, overall losses are disaggregated into the three key credit loss components. This disaggregation is important, since the behavior of PD, LGD, and EAD may differ under stressed economic conditions.

The first component, PD, measures how likely an obligor is to default and is an empirically derived estimate of credit quality. The quantification of PD requires a reference data set that includes obligors that defaulted. PD is generally modeled as part of a transition process in which loans move from one grade to another, where default is a terminal transition and PD represents the probability that an obligor will default during a given time period. PD is typically estimated at the segment level or at an individual borrower level.

Some commonly used approaches for PD estimation include: econometric models where PDs are conditioned on the macroeconomic environment and portfolio or loan characteristics; and rating transition models which are used to estimate stressed default rates. With the rating transition approach, the PD component is based on a stressed rating transition matrix for each quarter. The rating transition-based approaches use credit ratings applied to individual loans and they project how these ratings would change over time for a given stressed economic scenario. In linking the rating transitions to scenario conditions, this approach usually involves the following steps:

- Converting the rating transition matrix into a single summary measure;
- Estimating a time-series regression model that links the summary measure to scenario variables;
- Projecting the summary measure over the stress planning horizon using the parameter estimates from the time-series regression model, and;
- Converting the projected summary measure into a full set of quarterly transition matrices (See, e.g., Belkin, Suchower, and Forest (1998a, 1998b), Loffler and Posch (2007), and de Bandt, Dumontaux, Martin, and Medee (2013) for more details on the Z-score, or the M-factor approach, which is a one-parameter representation of credit risk and transition matrices).

The second component, LGD, measures the magnitude of the likely losses in the event of default. LGD is generally considered to be a conditional estimate of the average economic loss rate for obligors that default over a specified horizon and is computed as follows:

$$\text{LGD} = 1 - (\text{Recovery Value}/\text{EAD}),$$

where recovery value accounts for both positive and negative cash flows after default, including workout costs, accrued but unpaid interest and fees, losses on the sale of collateral, etc. These cash flows should reflect an appropriate discount rate. Factors that may affect LGD include timing in the economic cycle, the priority of claim, geography, industry, vintage, loan to value ratio, and covenants. The quantification of LGD requires a reference data set that includes obligors that defaulted, where a recovery amount can be determined. The reference data set may allow LGD to be calculated at the segment level or at the individual loan facility level, or LGD rates may be paired with facility level risk ratings. Some commonly used approaches for LGD estimation include using a long-run base scenario average, long-run average stressed scenarios, regression-based approach, and the Frye–Jacobs (2012) approach, which expresses LGD as a function of PD.

The third component, EAD, measures what the exposure amount likely will be if an obligor defaults. EAD typically represents a bank's expected gross dollar exposure of a facility upon default, recognizes that an obligor has an incentive to draw down all available in order to avoid insolvency as they approach default, and considers a bank's motivation and policy related to limiting exposure when it becomes aware of the increased credit risk of the obligor.

In the case of fixed exposures, such as term loans, EAD is equal to the amount outstanding. In contrast, for revolving exposures like lines of credit, EAD can be divided into drawn and undrawn commitments where typically the drawn commitment is known whereas the undrawn commitment needs to be estimated to produce a value for EAD. Two terms commonly used to express the percentage of the undrawn commitment that will be drawn and outstanding at the time of default are the Credit Conversion Factor (CCF) and the Loan Equivalent Factor (LEQ).

Quantification of EAD for loss modeling is typically focused on determining an appropriate LEQ or CCF. In the case of LEQ, EAD would be expressed as follows:

$$\text{EAD} = \text{Outstanding\$} + \text{LEQ} * (\text{Commitment\$} - \text{Outstanding\$}).$$

Common approaches for quantifying EAD are based on regressions or on averages under base and stressed scenarios.

10.2.3.2 FVO Loans

Unlike loans held in accrual portfolios, where losses are generally due to an obligor's failure to pay on its loan obligation (i.e., default risk), losses on fair value loans and commitments should reflect both expected changes in fair value of the loan, and any losses that may result from an obligor default under a given scenario. Changes in mark-to-market (MTM) value include changes in the economic and market environment. This could result from changes in macroeconomic factors such as interest rates, credit spreads, foreign exchange rates or any other factors that may capture idiosyncratic risks of a banking institution's portfolio. In addition, the market's perception of changes in an obligor's credit quality that is evidenced in obligor spread widening can affect the MTM value.

The loss estimation framework assumes that the value of assets depends on credit states that evolve by some process, which can be captured by some distribution function or a discrete state transition matrix. See Section 10.2.6 for details.

10.2.3.3 Other Wholesale Loss Modeling Approaches

In addition to the expected loss model approach discussed above, banks have used top-down charge-off models.

Charge-off models are top-down models used by banks to forecast net charge-off (NCO) rates by wholesale loan type as a function of macroeconomic variables. These models typically include lagged NCO rates, or autoregressive terms, as explanatory variables. There are several concerns with using NCO models, especially as primary or champion models for CCAR/DFAST:

- Charge-offs capture both PD and LGD components
- Variation in sensitivities to macroeconomic risk drivers across important portfolio segments is not captured
- Changes in portfolio risk characteristics are not accounted for over time, and
- Inclusion of lagged NCO rates as explanatory variables can dampen the impact of shocks to macroeconomic risk drivers and may cause a delayed response of the NCO rate to macroeconomic shocks (See, e.g., Carhill and Jones (2013) for further discussion of the problems associated with using autoregressive terms in stress-testing regression models).

10.2.4 C&I Loss Forecasting Models for Stress Tests

In this section, we describe various estimation approaches employed by banks to produce stressed PD, LGD, and EAD estimates that are used to generate expected loss forecasts for the accrual C&I portfolio. Since the first CCAR in 2011, there has been a proliferation of C&I loss forecasting approaches. As supervisory guidance has evolved, a larger variety and more granular loss forecasting models have been developed in order to achieve better model performance.

10.2.4.1 Stressed PD Modeling Approaches

Financial-Ratios Based Models: In this approach, borrowers' financial ratios such as the leverage ratio, loan to value, etc. are linked or sensitized to macroeconomic risk drivers. Financial factors are then adjusted based on the economic environment in the appropriate risk rating scorecard. This results in a new obligor risk rating that is linked to macroeconomic variables and which in turn yields a new PD. This approach is a bottom-up, granular approach that effectively uses a bank's risk management infrastructure. A potential weakness of this approach is that loan-level financial ratios may not always be available for all borrowers and rating grades may not be sensitive enough to financial ratios for stress testing purposes

Ratings-Migration Based Models: In this approach, the ratings transition matrix (TM) is conditioned on a systematic macroeconomic risk driver where the TM for each period is constructed relative to a through-the-cycle, or long-run average, historical TM (See, e.g., Belkin, Suchower, and Forest (1998) and Loffler and Posch (2007) for a discussion of the Z-factor approach, which uses a single systematic risk factor to shift transition matrices. There are also multi-systematic risk factor models that can be used in implementing the Z-factor approach (see, e.g., Wei (2003)). With the Transition Matrix Model (TMM) approach based on the Z-credit cycle factor, or alternatively called an M-factor by some banks, historical matrices are constructed using obligor-level rating migration data and then an average matrix is calculated. Each historical matrix can then be compared to the average, through-the-cycle matrix. The Z-factor can be derived that best fits the shift in transitions in a given historical matrix relative to the through-the-cycle average matrix. The derived Z-factor is used to shift the transitions of the average matrix to estimate the historical quarterly matrix.

The one-parameter representation of credit risk and transition matrices developed by Belkin, Suchower, and Forest (1998a, 1998b) is based on the Vasicek Asymptotic Single Risk Factor (ASRF) model. This model is the classic credit risk measurement framework used by CreditMetrics since 1997, and it also serves as the foundation for the Basel II Pillar 1 minimum regulatory capital requirement for AIRB banking institutions.

The model framework is:

$$X_{it} = Z_t\sqrt{\rho} + \varepsilon_{it}\sqrt{(1-\rho)},$$

where

X_{it} = normalized asset return of obligor i at time t,
Z_t = systematic risk factor at time t,

ε_{it} = idiosyncratic component unique to obligor i at time t,
$\sqrt{\rho}$ = sensitivity of the asset return of the obligor to the systematic risk factor, where ρ is the correlation among the obligors, and
Z and ε are mutually independent unit normal random variables.

In this model, the normalized asset return X_{it} is decomposed into two parts: a (scaled) idiosyncratic component ε_{it}, unique to an obligor, and a (scaled) systematic component Z_t, shared by all borrowers. The model assumes that uncertainty about the performance of obligor i is driven by the normalized asset return of obligor i at time t. When X_{it} breaches certain thresholds, the obligor's risk rating will migrate. The asset return is modeled as a function of the overall state of the economy and something that reflects idiosyncratic risk which is independent of the state of the economy. The overall state of the economy is denoted by Z, the systematic risk factor. Z_t measures how much the transition matrix in a given quarter deviates from the long-run average transition matrix. The idiosyncratic shocks that affect the asset return are denoted by ε_{it} and are independent from the systematic risk factor and which can be diversified away. At the end, the transition probabilities are expressed as analytical functions of Z_t, ρ and rating threshold boundaries. The rating threshold boundaries are typically estimated from the average transition matrix.

The Z_t and ρ values can be obtained using either Maximum Likelihood Estimation (MLE) or Weighted Least Squares (WLS) based on the entire transition matrix or on the default column. The Z values are then regressed on selected macroeconomic variables and the fitted Z values can be used to construct macro-conditional transition matrices.

There are several important underlying assumptions of the ASRF Model that are seldom met or even explicitly tested. These assumptions include: internal credit ratings follow a discrete, time-homogeneous, finite state space Markov chain; borrower credit migrations are statistically independent; the average (long-run) transition matrix is stable; rating transition matrices vary around the average transition matrix governed by a single exogenous systematic risk factor (Z factor); borrowers are risk homogeneous within a rating grade; unconditional rating thresholds do not change over time and conditional rating thresholds do not change during periods of stress; and borrower quality rating standards do not change over time.

In addition, the Z-factor regressions typically show a lack of sensitivity to macroeconomic risk factors. As a result, some banks need to make in-model adjustments to the coefficient estimates on the macroeconomic risk factors to increase sensitivity and to avoid under-estimation of losses. The use of the TMM approach based on the Z credit-cycle factor assumes that an internal risk rating system produces obligor risk ratings that properly rank-order credit risk and that credit rating migrations reflect changes in economic conditions. However, it is important to note that ratings transitions can be noisy and that management considerations can obscure a pure economic impact.

Regression-Based Models: In this approach, regressions are used to estimate transition probabilities conditioned on macroeconomic risk drivers.

There are two basic regression approaches used by banks, including multinomial and ordered logistic regression. For the purpose of illustration, we describe the multinomial approach. In implementing the multinomial regression-based approach, some banks have collapsed ratings transitions into three categories:

- Upgrades: obligors migrating to a better risk rating next period
- Downgrades: obligors migrating to a worse risk rating next period
- Defaults: obligors migrating to default (as defined by the firm) next period.

A loan's transition through various obligor rating states (including default or withdrawn) over time is modeled using a competing-risk framework. This allows the independent variables, or covariates, to change over time, which enables the probability of transition to be based on the specific values observed during that time period (or lagged periods). Multinomial logistic regression is used to predict the likelihood that a rating action occurred, and conditional transition matrices provide the probability of transitioning to particular ratings, given that a rating action occurred. Loan-level borrower and loan characteristics along with selected macroeconomic variables are used as inputs to the conditional PD model, and conditional transition matrices are generated based on historical rating transitions in the modeling dataset.

A multinomial logistic model with K possible end states is estimated by K-1 binomial logistic models, with one transition chosen as a reference, typically the state where the loan stays in the same rating by the end of the quarter. For a given risk rating group g, the K-1 outcomes regressed independently against the Kth outcome can be written as follows (we suppress group identification here for notational simplicity):

$$ln \frac{\Pr(Y_i = 1)}{\Pr(Y_i = K)} = \beta_1 \,.\, X_i$$

$$ln \frac{\Pr(Y_i = 2)}{\Pr(Y_i = K)} = \beta_2 \,.\, X_i$$

o ......

$$ln \frac{\Pr(Y_i = K-1)}{\Pr(Y_i = K)} = \beta_{K-1} \,.\, X_i,$$

where

Y_i = response variable, which has one of K possible outcomes, for observation *i*,
X_i = vector of covariates for observation i. The covariates include explanatory variables such as macroeconomic variables, previous upgrade, previous downgrade, and loan and borrower characteristics, and
β_k = vector of coefficients corresponding to covariate vector X on the probability of choosing outcome *k* over the last outcome.

Since the sum of the *K* probabilities must equal one, each of the *K* probabilities, $\Pr(Y_i = k)$, is explicitly expressed as ratios of exponential functions. The coefficients β_k can be estimated using maximum likelihood estimation. PROC LOGISTIC in SAS, or the mlogit command in Stata, can be used to implement multinomial logistic regression.

Often banking institutions do not have enough data to model individual rating-to-rating transitions and one practice has been to model similar rating transitions as a group (e.g., one or two notch downgrades for investment grade rating, one or two notch downgrades for non-investment grade rating, greater than two notch downgrades, one or two notch upgrades for non-investment grades, and default).

10.2.4.2 Stressed LGD Modeling Approaches

Stressed LGD should adequately reflect the impact of scenario conditions using relevant risk drivers with sufficient segmentation. Internal risk drivers may vary across geography, product, lending categories, and underwriting characteristics such as seniority and collateral. Empirically, it is difficult to uncover and establish a credible relationship between LGD and macroeconomic risk factors. Importantly, the use of a downturn LGD, which is a through-the-cycle estimate, is not sensitive to point-in-time changes in scenario conditions.

Possible predictor variables used in LGD models include seniority, collateral, facility type, time to resolution, loan size, and industry and regional credit cycles. The default process influences the design of LGD models. The LGD probability distribution function, which is bimodal with point masses at 0% and 100% and a diffuse distribution between those extremes, poses econometric challenges. In addition, academic research shows that PD and LGD are positively correlated due to the credit cycle. The treatment of incomplete workouts is a thorny issue in LGD modeling. Some banking institutions have unresolved defaults reaching 30%–50% of the total number of defaults which raises concerns about sample selection bias if these loans are excluded in modeling LGD.

Look-up Tables: In this approach, a look-up table of LGD values is used.

Parametric Regression Models: In this approach, LGD is regressed on macroeconomic risk drivers such as unemployment rate and a variety of internal risk drivers such as percentage collateralized, product indicator variable, region indicator variable, industry indicator variable, internal facility rating, etc. The predicted value (i.e., the conditional mean) from the regression is used as the LGD estimate.

Multi-Stage Regression Models: In this approach, a final LGD estimate is the outcome of a two-stage or three-stage regression. For example, a first-stage regression could involve estimating a time-to-resolution for the defaulted loan and then using the predicted time-to-resolution as an explanatory variable in a second-stage final LGD regression model. Another example of a two-stage logit regression model would involve a first stage in which the probability of a write-off $\propto$ is determined. In the second stage, LGD given a write-off is regressed on macroeconomic factors and facility characteristics using a fractional logit model, and LGD given no write-off is regressed on facility characteristics using a fractional logit model. In this two-stage model, LGD would be given as: $LGD = \propto * LGD_{write-off} + (1 - \propto) * LGD_{no\ write-off}$.

Tobit Models: In this approach, model inputs determine the mean and standard deviation of a latent normal distribution. Calibration of these models requires large amounts of data.

Zero-One Inflated Beta Models: In this approach, model inputs determine 0 and 1 probabilities and parameters of the beta distribution. Calibration of these models requires large amounts of data and is more complex than the Tobit model.

Fractional Response Models: These regression models are used when the dependent variable is in the range of [0,1] or (0,1) and is expressed as fractions, proportions, rates, indices, or probabilities. Fractional response estimators fit models on continuous zero to one data using probit, logit, heteroscedastic probit or beta regression. Beta regression can be used only when the endpoints zero and one are excluded. See, e.g., Papke and Wooldridge (1996) and Wooldridge (2010) for discussion. In Stata, the commands fracreg and betareg can be used to estimate fractional response and beta regression models, respectively.

Frye-Jacobs (2012) Model: In this approach, LGD is linked to the annualized default rate. There are some limitations associated with its use: it is based on a one-factor Vasicek model, with the annualized default rate as the single risk factor; the Vasicek model imposes the assumption of normality; the annualized default rate is used instead of a stressed annualized PD; and the default rate is not actually linked to macroeconomic variables.

Stressed EAD Modeling Approaches for Revolvers: Borrowers increase their utilization of credit lines during periods of distress. While covenant protections could impact EAD estimation, the impact is difficult to quantify. Empirical evidence of credit cycle sensitivity is much weaker for EAD than for LGD. There is a significant credit-cycle effect for some revolving products but not for all. In the case of closed-end C&I loans, the funded balance and the corresponding EAD equals the outstanding balance.

Typically, EAD is measured and estimated as a ratio to balance or line of credit (total or undrawn). There are three commonlyused approaches to model loan-level EAD. In the Loan Equivalent Factor (LEQ) approach, EAD is measured as the change in exposure from the current balance as a percentage of remaining line of credit amount: `

$$LEQ = \frac{EAD - Current\ Balance}{Current\ Total\ Line\ Amount - Current\ Balance}.$$

The LEQ uses information on both outstanding and line of credit at each point in time, but it is undefined or could be highly unstable where the current balance is either equal or close to the total available line of credit.

In the Credit Conversion Factor (CCF) approach, EAD is measured relative to the current balance:

$$Credit\ Conversion\ Factor = \frac{EAD}{Current\ Balance}.$$

While the CCF measure tends to be more stable than the LEQ, it is also undefined when current balance is zero. In addition, the CCF ignores information on the total line of credit amount.

In the third approach, which uses the so-called exposure at default factor (EADF) approach, EAD is expressed in terms of utilization rate:

$$EAD\ Factor = \frac{EAD}{Current\ Total\ Amount}.$$

Approach Based on Adjustments to Basel EAD: In this approach, adjustments are made to the AIRB EAD.

OLS Regression of EAD/Commitment on Macroeconomic Factors: In this approach, EAD is regressed on macroeconomic risk drivers such as unemployment rate and a variety of internal risk drivers.

Additional Utilization Factor (AUF) Regression: In this approach, additional utilization factor is regressed on macroeconomic factors and internal risk drivers such as a zero balance indicator, LOB indicator, obligor risk rating, etc.

10.2.5 CRE Loss Forecasting Models for Stress Tests

In this section, we describe various estimation approaches employed by banking institutions to produce stressed PD, LGD, and EAD estimates that are used to generate expected loss forecasts for the accrual CRE portfolio. There are two primary reasons why a borrower would default on a CRE loan. The first is that cash flows from the property are inadequate to cover scheduled mortgage payments. The second is that the underlying commercial properties, serving as secured collateral for most loans, are worth less than the mortgage. That is, a commercial mortgage borrower's ownership value, inclusive of property resale value, plus current and future incomes, less the market value of the mortgage (including current outstanding payments), becomes less than zero.

There are five key risk drivers in modeling CRE losses: debt service coverage ratio (DSCR), loan to value ratio (LTV), loan age, property type, and market vacancy. Among these risk drivers, the DSCR and LTV are commonly regarded as the key determinants of default in modeling CRE losses.

For example, DSCR, which is calculated as net operating income (NOI)/debt service, is inversely related to default probability. Whereas, LTV, which is calculated as outstanding balance/property value, is directly related to default probability. With regard to loan age, the PD peaks at around three to seven years, increasing before and declining thereafter. Finally, PD depends on property type, and higher Market Vacancy leads to higher default probability

These risk drivers appear as predictor variables in PD and LGD models, where DSCR and LTV are location-specific and depend on the macroeconomic variables. Vacancy, rent, and cap rates in turn depend on broader macroeconomic variables.

The typical CRE stress-loss estimation framework captures these dynamics within the following five modeling components where the functional dependence of DSCR and LTV on macroeconomic, regional and property-specific variables is modeled in the first two components (See, e.g., Day, Raissi, and Shayne (2014) or the Trepp White Paper on Modeling CRE Default and Losses (2016)):

Market Level Components: Market level rent, vacancy rate and cap rate (i.e., NOI/Property Value) and time-to-resolutions are forecast based on macroeconomic variables.

Cash Flow and Risk Driver Components: Repayment and balance schedules are computed using loan-level attributes and interest rate projections.

Default Model: Default probabilities are computed at the loan level using variables such as LTV, DSCR, Time-To-Maturity, loan age, property indicator and regional vacancy rate.

LGD Model: LGDs are computed at the loan level using property values and LTVs.

Expected Loss Computation: The output from the above components is used to compute a final expected loss for each loan.

The **Market Level Forecasting** component is used to predict the vacancy rate (e.g., per square foot), rent rate (e.g., per square foot), and cap rate at the property type-regional level based on macroeconomic variable projections usually from ordinary least squares (OLS) regressions. Variable transformations (e.g., difference, log difference, % log difference, or logit difference) are often employed to ensure that the time-series dependent variables are stationary. A separate regression is estimated for each region-property type combination at the desired level of granularity.

Historical cap rate data from vendors (e.g., REIS, CoStar) are used to develop cap rate models. Banking institutions have noted macro-variable sensitivity differences in the quality of cap rate data across vendors. Predictor variables in cap rate models typically include the CRE Price Index (CREPI), CMBS yield, and corporate bond yield. Some banking institutions have explored modeling property value directly because the approach of modeling cap rate and NOI separately to estimate the property value appears more complex than needed. Regardless of approach, the property value computed from the two components must fall as the economy worsens, and vice versa. Alternative models use the log-difference of the price index from the vendor data as the dependent variable.

The **Cash Flow** component uses simple calculations (no statistical estimation) to forecast loan-level balances and loan-level payment schedules based on loan-level data, forecasted loan-level data (e.g., vacancy, rent and cap rates) and scenario interest rates. Key outputs are the loan level NOI, property value and DSCR forecasts using the following steps:

- Compute gross operating income using rent rate, vacancy rate and average lease term
- Compute gross operating expenses using gross operating income, initial expense-to-income ratio and CPI
- Compute NOI forecasts (e.g. per square foot) as the difference of income and expenses starting with the initial NOI value
- Compute DSCR and property value forecasts using NOI and Cap rate forecasts as well as DSCR forecasts.

Default Component: This component typically uses a logistic regression to forecast probability of default based on a combination of static loan-level data, forecasted loan-level data (e.g., DSCR, LTV) and forecasted market data (e.g., vacancy rate, macro-variables). The PD models are typically segmented into two property types – construction and income producing real estate. The PD modeling range of practice for CCAR/DFAST includes:

- Regression models using internal data
- Regression models using external data (e.g., CMBS data from a vendor)
- Rules-based default model
- Ratings-migration regression models.

Regression Models: (Using internal or external data): A binary logistic regression framework is used to model the relationship between the default status of a loan y_i ($y_i = 1$ if the loan i has defaulted, $y_i = 0$ otherwise) and the explanatory variables X_i. The conditional probability of default of loan i, PD_i, given X_i has the form:

$$\text{Ln}\langle PD_i|1 - PD_i\rangle = \alpha + \beta \, . X_i$$

where the elements of the vector X_i include $\{LTV_i, DSCR_i, \delta_{1i}, \delta_{2i}, \ldots, \delta_{ni}\}$ and the indicator variables $\{\delta_{1i}, \delta_{2i}, \ldots, \delta_{ni}\}$ indicate the market, property type and other loan-specific information.

Rules-Based Models: As most CRE models are granular and compute DSCR and LTV at the loan level, some banks use these two metrics judgmentally to define loan level defaults. For example, by a default methodology logic, the stress LTV of 200% and a stress DSCR of .5x would default every loan. The reason is that the property is worth 50% of the loan amount at a 200% LTV, so the borrower would have no incentive to continue to make payments. In addition, the .5x DSCR implies that the property cash flow is only 50% of the debt service, so once again, the borrower would have no incentive to maintain the property. That is the business intuition that goes into defining the default logic thresholds for DSCR and LTV.

Ratings-Migration Regression Models: (See Regression-Based Models discussion in Section 10.2.4): PD regression models forecast transition movement across various risk rating grades (upgrade/downgrade/default) in terms of fundamental economic drivers. Matrix elements of the PD model can be estimated as multinomial logit probabilities as in Section 10.2.4.

LGD component: This component uses regression models (e.g., logistic, Tobit) to forecast final LGD based on a combination of static loan-level data, forecasted loan-level data and forecasted market-level conditions. The LGD range of practice for CCAR/DFAST includes:

- Loan level LGD formula based on internal variables such as LTV, liquidation expenses
- Regression models (e.g., fractional logistic, Tobit) using only internal variables
- Regression models using internal variables as well as macroeconomic variables.

An example of a simple model that accounts for property value dynamics in a stressed scenario as well as liquidation expenses depending on the property type and foreclosure proceedings in judicial and non-judicial states is:

$$\text{LGD} = \text{Maximum}((1 - 1/\text{LTV} + \text{Liquidation Expenses})\, \text{LGD}_{\text{Minimum}}).$$

This model sets a minimum LGD that is derived from either the credit LGD or regulatory LGD, or the combination of both depending on the scenario.

The LGD regression framework utilizes fractional logistic or Tobit regression with LTV (or transforms related to LTV), collateral shortfall percentage, property-type indicators and price changes (over four quarters following default) as the primary drivers to determine loss given default. LGD model estimation is often developed for different segments such as construction, wholesale income producing, and small real estate income producing loans. Some banks have developed LGD regression models for different region-property type combinations.

The **Expected Loss** component aggregates the output of the default, LGD and cash flow components and produces a loss forecast for each quarter.

CRE model validation activities for CCAR/DFAST applications have included:

(1) Critical assessment of the model theoretical framework and the conceptual soundness of each model component. Issues addressed in the critical assessment would include:

- Are PD and LGD sensitivities to different risk drivers intuitive for different business segments such as construction, and income-producing sub-classes such as multi-family, office, etc.?
- Do the sub-models (e.g., multi-family cap rate projection model for a given region) contain relevant risk drivers?

(2) Implementation verification and independent model replication, including model diagnostics.

(3) Evaluation of applicable performance tests for all components:
- Model component outputs and uses – vendor cash flow models, prepayment options
- Evaluate model component performances
- Review model Sensitivity and Scenario tests.

(4) Evaluation of data quality for each model component data, and relevance of using third-party data:
- Appropriateness of model inputs – are there sufficient data to model cap rate or vacancy rate for Office segment in region Y? If not, what proxies are used?
- Data sources for model development – market level forecasting data, PD and LGD models, blending of internal and external data
- Data reconciliation and integrity check process.

(5) Assessment of risk drivers and an evaluation of the segmentation schemes used in the model:
- Model segmentation scheme – income producing, construction, property types, regions? Appropriate granularity given business concentration?
- Model specification
- Variable selection
- Model fit
- Stationarity of market level time series data.

(6) Evaluation of the end-to-end model performance, and the reasonableness of the stress projections:
- Property value path under different stress severity.

10.2.6 FVO Portfolio Loss Modeling

Held for sale (HFS) loans are loans that are purchased or originated with the intent of being sold in a secondary market, while fair value option (FVO) loans are other loans to which the bank has elected to apply fair-value accounting practices. FVO loans and commitments are held for sale (HFS) or held for investment (HFI), and driven by fair value accounting. Losses on fair value loans and commitments reflect both expected changes in the fair value of the loan, and any losses that may result from an obligor default under a given scenario.

Unlike loans held in accrual portfolios, for which losses are generally due to an obligor's failure to pay on its loan obligation (default risk), losses on FVO loans under a given scenario are typically driven by:

- Changes in mark to market (MTM) value due to changes in the economic and market environment. This could result from changes in macroeconomic factors such as interest rates, credit spreads, foreign exchange rates or any other factors that may capture idiosyncratic risks of a banking institution's portfolio;
- The market perception of changes in an obligor's credit quality that is reflected in obligor spread widening.

When determining the fair value of a loan, the bank is required to include counterparty credit risk in the valuation on the basis that a market participant would include it when determining the price it would pay to acquire the loan (which is the price the bank would receive to sell the loan). For loans, counterparty credit risk is often included in the fair value by using a current market spread in the discount rate applied to the cash flows of the loan. Accounting practices (e.g., IFRS 13) prioritizes observable market inputs over unobservable inputs when using a valuation technique to measure a loan or commitment's fair value. Observable benchmarks are sometimes provided for the PD of certain counterparties through the implied PDs from CDS (credit default swap) contracts.

The loss estimation framework assumes that the value of assets depends on credit states that evolve by some process, which can be captured by some distribution function or a discrete state transition matrix [See, e.g., Agrawal, Korablev, and Dwyer (2008), Tschirhart, O'Brien, Moise and Yang (2007)]. While the assets in the portfolio are valued individually, the credit states of each obligor in the portfolio are not. This has the advantage of being analytically tractable and straightforward to implement but ignores the possibility of idiosyncratic migrations for assets of the same initial rating, as the distribution of the future ratings of all assets, given an initial rating, evolves in the same way. The distribution of future credit states of an obligor is determined by the repeated application of the forward stressed PD Transition Matrix for quarter t (as discussed in Section 10.2.4 on C&I portfolio PD models). The total estimated losses are determined by adding together the fair value losses, expected default losses, and gains from any associated hedges. The first loss component is the losses that occur if the facility is downgraded to a performing state, which is called the fair value pricing loss. The second is the losses that occur once a facility migrates to default, including incremental changes to the distressed prices, which is called the default loss. The third reflects the associated hedge gains, if any, calculated using the same framework as the first two loss components.

The cumulative loss from the change in fair value and default can be represented as:

$$Loss_t = (1 - PD_t) \times Fair\ Value\ Loss_t + PD_t \times Default\ Loss_t.$$

Similarly, for the hedges:

$$Hedge\ Gain_t = (1 - PD_t) \times Performing\ Hedge\ Gain_t + PD_t \times Default\ Hedge\ Gain_t.$$

10.2.6.1 Fair Value Loss

Following supervisory guidance, banking institutions generally forecast the credit spread path for given obligor rating classes (e.g., BBB, AA, CCC) in a given sector (differentiated by region, product, industry etc.). If a loan does not default in quarter *t*, one can use the PD Transition Matrix for quarter *t* to compute the probability that a loan in rating class *i* will migrate to rating class *j* in period *(t+1)* as follows:

$$M_{ij} = P_{ij}/(1 - P_{id}).$$

Since stressed credit spreads for each rating class j at quarter (t+1) are known, the spread of the loan at time (t+1), s_{t+1}, is obtained as the M-weighted sum of these spreads. For each quarter in the projection, the valuation of the non-defaulted loans is assessed by applying a relative credit spread move to the beginning quarter. The Mark-to-Market (MtM) losses are calculated for loans, single-name hedges using the following:

$$\text{Fair value pricing loss for quarter t} = [PV(s_t) - PV(s_{t-1})] \times (1 - PDQ_t),$$

where

$PV(s_t)$ = the fair value of the loan given the scenario spread widening at quarter t,
$PV(s_{t-1})$ = the fair value of the loan given the scenario spread widening at quarter $t-1$, and
PDQ_t = the cumulative PD through the specific quarter t of the projection (Obtained by multiplying Stressed Transition Matrices for each quarter for a given scenario).

For a facility that is performing in the current portfolio, there is some probability that it may default at time t over the CCAR/DFAST projection period. The Fair Value model cannot capture the price of a facility in default, so at the quarter in which a facility enters default its price will be approximated as a function of LGD (provided by the LGD Loan Model).

10.2.6.2 Computing Fair Value of a Loan

The Fair Value Model combines the future cash flows and discount rate to produce a fair-value:

$$\textit{Fair Value} = \mathrm{PV}(s_t) = \sum \frac{\textit{Future Cash Flows}_t}{(1 + \textit{Discount Rate})^t}.$$

The future cash flows are a function of payment commitments made by the obligor to service the outstanding balance of the facility, interest, and fees.

$$\text{Future Cash Flows} = \text{Facility Balance} + \text{Interest} + \text{Fees}.$$

Obligors make payments to the lender to return the balance lent to them (the drawn balance or principal). These payments reduce the outstanding balance and are paid over the tenor of the loan for amortizing facilities, or at the expiration of the facility for non-amortizing facilities. In addition to repayment, creditors expect incremental returns in the form of fees and interest. Obligors also pay fees (e.g., unused commitment fee) to the lender in exchange for the facilities. For example, a lender may charge a fee for the guarantee of providing capital, such as for a letter of credit, and maintaining the unused balance of the facility (e.g., a letter of credit) as a liability on its balance sheet.

Interest is a function of the balance of the loan and the lender's opportunity cost, which is expressed as an expected rate of return (interest rate):

$$\text{Interest} = \text{Facility Balance} * \text{Interest Rate}.$$

The interest rate is agreed to when the facility is contracted

$$\text{Floating Rate} = \text{Base Rate} + \text{Promised Spread}.$$

In setting rates, both the creditor and the borrower assume the risk that market rates will change as a result of market risk, borrower risk, and the cost of capital. Thus, the rate is a function both of the creditor's expected rate of return and a risk premium paid by the obligor in exchange for the creditor assuming the risk of non-repayment of the facility's balance. As the risk of default increases, so too does the risk premium and negotiated promised rate.

Risk ratings are the industry standard for assessing and describing the creditworthiness and risk of an obligor or facility. Lenders use either their own internally developed risk ratings standard or those provided by credit ratings agencies (e.g., Moody's and S&P) to assess credit risk. Historical observations have shown that credit ratings are an effective means of capturing the relationship between risk and expected returns. As a facility's risk rating worsens, the average credit spread (which is a function of market price) and commitment fee increase.

Discount rate: The market's expected return, which may differ from the rates promised to the borrower, is used as the discount rate to compute a market-defined fair value for the facility. The discount rate is a function of the market rate (MR), utilization (U), the combined base spread and spread shock (S), and market unused commitment fee (CF) for a given risk rating (RR) and macroeconomic conditions (MV):

$$\begin{aligned}
&Discount\ Rate(RR_t, MV_t) \\
&\quad = Market\ Rate(MV_t) + Base\ Spread(RR_t, MV_t) \\
&\qquad + Spread\ Shock(RR_t, MV_t) \\
&\qquad + Market\ Unused\ Commitment\ Fee(RR_t, MV_t).
\end{aligned}$$

Or,

$$\text{Discount Rate} = \text{MR} + \text{U}^{*}\text{S} + (1 - \text{U}) * \text{CF}.$$

The major modeling challenges result from the embedded prepayment option in the facility. Prepayment introduces uncertainty about the duration of the loan and the above spread calculation does not account for the loan prepayment option. The front-end pricing models typically use a credit state transition model framework to model the credit-dependent optionality of prepayments and drawdowns. A lattice of discount rates and credit state transitions over time is constructed and the loan is valued via backward induction on the lattice. The option to prepay, apply pricing grid reduction/increase and to draw down credit lines is evaluated at each node. This is referred to as the Full Revaluation model – it is typically used by desks to price risk, is battle-tested under many simulations, and is computationally intensive.

Because of the computational burden of the full revaluation approach, some banking institutions have used "sensitivities" or a "grid approach" to approximate changes in fair value in their CCAR/DFAST implementation. Under the sensitivities approach, fair value losses are derived from commonly used sensitivities such as CS01s and PV01s. While this approach is easy to use and provides a good approximation of price movements, it lacks pricing precision and relies on a linear approximation of a nonlinear relationship. The grid approach utilizes pre-calculated pricing model grids based on basis point changes (+50bps, +100bps, +150bps, etc.) and uses linear interpolation or nonlinear (cubic spline) interpolation of grid values for in-between spread values. This approach is more granular than the sensitivity approach, but not as granular as the Full Revaluation Approach.

While most banking institutions follow the principles outlined above in modeling their FVO loans for CCAR/DFAST stress testing, the actual implementations have differed. Accordingly, validation tends to emphasize the following:

- Hedging treatment: Hedges are carried at MTM/FV, but cover both the mark-to-market and accrual books. How are hedges allocated across portfolios?
- FVO portfolio for stress testing: FVO loan book varies with time. How is the seasonality issue dealt with in stress testing?
- CCAR/DFAST spread paths: How severe are the shocks and resulting losses? Is the recovery phase too aggressive?

- Risk Factors: Are the key risks captured? Are the risks captured in the model process granular enough? Key risks include default risk (which is a function of the credit state), recovery value in the event of default (LGD), maturity, market risk premium (current market rate of interest reflecting obligor's risk of default), base interest rate, prepayment, embedded optionality, utilization for revolving facilities. For example, the following important questions arise:
  - Is the spread shock applied to a migrated rating or the original rating? If not, how is this compensated for?
  - Is the granularity in credit spread stresses sufficient? Loan level models or sector models, where sector model granularity should be more than just Investment Grade vs. Non-Investment Grade spread paths.
  - Loans are inherently illiquid and tend to suffer from lack of observable pricing data. Does the methodology compensate for this by using appropriate data in more liquid markets (CDS, LCDS, CDX, LCDX, benchmark loan and bond indexes, etc.)?
- Revaluation approaches: How do the revaluation approaches estimate MTM/FV values? Treatment of option risk?
- Reasonability of business assumptions related to fees, sell-down and portfolio renewals.

10.2.7 The Core Components of an Effective Validation Framework

As laid out in SR 11-7 and OCC Bulletin 2011–12, an effective model validation framework should include three core elements:[3]

- Evaluation of conceptual soundness, including developmental evidence
- Ongoing monitoring, including process verification and benchmarking
- Outcomes analysis, including backtesting.

The first core component of the validation process is evaluation of a model's conceptual soundness. This element consists of assessing the quality of model design and construction and involves review of

[3] This section is based on language taken directly from SR 11-7 and OCC Bulletin 2011–12. Also, see SR15–18 and SR15–19 Appendices for consolidated guidance related to capital stress testing.

development documentation and empirical evidence supporting the methods used and variables selected for the model. Validation should ensure that judgment employed in model design and construction is well informed, carefully considered, and consistent with published research and with sound industry practice. Documentation and testing should convey an understanding of model limitations and assumptions. A sound development process will produce documented evidence that supports all model choices, including the theoretical construction, key assumptions, data, and specific mathematical calculations. Finally, validation should use sensitivity analysis to check the effect of small changes in inputs (separately, as well as simultaneously) and parameter values on model outputs to ensure they fall within an expected range. Unexpectedly large changes in outputs in response to small changes in inputs can indicate an unstable model.

The second core component of the validation process is ongoing monitoring, which demonstrates that the model is appropriately implemented and is being used and is performing as intended. Ongoing monitoring is key in evaluating whether changes in products, exposures, activities, clients, or market conditions necessitate adjustment, redevelopment or replacement of the model; and to verify that any extension or use of the model beyond its original scope is valid. As such, ongoing monitoring should include process verification and benchmarking: Process verification involves checking that all model components are functioning as designed and includes verifying that internal and external data inputs continue to be accurate, complete, and consistent with the model's purpose and design; and benchmarking consists of a comparison of a given model's inputs and outputs to estimates from alternative internal or external data or models. Any discrepancies between model output and benchmarks should trigger an inquiry into the sources and degree of the differences, and an assessment of whether they are within an expected, or appropriate range.

Finally, the third core component is outcomes analysis, which compares model outputs to actual model outcomes in order to evaluate model performance. The comparison depends on the nature of the objectives of the model, and might include assessing the accuracy of estimates or forecasts, an evaluation of rank-ordering ability, etc. Backtesting is one approach for outcomes analysis and involves the comparison of actual outcomes with model forecasts for a sample time period not used in model development.

10.3 Conclusions

In this chapter, we have examined modeling issues that are addressed in the validation of the quantitative wholesale credit risk models used by US banking institutions. Banking institutions use these models in decision making in the areas of credit approval, portfolio management, capital management, pricing, and loan loss provisioning for wholesale loan portfolios. Since the leading practice in wholesale credit risk modeling for loss estimation among large US banking institutions today is to use expected loss models typically at the loan level, our focus was on these models and the quantification of the three key risk parameters in this modeling approach, namely, probability of default (PD), loss given default (LGD), and exposure at default (EAD).

We addressed validation issues for wholesale credit risk models in the context of different regulatory requirements and supervisory expectations for the Advanced Internal Ratings Based (AIRB) approach of the Basel II and Basel III framework for regulatory capital and for the stress testing framework of CCAR and DFAST for assessing enterprise-wide capital adequacy. Given that the largest banking institutions use their obligor and facility internal risk ratings in PD and LGD quantification for Basel and also for quantification of stressed PD and LGD for CCAR and DFAST, we also addressed issues that arise in the validation of internal ratings systems used to grade wholesale loans.

References

Agrawal, D., Korablev, I., Dwyer, D. (2008). Valuation of Corporate Loans: A Credit Migration Approach, Moody's KMV Report, January 2008.

The Basel II Risk Parameters: Estimation, Validation, and Stress Testing, 2006, Edited by B. Engelmann and R. Rauhmeier, Springer.

BCBS. (1999). Credit Risk Modelling: Current Practices and Applications.

BCBS. (2005). Studies on the Validation of Internal Rating Systems, Working Paper No. 14.

BCBS. (2005). Update on Work of the Accord Implementation Group Related to Validation under the Basel II Framework, Basel Committee Newsletter, No. 4.

BCBS. (2005). Validation of Low-default Portfolios in the Basel II Framework, No. 6 (September 2005).

BCBS. (2009). Range of Practices and Issues in Economic Capital Frameworks,

BCBS. (2016). SIGBB Internal Discussion Memorandum

Board of Governors of the Federal Reserve System. (2011). *SR 11-7: Guidance on Model Risk Management.*

Board of Governors of the Federal Reserve System. (2013). *Capital Planning at Large Bank Holding Companies: Supervisory Expectations and Range of Current Practice.*

Board of Governors of the Federal Reserve System. (2015). *SR 15-18: Federal Reserve Supervisory Assessment of Capital Planning and Positions for Firms Subject to Category I Standards.*

Board of Governors of the Federal Reserve System. (2015). *SR 15-19: Federal Reserve Supervisory Assessment of Capital Planning and Positions for Firms Subject to Category II or III Standards.*

Bohn, J., and Stein, J. (2009). *Active Credit Portfolio Management in Practice, Wiley Finance.* John Wiley & Sons, Inc.

Belkin, B., Forest, L. and Suchower, S. (1998). A one-parameter representation of credit risk and transition matrices. *CreditMetrics Monitor (3rd Quarter).*

Cameron, A. and Trivedi, P. (2009). *Microeconometrics: Methods and Applications.* Cambridge University Press.

Carhill, M. and Jones, J. (2013). Stress-Test Modelling for Loan Losses and Reserves. In A. Siddique and I. Hasan, editors, *Stress Testing: Approaches, Methods and Applications.* Risk Books.

CCAR and Beyond: Capital Assessment, Stress Testing and Applications, 2013, edited by Jing Zhang, Risk Books.

Chen, J. (2013). Stress Testing Credit Losses for Commercial Real Estate Loan Portfolios, In J. Zhang, editor, *CCAR and Beyond: Capital Assessment, Stress Testing and Applications.* Risk Books.

Christodoulakis, G. and Satchell, S. (2008). *The Analytics of Risk Model Validation*, Quantitative Finance Series, Elsevier.

Crouhy, M., Galai, D. and Mark, R. (2001). *Risk Management.* McGraw Hill.

Day, T., Raissi, M., and Shayne, C. (2014). Credit loss estimation: Industry challenges and solutions for stress testing, Risk Practitioner Conference, October 2014.

De Bandt, O., Dumontaux, N., Martin, V. and Medee, D. (2013). A Framework for Stress Testing Banks' Corporate Credit Portfolio. In A. Siddique and I. Hasan, *Stress Testing: Approaches, Methods and Applications.* Risk Books.

Financial Accounting Standards Board, Financial Accounting Standards No. 157 Fair Value Measurements, Financial Accounting Series, No 284-A, September 2006.

Financial Accounting Standards No. 159 Fair Value Measurements, Financial Accounting Series, No 289-A, February 2007.

Forster, M. and Sober, E. (1994). How to tell when simpler, more unified, or less ad hoc theories will provide more accurate predictions, *The British Journal for the Philosophy of Science*, Vol. 45, No. 1, 1–35.

Godfrey, L. G. (1988). *Misspecification Tests in Econometrics, Econometric Society Monographs No. 16*, Cambridge University Press: Cambridge.

Glowacki, Jonathan B. (2012). Effective model validation. *Millman Insights*, December 24, 2012.

Hastie, T., Tibshirani, R. and Friedman, J. (2009). *The Elements of Statistical Learning: Data Mining, Inference, and Prediction*, Second Ed. Springer Series in Statistics, Springer.

Hirtle et al. (2001). Using Credit Risk Models for Regulatory Capital: Issues and Options, *FRBNY Economic Policy Review*.

James, G., Witten, D. Hastie, T. and Tibshirani, R. (2013). *An Introduction to Statistical Learning: with Applications in R*. Springer Texts in Statistics, Springer.

Klein, L., Jacobs, M and Merchant, A. (2016). Top Considerations in Wholesale Credit Loss, Accenture, 2016.

Ong, M.K., (editor). (2007). *The Basel Handbook: A Guide for Financial Practitioners*, Second Ed., Risk Books, London.

Office of the Comptroller of the Currency. (2011). *OCC 2011-12: Sound Practices for Model Risk Management: Supervisory Guidance on Model Risk Management*.

Quell, P. and Meyer, C. (2011). *Risk Model Validation: A Practical Guide to Address the Key Questions*. Risk Books.

Scandizzo, S. (2016). *The Validation of Risk Models, a Handbook for Practioners, Applied Quantitative Finance*. Palgrave Macmillan.

Shaikh, P., Jacobs, M. and Sharma, N. (2016). Industry practices in model validation. *Accenture*, June 2016.

Stress Testing: Approaches, Methods and Applications, edited by A. Siddique and I. Hasan, Risk Books, 2013.

Tschirhart, John, O'Brien, James, Moise Michael and Yang, Emily. (2007). Bank Commercial Loan Fair Value Practices, *Finance and Economics Discussion Series, Division of Research & Statistics and Monetary Affairs*, Federal Reserve Board, Washington D.C., 2007–29, June 2007.

Vasicek, O. (1991). Limiting Loan Loss Probability Distribution. *KMV Working Paper*.

White Paper: Modeling CRE Default and Loss, 2016, Trepp.

Yang, J. and Chen, K. (2013). A Multiview Model Framework for Stress Testing C&I Portfolios, Chapter 7 in *CCAR and Beyond: Capital Assessment, Stress Testing and Applications*, edited by J. Zhang, Risk Books.

11 Case Studies in Wholesale Risk Model Validation*

DEBASHISH SARKAR**

11.1 Introduction

In this chapter, we describe in more detail validation issues and activities surrounding PD, LGD, and EAD modeling and internal borrower and facility ratings. To accomplish this task, we present several case studies. The six case studies are based on banking institutions' practices observed by the author and other regulators, and they focus on important issues identified in the validation process.

This chapter is organized according to the various major steps that a complete model validation would take in addressing the following issues: (1) use of the model; (2) internal and external data; (3) model assumptions and methodologies; (4) model performance; (5) outcomes analysis; and (6) the quality and comprehensiveness of development documentation (see, e.g., Glowacki 2012). This chapter also includes some observations on partial model validation and review of vendor models.

11.2 Validation of Use

A model validation generally begins the way one would start to develop a financial model; that is, by understanding the use of the model. This will help determine the level of detail of the model validation and allow the model validation group to focus on key areas of the model. For example, while reviewing a loss model for the purpose of CCAR/DFAST stress tests, it is important that the results produced by the model are reasonable and robust under a stressful environment. In contrast, for pricing models, where the focus is to develop an average cost, the results produced by the model for extremely stressful scenarios may not be as

* Please refer to Chapter 10 for background on Wholesale Risk Models.

** Federal Reserve Bank of New York. The views expressed in this chapter are those of the author alone and do not represent those of the Federal Reserve Bank of New York.

important in the model validation. A model validation should identify the use of the model, whether the model is consistent and applicable for the intended use, and it should ensure that the model is not being used for purposes beyond the capabilities of the model.

11.2.1 Use Validation: AIRB Regulatory Capital Models

Basel II AIRB Models Guidance: IRB components should be integrated for internal risk management purposes and thus, validation activities related to uses are required. The use test for estimates is broader and requirements are based on paragraph 444 of Basel II (June 2006).

The IRB use test is based on the conception that supervisors can take additional comfort in the IRB components where such components "play an essential role" in how banks measure and manage risk in their businesses. If the IRB components are solely used for regulatory capital purposes, there could be incentives to minimize capital requirements rather than produce accurate measurement of the IRB components and the resulting capital requirement. Moreover, if IRB components were used for regulatory purposes only, banks would have fewer internal incentives to keep them accurate and up-to-date whereas the employment of IRB components in internal decision making creates an automatic incentive to ensure sufficient quality and adequate robustness of the systems that produce such data.

In an internal Basel survey (BCBS SIGBB Internal Discussion Memo 2016), supervisors acknowledged that universal usage of the IRB components for all internal purposes is not necessary. In some cases, differences between IRB components and other internal risk estimates can result from mismatches between prudential requirements in the Basel II Framework and reasonable risk management practices, business considerations, or other regulatory and legal considerations. Examples include different regulatory and accounting requirements for downturn LGD, PD and LGD floors, annualized PDs and provisioning. Other examples of where differences could occur include pricing practices and default definitions.

In general, there are three main areas where the use of IRB components for internal risk management purposes should be observable: strategy and planning processes, credit exposure management, and reporting. Uses in any of these areas provide evidence of internal use of IRB components. If IRB components are not used in some of these areas, the supervisor may require an explanation for such non-use, or may raise concerns about the quality of the IRB components.

In many instances, supervisors will need to exercise considerable judgement in assessing the use of IRB components. For example, supervisors have noticed use of adjusted IRB parameters in key business processes. The types of adjustments that require justifications include:

- Removal of conservative layers, like a downturn adjustment or application of floors
- Adjustments to have point in time (PIT) parameters rather than through the cycle (TTC) parameters
- Adjustments of the time horizon which can be different from the twelve months used for regulatory capital.

Banking institutions are responsible for proving that they comply with the use test requirement. They should document and justify adjustments made to IRB components for use in key operational processes such as:

- Risk appetite / capital allocation
- Credit granting (including pricing, limits)
- Credit monitoring /early warning
- Internal reporting
- NPL management /recovery
- Provisioning/cost of risk
- Performance, RAROC, remuneration
- Economic capital and ICAAP
- Stress testing.

Case Study 1 Validation of Use for LGD and PD Estimates and Facility and Obligor Ratings

While one banking institution's approach to wholesale IRB was consistent with risk management practices at the institution, the bank's model validation team noted several important areas of divergence: First, the banking institution's facility risk ratings (FRRs) were judgmental adjustments to the obligor risk ratings (ORR), achieved through a notching process. Second, when combined with the final ORR, the FRR approximates an expected loss. This is different from LGD, which

Case Study 1 *(cont.)*

is a stressed loss number based on facility characteristics only. Third, for internal credit risk management purposes, the banking institution was not using a dual risk ratings system, which strictly separates obligor and facility characteristics.

Since the banking institution's FRRs approximate expected loss, the resulting internal risk capital calculation would likely underestimate the amount of capital required to be held against a given loan under Basel II rules. The bank's management believed that the FRR is a better assessment of facility risk than LGD because the latter's numerous LGD segments may not contain enough actual data to support estimates. The layer of conservatism that is required, given the lack of LGD data, would therefore overestimate the capital requirement. The bank was also using its FRRs in the allowance for loan and lease losses (ALLL) calculations.

While baseline and final ORRs were consistent and were validated against PDs used in the AIRB approach, the bank was layering on a further qualitative assessment in determining obligor limit ratings (OLRs) for committed facilities beyond one year. OLRs were used to determine risk tolerance for individual borrowers as well as related groups of borrowers and they were generally viewed to be a compensating adjustment for facilities with a longer term. The ability to predict default becomes more uncertain for longer-term facilities and relies upon a judgmental process that calls for expertise that credit analysts may not possess. In reality, the vast majority of OLRs were the same as the ORRs, but management was unable to produce a reliable analysis of these data. The OLR is standardized at the economic group level of the borrower and it was usually based on consolidated financial information. It did not take into account individual group member (obligor) PD. So while each obligor, in compliance with Basel II standards, is assigned a PD, this PD was not used for limit setting.

11.2.2 Use Validation: CCAR/DFAST Models

Stress Testing Models: The validation focus for model use is the reasonability and robustness of outcomes. Consequently, in addition to performance and back-testing, guidance emphasizes validation related to:

- Model assumptions and limitations
- Model overlays
- Sensitivity analysis
- Challenger/Benchmark models.

Supervisory Guidance: Models used in the capital planning process should be reviewed for suitability for their intended uses. A firm should give particular consideration to the validity of models used for calculating post-stress capital positions. In particular, models designed for ongoing business activities may be inappropriate for estimating losses, revenue, and expenses under stressed conditions. If a firm identifies weaknesses or uncertainties in a model, the firm should make adjustments to model output if the findings would otherwise result in the material understatement of capital needs (SR15–18 guidance,[1] pp 9–10.) SR 15–18 also outlines expectations for model overlays, benchmark models, and sensitivity analysis.

Model Assumptions and Limitations: Banking institutions make modeling assumptions that are informed by their business activities and overall strategy. For example, in CRE stress-loss modeling, banks facing a lack of historical data may assume LTV or DSCR default threshold triggers based upon LOB specialist judgment. Such assumptions can significantly impact model effectiveness, to the extent that the resulting model output differs from what is realized in practice. As a result, banks should mitigate model risk by quantifying the effects of assumptions to demonstrate:

- Consistency of results with economic scenarios
- Outcomes conservatism and the consideration of adjustments to account for model weaknesses
- Comprehensive documentation of specialist panel discussions
- Reasonableness from a business perspective
- Use of benchmark data to the extent possible
- Testing of assumptions and quantifying the impact of these on model output.

Model Overlays (SR15–18, Appendix B): A BHC may need to rely on overrides or adjustments to model output (model overlay) to compensate for model, data, or other known limitations. If well-supported, use of a model overlay can represent a sound practice.

Model overlays (including those based solely on expert or management judgment) should be subject to validation or some other type of effective challenge. Consistent with the materiality principle in SR 11-7 and OCC Bulletin 2011–12, the intensity of model risk management for overlays should be a function of the materiality of the model and

[1] For category I firms.

overlay. Effective challenge should occur before the model overlay is formally applied, not on an *ex post* basis.

Sensitivity Analysis: Sensitivity analysis is an important tool for stress testing model robustness and checking for model stability. In sensitivity analysis, a model's output is evaluated by changing or stressing individual input factors to understand the model's dependency on these individual factors. Sensitivity analysis can be used as part of a bank's champion/challenger process: model validation testing; quantifying a model risk buffer; and demonstrating the conservatism of model assumptions.

Sensitivity analysis should be conducted during model development and as well as in model validation to provide information about how models respond to changes in key inputs and assumptions, and how those models perform in stressful conditions (SR 15–18.)

Challenger/Benchmark Models: Champion/challenger frameworks are important for model governance, delivering model robustness, usability and long-term performance. They are a critical source of performance benchmarking to assess:

- Appropriateness of chosen methodology
- Alternative estimation techniques or different risk factors considered
- Comparability of model output
- Use of a common reference dataset.

11.2.3 Use Validation: Summary and Conclusions

The use test's ultimate goal is to enhance the quality of IRB parameters or stress model estimates, through continuous emphasis on improving the estimation processes. The conditions to create continuous emphasis on the quality of model outputs are: active interaction between users and modelers, and a good understanding of the model, its assumptions, and its limitations among model developers and users.

Active involvement of model users is expected in model development and model maintenance. This should be clearly described in the model development or governance policy and verified through the analysis of modeling workgroup minutes (regular presence of business representatives, suggestions made by the business etc.). For CCAR/DFAST, supervisors look for evidence of active LOB engagements during the risk identification (e.g., segmentation, risk drivers, variable selection) and outcomes challenge processes.

Model developers should demonstrate the efforts made to explain their models to users. This can be found in the agenda of the modeling workgroup, supported by an assessment of the clarity of the presentations and minutes of that workgroup and of the model documentation. The number and quality of the training sessions with users could also be checked. In their discussions with users, modelers should be especially transparent regarding key modeling assumptions and the main constraints and shortcomings of the model. Senior management should also be aware of the main features of the models and all major shortcomings. The validation report must clearly state the constraints, shortcomings, and the corrective actions, if any.

11.3 Validation of Data (Internal and External)

The data and other information used to develop a model are of critical importance. As a result, there should be a rigorous assessment of data quality and relevance, along with appropriate documentation. The second step of a model validation is to review the data used to develop the model. The model validation group would start with the same data that were used to develop the model. The model validation review of the data could include: univariate analyses to independently identify potential variables to include in the model; a review of the range of the response or outcome variable being modeled (e.g., the minimum and maximum default rate in the data by calendar quarter); a review of the number and magnitude of stressful events included in the data; data exclusions; and other tests. External data not used in model development could be added to the validation dataset to check for other risk drivers that were not considered in the development stage of the model. The intent of this part of model validation is to understand limitations of the data used to develop the model and their implications for the estimates produced by the model (see, e.g., Glowacki (2012)).

Data availability for wholesale portfolio loss modeling is a challenge for many banking institutions. Several types of portfolios may have very few defaults. For example, some portfolios historically have experienced low numbers of defaults and are generally – but not always – considered to be low-risk (e.g., portfolios of exposures to sovereigns, banks, insurance companies or highly rated corporates). Other portfolios may be relatively small in terms of total exposures, either globally or at an individual bank level (e.g. project finance, shipping), or a banking institution may be a recent market entrant for a given portfolio. Other portfolios may not have incurred recent losses, but historical experience, or other analysis, may suggest there is a greater likelihood of losses than is captured in recent data.

11.3.1 Data Validation: AIRB Regulatory Capital Models

The Basel II framework recognizes that relatively sparse data might require increased reliance on alternative data sources and data-enhancing tools for quantification and alternative techniques for validation. The Basel guidance (BCBS (2005), No. 6) also recognizes that there are circumstances in which banking institutions will legitimately lack sufficient default history to compare realized default rates with parameter estimates that may be based in part on historical data. In such cases, greater reliance must be placed on validation techniques such as:

- Pooling of data with other banks or market participants, the use of other external data sources, and the use of market measures of risk can be effective methods to complement internal loss data. A bank would need to satisfy itself and its supervisor that these sources of data are relevant to its own risk profile. Data pooling, external data and market measures can be effective means to augment internal data in appropriate circumstances. This can be especially relevant for small portfolios or for portfolios where a bank is a recent market entrant.
- Internal portfolio segments with similar risk characteristics might be combined. For example, a bank might have a broad portfolio with adequate default history that, if narrowly segmented, could result in the creation of a number of low default portfolios. While such segmentation might be appropriate from the standpoint of internal use (e.g., pricing), for purposes of quantifying risk parameters for regulatory capital purposes, it might be more appropriate to combine the sub-portfolios.
- In some circumstances, different rating categories might be combined and PDs quantified for the combined category. A bank using a rating system that maps to rating agency categories might find it useful, for example, to combine AAA, AA and A-rated credits, provided this is done in a manner that is consistent with paragraphs 404–405 of the Basel II Framework. This could enhance default data without necessarily sacrificing the risk-sensitivity of the bank's internal rating system.

- The upper bound of the PD estimate can be used as an input to the formula for risk-weighted assets for those portfolios where the PD estimate itself is deemed to be too unreliable to warrant direct inclusion in capital adequacy calculations.

Banks may derive PD estimates from data with a horizon that is different from one year. Where defaults are spread out over several years, a bank may calculate a multi-year cumulative PD and then annualize the resulting figure. Where intra-year rating migrations contain additional information, these migrations could be examined as separate rating movements in order to infer PDs. This may be especially useful for the higher-quality rating grades.

If low default rates in a particular portfolio are the result of credit support, the lowest non-default rating could be used as a proxy for default (e.g., banks, investment firms, thrifts, pension funds, insurance firms) in order to develop ratings that differentiate risk. When such an approach is taken, calibration of such ratings to a PD consistent with the Basel II definition of default would still be necessary. While banks would not be expected to utilize all of these tools, they may nevertheless find some of them useful. The suitability and most appropriate combination of individual tools and techniques will depend on the bank's business model and characteristics of the specific portfolio.

11.3.2 Data Validation: CCAR/DFAST Models

The CCAR Range of Practice Expectations (ROPE) guidance states that banking institutions should ensure that models are developed using data that contain sufficiently adverse outcomes. If an institution experienced better-than-average performance during previous periods of stress, it should not assume that those prior patterns will remain unchanged in the stress scenario. As such, institutions should carefully review the applicability of key assumptions and critically assess how historically observed patterns may change in unfavorable ways during a period of severe stress for the economy, the financial markets, and the institution.

For CCAR/DFAST loss and revenue estimates, banking institutions should generally include all applicable loss events in their analysis, unless an institution no longer engages in a line of business, or its activities have changed such that the institution is no longer exposed to a particular risk. Losses should not be selectively excluded based on arguments that the nature of the ongoing business or activity has changed – for example, because certain loans were underwritten to standards that no longer apply, or were acquired and, therefore, differ from those that would have been originated by the acquiring institution.

The supervisory expectations for model validation as laid out in SR11–7 and OCC Bulletin 2011–12 address all stages of the model development lifecycle, including the review of reference data. Specifically, data quality assessment would include:

- Assessing the appropriateness of the selected data sample for model development; for stress testing purposes the data sample should include at least one business cycle
- Evaluating the portfolio segmentation scheme in accordance with FR Y-14A reports submitted to the Federal Reserve
- Data reconciliation (e.g., exclusions) and validity checks
- Assessing treatment of missing values and outliers
- Assessing suitability of using proxy data where applicable.

Case Study 2: Validation of Rating Transition Model Data

The bank uses a credit ratings transition matrix model (TMM) framework to forecast quarterly transition rates under specified macroeconomic scenarios. The TMM is developed for each of a dozen segments defined by business type and region (including international segments). The TM model forecasts key credit ratings migration rates, i.e., upgrade, downgrade and default, at a segment level.

The Bank's Model Validation assessed the model development data inputs and sources; the quality and relevance of the model development data; the data processing and data exclusions; and the dependent and independent variable definitions and transformations.

Data Inputs and Sources: The TMM was developed using internal historical ratings and default data and external data from Moody's Default and Recovery Database (DRD). Validation reviewed Loan data; Risk Rating Data; Historical Defaults; and Moody's DRD. Validation reported the following observations:

- Obligor ratings were not actually refreshed every quarter. Therefore, historical quarterly transitions may appear muted and rating inertia may be overstated in the calibration dataset.

Case Study 2: *(cont.)*

- Based on independent analysis of the raw datasets for the TMM and the LGD models, discrepancies existed in the default counts between the two datasets.
- Inconsistencies exist with respect to assignment of risk segment, risk ratings and defaults for the population of common obligors in both the internal and external data.

To assess data quality and completeness, validation:

- Performed data reconciliation and found discrepancies between position data and the development data.
- Checked Accuracy of Raw Data: Verified that the default flag provided in the raw dataset was accurate.
- Checked for Completeness of External Data: Verified that complete external data were used and all exclusions were reasonable and documented.
- Checked for Quality of External Data: Ensured that key fields were populated with intuitive and valid data points.

Review of Model Development Data Relevance: Validation noted that the historical data ranges for all segments were not identical, which is not a good practice. The internal dataset was augmented with external data to address the issue of insufficient data, particularly for international segments ratings-transition data. Developers presented an analysis of consistency of external data with internal data with respect to the definition of default, risk rating and risk segment. Validation observed that, while the results for default rates and risk segment were comparable between internal and external data, results for mapping Moody's to internal risk ratings were less satisfactory. Validation also noted that the model reference data period was sufficiently long and included a period of severe economic stress (as per supervisory guidelines).

Data Processing and Exclusions: The model developers did not perform an analysis of the impact of data exclusions on the TMM component. Validation independently implemented the exclusions applied to the development dataset and assessed the rationale for each exclusion in light of business intuition and impact of observed default in the development data. Validation observed that, due to the exclusion of scorecards with data anomalies, upgrade and downgrade rates in several risk segments within the TMM framework changed significantly.

11.3.3 Data Validation: Summary and Conclusions

Effective data validation practices include:

- Checking data samples used for model development, calibration or validation to verify the accuracy, consistency and completeness of the data used
- Checking a sample of observations to verify whether rating processes are applied appropriately
- Investigating missing data and data exclusions to ensure the representativeness of data used
- Reconciling figures between business reports (e.g., accounting information) and model development (e.g., risk databases)
- Understanding the bank's rationale for certain data aggregations, as well as evaluating inconsistences between the source data and the data actually used for model development
- Evaluating the exclusion or filtering criteria used for creating model development and validation data samples
- Reviewing the adequacy of the data cleaning policy
- Reviewing computer codes (e.g., SAS, Stata, R, MATLAB, Excel) used for the risk rating, parameter estimation, or model validation processes.

11.4 Validation of Assumptions and Methodologies

This step of a model validation process involves a review of the selection of the type of model and the associated modeling assumptions to determine if they are reasonable approximations of reality. The selection of the model type should be justified by the model development team and include a discussion of the types of models considered but not selected. The structure of the model should reflect significant properties of the response or outcome variable being modeled. As noted by Glowacki (2012), a logistic model is commonly selected to estimate PDs as it has desirable attributes such as the ability to model dichotomous events (default or no default) and produce a probability estimate between 0 and 1. The logistic model is not always appropriate, however, particularly when average default rates are small (around 1%). For stress-test applications, stressed default rates can easily spike to greater than 10% or 20%, due to the shape of the logistic curve.

This can be problematic, since these results are generally not consistent with actual experience. In sum, the model validation group must be aware of the properties of a logistic model and be able to determine and to assess the appropriateness of the assumptions underlying use of the model.

If the model under review is a regression model, a model validation should include a review of the variables and coefficient estimates in the model, the methodology used for selecting the variables, and the goodness-of-fit results for the model. This review would include an understanding of any transformations performed on the data in the regression model for reasonableness, as well as discussions with the model development team on variable selection to understand the process utilized in developing the model.

If the model is not a regression model, a model validation should include a review of the form of the model, the inputs into the model, and the sensitivity of the model to these inputs. Part of the model validation should also include discussions with the model development team on how the model was developed, the reasoning for ultimate model selection, and limitations of the model.

11.4.1 Validation of Assumptions and Methodologies: AIRB Regulatory Capital Models

The validation process involves the examination of the rating system and the estimation process and quantification methods for PD, LGD and EAD. It also requires verification of the minimum requirements for the AIRB approach. The application of validation methods is closely linked to the type of rating system and its underlying data, e.g., ratings for small business lending will typically be of a more quantitative nature, based on a rather large quantity of data. Sovereign ratings instead will typically place more emphasis on qualitative aspects because these borrowers are more opaque and default data are scarce (see, e.g., BCBS (2005), No. 14, p. 8 and BCBS (2005) No. 6).

Validation by a banking institution consists of two main components: validation of the rating system and estimates of the risk components PD, LGD, and EAD; and validation of the rating process, focusing on how the rating system is implemented.

In the case of a model-based rating system, the validation of the model design should include, for example, a qualitative review of the statistical model building technique, the relevance of the data used to build the model for a specific business segment, the method for selecting the risk factors, and whether the selected risk factors are economically meaningful.

Evaluation of an internal rating process involves important issues like data quality, internal reporting, how problems are handled and how the rating system is used by the credit officers. It also entails the training of credit officers and a uniform application of the rating system across different branches. Although quantitative techniques are useful, especially for the assessment of data quality, the validation of the rating process is mainly qualitative in nature and should rely on the skills and experience of typical banking supervisors. The following paragraph provides more detail on these issues.

Banking institutions must first assign obligors to risk grades. All obligors assigned to a grade should share the same credit quality as assessed by the bank's internal credit rating system. Once obligors have been grouped into risk grades, the bank must calculate a "pooled PD" for each grade. The credit-risk capital charges associated with exposures to each obligor will reflect the pooled PD for the risk grade to which the obligor is assigned. While supervisory guidance presents permissible approaches to estimating pooled PDs, it permits banks a great deal of latitude in determining how obligors are assigned to grades and how pooled PDs for those grades are calculated. This flexibility allows banks to make maximum use of their own internal rating and credit data systems in quantifying PDs, but it also raises important challenges for PD validation. Supervisors and bank model validators will not be able to apply a single formulaic approach to PD validation, because the dynamic properties of pooled PDs depend on each bank's particular approach to rating obligors. Supervisors need to exercise considerable skill to verify that a bank's approach to PD quantification is consistent with its rating philosophy. The underlying rating philosophy definitely has to be assessed before validation results can be judged, because the rating philosophy is an important driver for the expected range for the deviation between the PDs and actual default rates.

Banking institutions typically employ two stages in the validation of PD: validation of the discriminatory power of the internal obligor risk rating; and validation of the calibration (i.e., accuracy) of the internal rating system.

Quantitative measures used to test the discriminatory power of a rating system include (see, e.g., Scandizzo (2016), Loffler and Posch (2007), Bohm and Stein (2009), and Christodoulakis and Satchell (2009)):

- Cumulative Accuracy Profile (CAP) and Gini Coefficient
- Receiver operating characteristic (ROC), ROC measure and Pietra index
- Bayesian error rate
- Entropy measures (e.g., conditional information entropy ratio (CIER))
- Information value
- Kendall's Tau & Somers' D
- Brier score
- Divergence

Commonly-used calibration methodologies include:

- Binomial test with an assumption of independent default events
- Binomial test with an assumption of non-zero default correlation
- Chi-square test
- Brier score

For LGD and EAD models, quantitative validation techniques are significantly less advanced than those used for PD. There are four generally accepted methods for assigning LGD to non-default facilities: workout LGD; market LGD; implied historical LGD; and implied market LGD. Of these four methods, workout LGD is the most commonly used in the industry. Risk drivers such as the type and seniority of the loan, existing collateral, the liquidation value of the obligor's assets, and the prevailing bankruptcy laws should be considered for LGD estimation.

For EAD models, banking institutions typically use either the cohort method or fixed-horizon method in the construction of the development dataset for EAD estimation. The requirements for the estimation process of EAD and the validation of EAD estimates are similar to those for LGD.

11.4.2 Validation of Assumptions and Methodologies: CCAR/ DFAST Models

Case Study 3: Segmentation for C&I Stress PD Modeling

In C&I stress loss modeling, estimations are typically made at the loan level with reporting by segments. There are many dimensions to segmentation, but industry classification is one of the most statistically significant. To show that a particular segmentation approach has appropriate granularity (i.e., segments have sufficient data to develop robust and testable estimates that capture different underlying portfolio risk characteristics), given the modeling objective of forecasting losses under normal and stressed macroeconomic environments, banking institutions provide:

- Business rationale for the segmentation, which could be either the business requirements driving a non-statistical segmentation, or the business intuition for the segmentation variables of a statistical segmentation
- Evidence that developing a model based on the segmentation approach is feasible (e.g., the number of defaults per segment is adequate based on some criterion)
- For statistical segmentations, discussion of the trade-offs compared to alternative segmentations such as a methodology with appropriate explanatory variables but no or fewer segmentation
- For statistical segmentation, if available, analysis to justify differences between segments (e.g., central tendency and / or dispersion of distributions, risk factors, sensitivities to common risk factors).

One bank used a five-step, iterative segmentation process that combined business intuition with statistical analysis to define segments for the PD and Rating Migration Models:

Step 1: Risk managers, in consultation with representatives from the front-line business and risk units, propose initial industry and geographic segments.

Step 2: Model developers statistically test the proposed segments, working closely with the risk unit to refine the segmentation. The model developers may also suggest additional risk drivers for each segment based on any statistical analyses conducted.

Case Study 3: *(cont.)*

Step 3: Risk and model developers work iteratively to refine the list of segments and determine appropriate and statistically relevant risk drivers.

Step 4: Risk and model developers propose industry and geographic segments to the senior committee for review. Alternative segmentation schemes may be proposed at this stage.

Step 5: The senior committee reviews, challenges, and decides on the segmentation approach with the understanding that some segments may be adjusted and re-approved following model calibration.

Model validation observed that model developers systematically refined and combined the initially proposed segments and tested the adjusted-segment models against historical data to measure the impact on the model's performance across industries and geographies. Key statistical performance measures including ROC, variance inflation factor (VIF), among others, were provided and the values were found to be stable across all segments. However, no quantitative analysis was provided in support of the stated objective – "First, portfolios must exhibit relatively homogenous behavior within a given segment (i.e., relatively uniform default and rating migration behavior with respect to changes in the model inputs). Second, portfolios must exhibit differentiated risk characteristics across segments." Segmentation issue was extensively discussed by the senior committee from a functional soundness perspective.

11.4.3 Validation of Assumptions and Methodologies: Summary and Conclusions

Effective validation practices should include:

- Assessing conceptual soundness of the model and relevance to published research and/or sound industry practices
- Testing assumptions and assessing appropriateness of the chosen modeling approach for intended business purposes
- Reviewing alternative methodologies and designs
- Evaluating the segmentation and variable selection processes reflecting appropriate consideration for portfolio risk characteristics.

11.5 Validation of Model Performance

Quantitative credit risk models, particularly those that are complex, can produce inconsistent results. One such example is forecasting CRE property values under stressed macroeconomic scenarios. Some banking institutions develop NOI and Cap Rate models separately in deriving stressed property values (where Property Value = NOI/Cap Rate) for income-producing CRE properties as functions of CRE-related macroeconomic variables such as the mortgage rate, interest rate, and federal funds rate. These NOI and Cap Rate models, when developed separately, can lead to inconsistent forecasts, such as property values rising during stress periods. Therefore, an important step in a model validation is to assess the reasonableness of model outputs. This aspect of model validation relies heavily upon a model validator's professional expertise and judgment. The review of model performance should include sensitivity analysis, statistical tests (performed either independently from or with the model development team), and other evaluations commensurate with the type of model and scope of the validation. The focus here is to understand the limits of the model and the conditions that indicate whether the model is performing appropriately or not.

Sensitivity analysis is an important tool for assessing model robustness and for checking model stability. In sensitivity analysis, a model's output is evaluated by changing individual or a set of inputs to understand the model's dependency on these individual inputs.

11.5.1 Validation of Model Performance: AIRB Regulatory Capital Models

Basel II (2006) paragraphs 388, 389, 417, 420, 449, 450 and 500–504 provide guidance related to the performance of internal rating systems and the accuracy of risk estimates. Paragraph 389 emphasizes that a banking institution's "rating and risk estimation systems and processes provide for a meaningful assessment of borrower and transaction characteristics; a meaningful differentiation of risk; and reasonably accurate and consistent quantitative estimates of risk." However, "it is not the Committee's intention to dictate the form or operational detail of banks' risk management policies and practices."

Based on an internal Basel survey (BCBS (2016)), no jurisdiction has defined a minimum standard for the discriminatory power of rating systems or minimum standards for PD calibration. Banks define their own standards for model performance, informed by Basel Committee guidelines and industry standards and, for certain performance metrics, benchmark themselves against industry practices. The banks' own standards are then reviewed and challenged by their supervisors. For low-default portfolios, banks and supervisors seek "alternatives to statistical evidence" or take recourse to benchmarking. The internal Basel survey also identified commonly used statistical tests and statistics for backtesting purposes. Table 11.1 summarizes statistical tests and related statistics used by banks for back-testing.

Most of these statistical tests are sensitive to the assumption of independent observations. However, such independent tests give conservative results. Backtesting generally includes out-of-sample and out-of-time tests. Backtesting failure is generally not a standalone trigger for rejection of a model. Instead of rejecting a model because of back-testing failures, less strict reactions such as capital add-ons may be applied until the model weaknesses are addressed.

11.5.2 Validation of Model Performance: CCAR/ DFAST Models

11.5.2.1 Federal Reserve SR 15–18 Guidance on Assessing Model Performance

A firm should use measures to assess model performance that are appropriate for the type of model being used. The firm should outline how each performance measure is evaluated and used. A firm should also assess the sensitivity of material model estimates to key assumptions and use benchmarking to assess reliability of model estimates (see Appendix C, "Use of Benchmark Models in the Capital Planning Process" and Appendix D, "Sensitivity Analysis and Assumptions Management").

A firm should employ multiple performance measures and tests, as generally no single measure or test is sufficient to assess model performance. This is particularly the case when the models are used to project outcomes in stressful circumstances. For example, assessing model performance through out-of-sample and out-of-time backtesting may be challenging due to the short length of observed data series or the paucity of realized stressed outcomes against which to measure the model performance. When using multiple approaches, the firm should have a consistent framework for

Table 11.1. ***Backtesting tests.***

Statistical tests and related statistics used by banks for backtesting (BCBS (2016))

Discriminatory power of rating systems	PD calibration	LGD and EAD calibration
– Gini index or Accuracy Ratio (AR) – Receiver Operating Characteristic (ROC) and Area under ROC – Cumulative Accuracy Profile (CAP) – Kolmogorov–Smirnov Statistic (KS) or D Statistic – Pietra Index – Bayesian Error Rate (BER) – Information Statistic (I) – Kullback-Leibler Statistic (KL) – Kendall's Tau-b – Somers' D	– Binomial test at portfolio or grade level – Hosmer-Lemeshow or Chi-Square test, Spiegelhalter test at portfolio level – Normal distribution and one-factor model calibration tests, sometimes based on the Merton model – Beta test: Does the ratio of observed vs predicted default rates equal one? – Mean Squared Error (MSE), Mean Absolute Deviation (MAD), and Mean Absolute Percent Error (MAPE) – Observed versus Estimated Index – Traffic Lights Test – Tests for the comparison of PD and observed default rates over several years	– Normal and Student t tests – Mean Squared Error (MSE) – Receiver Operating Characteristic (ROC) – Beta test: Does the ratio of observed vs predicted loss rates (exposures in case of EAD) equal one? – Rank correlation of observed and predicted loss rates (exposures in case of EAD)

evaluating the results of different approaches and supporting rationale for why it chose the methods and estimates ultimately used.

A firm should provide supporting information about models to users of the model output, including descriptions of known measurement problems, simplifying assumptions, model limitations, or other ways in which the model exhibits weaknesses in capturing the relationships being modeled. Providing such qualitative information is critical when certain quantitative criteria or tests measuring model performance are lacking.

Quantitative validation of loss models involves backtesting, sensitivity analysis and application of key statistical tests to gauge overall model robustness. Depending on the underlying modeling approach, the most appropriate metrics should be selected covering relevant validation areas. These metrics may be evaluated in-sample, out-of-sample or across multiple sub-samples. Table 11.2 describes various validation areas and the associated key metrics.

Case Study 4: CRE LGD Model Validation

A banking institution modeled LGD for income-producing CRE loans using a Tobit regression with the inverse of LTV, i.e., 1/LTV, property value, and macroeconomic variables as predictor variables. The LGD model was segmented by property types, where the region-specific indicators were used for the US loans to account for the LGD variation across regions. LGD regressions were estimated using a combination of the bank's internal default data and external Trepp default data. Model risk management (MRM) evaluated the following items:

- The modeling methodology and pros and cons of the selected modeling approach
- The economic intuition behind the choice of explanatory variables used in the model
- Consistency of the explanatory variables across the different property type and regional segments.

More specifically, MRM evaluated the pros and cons of the selected modeling approach with respect to industry publications and academic research in the public domain and observed that the model may not sufficiently capture the following effects: (1) impact of the rent rate on vacancy rate; (2) impact of new construction on the vacancy rate and

Case Study 4: *(cont.)*

rent rate; (3) impact of usage factor on vacancy rate and rent rate; (4) impact of property-type specific risk drivers on vacancy rate and rent rate; (5) cyclical nature of CRE market dynamics; and (6) impact of rent rates on cap rates.

Additionally, the validation tests conducted by MRM showed:

- Residuals for all LGD regressions (Tobit model) failed normality and homoscedasticity tests. This is important, since the Tobit model makes normality and homoscedasticity distributional assumptions for regression residuals.
- The LGD model does not capture differences due to default type (term default vs maturity default) or recourse type (recourse vs non-recourse).
- The model underpredicts losses for specific property classes (retail, multifamily, industrial, etc.) based on in-sample and out-of-sample backtesting results. The underprediction in the LGD model is partially mitigated by a defaulted property value adjustment applied to the loss forecasts.
- The coefficients for GDP growth rate in the retail segment and for property value in the multifamily segment showed statistically significant counter-intuitive signs, when the model was calibrated using a different time frame.
- When re-estimated at a regional level, the GDP growth rate variable in the Retail LGD model shows a statistically significant counter-intuitive sign for a geographic segment.
- When the model is re-estimated separately using the bank's internal data only and the external Trepp CMBS data only, the coefficient estimate on the Unemployment rate in the retail and industrial segments shows opposite signs between the two datasets, which is not intuitive.

11.5.3 Model Performance Validation: Summary and Conclusions

In validating model performance, sensitivity analysis is an important and effective tool for assessing model robustness and checking for model stability and can be used for:

- Model validation testing
- Quantifying a model risk buffer
- Demonstrating the conservatism of model assumptions

Table 11.2. ***Metrics for outcomes analysis (Shaikh et al. (2016)).***

Validation Areas	Description	Key Metrics
Accuracy	Comparison of actual to model predictions (e.g. default, upgrade, downgrade rates by risk ratings.)	Mean absolute percentage error (MAPE); Mean absolute error (MAE) Root mean square error (RMSE) Cumulative percentage error (CPE) McFadden pseudo R-squared
Stability	Analysis of shift in population characteristics from the time of model development to any reference time period.	Population stability index (PSI) Character stability index (CSI)
Sensitivity	Capturing the sensitivity of models to macroeconomic factors by performing factor prioritization and factor mapping.	Sensitivity ratio.
Model discrimination	Validation of the statistical measure of models' ability to discriminate risk.	Kolmogorov–Smirnov (KS) C-statistic Gini Coefficient Concordance
Vintage analysis	Comparison of behavior of loss over time.	MAPE RMSE

11.5.4 Outcomes Analysis

Outcomes analysis compares the actual estimates produced by a model against historically observed outcomes, as opposed to identifying the limitations of a model. Examples of outcomes analysis include backtesting, out-of-sample testing, and actual-to-expected comparisons on an ongoing basis. Outcomes analysis should be performed prior to implementing the model and done at least on an annual basis after implementation to ensure it is performing as expected. Error limits should be developed for the outcome analysis results, and if the actual errors from the model exceed those limits, predetermined actions should be required. If the model is recalibrated or updated on an annual basis, limits should also be developed that monitor the size and frequency of re-estimating the model. If updating the model repeatedly results in large changes in the estimates produced by the model, then certain actions should be required, including external model validation, a recalibration of the model, or even development of an entirely new methodology or type of model. The action type and triggers for the specific action should be set out in advance of, and in accordance with, the use and risk of the model. These policies should be written and included in the model governance policies of the banking/institution. The initial model validation could be used to help set error limits for the model.

11.5.4.1 Outcomes Analysis: AIRB Regulatory Capital Models

Banking institutions are expected to conduct a number of exercises to demonstrate the accuracy of their IRB estimates (Paragraphs 388 and 389 of the Basel II Accord.) Such exercises should include comparisons of estimates to relevant internal and external data (benchmarking), comparisons of estimates to those produced by other estimation techniques (often referred to as Challenger Models), and the comparison of model estimates to realized outcomes (backtesting). The benchmarking exercises could be any of the following (BCBS internal observations):

- **Cross-bank comparisons:** These exercises involve aggregating IRB estimates or internal ratings across portfolios and portfolio segments, and comparing the results with those of other peer banks or external sources (e.g., external agency ratings such as those provided by Moody's and S&P).
- **Common obligor analysis:** These exercises involve aggregating IRB estimates for a subset of exposures where multiple banks are exposed to an identical set of obligors. Identifying commonly held

obligor sets effectively controls for deviations in the three key parameters from the benchmark that can be attributed to differences in risk.

- **Hypothetical portfolio exercises:** In these exercises, banks are asked to develop IRB estimates for a hypothetical set of exposures.
- **Backtesting exercises:** Backtesting exercises involve the comparison of realizations of historical defaults and losses to IRB estimates. Specifically, historical realizations of default rates are compared to PD estimates, historical realization of loss rates on defaulted exposures are compared to LGD estimates, and historical realizations of exposure sizes on defaulted exposures are compared to EAD estimates. Such comparisons can show whether bank estimates show a reasonable relationship to actual risk-determined outcomes.
- **Thematic reviews of modeling practices (mostly conducted by supervisors):** Benchmarking exercises need not be restricted to quantitative considerations. Some supervisors mentioned thematic reviews of specific modeling practices across banks. The "benchmark" in this case might be practices observed to be common or expected, with an objective to identify bank practices that deviate from this benchmark. Such exercises are resource-intensive in that they typically require on-site interactions and in-depth reviews of model development documentation.
- **Regression-based exercises (mostly conducted by supervisors):** Some supervisors apply regression techniques to the development of benchmarks for PD, LGD and EAD estimates. Regression specifications and techniques vary but they all necessarily rely on risk-driver information obtained through supervisory reporting to produce benchmark estimates that can then be compared to banks' estimates.

Benchmarking and challenger models are both important analytical tools that can be used in a bank's validation efforts. However, it is important to note that the two types of tools focus on different aspects of model validation. Benchmarking provides insights into the performance of IRB parameter estimates (outcomes analysis) relative to a benchmark; whereas, challenger models provide insights into the bank's chosen modeling approach (process analysis) relative to alternative modeling approaches.

Case Study 5: Outcomes Analysis of AIRB LGD

A benchmark model was developed by a banking institution as a part of its LGD validation using external Moody's URD data. The benchmark model assumed a linear relationship between LGD and several risk drivers. For each observation, the dataset included risk drivers and other attributes such as instrument type and default type, which were used to build a statistically based benchmark model. The LGD was estimated as a linear function of the following variables: debt cushion; instrument type; default type; instrument ranking; issuer total debt; and principal amount at default. All estimated coefficients were statistically significant at the 95% confidence level and the R-square was above 40%. Predicted LGDs from the benchmark model developed on Moody's data were higher than the observed LGDs.

The validation report noted, among other issues, the following limitations for the benchmark model:

- The majority of Moody's URD data used to construct the benchmark model used corporate bonds; whereas, the bank's LGD data used bank loans.
- The bank faced challenges in mapping its internal data to external data in order to use the benchmark model that was developed on Moody's data. The selected risk drivers in the benchmark model, for example, debt cushion, may not have been mapped perfectly to an equivalent variable in the internal data.
- Facility LGD in a segment typically exhibits distributions such as a bi-modal or beta distribution by common risk mitigants such as collateral, seniority, or type of business or products. LGD performance can be related to the macroeconomic factors in a country or a sector, and to a bank's recovery process or practice.
- The predicted LGDs from the benchmarking model exhibit a Gaussian-like distribution, which differs from the observed LGD distribution based on Moody's URD data. This result indicates that a linear regression model based on the statistically selected risk drivers is not adequate to capture the LGD profile.
- The predicted facility-level LGDs were mostly concentrated in the 30%–45% facility grades, indicating the performance of the benchmarking model was poor in differentiating facility-level LGDs.

11.5.4.2 Outcomes Analysis: CCAR/DFAST Models

In CCAR/DFAST, benchmark models[2] should provide a significantly different perspective (such as different theoretical approach, different methodology, and different data) as opposed to just tweaking or making minor changes to the primary or champion approach.

Examples of good or leading practices would include the following:

- Identification of material portfolios that require a benchmark
- Having a set process for developing and implementing benchmark models (as banks have for all models)
- Clear expectations for benchmarks to supplement results of the primary or champion model
- Using several different benchmark models, each with their own different strengths, thereby allowing the bank to triangulate around an acceptable model outcome
- Using benchmark models to alter primary or champion model results as a "bridge" or transition to eventual better modeling in the future.

Examples of bad or lagging practices would include the following:

- No benchmark model, not a good fit, or not evaluated for quality
- Overreliance on developer benchmarks by validation staff
- Differences in results not reconciled or explained
- Change a variable or two, or otherwise make slight tweaks to the model, and then claim that is a benchmark model

Results of benchmarking exercises can be a valuable diagnostic tool in identifying potential weaknesses in a bank's risk quantification system. However, benchmarking results should never be considered definitive indicators of the relative accuracy or conservativeness of banks' estimates. The benchmark itself is an alternative estimate, and differences from that estimate may be due to different data, different levels of risk, or different modeling methods. The identification of outliers from the benchmark should always be investigated further to determine underlying causes of divergences.

Because no single benchmarking technique is likely to be adequate for all situations, the development of underlying benchmarks should also consider multiple approaches to arrive at more informed

[2] Firm guidance differs by categories (see SR 15–18 and SR 15–19)

conclusions. As examples, benchmarks can be constructed using unweighted or exposure-weighted averages, PIT or TTC estimates, or with or without regulatory add-ons.

Benchmarking exercises should consider multiple layers of analyses to avoid drawing misleading conclusions. For example, analysis at a portfolio level may suggest alignment with the benchmark when a bank's estimates overpredict for some sub-portfolios or segments (by product type, by geography, or by rating grade) but underpredict for others.

Benchmarking analyses that rely on multiple data sources are likely to produce more robust analyses than those that rely on a single data source. Similarly, benchmarking analyses that also consider qualitative factors (differing modeling approaches and environmental factors) are likely to be more informative than strictly quantitative exercises.

11.6 Model Validation Report

The final step of a model validation is communication of the results through a model validation report. The model validation report should be a written report that documents the model validation process and results. The report should highlight potential limitations and assumptions of the model and it may include suggestions on model improvements.

11.6.1 Model Validation Report: AIRB Regulatory Capital Models

Validation reports should be transparent. Transparency refers to the extent to which third parties, such as rating system reviewers and internal or external auditors and supervisors, are able to understand the design, operations and accuracy of a bank's IRB systems and to evaluate whether the systems are performing as intended (US Final Rule, Section 22(k)). Transparency should be a continuing requirement and achieved through documentation. Banks are required to update their documentation in a timely manner, such as when modifications are made to the rating systems.

Documentation should encompass, but is not limited to, the internal risk rating and segmentation systems, risk parameter quantification processes, data collection and maintenance processes, and model design, assumptions, and validation results. The guiding principle governing documentation is that it should support the requirements for the quantification, validation, and control and oversight mechanisms, as well as the bank's broader credit risk management and reporting needs. Documentation is critical to the supervisory oversight process. A bank's validation policy should outline the document requirements.

Case Study 6: Validation Report for AIRB Models

One bank's validation policy specified the documentation template for model assessment along the following topics:

- Validation timeline
- Summary of validation
- Intended uses of the Model
- Model input and data requirement
- Data processing procedures and transformations
- Model assumptions
  - Market, business or data related assumptions and decisions
  - Mathematical, statistical or technical assumptions and decisions
  - General assessment of model assumptions
- Model review
  - General model review
  - Alternative modeling approach
  - Assessment of business model documentation and testing
- Limitations and compensating controls
  - Limitations of the general modeling framework
  - Limitations of the model implementation and technical assumptions
  - Compensating controls
- Validation restrictions and corrective actions
- Model or system control environment
- Model implementation and approximation
- Testing approach and validation procedures
  - Justification for choice of the testing approach
  - Independent implementation of business model
  - Independent implementation of benchmark model
  - Comparison of business models/engines
  - Business test results
- Conclusions

11.6.2 *Validation Report: CCAR/DFAST Models*

SR 15–18 guidance (p. 9): "A firm's documentation should cover key aspects of its capital planning process, including its risk-identification, measurement and management practices and infrastructure; methods to estimate inputs to post-stress capital ratios; the process used to aggregate estimates and project capital needs; the process for making capital decisions; and governance and internal control practices. A firm's capital planning documentation should include detailed information to enable independent review of key assumptions, stress testing outputs, and capital action recommendations."

CCAR/DFAST validation reports should include assessment of model overlays, if any.

11.6.3 *Model Validation Report: Summary and Conclusions*

The Model Validation Report should be sufficiently detailed so that parties unfamiliar with a model can understand how the model operates, its limitations, and its key assumptions.

For a complex model with many components (i.e., segments or sub-models), model developers are required to provide all the tests for each segment/sub-model in a comprehensive document, which provides sufficient evidence that a test conducted for one segment is still valid for another segment, so that a model performance can be compared and reported separately for each segment/sub-model. Technical soundness must be assessed for the overall model and every model component contained in the same model submission.

11.7 Vendor Model Validation and Partial Model Validation

The regulatory expectation is that banks will apply the same rigor in validating vendor models as they do for their internally developed models. Comprehensive validations on so-called black box models developed and maintained by third-party vendors are therefore problematic, because the mathematical code and formulas are not typically available for review (in many cases, a validator can only guess at the cause-and-effect relationships between the inputs and outputs based on the model's documentation provided by the vendor). Where the proprietary nature of these models limits full-fledged validation, banking institutions should perform robust outcomes analysis including sensitivity and benchmarking analyses. Banking institutions should monitor models periodically and assess the model's conceptual soundness, supported by adequate documentation on model customization, developmental evidence, and applicability of the vendor model applied to the bank's portfolio.

Applicable standards from supervisory guidance include:

- The design, theory, and logic underlying the model should be well documented and generally supported by published research and sound industry practice.
- The model methodologies and processing components that implement the theory, including the mathematical specification and the numerical techniques and approximations, should be explained in detail with particular attention to merits and limitations.

Banking institutions are expected to validate their own use of vendor products and should have systematic procedures for validation to help it understand the vendor product and its capabilities, applicability, and limitations. Validation should begin with a review of the documentation provided by the vendor for the model with a focus on the following:

- What is the level of model transparency?
- Does the system log results of intermediate calculations?
- How complete/detailed and granular is the level of reporting?
- Are limitations of the model clearly communicated with the magnitude/scope of possible effects?
- Are boundary conditions (i.e., conditions under which the model does not perform well) described in the documentation?
- What is the level of documentation provided?
    - Are calculations explained sufficiently?
    - Are formulas and supporting theory provided?
    - Are there detailed examples of calculations and set-up? Can these be duplicated by the firm?
    - Does the implemented model match current industry practice?

11.7.1 Partial Model Validation

As noted previously, comprehensive model validations consist of three main components: conceptual soundness, ongoing monitoring and benchmarking, and outcomes analysis and backtesting. A comprehensive validation encompassing all these areas is usually required when a model is first put into use. Any validation that does not fully address all three of these areas is by definition a limited-scope or partial validation.

Four considerations can inform the decision as to whether a full-scope model validation is necessary:

1. What feature of the model has changed since the last full-scope validation?
2. How have market conditions changed since the last validation?
3. How mission-critical is the model? How often have manual overrides of model output been necessary?

References

BCBS. (2005). Studies on the Validation of Internal Rating Systems, Working Paper No. 14.

(2005). Update on Work of the Accord Implementation Group Related to validation Under the Basel II Framework, Basel Committee Newsletter, No. 4.

(2005). Validation of low-default portfolios in the Basel II Framework, No. 6 (September 2005).

(2006). International Convergence of Capital Measurement and Capital Standards (June 2006).

(2016). SIGBB Internal Discussion Memorandum.

Board of Governors of the Federal Reserve System, 2011. SR 11-7: Guidance on Model Risk Management.

Board of Governors of the Federal Reserve System, 2013. Capital Planning at large Bank Holding Companies: Supervisory Expectations and Range of Current Practice.

U.S. Final Rule. Federal Register/ Vol 78, No 198, Oct 2013.

Glowacki, Jonathan B. Effective Model Validation, *Millman Insights*. December 24, 2012.

Shaikh, P., Jacobs, M and Sharma, N. (2016). Industry Practices in Model Validation, *Accenture*, June 2016.

12 *Validation of Models Used by Banks to Estimate Their Allowance for Loan and Lease Losses*

PARTHA SENGUPTA*

12.1 Introduction

The allowance for loan and lease losses (henceforth ALLL) represents a bank's estimate of losses expected to be experienced on its current loan portfolio over a specified period of time. Sometimes termed "reserves," ALLL is one of the most significant estimates that appear on banks' financial statements and regulatory filings. Table 12.1 summarizes allowance information for US banks. For example, average ALLL reported by the four mega banks in the United States (BAC, C, JPM, and WFC) on 12/31/17 was $10.2 billion. The median reserve ratio (ratio of ALLL to total loans) of these banks was about 1.2 percent whereas on average allowances were about 1.4 times the nonperforming loan balance. Given the significance of these numbers, it is not surprising that ALLL is under significant scrutiny from bank regulators, auditors and security analysts.

Bank regulators focus on ALLL for a number of reasons. First, often viewed as an indicator of a bank's "expected" losses on its loan portfolios, ALLL is informative about the credit risk of a bank's loan portfolios. The Comptroller's Handbook on Allowance for Loan and Lease Losses (2012) states that (page 3 of [1]):

> The allowance must be maintained at a level that is adequate to absorb all estimated inherent losses in the loan and lease portfolio.

Second, ALLL directly impacts the bank's capital calculations; therefore, if a bank is facing capital constraint (regulatory capital requirements are binding), increases in ALLL may have to be accompanied by other active policies to increase capital (e.g., restricting dividend

* Office of the Comptroller of the Currency. The views and opinions expressed in this essay are those of the author only and do not necessarily correspond to those of the Office of the Comptroller of the Currency, the United States Treasury, or those of its employees.

Table 12.1. *Allowance (ALLL) data for 2017: US banks.*

Q4–2017 median values across banks:	*Top 4 banks*	*>$1 billion*	*All banks*
Total allowance ($ millions)	10,170	16.55	1.71
Total allowance to loans (%)	1.18	1.02	1.20
Total allowance to non-performing loans (%)	144.28	196.47	194.69
Allowance to loans – residential real estate* (%)	0.33	0.61	
Allowance to loans – commercial loans* (%)	0.86	1.14	
Allowance to loans – credit cards* (%)	3.91	2.98	

*Portfolio-level allowance information is provided by the larger banks only. Numbers are based on Bank Call Report data.

payments). Finally, some policymakers and regulators view ALLL as a buffer that helps protect banks and reduce their risk of insolvency although this view is not universally supported.

In this chapter I focus on potential issues and challenges bank examiners may face while attempting to review the quality of a bank's model risk management practices and its validation of the modeling methodologies used to estimate ALLL. Unfortunately, this task is complicated by the fact that the accounting for ALLL is undergoing significant changes with new accounting standards scheduled to be implemented in 2020. Therefore, by the time this book is published, many of the current modeling methodologies and validation concerns will cease to be relevant. Furthermore, since the new standards are yet to be implemented, we are not privy to banks' new modeling methodologies and validation practices surrounding these new models will take a few years to evolve fully. In order to make this chapter relevant to readers, I take the approach of extracting modeling and validation concerns of today that I expect to be relevant under the new accounting regime. I also provide my hypotheses on the potential modeling and validation challenges that I expect to arise as the new accounting standards get implemented.

The rest of the chapter is set up as follows. I start with a brief description of the current incurred loss methodology of reserve computations in Section 12.2. Next I provide some discussion on the potential concerns raised about this reserve methodology that might have precipitated the change in reserve accounting. In Section 4, I provide a discussion of the Current Expected Credit Loss (CECL) methodology. In Section 5, I identify some of the modeling and validation challenges that seem to be unique to the CECL methodology. Next, I transition into other concerns that could be common to the current reserve methodology and the upcoming approach. The last section concludes.

12.2 Pre-2020 Accounting for ALLL

The current accounting requirements for computing ALLL vary according to (1) whether loans are expected to have been impaired or not, and (2) whether the loans have been purchased or originated. A number of accounting standards, including ASC 450-20, ASC 310-10, and ASC 310-20 provide guidance on how allowances on various portfolios should be computed. For example, ASC 310-10 refers to impaired loans and prescribes that banks should use the estimated fair value of the loans to compute the ALLL. This approach implies a lifetime view for reserve computation. On the other hand, ASC 450-20 relates to non-impaired loans and for these loans reserves are computed to estimate losses that are probable and estimable. This is the largest portion of ALLL at most banks.

A brief description of all relevant accounting standards applicable today is provided below.[1] Note that loans that are held for sale are listed at fair value and allowances are not computed for these loans.

12.2.1 Reserves for Non-impaired Loans

ASC 450-20 (previously FAS 5) drives the recognition of reserves for loans that are currently not impaired. These include all loans *except* those that were individually evaluated and found to be impaired. These are evaluated in pools with similar risk characteristics.

The allowance methodology under ASC 450-20 is popularly known as the Incurred Loss Methodology which requires banks to record reserves for "probable losses that have already been incurred that

[1] The new accounting standards becoming effective from 2020 is discussed in Section 4.

can be reasonably estimated" (page 9 of [2]). Since the point at which a loss is incurred is typically not observable, banks estimate the average length of time it takes for a loss trigger (e.g., the loss of a job) to be observed by the bank (e.g., non-payment of the loan) and reserve for expected losses over this period. This period is often called the Loss Emergence Period. Typically this period is one year or more: "Generally, institutions should use at least an 'annualized' or 12-month average net charge-off rate for such loans" (page 10 of [2]).

Since this is the largest component of reserve for most banks, a wide variety of methodologies are in use to compute this reserve. Methodologies range from simple (e.g., using some type of historical average of loss rates or net charge-off rates) to sophisticated (models estimating PDs, LGDs, and EADs using detailed loan-level data to capture loan attributes, borrower attributes and – to some extent – economic conditions). Methodologies vary across the type of portfolio examined (e.g., mortgages, home equity, credit card, commercial). All portfolios have their unique features that add to the modeling challenge. For example, for lines of credit, defaults on additional draws expected over the LEP have to be estimated. This is not a concern for mortgages. For commercial loans made to borrowers that do not have public debt ratings, banks have to develop their own rating methodology to rank these borrowers and track their credit risk over time.

12.2.2 Reserves for Impaired Loans

A loan is impaired when it is probable that an institution will be unable to collect all amounts due (both principal and interest) according to the contractual terms of the original loan agreement. The accounting guidance for the loans that are individually identified as impaired is provided in ASC 310 (Receivables). This states that once impaired, the amount of impairment (allowance) is computed based on either (1) the present value of expected cash flows, (2) observable market price, or (3) the fair value of the collateral (if the loan is collateral-dependent), less estimated costs to sell. Therefore, on these loans reserves capture expected losses over the full life.

One type of loan that falls into this category is a troubled debt restructuring (TDR). A loan is considered a TDR if (1) the restructuring constitutes a concession and (2) the debtor is experiencing financial difficulties. FASB Update 2011-02 [9] defines the conditions under which a restructuring is a TDR. All of the following conditions must be met:

- The borrower must be experiencing financial difficulty at the time of the modification, or the lender must anticipate that the borrower will experience difficulty making their near-term payments on the existing loan.
- The lender has granted a concession to the troubled borrower that they would not otherwise have granted to a non-troubled borrower.
- The concession granted by the lender must be something other than an interest-only concession of three months or less.

Note that impaired loans should not be included in the pool of loans that are evaluated under ASC 450 (non-impaired loans).

12.2.3 Reserves for Purchased Credit-Impaired Loans

ASC 310-30 (SOP 02-3) applies to loans that are acquired and meet both of the following conditions: (1) deterioration in credit quality occurred *after* origination and (2) it is probable that the acquirer will be unable to collect all contractually obligated payments from the borrower. For these purchased credit-impaired loans, declines in expected collections over time would be recorded as allowances using present value of expected future cash flow method.

12.3 The Financial Crisis and Criticisms of the Incurred Loss Methodology

After the financial crisis in 2008, policymakers, bank regulators, and researchers devoted significant attention to determine its causes. Many potential problems were highlighted, and reserve accounting was one of them. It was observed that reserves fell short of actual (one-year-ahead) charge-offs at many banks in the 2008–2009 period.[2] Some argued that the current accounting rules hampered banks' ability to

[2] Using quarterly call report data for all banks, I observe that during 2008–2009 in about 18 percent of the cases, allowances fell short of future four-quarter net charge-offs. For all bank-quarter data for the 26-year period of 1990–2015, I observe the same in less than 5 percent of the cases. Focusing on the larger (>$1 billion) banks, I find that during 2008–2009 in about 33 percent of the cases, allowances fell short of future four-quarter net charge-offs.

increase reserves ahead of the crisis because the rules required that losses have to be "probable" and "incurred" to be reserved for. While in practice banks had the flexibility to adjust reserves as economic conditions changed, it is true that the standards prescribe that expectations about future economic conditions should not be explicitly incorporated in reserve computations. Therefore, the standards could be interpreted as backward-looking rather than forward-looking and a bank following the standards carefully could decide to wait until actual losses started increasing in a downturn before increasing reserves substantially. Some standard-setters, policymakers and regulators have used this argument to push for a more forward-looking approach to computing reserves. While the case for making the reserve computations more forward-looking is fairly compelling, there is little empirical research to indicate that reserve accounting actually caused or accentuated the financial crisis. Nor is there conclusive evidence to indicate that a different accounting approach to reserve accounting would have prevented the financial crisis or allowed regulators to identify problem-banks early. In his 2013 speech, Tom Curry – the Comptroller of the Currency at that point – notes [4]:

> The simple fact is that no loan loss methodology would have kept us out of trouble during the financial crisis.

A second criticism raised against the existing accounting standards is that it might have made loan reserves pro-cyclical. This viewpoint can be summarized by the following extracted from the 2013 speech of Tom Curry, the Comptroller of the Currency [4]:

> By requiring banks to wait for an "incurred" loss event to recognize the resulting impairment, the model precludes banks from taking appropriate provisions for emerging risks that the bank can reasonably anticipate to occur. The result too often has been the need for banks to make large loan loss provisions in the midst of a credit downturn, often when earnings and lending capacity are already stressed. This leads to pro-cyclicality and results in delayed loss recognition.

In other words, the "incurred loss" methodology might have precluded banks from raising reserves in benign economic times in anticipation of a future crisis. As the economic downturn started, banks then raised reserves quickly, causing reserves to be pro-cyclical. To the extent that a bank faced capital constraints in the downturn, increases in reserves in these times would have reduced their capital and this might have caused them to reduce their new lending activity, accentuating the economic downturn. This argument does sound reasonable but two caveats are worth mentioning. First, the argument applies only when a bank faces a capital constraint; otherwise increases in reserves, by itself, should not impact its lending activity. Second, it is not clear why reducing pro-cyclicality should be a criteria for evaluating the appropriateness of financial accounting standards.

12.4 The New Current Expected Credit Loss (CECL) Methodology

Criticisms of the Incurred Loss Methodology raised in the post crisis period culminated in the Financial Accounting Standards Board (FASB) issuing Accounting Standards Update 2016-13 (Topic 326) in June 2016 [5]. The proposed new methodology – commonly referred to as the Current Expected Credit Loss (CECL) methodology – is a major shift in the way reserves would be computed. Effective for fiscal years beginning after December 15, 2019, public business entities that are SEC filers will have to reserve for losses expected over the contractual life of a loan they hold for investment.[3] In computing the reserves, banks can use information on past events, current conditions, and reasonable and supportable expectations about the future.

CECL brings in a major paradigm shift in the way allowances are to be computed. Its two most significant innovations are: (1) an extension of the measurement window to full contractual life of the loan, and (2) the incorporation of reasonable and supportable expectations about future economic conditions in the loss forecasts. CECL also removes the requirement that losses have to be "incurred" and "probable" to be reserved for. Therefore, allowances would be recorded even if the probability of losses are low and these are expected to result from a future loss-triggering event.

As banks reveal more information on how they actually plan to implement CECL, various modeling and validation challenges emerge. I discuss these in more detail in the next section. There is also some confusion in the industry about the appropriate interpretation of certain

[3] Allowances would not be computed for loans held for sale.

components of the standards. In cases where alternative interpretations of CECL standards have been proposed, I discuss the potential pros and cons of these interpretations in the next section as well.

12.5 Potential Modeling and Validation Concerns surrounding CECL

As of writing this chapter the effective inter-agency guidance on allowance computations is the one published in 2006 pertaining to the incurred loss methodology in use today [2]. Upcoming issues on CECL implementation are addressed through the inter-agency Frequently Asked Questions bulletin [6]. Regarding the validation of allowance methodologies, there is no separate guidance pertaining to validation and model risk management of allowance methodologies. Therefore, current validation practices of ALLL models are primarily driven by OCC 2011–12 [3]. Drawing from these documents I highlight some modeling and validation challenges that can arise during CECL implementation. In Section 12.6, I discuss issues that could be common to both CECL and the current allowance methodologies.

12.5.1 Issues from Extending the Loss Measurement Window to Contractual Life

Arguably, the biggest innovation of CECL is the extension of the loss-measurement window to the contractual life of loans. For banks with thirty-year mortgages, this is a significant shift. Even incorporating the likelihood of prepayments, banks could be looking at effective lives (or measurement windows) of seven years or more, for this portfolio. The extension of the measurement window results in a number of model development and validation challenges that I discuss below.

Observation 5.1.1: Iterative applications of one-year PDs (or loss rates) over some average loan life may not yield the "correct" lifetime PD (or CECL reserves). I illustrate this point using default rates and loss rates generated by the Department of Housing and Urban Development (HUD) and reported in their 2016 study [7]. HUD uses their rich historical loan-level data on mortgages to estimate claim rates (can be viewed as the probability of default), and loss rates over the

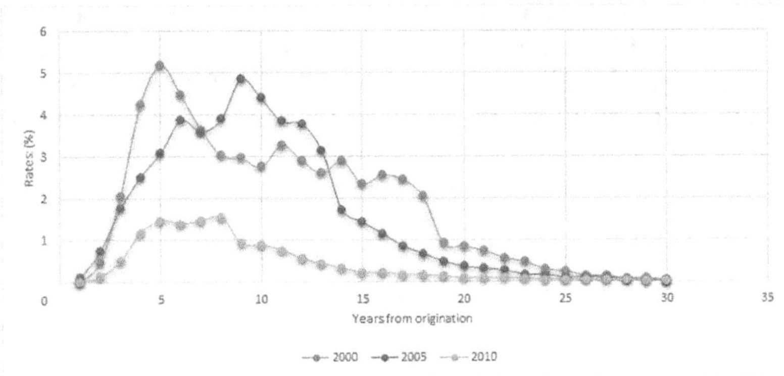

Figure 12.1 Conditional claims rates over different horizons for the 2000, 2005 and 2010 loan chorts.

full contractual life of the loans.[4] Figure 12.1, generated from this study, shows that for each cohort of loans, PDs first increase with loan age and then decrease gradually. This "maturation" effect has been observed for most types of mortgage loans, suggesting that a simple multiplication of one-period PD with some measure of life is unlikely to yield the true lifetime PD. Beyond the first few periods, PDs and loss rates may go down as LTVs improve (with gradual home price increase) and debt-income rise (improvements in income over time).[5] Over long horizons, prepayments may also play a big role in affecting PDs. Therefore, banks should explore methodologies that allow them to capture the effect of loan age and prepayments on PDs/loss rates. Appendix B provides an example illustrating the effects of this maturation on loss estimation. It shows that in situations where the probability of default varies with loan age, CECL loss forecasts cannot be accurately computed based on one-year loss rates and average loan life estimates. This is true even when the effects of changes in loss rates due to changes in macroeconomic conditions over time.

[4] The HUD study uses loan-level data from 1975 to 2016 on over 32 million loans to estimate claim rates, prepayment rates and loss rates over the full life of mortgage loans, making their computations consistent with CECL. They also incorporate expectations of key macroeconomic factors, again along the lines of CECL. More details of the HUD study and the data are provided in Appendix A.

[5] Of course, during economic downturns these trends may reverse.

Observation 5.1.2: Data over one economic cycle or the average effective life of loans in the portfolio might not necessarily be adequate. Suppose a bank makes the determination in 2020 that the average length of its mortgage portfolio is seven years. Would data from 2013–2019 be adequate for loss estimation? Note that if this is done, actual seven-year cumulative PDs (and full maturation curves) can be obtained only for the 2013 cohort of data – the rest of the data can only paint a partial picture. The fact that the seven-year PD information comes from only one cohort makes it difficult to estimate how this might change over time as economic conditions change. As Figure 12.1 above shows, cumulative PDs vary significantly from one cohort to another, at least partly due to the effect of differing economic conditions on PDs.

Observation 5.1.3: CECL creates a bigger disconnect between loss forecasts and observed charge-offs. Under the incurred loss methodology, validators would often compare allowance forecasts to actual charge-offs over the next few quarters. The problem is that charge-offs in a quarter represent realized losses on a mixed portfolio of loans consisting of different vintages (including loans originated during the quarter). CECL should be computing cumulative lifetime losses on a fixed cohort of loans existing on the measurement date. The impact of this problem might be low when the measurement window is short (e.g., one year) since losses on loans originating during this window might be low. However, under CECL, since the measurement window can be fairly lengthy for certain portfolios such as mortgages, actual charge-offs need to be segregated to identify those that relate to loans existing at a fixed point for proper performance measurement. Therefore, new methodologies for model monitoring and performance measurement have to be developed.

Observation 5.1.4: Certain methodologies used for backtesting and out-of-time testing might become impractical under CECL. Generally, for true out-of-time testing one would need out-of-time data over the period of reserve measurement (e.g., LEP). In the context of CECL this would mean that for a mortgage portfolio with an average effective life of seven years, a bank would need to leave out seven years of data in order to evaluate its out-of-time performance. This of course may not be practical so some alternative ways of measuring model performance would have to be developed. One potential risk under CECL might be that one may rely more on the short-term performance measures of long-term loss forecasting models, which might not be optimal.

Observation 5.1.5: While CECL allows banks to incorporate the time value of money through appropriate discounting techniques, model validators and regulators should make sure that the bank's approaches are correctly incorporating the time value information.

CECL increases the loss-measurement window for a number of portfolios – particularly mortgages – raising the question of whether discounting is allowed in the computation of CECL allowances. The FASB has specifically indicated that discounting is an acceptable approach:

> The allowance for credit losses may be determined using various methods. For example, an entity may use discounted cash flow methods, loss-rate methods, roll-rate methods, probability-of-default methods, or methods that utilize an aging schedule. (Paragraph 326-20-30-3 of FASB's Topic 326)

Given that the accounting standard discusses the possibility of discounting in the context of a cash-flow-based method, the question arises whether CECL allowances can be computed by discounting forecasted losses (instead of forecasted cash flows). The answer to this question depends on how losses are defined and on the timing of these losses. Regarding loss measurement, these should capture all contractual cash flows (both principal and interest) not expected to be collected. Regarding the timing, these should be measured at the point cash inflows were scheduled to be received but were not received. I illustrate these points through a comprehensive mortgage loan example provided in Appendix C and discuss a few takeaways from the example here. First, it is important to note that while losses are often defined in accounting as losses of principal amounts only, discounting of principal losses only will be inappropriate since present value approaches hinge on interest foregone as the time value of money. Second, in accounting the timing of loss recognition is often driven by regulation and therefore may not correspond to the timing of cash inflows or outflows. For example, if an asset is written down to zero 180 days after a customer stops payment, there is no real cash inflow or outflow taking place on that date. Therefore, computing a loss at that point and discounting this loss would not yield a correct reserve amount. In summary, model validators and regulators should ensure that banks using a present value approach to computing reserves are properly identifying the timing of cash flows and properly measuring cash inflows or "losses."

12.5.2 Issues from Incorporating Reasonable and Supportable Forecasts of the Future

A second major innovation of CECL is the incorporation of expectations about the future in allowance estimates. Paragraph 326-20-30-7 of Topic 326 states: "..an entity shall consider available information relevant to assessing the collectability of cash flows...information relating to past events, current conditions and reasonable and supportable forecasts." This removes one long-standing criticism of the incurred loss methodology which specifically excludes the possibility of incorporating expectations about the future in allowance estimation. Therefore, CECL improves upon the current allowance methodology by expanding the information set banks can use to generate allowance forecasts. However, this can add to the complexity of allowance computations and raises important issues about how to validate economic forecasts. I list a few important issues that model validators should pay attention to, while reviewing banks' CECL methodologies.

Observation 5.2.1: The appropriateness of the economic forecasts used should be carefully validated. As banks start incorporating information about their expectations about the future, it is important to carefully validate this process. Is the bank using forecasts of inputs (such as house prices, unemployment rates) in a model to generate its loss forecasts or are they forecasting losses directly? If forecasts of inputs are used, are these internally generated or obtained from an external source? Irrespective of the source, the quality of these forecasts should be assessed carefully. Some banks may choose to explore multiple scenarios and combine them in some way. In this case, the choice of the scenarios and the process of weighting them should be carefully evaluated.

Observation 5.2.2: The choice of the length of the forecasting horizon used should be carefully evaluated. The FASB does not require banks to forecast the economic environment over the full contractual life of its loan portfolio. It states that:

.. an entity is not required to develop forecasts over the contractual term of the financial asset or group of financial assets. Rather, for periods beyond which the entity is able to make or obtain reasonable and supportable forecasts of expected credit losses, an entity shall revert to historical loss information that is reflective of the contractual term of the financial asset or group of financial assets. (Paragraph 326-20-30-9)

The language allows for significant variability in the forecast horizon across portfolios and banks. Bank examiners should carefully evaluate how a bank determines its forecast horizon. While it might be reasonable for one bank to be more confident about its future loss estimates than another (and choose a longer forecast horizon) it is not necessarily clear whether one bank might be better than another in forecasting the future economic conditions that are used as inputs in the loss estimation models. Horizontal comparisons of banks' practices may be useful here.

Observation 5.2.3: The methodology used to revert to some loss history should be carefully reviewed. The FASB states that:

. . .periods beyond which the entity is able to make or obtain reasonable and supportable forecasts of expected credit losses, an entity shall revert to historical loss information. (Paragraph 326-20-30-9)

The standards do not provide guidance on the exact nature of reversion to be applied. One of the questions that arise is whether the standard requires reversion to a bank's historical loss experience or whether it can revert to historical values of inputs and use the resulting loss forecasts. In the absence of further guidance, both methods may be permissible. A second question relates to the speed of reversion. Again, in the absence of further guidance a number of alternatives have been proposed including immediate reversion and straight-line reversion over a certain period. One point I note here is that historically economic conditions have been observed to change only gradually. This is illustrated in the graph of monthly unemployment rates over 1990–2016 in Figure 12.2. Similar patterns are observed for many other macroeconomic variables. Therefore, one may question the appropriateness of an immediate reversion to mean inputs after a one-year forecast at the start of an economic downturn.

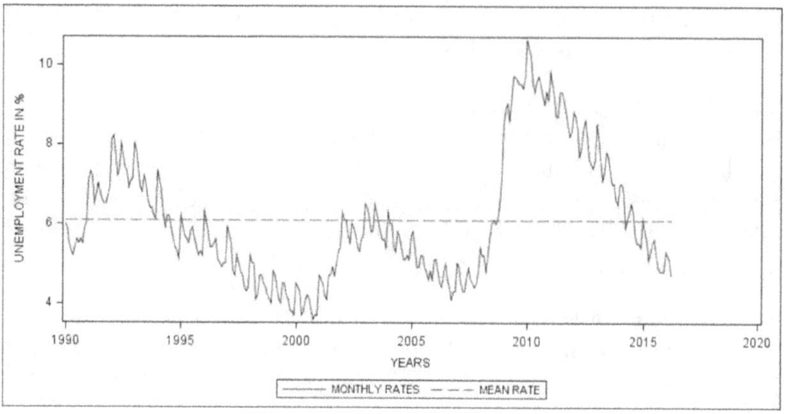

Figure 12.2 Time series of monthly unemployment rates 1990–2016.

12.5.3 Other Issues from Changes Brought in by CECL

CECL also brings in a few other changes that are worth highlighting:

Observation 5.3.1: CECL may not be capturing expected losses over the full economic life on a loan. CECL requires the computation of allowances capturing expected losses over the contractual life of an asset rather than the full economic life of an asset. The distinction can be significant for loans that typically get extended and/or renewed. FASB Update 2016-13 states:

> An entity shall not extend the contractual term for expected extensions, renewals, and modifications unless it has a reasonable expectation at the reporting date that it will execute a troubled debt restructuring with the borrower. (Paragraph 326-20-30-6)

The issue has raised a debate along a number of fronts. Some have argued that the standards fail to capture the risk of extending loans of substandard borrowers. Others argue that the change may result in a reduction in allowances if under the current practice losses over a longer horizon are captured. Some have debated whether the standard's language of "troubled debt restructuring (TDR)" can be exploited to capture potential losses expected beyond the initial contract period. The possibility of forecasting future TDRs have also been discussed. However, the FASB has clarified that it expects banks to

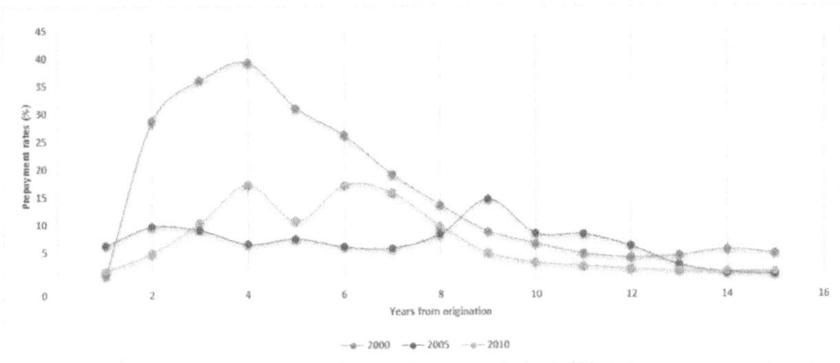

Figure 12.3 Conditional prepayment rates over different horizons for the 2000, 2005 and 2010 loan cohorts (30-year fixed mortgages).

identify expected TDRs at the reporting date on a loan-by-loan basis rather than on a pooled (probabilistic) basis.

Observation 5.3.2: Modeling (or forecasting) prepayments will likely become more important under CECL. Although it is not necessary for banks to model prepayments explicitly, it is clear that prepayments can significantly reduce the likelihood of default and losses. Figure 12.3 shows the prepayment rates for different loan cohorts based on the HUD study [7]. The graphs show that prepayments continue to be significant for mortgages even beyond five years. Since prepayments can cause the loss rates on a particular loan portfolio to go down with loan age, simple iterative applications of yearly loss rates or charge-off rates over some average loan life may differ significantly from the true cumulative loss rates experienced in these portfolios that CECL is expected to capture.

Observation 5.3.3: Reserves may not be needed to capture undrawn commitments on open lines. The FASB's position on commitments is summarized as follows:

> In estimating expected credit losses for off-balance-sheet credit exposures, an entity shall estimate expected credit losses on the basis of the guidance in this Subtopic over the contractual period in which the entity is exposed to credit risk via a present contractual obligation to extend credit, unless that obligation is unconditionally cancellable by the issuer. (Paragraph 326-20-30-11)

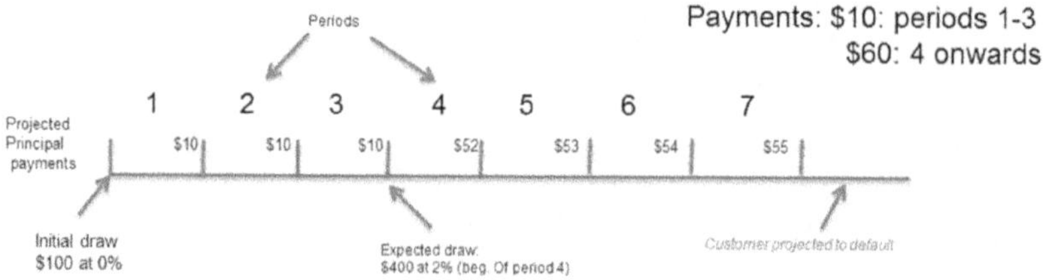

Figure 12.4 Illustration of payments on a credit card and allowance.

This has raised the question of how to determine if an obligation is unconditionally cancellable or not. While a bank may claim that their lines are cancellable at will, for certain types of loans such as HELOCs, various state and federal regulations restrict banks' ability to terminate, reduce or suspend these contracts (e.g., Regulation Z). In cases where banks designate portfolios with significant on-balance sheet commitments as unconditionally cancellable, bank examiners should review the specific language of the contract and applicable governmental requirements to determine if the obligation is truly unconditionally cancellable.

Observation 5.3.4: Computing reserves to cover the on-balancesheet portion of revolving lines (such as credit cards) may require various assumptions that should be carefully evaluated. The problem can be illustrated in terms of a simple example of a credit card that originates with an initial draw of $100 at the promotional rate of 0%. Suppose the bank anticipates receiving periodic (e.g., monthly) payments of $10 towards this balance. Furthermore, suppose the bank anticipates that the customer will make an additional draw of $400 at the beginning of period 3 and consequently his payments will rise to $60/period thereafter. The $400 draw is expected to be at a 2% (per period) interest rate. Finally, the bank expects the customer to default in period 8. Figure 12.4 summarizes these assumptions. If credit cards' open lines are assumed to be unconditionally cancellable, in periods 1, 2 and 3 the bank should compute reserves based on the likelihood of default on the unpaid balance (based on the initial $100 draw) only. Note however, that from period 4 onwards, the customer's payments could be viewed as going towards either the original draw, or the new borrowing, or both. The way allowances are computed would depend on the way the payments are allocated to various balances. Many possibilities exist but I show a few here:

1. *Option 1*: Over periods 1–3, the bank ignores the information on possible future draw and expects payments of $10 each period. In this case the initial draw is anticipated to be paid off in 10 periods. If the customer is expected to default in period 8, reserves of $30 would be recorded at the beginning of period 0.

2. *Option 2*: Over periods 1–3, the bank anticipates the future draw and the increase in payments from period 4 but assumes FIFO in allocating all the payments. That is, all principal payments are assumed to go towards paying off the oldest balance first. Therefore. in period 4, $52 (after deducting $8 for interest) would go towards paying off the initial draw.[6] Proceeding in this way, the bank would anticipate collecting full payment on the initial draw by period 5.[7] Therefore, if it expects the customer to default in period 8, it would not record any reserves until the new draw originates in period 4.
3. *Option 3*: As in option 2, the bank anticipates the additional draw and increase in payments following this draw. However, it allocates the payments from period 4 onwards pro rata to the beginning balance and the new draw. If we assume that the 20% of the $60 projected payments are towards the initial draw, it will take about 9 periods to pay off the initial balance. Therefore, an allowance of about $27 would be recorded in period 0 if a default is expected in period 8.
4. *Option 4*: A fourth option would be to allocate payments to balances according to the Card Act. The Card Act requires banks to allocate payments to the highest interest draw first for interest computations. This would mean that from period 4 onwards, payments go towards the $400 draw only, until this balance is paid off, indicating that $70 of the initial draw will remain unpaid by the time the customer defaults in period 7 yielding an allowance of $70.

The illustration above, shows how the payment allocation scheme may impact the timing of when reserves are to be recorded. The FIFO approach (option 2) results in the lowest allowance balance and may

6 Interest calculations are rounded to the nearest dollar.

7 Note that the CARD Act requires that banks compute interest according to the assumption that payments go towards paying off the higher balance first. Therefore, for interest computations period 4's payment will be assumed to go towards the $400 draw rather than the initial draw.

be computationally the simplest. However, if one believes that future payments are associated with future draws and balances, the process using information on future payments and allocating *all* of it to current balances may be viewed as a selective use of future information. If one is to forecast payments on current balances only, should banks attempt to forecast (or mimic) payments under the hypothetical situation where there are no future borrowings taking place? Alternatively, if a bank indeed forecasts all future payments, the question may arise as to why the CARD Act would not be followed which would allocate payments to the highest interest balance first. However, I also note that the CARD Act is to be used for interest computations and banks are not required to use the same methodology for financial reporting (and reserve computation) purposes.

As the example and the discussion above shows, the question of how to forecast payments on *current draws* is a tricky one and various payment allocation assumptions are possible. Bank examiners and model validators should carefully evaluate the reasonability of these assumptions and evaluate the impact of these assumptions on reserve computations.

12.6 General Model Validation Concerns of ALLL Models

12.6.1 Data Issues

Observation 6.1.1: Loss estimates derived primarily using external data may not effectively capture a bank's own credit risk. If a bank has a very short history of loss data and/or has experienced limited losses historically, they may prefer to use external data for reserve computations. The main drawback of using external data is that the population from which the external data is collected may not be representative of the bank's own geographic footprint or risk profile. Therefore, efforts should be made to obtain an external sample that is as representative of the bank as far as possible. The following, from OCC 2011–12, alludes to this concern:

> The relevance of the data used to build the model should be evaluated to ensure that it is reasonably representative of the bank's portfolio or market conditions, depending on the type of model. This is an especially important exercise when a bank uses external data or the model is used for new products or activities. (page 11 of [3])

Model validators should look for support that the external data is indeed appropriate for the bank to use. In some cases banks would use all available external data to estimate losses and then apply scaling adjustments to these estimates to match its own loss experience. This could be problematic since the bank had resorted to using external data because they did not consider their own data appropriate for use. A better practice is to derive a sub-sample from the external population that best matches the bank and use the results based on this sub-sample.

Observation 6.1.2: Loss forecasts generated using aggregate (portfolio-level) data may not effectively capture expected credit losses, particularly for loan portfolios with long contractual lives under CECL. If a bank does not maintain a good history of loan-level data but does maintain the information at certain portfolio levels, it is possible to use this data to generate loss forecasts based on this information as well. The drawback of this approach is that it averages out the effects of loans within the portfolio. Therefore, if the bank's portfolio structure is undergoing significant changes, the model's forecasts' errors may increase. One way to mitigate this problem is to segment the data (if data permits) across the main components.

Observation 6.1.3: Feeder data and/or feeder models that are expected to have a significant impact on allowance estimates should be carefully scrutinized. In some cases, a bank will use inputs that are generated by another model. An example could be forecasts of home values used to generate CLTVs for mortgage loans. While this practice by itself is not inappropriate, there are a few practical complications of validating these models. First, when model errors are computed, forecasts of the input variables (including those coming from feeder models) should be used so the true downstream performance of the model can be properly evaluated. Second, the process through which the input variables are generated should be separately validated as well. Under CECL, economic forecasts are expected to be a significant component of allowance computations. Irrespective of whether these are internally generated or externally generated or obtained from an external source, the validity and appropriateness of these forecasts should be carefully evaluated.

Observation 6.1.4: If one of the significant variables in a loss forecasting model have a large fraction of missing data, the specific treatment of these missing observations may add a bias to loss estimates. Banks rarely have complete data for all the variables they use in model estimation. In cases where some observations are missing data on a certain variable, banks may replace these with the mean or median value for that series. This helps in maximizing the number of observations that can be used for model estimation. However, this practice assumes that the sub-sample of loans for which the data are missing do not have a systematically different risk profile from the rest of the population. For example, if some variable was missing because the borrower chose not to report it, maybe these borrowers were of higher risk (choosing not to report the data to avoid a red flag) than those reporting the variable. If this is true, replacing these variables by population averages is not appropriate. Therefore, the choice of replacing missing variables should be carefully evaluated. In some cases, it might be more reasonable to completely drop observations with missing variables.

Observation 6.1.5: Errors or biases can result from the application of certain sampling and weighing techniques. When using large datasets of loan-level data, banks sometime choose to estimate models using a subset of the data population. Various sampling approaches are possible. Apart from simple random sampling, other techniques used are stratified sampling, systematic sampling and cluster sampling. In some cases, weights may also be applied to the sampled data. Sampling techniques should be carefully evaluated for their appropriateness as certain methods of weighing and re-sampling may yield biased results.

Observation 6.1.6: Model validators should carefully evaluate the appropriateness of various data exclusions. For example, a bank may be estimating a model using data from a few large segments and then applying the results to all segments. If the bank's estimation data does not fully cover all segments and products, it is important to explain why data for certain sub-segments were ignored, and provide evidence that the model results are indeed applicable to the other segments. Is it possible that the excluded segments have significantly different risk characteristics and are expected to behave differently from other segments?

Observation 6.1.7: Model validators should be on the lookout for certain problems that can arise from pooling observations and stacking data. Sometimes time-series data are combined into panel data for estimation. Depending on the nature of data stacking and panel setup, some estimation concerns may arise. For example, heteroscedasticity could be a problem in this type of data affecting hypothesis testing. Appropriate corrections should be made to deal with this type of problems. The stacking of data could also cause certain types of observations to be weighted more heavily than others. For example, if monthly mortgage loan data for a period are combined, loans that survive longer would be repeated in the sample more often causing loans with longer maturity to be weighed more heavily in the sample. Depending on the estimation methodology, some adjustments might be needed to generate accurate estimates of model parameters.

12.6.2 Modeling Issues

Observation 6.2.1: A bank's selection of a certain model structure should be properly supported. For example, if a bank uses the proportional hazard model for estimating losses on their mortgage portfolio, the relevant question is why this structure was deemed better than some other alternatives such as the panel logistic model. Were the pros and cons of these approaches explored? The choice of the model should be driven by its purposes. For example, a model that empirically separates maturation effects, vintage effects and economic effects may have difficulty in identifying the effects of macroeconomic variables since vintage effects may capture part of this effect. Therefore, if the model's goal is to explore the sensitivity of losses to economic conditions, this methodology may not be the best choice. (This is less of an issue currently since allowances are not supposed to incorporate expectations about the future economic environment; however, this would become more of a concern under CECL when expectations about future economic conditions will play more of a role).

Observation 6.2.2: The process of variable selection should be properly supported. Validators should examine whether the bank provides a clear description of the process through which the variables were selected and whether this process makes business sense. The process should not be driven purely by model fit. Similarly, the reasoning behind using transformations, splines, lags, and interactions used should be adequately documented and supported.

Observation 6.2.3: Model reviewers should examine whether all variables used in a model are defined in a way consistent with regulations and the bank's policies. For example, if the bank's internal definition of default is 90DPD, it may not be appropriate to define 120DPD as default for modeling purposes.

Observation 6.2.4: Model validators should be aware of all model calibration and overrides that are in place and carefully evaluate the impact of these adjustments to model results. Some models have dials built-in that can be adjusted to calibrate model performance. Sometimes a bank may manually override certain input or output values. In general, these types of adjustments raise various concerns about model quality and governance. If these types of ad hoc adjustments are deemed necessary, the bank should provide detailed comparisons of model performance with and without the adjustments, support for the adjustments made, and explain what criteria it uses to determine the nature and size of adjustments, and evidence that management has been made aware of these adjustments and approved them.

Observation 6.2.5: Model validators should evaluate the model limitations and understand how these are captured in the estimation process. For example, a bank's loss estimation model may not be capturing various risks, such as those arising from balloon payments, interest rate resets etc. Therefore, validation should carefully evaluate the bank's exposures to these special types of risks, and evaluate the need for separate component models to be built or overlays to capture these special risks. The Interagency Supervisory Guidance on Allowance for Loan and lease Losses Estimation practices for Loans and Lines of Credit Secured by Junior Liens on 1–4 Family Residential Properties specifically identifies these issues (page 4 if [8]):

> . . .institutions should ensure their . . . methodology adequately incorporates the elevated borrower default risk associated with payment shocks due to (1) rising interest rates for adjustable-rate junior liens, including HELOCs, or (2) HELOC converting from interest-only to amortizing loans.

Observation 6.2.6: The use of certain period/event dummies should be well-supported. Banks sometimes include special dummies in their models to capture certain shocks that cannot be otherwise explained (through the inclusion of other model variables). These dummies improve the in-sample fit of the model but their impact on out-of-sample (particularly out-of-time) forecasts is not clear. Therefore, it is important to examine the impact of these dummies on loss forecasts and determine whether these are warranted or not.

Observation 6.2.7: Loss forecasting models with autoregressive structures should be carefully evaluated. Sometimes loss rates are forecasted in terms of lagged loss rates. This methodology is not very useful in picking up the underlying drivers of losses or identifying factors that might cause loss rates to rise (often a concern of regulators). These models also become less and less effective as the forecasting horizon gets longer. Finally, validators should be careful to ensure that for performance testing of these models, fitted values of the lagged dependent variable (rather than actual values) are used (obviously five-quarter-ahead loss rates could be fairly accurately estimated if we knew quarter-four actual loss rates but quarter-four loss rate is a model output too). Similar problems exist when delinquency rates in one bucket (e.g., 60DPD) are forecasted in terms of the previous delinquency rate (30DPD).

Observation 6.2.8: The impact of restricting the LGD measurement window on loss rates should be evaluated. Since complete loss resolution can take a fairly long time (sometimes many years), most banks incorporate charge-offs and recoveries over a fixed horizon only. Depending on the horizon chosen, a significant portion of losses (or recoveries) may be ignored. Model reviewers should carefully evaluate the assumptions banks are using to forecast additional losses beyond the measurement window and carefully evaluate the appropriateness of the LGD measurement window used.

Observation 6.2.9: The choice between using origination information and updated information in models should be carefully evaluated. Sometimes banks use information as of the loan origination date to estimate losses. This structure ignores newer information that might become available prior to the measurement date suggesting that the model specification could be improved. For example, if allowances on mortgage loans as of 12/31/2016 are computed for loans of 2010 vintage, using FICO information as of origination may not be very useful. Some of the loans may have been modified and terms changed, and this information is ignored as well. A better structure would be to use information as of a measurement (snapshot) date. Model reviewers should carefully evaluate the impact of using origination information (rather than updated information) on model performance.

Observation 6.2.10: The value added from using overly complex models should be evaluated. Sometimes the benefits of building complex models are not enough to justify the costs of developing and maintaining this complex model structure. Complex models could also lack intuition making it hard for a user to interpret the results and devise a remediation plan if performance deteriorates. Therefore, a bank should start from a simple framework and add complexity so long as the additional layer of complexity improves model performance appreciably.

Observation 6.2.11: Model reviewers should evaluate whether the models are estimated at a level of granularity that appropriately captures the risks of the portfolio. While FASB's Topic 326 does not directly opine on the level of segmentation to be used for reserve modeling, it indicates that the disclosures of reserves should be segmented by the type of financing receivable, industry sector of the borrower, and by risk rating (paragraph 326-20-55-10). If a bank chooses to use a single model to estimate its mortgage PDs using all its mortgage data, it is essentially assuming that the model variables impact PDs the same way across these potential portfolio pools. Bank examiners and model validators should look for support of this assertion. The lack of segmentation could be justified if model coefficients are observed to be stable across segments and the bank's current portfolio mix is very similar to that observed for its historical (estimation) data.

Observation 6.2.12: Model reviewers should evaluate whether the model results are applied to the proper loan portfolios. Suppose a bank estimates its credit card losses using data on consumer credit cards only, but it applies this model to forecast losses on both its consumer and business credit card loans. The bank may choose to support this decision based on the argument that it did not have enough data on business credit card loans. Implicit in this decision are the assumptions that the loss drivers of these two portfolios are the same and these drivers impact losses in the same way. These assumptions should be empirically supported.

12.6.3 Documentation Issues

Adequate documentation is an important prerequisite to effective model validation. If the model documents do not reveal enough details of the models, it is difficult to pass judgment on the model. Here is a list of some documentation deficiencies I have observed:

Observation 6.3.1: The model document should provide the final model results in a clear readable way. Model documents sometimes provide a long and rambling description of the path through which the final model specification is picked and the various alternatives that were examined and rejected. While this discussion is important, it would be useful to provide full details of the final model selected at the very beginning. Regression coefficients, t-values/p-values, variable definitions, and results of model diagnostics should be reported in a clear precise manner before other alternative model specifications and variable selection procedures are described.

Observation 6.3.2: The model document should provide an adequate description of the data used. A detailed description of the data should include summary statistics of all model variables used (not just means and number of observations) and this should also be broken down by major portfolio characteristics (FICO buckets, fixed rate loans versus ARM loans, etc.) and sample period (e.g., by year). If the bank uses external data, it should provide some comparisons of this data with internal data for the periods/segments for which internal data are available.

Observation 6.3.3: The model document should provide a clear description of variable transformations and replacements. A bank may be replacing missing values of observations with mean or median vales. In this case model reviewers should look for support that this type of replacement is not creating a bias in the results. Could the loans with missing data be associated with higher risk than the rest? The model document should include adequate support for data replacements. Similarly, if the bank performs other types of data cleaning (e.g., removal of outliers), these should be clearly explained and, in some cases, an empirical assessment of the consequences of such transformation should be provided. Finally, if the bank performs variable transformations, it should clearly explain the reasons for these and explain their consequences.

Observation 6.3.4: The model document should provide a clear and comprehensive description of all performance tests conducted. Model reviewers should look for in-sample and out-of-sample test results and side-by-side comparisons of these. Statistical tests of model fit such as mean absolute percentage error should be reported along with graphs showing forecasts and actuals. If the model has different components (e.g., PDs and LGDs) separate performance results for each should also be provided. Simple cut-and-paste from statistical packages often result in missing labels, missing description etc. Model reviewers should ensure that the results are clearly explained rather than simply dumped from SAS or STATA.

Observation 6.3.5: Model reviewers should look for detailed support on how model issues raised by model validation were remediated by model developers. A brief note such as "the issue was closed on xx/xx/xx" is not sufficient. A clear description of how the issue was remediated should be provided. If the bank provides arguments supporting their choice, this should be documented as well. In some cases, the bank's response might have to be evaluated by model validation again. Descriptions of all empirical work in support of various positions taken should be clearly documented.

12.6.4 Performance Testing Issues

Understanding model performance is ultimately the key to determining the effectiveness of the models used. Model validators play a key role in evaluating model performance, conducting sensitivity tests, and responding to the results appropriately. A large variety of sensitivity tests can and should be conducted. OCC 2011–12 provides guidance on this:

> . . .banks should employ sensitivity analysis in model development and validation to check the impact of small changes in inputs and parameter values on model outputs to make sure they fall within an expected range. Unexpectedly large changes in outputs in response to small changes in inputs can indicate an unstable model. Varying several inputs simultaneously as part of sensitivity analysis can provide evidence of unexpected interactions, particularly if the interactions are complex and not intuitively clear. (page 11 of [3])

Here I describe some of the features to look for in validating model performance:

Observation 6.4.1: Analyses of model performance should include various tests of model performance. Sometimes banks show model performance using graphs only. While graphs are useful, they cannot be completely relied upon. Therefore, the bank should report fit statistics such as mean square error, mean absolute percentage error, and Kolmogorov–Smirnov goodness-of-fit statistics. Sometimes banks report cumulative percentage errors only. These, however, may not be very reliable since positive forecasts in one period would be offset by negative forecast error in another period hiding the volatility in forecast errors over time.

Observation 6.4.2: When feeder models or lagged values are used, fitted values rather than actual values (of inputs from these sources) should be used in performance results. Suppose a bank is using monthly transition rates for forecasting reserves for its mortgage portfolio. Suppose these transition rates are forecasted using lagged transition rates. In this case, when reserves are to be computed for one year, the independent variables to be used in the second, third and four quarter forecasts are unknown and have to be forecasted. Therefore, the accuracy of reserve estimates would depend on how accurately the independent variables in the last three quarters are forecasted. Validators should be careful to evaluate true model performance for the forecast horizon which should be based on information available at the beginning of the horizon only.

Observation 6.4.3: Model validators should look for true out-of-time and pseudo out-of-time performance test results. Banks should report results of out-of-time tests whenever possible. Pseudo out-of-time results (results using data as of a certain jump-off point only) should also be reported. This is particularly useful in determining how the model would perform at different time periods.

Observation 6.4.4: Model validators should look for tests of stability of model coefficients over time and examine the sensitivity of the results shocks in key model parameters. For example, banks should be evaluating whether the parameter estimates are stable over time by estimating the coefficients using data for various sub-periods and/or sub-segments.

Observation 6.4.5: Model validators should examine whether the bank has performance thresholds for triggering model review and redevelopment. Under what circumstances would the bank determine that the model in production is not performing adequately and work on redeveloping it? How often would the modeler update the coefficients?

12.6.5 Other Issues

I list a few other validation concerns that do not fit directly into the categories listed above.

Observation 6.5.1: Special issues arise when third-party vendors are used for model development. First, the choice of the particular vendor model and its appropriateness for the bank should be clearly documented. Second, the bank's management should demonstrate sufficient knowledge of the components of the vendor model. If the vendor is not willing to reveal specifics of the model methodology, additional sensitivity analysis should be conducted to assure the reviewers that model risk is appropriately estimated and controlled for. If the model structure is too opaque to assess model risk, the use of the vendor model might be questioned. Finally, additional issues arise if external data are used; these are described in Section 12.6.1.

Observation 6.5.2: In some cases, the involvement of model validation in model documentation and refinements raises concerns of independence. One may observe significant overlap between the model document and the validation document. Portions could be cut and pasted from one to the other making it difficult to determine who generated the content. If the validation team performs tests of its own, it needs to make sure that these are reported as such. The demarcation also gets foggy when validation is conducted in pieces as the model gets built (parallel validation). In this case the validation team should clearly document all the issues raised at various stages and explain how these were remediated over time. A clean model document with few or no final issues raised by validation may cause regulators to question the adequacy of the validation. Therefore, the validation team should make extra efforts to differentiate their documentation from that produced by model development and ensure that regulators see their role in providing effective challenge.

Observation 6.5.3: Banks that switch models too frequently should be scrutinized more carefully. If a bank is switching models too often it becomes difficult to evaluate the long-term performance of any model. Therefore, these banks may face model risk that cannot be reasonably assessed. Furthermore, regulators may be concerned that these models were not developed carefully. Situations where models are developed late in the year providing little time for validation should raise red flags. It is useful to find out whether the bank has well-defined criteria for determining when to rebuild models, when to re-run them, and when to use overlays. Can the bank document whether model refinements over time are helping to improve model performance?

12.7 Conclusions

Banks' methodologies for computing loan loss reserves will undergo significant changes in 2020 due to the new accounting standards becoming effective at that point. As banks' methodologies change, regulators will have to adapt by developing new validation practices and refining existing practices to meet the new requirements. In this chapter I have made an effort to gauge some of the validation concerns that might arise when CECL gets implemented and list those concerns of today that might continue to be a concern in the future. However, since there is significant uncertainty surrounding the exact modeling methodologies that banks would use under CECL, this is a challenging task. Therefore, this chapter should be considered as representing my own expectations of upcoming issues, rather than a definitive discussion on the topic.

Appendix A Description of HUD data and Analysis

The Federal Housing Administration (FHA) maintains a Mutual Mortgage Insurance Fund to cover expected losses on the FHA loans. Every year the Housing and Urban Development (HUD) conducts an actuarial review of the Fund's value using a long time series of historical data on the FHA loans. In estimating the Fund value, the HUD study estimates conditional claims rates, conditional prepayment rates and loss rates. These rates are conditional on the values of variables used to forecast these components. Claim rate is defined as the number of loans that become claims during a time period divided by the number of surviving loans-inforce at the beginning of that period. This can be viewed as the rate of default on loans. Conditional prepayment rate is defined as the number of loans that are completely prepaid during a time period divided by the number of surviving loans-in-force at the beginning of that period.

The 2016 HUD study [7] estimated its models using the full population of loan-level data from the FHA single-family data warehouse as of 2016. This produced a population of around 32 million single-family loans originated between FY 1975 and second quarter of FY 2016. The study identified the quarterly status of loans as current, prepaid, defaulted (90+ delinquent) and blemished (prior ninety-day delinquent). The study also separately identified loans that were streamline refinanced (prepaid loans that are recaptured into FHA endorsements via streamline financing). Multinomial logit was used for model estimation. Explanatory variables in the models included mortgage age, current LTV, payment-to-income ratio, spread at origination, short-term home appreciation, relative loan size, refinance incentive, and borrower credit scores. Splines were used to model the impact of some continuous variables. Beyond the model to estimate the conditional claim rate, the study also modeled loss severity and loan volume. The study used forecasts of home prices, treasury rates, and unemployment rates in their computations.

I use various figures drawn from their analysis in this chapter because it is one of the few comprehensive studies that report cumulative loss rates and prepayment rates using a long history of time series data. The numbers reported pertain to FHA loans only and therefore may not be representative of the experiences of any particular bank. Furthermore, these numbers relate to mortgage loans only and therefore any conclusions drawn may not apply to allowance computations for other loan portfolios.

Appendix B An Example on Maturation Effect and CECL Loss Computations

Suppose a bank starts business in 2004 by issuing \$500 in new loans. This could be viewed as the bank issuing 500, \$1 loans. These loans are contracted to be paid off in four annual (equal) installments. Loans are assumed to be issued at the beginning of 2004 and payments are scheduled to be made at the end of each year. The loans are associated with no collateral. The interest rate on the loans is 5%.

Suppose the bank assumes (forecasts) losses on the loans over the four years as follows:

	yr 1	yr 2	yr 3	yr 4
Assumed loss rates (fraction of par)	0.003	0.023	0.012	0.002

In terms of beginning-of-the-year balances these translate to:

	yr 1	yr 2	yr 3	yr 4
Assumed loss rates (fraction of beg. Balance)	0.003	0.017	0.006	0.001

The bank uses these forecasted loss rates to compute CECL allowances. For simplicity, we also assume that each year the defaulting customers are those that have balances due that year. For example, out of the \$500 loans outstanding as of 1/1/2004, \$125 is due on 12/31/2004. The bank expects that \$1.50 (0.003 × \$500) of this would not be collected. Similarly, on 12/31/2004, the bank expects that out of the

		Forecasted losses (Charge-offs)				
Origination Year	Originations	Year 1	Year 2	Year 3	Year 4	Total
2004	500.00	1.50	11.50	6.00	1.00	20.00
2005	525.00	1.58	12.08	6.30	1.05	21.00
2006	551.25	1.65	12.68	6.62	1.10	22.05
2007	578.81	1.74	13.31	6.95	1.16	23.15
2008	607.75	1.82	13.98	7.29	1.22	24.31
2009	638.14	1.91	14.68	7.66	1.28	25.53
2010	670.05	2.01	15.41	8.04	1.34	26.80
2011	703.55	2.11	16.18	8.44	1.41	28.14
2012	738.73	2.22	16.99	8.86	1.48	29.55
2013	775.66	2.33	17.84	9.31	1.55	31.03
2014	814.45	2.44	18.73	9.77	1.63	32.58
2015	855.17	2.57	19.67	10.26	1.71	34.21
2016	897.93	2.69	20.65	10.78	1.80	35.92

Figure 12.5 Sequence of originations and losses (charge-offs).

	CECL Allowance components				Current ALLL
End of the year	1 yr. old loans	2 yr. old loans	3 yr old loans	Tot CECL ALLL	(1-yr-ahead c/o)
2004	18.50			18.50	11.50
2005	19.43	7.00		26.43	18.08
2006	20.40	7.35	1.00	28.75	19.98
2007	21.42	7.72	1.05	30.18	20.98
2008	22.49	8.10	1.10	31.69	22.03
2009	23.61	8.51	1.16	33.28	23.13
2010	24.79	8.93	1.22	34.94	24.28
2011	26.03	9.38	1.28	36.69	25.50
2012	27.33	9.85	1.34	38.52	26.77
2013	28.70	10.34	1.41	40.45	28.11
2014	30.13	10.86	1.48	42.47	29.52
2015	31.64	11.40	1.55	44.59	30.99
2016	33.22	11.97	1.63	46.82	32.54

Figure 12.6 CECL and current ALLL computations.

	Computing loan balances oustanding at year end				
End of the year	1 year life	2 year life	3 year life	tot bal.	WAL
2004	125.00	125.00	125.00	375.00	2.00
2005	256.25	256.25	131.25	643.75	1.81
2006	394.06	269.06	137.81	800.94	1.68
2007	413.77	282.52	144.70	840.98	1.68
2008	434.45	296.64	151.94	883.03	1.68
2009	456.18	311.47	159.54	927.19	1.68
2010	478.99	327.05	167.51	973.54	1.68
2011	502.93	343.40	175.89	1022.22	1.68
2012	528.08	360.57	184.68	1073.33	1.68
2013	554.49	378.60	193.92	1127.00	1.68
2014	582.21	397.53	203.61	1183.35	1.68
2015	611.32	417.40	213.79	1242.52	1.68
2016	641.89	438.27	224.48	1304.64	1.68

Figure 12.7 Weighted-average-life (WAL) computations.

\$125 due at that point \$1.13 ($0.023 \times \$500$) would be uncollectible. The process continues in this way.

Suppose the bank continues to issue new loans each year with a 5% increase in loan volume from year to year. In this case, the sequence of originations and losses (charge-offs) are expected to be as follows in Figure 12.5.

Based on the above information, CECL and current ALLL allowances would be computed in the Figure 12.6.

The important question is whether one could start from a one-year loss estimate (current ALLL amount) and use this in conjunction with an estimate of weighted-average loan life to get to the CECL allowance. The weighted-average-life (WAL) computations for the example are provided in Figure 12.7.

One can check that the CECL allowance ≠ (current ALLL * WAL). For example, for 2010, CECL allowance = \$34.94 whereas the current ALLL (\$24.28) multiplied by the WAL (1.68) yields \$40.79.

In order to verify that the problem is indeed a manifestation of the maturation effect of losses, we redo the example by removing the maturation effect. In order to achieve this, we change the above example by assuming the following loss projections:

	yr 1	yr 2	yr 3	yr 4
Assumed loss rates (fraction of par)	0.003	0.002	0.002	0.001

This translates to the following based on beginning-of-the-year balances:

	yr 1	yr 2	yr 3	yr 4
Assumed loss rates (fraction of beg. balance)	0.003	0.003	0.003	0.003

Since the loss rates do not vary by loan age, there is no maturation effect in play.

We keep all other information in the example the same. Under the new assumptions, the forecasted charge-offs are in Figure 12.8.

The allowance computations are shown on the next page. The Weighted-average loss (WAL) calculations remain unchanged (provided on the last page) as the loan payment assumptions do not change. In this case, we do get:

One can check that now the CECL allowance = (current ALLL * WAL). For example, for 2010, CECL allowance = \$4.91 whereas the current ALLL (\$2.92) multiplied by the WAL (1.68) yields \$4.91 as well. Figure 12.9 presents these calculations.

		Forecasted losses (Charge-offs)				
Origination Year	Originations	Year 1	Year 2	Year 3	Year 4	Total
2004	500.00	1.50	1.13	0.75	0.38	3.75
2005	525.00	1.58	1.18	0.79	0.39	3.94
2006	551.25	1.65	1.24	0.83	0.41	4.13
2007	578.81	1.74	1.30	0.87	0.43	4.34
2008	607.75	1.82	1.37	0.91	0.46	4.56
2009	638.14	1.91	1.44	0.96	0.48	4.79
2010	670.05	2.01	1.51	1.01	0.50	5.03
2011	703.55	2.11	1.58	1.06	0.53	5.28
2012	738.73	2.22	1.66	1.11	0.55	5.54
2013	775.66	2.33	1.75	1.16	0.58	5.82
2014	814.45	2.44	1.83	1.22	0.61	6.11
2015	855.17	2.57	1.92	1.28	0.64	6.41
2016	897.93	2.69	2.02	1.35	0.67	6.73

Figure 12.8 Sequence of originations and losses (charge-offs) with new assumptions.

CECL Allowance components					Current ALLL
End of the yea	1 yr. old loans	2 yr. old loans	3 yr old loans	Tot CECL ALLL	(1-yr-ahead c/o)
2004	2.25			2.25	1.13
2005	2.36	1.13		3.49	1.93
2006	2.48	1.18	0.38	4.04	2.40
2007	2.60	1.24	0.39	4.24	2.52
2008	2.73	1.30	0.41	4.45	2.65
2009	2.87	1.37	0.43	4.67	2.78
2010	3.02	1.44	0.46	4.91	2.92
2011	3.17	1.51	0.48	5.15	3.07
2012	3.32	1.58	0.50	5.41	3.22
2013	3.49	1.66	0.53	5.68	3.38
2014	3.67	1.75	0.55	5.96	3.55
2015	3.85	1.83	0.58	6.26	3.73
2016	4.04	1.92	0.61	6.58	3.91

Figure 12.9 CECL and current ALLL computations (new assumptions).

Appendix C An Example on Discounting of Cash Flows and Losses

Suppose a bank issues a \$500,000 thirty-year mortgage on 1/1/2018. The loan pays 12% interest (1% per month) yielding monthly payments of \$5,413.06. You should be able to check that the present value of these monthly payments (360 months) at 1% interest yields \$500,000 (subject to some rounding).

	Principal payment	Interest payment	Principal balance	Monthly interest rate	Forecasted cash flows
1/1/2018			500,000.00	0.01	
1/31/2018	143.06	5,000.00	499,856.94	0.01	5,143.06
2/28/2018	144.49	4,998.57	499,712.44	0.01	5,143.06
3/31/2018	145.94	4,997.12	499,566.50	0.01	5,143.06
4/30/2018	147.40	4,995.67	499,419.11	0.01	5,143.06
5/31/2018	148.87	4,994.19	499,270.23	0.01	5,143.06
6/30/2018	150.36	4,992.70	499,119.87	0.01	5,143.06
7/31/2018	151.86	4,991.20	498,968.01	0.01	5,143.06
8/31/2018	153.38	4,989.68	498,814.63	0.01	5,143.06
9/30/2018	154.92	4,988.15	498,659.71	0.01	5,143.06
10/30/2018	156.47	4,986.60	498,503.24	0.01	5,143.06
11/30/2018	158.03	4,985.03	498,345.21	0.01	0.00
12/31/2018	159.61	4,983.45	498,185.60	0.01	0.00
1/1/2019	161.21	4,981.86	498,024.40	0.01	0.00
1/31/2019	162.82	4,980.24	497,861.58	0.01	0.00
2/28/2019	164.45	4,978.62	497,697.13	0.01	0.00
3/31/2019	166.09	4,976.97	497,531.04	0.01	0.00
4/30/2019	167.75	4,975.31	497,363.29	0.01	0.00
5/31/2019	169.43	4,973.63	497,193.86	0.01	0.00
6/30/2019	171.12	4,971.94	497,022.73	0.01	0.00
7/31/2019	172.84	4,970.23	496,849.90	0.01	0.00
8/31/2019	174.56	4,968.50	496,675.33	0.01	0.00
9/30/2019	176.31	4,966.75	496,499.02	0.01	0.00
10/30/2019	178.07	4,964.99	496,320.95	0.01	0.00
11/30/2019	179.85	4,963.21	496,141.10	0.01	400,000.00

Figure 12.10 Reserve computations based on discounted (expected) cash flows.

Suppose we now incorporate the possibility of default. If the bank expects the customer to stop payment in month 11, charge off the account to collateral value of $400,000 in month 17 and liquidate the property in month 24 for $400,000, the reserve computations based on discounted (expected) cash flows can be shown in Figure 12.10.

An alternative to computing allowances based on cash flows expected to be received would be to do the computations based on expected losses. For this approach to work, the monthly expected losses should be computed as the difference between contractual monthly payments (column 3) and actual payments received or cash collected (column 6). If this is done for all the months and discounted at the 1% monthly interest we should get the same CECL reserve as above.

Note that other "hybrid" approaches such as measuring the loss at month 17 (charge-off point), or discounting principal losses (e.g., difference between $498,503 and $400,000) are not incorporating the time value of money correctly and therefore these approaches should be avoided.

References

[1] Office of the Comptroller of the Currency. (2012). *Comptroller's Handbook: Allowance for Loan and Lease Losses.*

[2] Office of the Comptroller of the Currency. (2006). *Interagency Policy Statement on the Allowance for Loan and lease Losses.* 2006-47.

[3] Office of the Comptroller of the Currency. (2011). *OCC 2011-12: Sound Practices for Model Risk Management: Supervisory Guidance on Model Risk Management.*

[4] Remarks by Thomas J. Curry, *Comptroller of the Currency before the AICPA Banking Conference.* Washington D.C. September 16, 2013.

[5] FASB Accounting Standards Update No 2016-13. (June 2016). Financial Instruments – Credit Losses (Topic 326).

[6] Office of the Comptroller of the Currency. (September 2017). *Frequently Asked Questions on the New Accounting Standard on Financial Instruments – Credit Losses.*

[7] Actuarial Review of the Federal Housing Administration Mutual Mortgage Insurance Fund Forward Loans for Fiscal Year 2016. U.S. Department of Housing and Urban Development. November 2016.

[8] Office of the Comptroller of the Currency. (2012). *Interagency Supervisory Guidance on Allowance for Loan and lease Estimation Practices for Loans and Lines of Credit Secured by Junior Liens on 1-4 Family Residential Properties.*

[9] Accounting Standards Update No. 2011-02: Receivables (Topic 310). Financial Accounting Series; Financial Accounting Standards Board.

13 *Operational Risk*

FILIPPO CURTI, MARCO MIGUEIS
AND ROBERT STEWART*

13.1 Introduction

In the late 1990s and early 2000s, the Basel Committee recognized increasing bank losses unrelated to credit risk or market risk, including the dramatic collapse of Barings Bank due to a rogue trader. As a result, the committee created a third risk stripe – operational risk – and required that banking organizations explicitly assign risk weighted assets for operational risk.

The largest, most complex banks were encouraged to adopt the Advanced Measurement Approach (AMA), where banks model operational risk capital requirements explicitly. US regulators took a step further and required large, internationally active banks to adopt the AMA. In the US rules, operational risk is defined as "The risk of loss resulting from inadequate or failed processes, people, and systems or from external events. It includes legal risk, but excludes strategic risk and reputation risk."[1] Given this definition, operational risk covers a wide breadth of losses including rogue traders, terrorist attacks, transaction processing errors, computer system failures, and even bank robberies. Nevertheless, in the USA over 80% of operational losses stem from legal events. Many of these legal events have garnered significant attention and led to numerous multi-billion dollar settlements for large US banks. These include the well-publicized settlements stemming from the manipulation of the LIBOR and FX markets, the violation of anti-money laundering laws, and the misrepresentation of securitized products.[2] These large legal losses have driven up the

* The views expressed in this chapter are those of the authors only and do not reflect those of the Federal Reserve System.

[1] See 12 CFR part 217 for the Federal Reserve version of the capital rule.

[2] http://violationtracker.goodjobsfirst.org/prog.php?major_industry_sum=financial+services.

Table 13.1. *US banking organizations operational risk RWA ratios.*

Institution Name	Operational Risk Risk-Weighted Assets ($000s)	Total Risk-Weighted Assets ($000s)	Operational Risk RWA/ Total RWA
Wells Fargo	267,200,000	1,303,100,280	21%
Goldman Sachs	130,737,500	581,699,000	22%
U.S. Bancorp	61,750,000	267,308,856	23%
Northern Trust	16,576,875	69,153,613	24%
JP Morgan Chase	400,000,000	1,497,870,000	27%
Citigroup	325,000,000	1,210,106,971	27%
Bank of America	500,000,000	1,586,992,604	32%
Morgan Stanley	129,837,500	373,931,000	35%
Bank of NY Mellon	65,887,500	170,709,400	39%
State Street	44,230,988	100,632,846	44%
		Average	**29%**

percentage of risk-weighted assets (RWA) that firms hold for operational risk relative to total RWA. As of the first quarter of 2016, ten US banking organizations were subject to public disclosure of their AMA estimates, and their operational risk RWA to total RWA ratios are as follows in Table 13.1.[3]

Given the risk-weighted assets computed in the first quarter of 2016, operational risk is the second largest risk US banks face behind only credit risk.

Because operational risk has such a dramatic impact on bank profits and capital requirements, modeling operational risk losses is a priority for banking organizations. This chapter provides an overview of operational risk modeling techniques used by industry participants and regulators in the USA, recommendations for how modeling techniques can be improved, and a summary of the model risk tools necessary for any operational risk modeling framework. The remainder of this chapter is organized as follows: Section 13.2 discusses the loss distribution approach, Section 13.3 discusses regression modeling, Section 13.4 discusses techniques to minimize model risk, and Section 13.5 concludes.

[3] Regulatory Capital Reporting for Institutions Subject to the Advanced Capital Adequacy Framework (FFIEC 101).

13.2 Loss Distribution Approach (LDA)

The Loss Distribution Approach (LDA) is an empirical modeling technique that can be used to estimate Value-at-Risk measures for operational losses. With the LDA, probability distributions for the frequency of losses and the severity of losses are estimated separately and assumed independent. If this assumption holds, the LDA framework is likely to produce more accurate results than alternatives that do not model severity and frequency distributions separately. After the frequency and severity distributions are estimated, the distributions are combined through Monte Carlo simulation or similar numerical techniques to secure an annual operational loss distribution from which Value-at-Risk measures can be calculated.

Under the 2007 US Advanced Approaches risk-based capital rule, banking organizations with greater than $250 billion in total assets or more than $10 billion in foreign exposure must use the AMA to calculate a capital requirement for operational risk. The AMA is a flexible framework that requires banks to build their own models to produce "an estimate of operational risk exposure that meets a one- year, 99.9th percentile soundness standard."[4] Furthermore, the rule requires that firms use four data elements: internal loss data, external loss data, scenario analysis, and business environment and internal control factors (BEICFs). Although not required, all US AMA firms have chosen to build LDA models using primarily internal and external loss data to produce capital estimates. Many banks have also explored using the LDA to model stressed operational losses in the Comprehensive Capital Analysis and Review (CCAR) and the Dodd–Frank Act Stress Tests (DFAST) exercises.

13.2.1 LDA and the 99.9th Quantile

Actuaries have used the LDA for more than three decades to estimate potential losses stemming from insurance contracts and, consequently, the LDA is a staple of actuarial exams across the world (Heckman and Meyers, 1983). Despite the LDA's success in the insurance industry, the use of the LDA to model operational risk has caused mixed reactions in the banking industry and supervisory communities. The Basel Committee criticized the AMA for not "balancing simplicity, comparability, and

[4] 12 CFR part 217.

risk sensitivity" at least partly due to the use of LDA models.[5] Also, Federal Reserve stress testing guidance has discouraged banks from using complicated models that would likely include the LDA.[6]

The main difficulty in applying the LDA to operational risk is the uncertainty associated with tail operational losses. When applied to insurance contracts, the LDA benefits from virtually all insurance contracts having caps specifically defining the maximum payment. Caps on potential losses make estimating severity loss distributions simpler because this extra information is used in the model. There are no maximum payouts in operational risk, and therefore operational risk models are forced to extrapolate those estimates, causing uncertainty.

The AMA applies a one-year, 99.9th quantile soundness standard which means that banks should estimate a one-in-a-thousand-year annual loss. But even the most advanced banks have only ten to fifteen years of representative data, so estimating a one-in-a-thousand year annual loss involves radical extrapolation. Even with ample data, estimating a quantile so far out on the tail may not be realistic (Daniellson, 2002). The difficulty in estimating the 99.9th quantile is amplified when a bank has limited loss data for a particular operational risk category and when tail losses of the risk category are particularly volatile, such as legal losses.

Following earlier research by Cope et al. (2009), the example below illustrates the uncertainty of the 99.9th quantile in the best-case scenario where the loss frequency and severity distributions are known, but the parameters are unknown. We simulate ten years of data for 100 banks from the same distributions, where frequency is assumed to follow a Poisson distribution and severity a lognormal distribution. To show the impact of loss volatility and data scarcity on uncertainty, we consider two scale parameters of the lognormal distribution ($\sigma = 2$ or $\sigma = 3$) and two intensity parameters of the Poisson distribution ($\lambda = 2$ or $\lambda = 20$) for four possible scenarios. In all the scenarios, the location parameter of the lognormal distribution is constant ($\mu = 10$). Then, for each bank, we use the LDA with the simulated data to estimate the 99.9th quantile of annual operational losses.[7] We assume the hypothetical

[5] www.bis.org/press/p160304.htm.

[6] www.federalreserve.gov/bankinforeg/srletters/sr1518.htm.

[7] For each bank, after the frequency and severity distributions were estimated, we used Monte Carlo simulation to estimate the 99.9th quantile of the annual operational loss distribution. We performed one million replications in the Monte Carlo simulations of each bank.

Table 13.2. *Descriptive statistics for 99.9th quantile estimates.*

$\sigma = 2$ and $\lambda = 20$		$\sigma = 2$ and $\lambda = 2$	
Mean	54,208,410	Mean	31,255,235
St Deviation	17,997,923	St Deviation	40,913,624
Median	50,531,734	Median	15,946,067
Coeff Variation[9]	33%	Coeff Variation	131%
True 99.9	56,337,692	True 99.9	16,223,133
$\sigma = 3$ and $\lambda = 20$		**$\sigma = 3$ and $\lambda = 2$**	
Mean	2,577,796,121	Mean	1,751,586,112
St Deviation	1,338,702,076	St Deviation	3,533,153,256
Median	2,219,597,444	Median	416,356,913
Coeff Variation	52%	Coeff Variation	202%
True 99.9	2,611,446,065	True 99.9	428,017,545

banks know the distributions that generate the data, but not the parameters. Table 13.2 provides descriptive statistics for the estimated 99.9th quantile for each of these scenarios plus the true 99.9th quantile resulting from these distributions.[8]

When a bank knows the distributions of the losses, loss severity sigma is low ($\sigma = 2$), and loss data is plentiful ($\lambda = 20$),[10] then the 99.9th quantile estimates are fairly accurate. The mean and median estimates of the 99.9th quantile are close to the true 99.9th quantile and the variation of estimates is relatively small with a coefficient of variation equal to 33%. But this must be considered a best-case scenario because in the real-world we do not have known distributions, loss severity is often highly volatile, and data is frequently scarce.

Uncertainty increases markedly when loss severity sigma is high or when loss data is scarce. When the volatility of loss severity is high ($\sigma = 3$), volatility of estimates increases. Mean and median estimates remain close to the true 99.9th quantile, but the coefficient of variation

[8] To estimate the true 99.9th quantile, we produced one hundred million years of data from the frequency and severity distributions and calculated the 99.9th quantile of this simulated data.

[9] Coefficient of variation is the standard deviation divided by the mean.

[10] Under $\lambda = 20$ and given that banks have ten years of data, each simulated bank has on average 200 losses in this risk category.

Table 13.3. *Descriptive statistics for ratio of alternative estimates of the 99.9th quantile to lognormal estimates.*

Percentile of Ratio	Loglogistic/Lognormal	Gamma/Lognormal
5th percentile	5.13	0.005
Median	18.00	0.041
95th percentile	75.28	0.207

grows to 52%. Data scarcity results in an even larger increase in estimated volatility. When $\lambda = 2$, but σ remains 2, the coefficient of variation of estimates grows to 131%. Also, the mean estimate becomes much larger than the median estimate or the true 99.9th quantile because of outliers. Finally, when severity volatility is high ($\sigma = 3$) and loss data is scarce ($\lambda = 2$), the coefficient of variation on the 99.9th quantile increases to over 200%.

When the distributions are known, the example illustrates considerable uncertainty in estimates of the 99.9th quantile. In real-world applications, modelers face not just parameter uncertainty, but also model uncertainty. Even in cases where the number of losses is high, there is uncertainty whether tail losses follow the same loss generating process as losses in the body of the distribution. Building upon the previous example, we use the loss data generated for 100 banks under scenario four ($\sigma = 3$ and $\lambda = 2$) and estimate the 99.9th quantile of the loss distribution using two alternatives to the lognormal distribution: the loglogistic distribution and the gamma distribution. Table 13.3 displays descriptive statistics for the ratio of alternative estimates of the 99.9th quantile to lognormal estimates.

For the 100 hypothetical sets of simulated loss data, incorrectly assuming that the loss severity follows a loglogistic distribution results in significantly higher estimates of the 99.9th quantile. Conversely, the incorrect use of the gamma distribution results in significantly lower estimates. These differences are dramatic: The 5th percentile of the loglogistic to lognormal ratio is 5 and the 95th percentile is 75, while the 5th percentile for the Gamma to lognormal ratio is 0.005 and the 95th percentile is 0.207.

Practitioners try to resolve model uncertainty through sophisticated model selection criteria that include goodness-of-fit criteria balanced with over-fitting criteria. So, the typical model selection frameworks of

US AMA banks that follow the guidelines outlined in supervisory guidance BCC 14-1 should rule out the loglogistic or the gamma distribution in this example. But in real world applications even well-developed model selection techniques cannot narrow the range of options algorithmically, tradeoffs will always exist, and modelers will always have to make judgmental model selection decisions.

13.2.2 Using the LDA Appropriately

Estimating the 99.9th quantile suffers from substantial uncertainty even when the loss distribution is known. The simple examples in the last subsection illustrate what many researchers and practitioners have written about the uncertainty in measuring the 99.9th quantile: Mignola and Ugoccioni, 2006; Nešlehová et al., 2006; Cope et al., 2009; and Opdyke and Cavallo, 2012. However, uncertainty can be diminished by focusing on lower quantiles. We compute summary statistics for the 99.9th, 99th, 95th, 90th, and 50th quantile estimates for the 100 banks simulated over ten years under the lognormal ($\sigma = 3$ and $\lambda = 2$) scenario. Table 13.4 displays statistics for different quantile estimates using the lognormal distribution.

Uncertainty decreases as we move down the quantiles. While the coefficient of variation of the estimates is 202% at the 99.9th quantile, the coefficient of variation decreases to 157% at the 99th quantile, to 126% at the 95th quantile, and to 113% at the 90th quantile. Thus, by moving from the 99.9th quantile to the 90th quantile, we see a 44% decrease in the relative volatility of estimates.

The effect of model uncertainty on quantile estimates is also reduced at lower quantiles, as the impact of a wrong distribution choice is diminished. Table 13.5 compares the estimates of the 99.9th, 99th, 95th, 90th, and 50th quantiles when different severity distributions are used to estimate the loss distribution.

The variation of estimates decreases as we move down the quantiles. The median bank ratio of the log-logistic estimate to the log-normal estimate of the 99.9th is 18. But this median ratio decreases to 3.35 when estimating the 99th quantile, to 1.37 when estimating the 95th quantile, and to 1.05 when estimating the 90th quantile. Similarly, the median ratio of gamma distribution quantile estimates to log-normal quantile estimates moves closer to one as we move down the quantiles. This median

Table 13.4. *Descriptive statistics for quantile estimates.*

Statistics	99.9th Quantile	99th Quantile	95th Quantile	90th Quantile	50th Quantile
Mean	1,751,586,112	132,849,456	15,805,428	5,386,383	123,572
St Deviation	3,533,153,256	208,668,352	19,881,664	6,086,133	121,171
Median	416,356,913	49,591,245	7,735,879	2,909,604	86,750
Coeff Variation	202%	157%	126%	113%	98%
True Quantile	428,017,545	51,179,696	8,221,633	3,162,613	87,024

Table 13.5. ***Descriptive statistics for ratio of alternative estimates to lognormal estimates.***

	Loglogstic/Lognormal				
Statistics	99.9th Quantile	99th Quantile	95th Quantile	90th Quantile	50th Quantile
5th Percentile	5.13	1.41	0.81	0.67	0.71
Median	18.00	3.35	1.37	1.05	0.93
95th Percentile	75.28	7.25	2.13	1.42	1.25
	Gamma/Lognomal				
Statistics	99.9th Quantile	99th Quantile	95th Quantile	90th Quantile	50th Quantile
5th Percentile	0.005	0.042	0.215	0.414	1.593
Median	0.041	0.183	0.566	0.954	3.357
95th Percentile	0.207	0.877	2.587	3.877	10.167

ratio is 0.183 at the 99th quantile, 0.556 at the 95th quantile, and 0.954 at the 90th quantile. Therefore, model misspecification errors decrease dramatically when lower quantiles are estimated.

We believe the LDA becomes a more useful modeling framework when applied to lower percentiles. Estimates of lower percentiles are more precise and, thus, when applied to lower percentiles LDA models are useful quantification tools that should be used by risk managers and bank management to understand operational risk in cases where the loss profile is stable over time. A capital framework that targeted a lower confidence level and relied on a supervisory determined multiplier to ensure appropriate conservatism would be preferable to the current AMA framework. This idea has been proposed by Mignola and Ugoccioni (2006), Cope et al. (2009), and Ames et al. (2015), who suggested using a lower percentile as a soundness standard and a regulatory created multiplier to scale this number up to create a margin of safety above what is realistically measureable. This approach mirrors what is done in other domains, such as engineering, physics, and even other areas of finance, where multipliers or safety factors are used to adjust for our inability to measure extremes accurately. The same logic could be used in operational risk. The mistake of creating a one-in-a-thousand year soundness standard should not denigrate the LDA.

LDA models are not the best fit for stress testing exercises such as CCAR. These exercises typically require modeling the relation of operational loss exposure to macroeconomic factors, with the goal of quantifying operational losses under stressful macroeconomic conditions. The static LDA framework cannot be directly applied to answer this question, and the mapping of quantiles of an annual operational loss distribution to particular macroeconomic scenarios is not clear. Nevertheless, we believe LDA models are useful benchmarking tools for stress testing models as we will discuss in the model risk section.

Practitioners, regulators and analysts often see what they want in tangled operational risk data. While bankers may emphasize the low frequency of large losses, regulators may emphasize that these large losses represent the preponderance of the risk. Both sides may be correct. The LDA provides a useful paradigm for understanding, organizing, and explaining the operational risks faced by banks. So, while we cannot know if future losses will imitate past losses and no model provides the proverbial silver bullet, the LDA should be part of any complete operational risk modeling framework.

13.3 Regression Modeling

Regression techniques are commonly used tools of finance and risk management practitioners, including in operational risk measurement. Multiple financial institutions have tried to model the relationship between operational losses and potential drivers, such as business volumes and control factors. Nevertheless, the biggest push to use regression models on operational risk has come with the stress testing frameworks of the CCAR and DFAST, which directed banks to explore the relationship between operational losses and the macroeconomy.[11]

[11] Pub. L. No. 111–203, 124 Stat. 1376 (July 21, 2010).

Finding stable and measurable relationships between the macroeconomy and operational losses is daunting. Both the macroeconomy and operational losses are: dynamic, nonlinear, complex, and likely related to a variety of factors, many unknown. Thus, regressions using macroeconomic factors to explain operational losses suffer from both exogeneity and endogeneity issues as establishing meaningful factors to determine causality is not straightforward. Still, researchers have used regression modeling to improve our understanding of relationships between operational losses and the macroeconomy: Chernobai et al., 2011; Hess, 2011; Sekeris, 2012; Cope and Carrivick, 2013; and Abdymomunov et al., 2015. The next three sub-sections detail three difficulties in applying regression analysis to model the relation between the macroeconomy and operational losses: dates, large loss events and small sample sizes.

13.3.1 Dates

The first challenge is that the dates that operational losses occur are not definitive. As part of CCAR, US banks are required to collect three dates in operational loss datasets: the occurrence date, the discovery date, and the accounting date. The occurrence date is the date when a loss event occurred; the discovery date is the date when the loss event was discovered by the bank's control processes; and the accounting dates of an operational loss event are the dates where a loss event produces a loss on the bank's financial statements.

Certain types of losses occur over an extended period of time, so loss dates are uncertain and open to interpretation. For example, unauthorized trading was ongoing for at least three years prior to the Baring's bankruptcy (Leeson, 1996). Therefore, choosing an occurrence date for this operational loss and other fraud losses is highly judgmental. While researchers have theorized a link between fraud losses and the macroeconomy (Akerlof and Romer, 1993; Aliber and Kindleberger, 2005; Stewart, 2016), assigning a specific date to use for regression analysis is ambiguous. Similarly, legal losses do not always have definitive dates because cases can take years to resolve. For example, in February 2012 the federal government and forty-nine state attorneys general reached a settlement agreement with the nation's five largest mortgage servicers – Bank of America Corporation, JP Morgan Chase & Co., Wells Fargo & Company,

Citigroup Inc. and Ally Financial Inc. – to address mortgage servicing, foreclosure and bankruptcy abuses, including "robo-signing."[12] These offenses were committed in the run-up to the crisis, five plus years before the settlement was announced. Then, the offenses were unearthed and lawsuits filed around the crisis peak in 2008. Lastly, the banks reserved for the pending losses in the years following the crisis, with each bank reserving losses on separate dates based on the stage of the settlement agreements. There is no unambiguous date to use for analysis.

Using loss data from the Federal Reserve's Y-14Q report,[13] Table 13.6 provides descriptive statistics for the time between the occurrence date and the discovery date, and for the time between the discovery date and the accounting date by Basel event type.[14]

Lags between occurrence date and discovery date, and between discovery date and accounting date are substantial. Lags between occurrence and discovery dates are on average less than 80 days for external fraud (EF), damage to physical assets (DPA), and business disruption and system failures (BDSF), but the lag for clients, products, and business practices (CPBP) which includes legal losses is more than a year at 447 days. Lags between discovery and accounting dates are similarly large, although the ranking of different events changes somewhat. On average, CPBP events compare somewhat more favorably to other event types regarding the discovery date to accounting date lag relative to the occurrence date to discovery date lag.

The data also show that large losses have larger lags than small losses. The weighted average shown in Table 13.6 is computed by first

[12] www.justice.gov/ust/eo/public_affairs/articles/docs/2012/abi_201203.pdf; www.nationalmortgagesettlement.com/about

[13] As part of Comprehensive Capital Analysis & Review (CCAR), bank holding companies (BHCs) with assets over $50 billion are required to provide operational loss data to the Federal Reserve, and this data is used in this analysis. At the time of analysis, data was submitted by thirty-four BHCs. BHCs must report information on all their operational loss events above an appropriate collection threshold including: dollar amount, occurrence date, discovery date, accounting date, Basel II event type, and Basel II business line.

[14] The seven Basel event types are Internal Fraud (IF); External Fraud (EF); Employment Practices and Workplace Safety (EPWS); Clients, Products, and Business Practice (CPBP); Damage to Physical Assets (DPA); Business Disruption and System Failures (BDSF); and Execution, Delivery, and Process Management (EDPM).

Table 13.6. ***Descriptive statistics by Basel event type.***

	Occurrence date to discovery date				Discovery date to accounting date[15]			
Event Type	Average	Wgt Avg[16]	Median	90 Prct	Average	Wgt Avg	Median	90 Prct
IF	182	375	0	500	128	224	21	330
EF	57	188	0	105	77	257	30	130
EPWS	129	167	0	349	467	1237	123	1314
CPBP	447	583	0	1670	382	1275	210	975
DPA	78	127	0	104	223	313	74	695
BDSF	56	192	0	61	46	95	0	120
EDPM	170	258	0	371	134	831	4	394

weighting the losses by the size of the loss, and then computing an average. The difference between the average lag and the weighted average lag is substantial, and highest in the CPBP event type. Legal events can take multiple years before banks can take reserves according to accounting rules that require legal losses to be "estimable and probable" before reserves can be set. These large lags, particularly for large legal events, introduce significant challenges to modeling operational losses in dynamic settings as they introduce large uncertainty around the appropriate dates to use.

Modeling operational losses based on occurrence date is challenging. There is uncertainty regarding the proper date and, when data from multiple banks is used, practices around when occurrence dates are set differ dramatically. Discovery dates can be more objectively determined, but discovery dates also suffer from discrepancies across lines of business within a bank and across banks due to different collection practices. Also, when discovery dates differ significantly from occurrence dates, the use of discovery dates to assess the relationship between operational losses and potential explanatory factors may not

[15] For events with multiple accounting dates, the accounting date used in this analysis results from the weighted average of the loss impacts of the different accounting dates.

[16] In calculating the weighted average lag, loss events are weighted according to the size of the loss.

be sensible because loss discovery may be unrelated to the factors driving losses. Therefore, in most research we have pursued, the accounting date is used.

Accounting date seems like a reasonable choice for at least three reasons. First, accounting dates are the most objective date available, as the date banks take an accounting loss is governed by accounting rules that should ensure more comparability than occurrence date or discovery date. Second, modeling based on accounting date allows practitioners to break down loss events into each accounting impact, which can be useful when modeling loss events spanning multiple years.[17] Third, while the criticism that discovery dates may be unrelated to explanatory factors certainly also applies to accounting dates, accounting dates are intrinsically relevant in a way that discovery dates are not. Accounting dates correspond to when banks subtract losses on their income statement; thus, accounting dates are when operational losses can trigger banks falling below regulatory thresholds or, ultimately, bankruptcy. So, even if accounting dates do not provide the ideal basis to assess the relation between operational losses and their drivers, understanding the factors that best predict the impact of losses on accounting dates is important. However, despite favoring the use of accounting dates, we believe these dates can still be problematic. Particularly for legal events, banks have discretion when to set their legal reserves and thus when to set accounting dates. When attempting to model losses across multiple banks, this problem is magnified and tends to obscure the relationship between operational losses and macroeconomic events such as the 2008 financial crisis.

13.3.2 Large Loss Events

Rare, large loss events occur across all seven event types. For example, banks with credit card portfolios have extensive external fraud losses, most of them small amounts because banks use point of sale fraud models and limits on lines of credit to control loss sizes. But occasionally, a more sophisticated thief steals large quantities of credit card

[17] For example, most large legal events result in multiple accounting impacts because the reserves associated with the loss event are frequently adjusted to reflect more recent assessments of expected loss. Each time the reserve for a legal loss event is increased, an accounting impact is produced as the bank needs to record this loss in their financial statements.

numbers causing banks to suffer large losses, such as the Home Depot breach that compromised 56 million credit and debit cards in 2014 and the Target breach that affected 40 million cards in 2013.[18] These more sophisticated crimes lead to much larger and uncertain losses. Similar large and rare events occur across all the Basel event types. IBM's Algo OpData collects publicly available operational losses from various news outlets and provides descriptions of the losses.[19] For all events, the range of impacts is very broad. For example, the damage to physical assets (DPA) event type describes the smallest loss in the dataset as follows:

In an external risk case, a fire destroyed a Bank of America building in October 2001 in Winter Haven, Florida. The fire caused approximately $1 million in damage to the two-story building. The taxable value of the old bank was in the range of $1.4 million according to records filed with the local appraiser's office.

While the largest loss event in DPA is described:

Bank of New York – the largest clearing and settlement firm in the United States – found itself without access to its four downtown premises, and to basic utilities, including electricity, and phone service immediately after the destruction of the World Trade Center on September 11, 2001. The loss amount is approximately $749 million.

The prevalence of such large events is demonstrated by the descriptive statistics of the severity of loss events of the seven event types calculated from pooled losses of all CCAR banks using FR14-Q data, in Table 13.7.[20] For all event types, standard deviations are substantially larger than average losses and average losses are meaningfully larger than median losses.

The disproportionate impact of large operational loss events and the ambiguity around dates poses challenges to using regression techniques to model the relationship between operational risk and macroeconomic drivers. When modeling total operational losses or loss severity, a few large loss events tend to dominate results. So, while a majority of the large operational loss events following the

[18] www.wsj.com/articles/home-depot-breach-bigger-than-targets-1411073571.

[19] www-03.ibm.com/software/products/en/algo-opdata.

[20] To ensure consistency across banks, only loss events with severity above $20k are included in this analysis.

Table 13.7. *Descriptive statistics of the severity of loss events.*

Event Type	N	Average	Median	St Deviation
IF	6,331	535,467	53,155	7,165,867
EF	124,742	99,848	31,683	2,976,935
EPWS	33,675	266,518	63,027	3,247,419
CPBP	50,429	4,666,509	69,129	165,685,712
DPA	3,064	995,617	48,523	26,332,873
BDSF	3,408	508,676	67,058	3,981,882
EDPM	109,280	392,331	50,202	16,294,342

2008 financial crisis – losses related to securitization litigation, representations and warranties, improper underwriting, and improper foreclosure – are linked to the financial crisis because the losses are related to the downturn in the mortgage market, the infrequent occurrence of large loss events and the infrequent occurrence of financial crisis combined with the difficulties in establishing accurate loss dates makes producing reliable estimates difficult, even when links between operational losses and macroeconomic events are apparent.

13.3.3 Small Sample Size

Basel II was introduced in the early 2000s, so US banks are relatively new at collecting and organizing operational losses. The most advanced banks have a little more than ten years of reliable data. Ten years of data are insufficient to measure meaningful correlations between operational losses and the macroeconomy, so any results will be subject to a great deal of uncertainty. For any individual bank, the prospect of finding spurious relationships is high.

To illustrate this challenge, we present an example that uses Federal Reserve Y-14Q data from thirty-four CCAR banks. Independently for each bank, we run a linear regression between total quarterly operational losses and GDP growth. Let Y_t be the dependent variable representing the observed total quarterly operational loss at time t and let X_t represent the one-year percentage change in GDP between five quarters prior and the previous quarter: $(GDP_{t-1} - GDP_{t-5})/GDP_{t-5}$. The model assumes a linear relationship between $ln(Y)$ and X such that

$$\ln(Y_t) = \alpha + \beta X_t + \varepsilon_t,$$

where α and β are the regression parameters and ε_t is a random disturbance term assumed to be independently and identically distributed with a normal density function.

Results are inconsistent. For nineteen out of the thirty-four banks, the relation between losses and GDP growth is not statistically significant, while for twelve banks this relationship is negative and statistically significant, and for three banks this relationship is positive and statistically significant. The sign of the relationship between operational losses and macroeconomic conditions may change from bank to bank, or there may not be a relationship in some cases. However, in our view a more likely explanation for the inconsistency found in these regressions are the small sample sizes used together with the other challenges mentioned in earlier subsections. The number of quarters of data in these regressions ranges from sixteen to sixty-five, for an average of forty-eight. Such small samples are insufficient to unearth relationships that suffer from large uncertainty due to the effect of large loss events and the uncertainty of loss dates.

13.3.4 Using Regression Analysis Appropriately

When pooling data from multiple banks, researchers have been able to show relationships between operational losses and the macroeconomy. Using Algo FIRST data, Chernobai et al. (2011) showed that operational loss frequency is negatively related to GDP growth. Building on the Chernobai et al. results, Abdymomunov et al. (2015) confirmed that loss frequency is negatively correlated with GDP growth and, in addition, showed that total losses are also negatively correlated to GDP growth using Federal Reserve Y-14Q data. Similarly, using ORX data, Cope et al. (2012) showed that external fraud losses and employment practices and workplace safety losses are positively correlated with income per capita. The Federal Reserve has also found success building factor driven models for the CCAR exercises. Specifically, the Federal Reserve has modeled loss frequencies using factors:

Loss frequency is modeled as a function of macroeconomic variables and BHC specific characteristics. Macroeconomic variables, such as the real GDP growth rate, stock market return and volatility, credit spread, and the unemployment rate, are included directly in the panel regression model and/or used to project certain firm specific characteristics.[21]

The Federal Reserve's access to multiple banks' data strengthens confidence in the relationships found. To illustrate the increased robustness of regressions that use data from multiple banks, we build from the example presented in Section 13.3.3 by estimating the relationship between operational losses and GDP growth in an unbalanced panel data set consisting of the thirty-four CCAR banks. Let Y_{it} be the dependent variable representing the observed total quarterly operational loss of bank i at time t, and let X_t represent the one-year percentage change in GDP: $(GDP_{t-1} - GDP_{t-5})/GDP_{t-5}$. The model assumes a linear relationship between $ln(Y)$ and X and includes bank invariant unobserved factors such that

$$\log(Y_{it}) = \alpha + \beta X_t + a_i + \varepsilon_{it},$$

where α and β are regression parameters, ε_{it} is the random disturbance term assumed to be independently and identically distributed with a normal density function, and a_i is a bank fixed effect that accounts for bank-specific factors that are invariant through time.

The pooled regression shows a robust negative relationship between operational losses and GDP growth. β is –0.09, which means that when GDP increases 1%, operational losses decrease 0.09%. This is a small effect, but significant at a 1% level with a p-value of 0.000004. The confidence in these results stems from the large sample used for its derivation, which includes 1,621 bank-quarter observations. We believe banks should continue data pooling efforts such as currently practiced through the Operational Risk Data Exchange (ORX) and the American Bankers Association Operational Loss Data Consortium.[22] These organizations allow banks to better understand the relationship between operational losses and macroeconomic drivers that will not likely be apparent in an individual bank's data because of all the noise that long tails and short datasets create.

Some banks have used regressions reasonably as part of their operational loss stress test projections in the execution delivery and process

[21] Appendix B of Board of Governors of the Federal Reserve System (2015), Dodd–Frank Act Stress Test 2015: Supervisory Stress Test Methodology and Results.

[22] www.orx.org/Pages/HomePage.aspx and www.aba.com/products/surveys/pages/operationalrisk.aspx.

management (EDPM) and the external fraud (EF) event types where there is more data. Significant correlations have been found with macroeconomic variables such as the Chicago Board of Options Exchange Volatility Index (CBOE VIX), and bank specific variables such as the quarter used in the annual accounting cycle, the number of open credit card accounts, and mortgage origination volume. Still, factor models are not currently used extensively in operational risk models, and this offers an opportunity for further research.

13.4 Model Risk

Ambiguous dates, small sample sizes, and long tails subject operational risk models to substantial model risk. Parameter uncertainty, model selection ambiguity, and unknowns around data quality are all sources of model risk that must not be downplayed or ignored. Economists and all scientists are often not transparent about the limitations of their findings, particularly when it comes to their statistical reliability (Leamer, 1983). Due to cognitive biases, faulty incentives, or an overreliance on statistical significance, the tendency for practitioners to overstate results is large and consistent across disciplines and over time (Kahneman and Lovallo, 1993; Ioannidis, 2005). These issues may be more severe in the banking industry where government guarantees encourage banks to underestimate risk (Admati, 2014; International Monetary Fund, 2014; Hoenig, 2016). To overcome these model risk issues, we believe any operational risk modeling framework must include ample benchmarking, backtesting, and sensitivity analysis. Furthermore, modelers must communicate results, including the uncertainty inherent in the results, clearly and unequivocally.

13.4.1 Backtesting

Velleman (2008) wrote: "A model for data, no matter how elegant or correctly derived, must be discarded or revised if it doesn't fit the data or when new or better data are found and it fails to fit them." Similarly, Gabaix and Laibson (2008) argued that models should be empirically consistent such that useful models must either be consistent with past data or have proven effective in making predictions. Backtesting is an approach to judge the empirical consistency of models based on comparing actual outcomes of the variables of interest to model outputs based on data that does not include the actual comparison outcomes (Campbell, 2006; Board of Governors of the Federal Reserve System, 2011). For example, data from 2000 to 2014 would be used to estimate the model, which would then be combined with projections for the modeled loss drivers for 2015 and 2016 to estimate losses in 2015 and 2016. These modeled losses would then be compared to actual losses in 2015 and 2016.

Backtesting provides a framework for informed discussions around a model's usefulness by enhancing practitioners understanding of how real losses compared to model outputs and helping unveil deficiencies in the model. In the operational risk context, backtesting is particularly important because it offers a tool to counter the effects of the skewed incentives faced by bank modelers. All operational risk modeling frameworks should use extensive and transparent backtests. Regardless of the modeling techniques used – LDA, regressions, scenarios – banks should develop simple, easily communicated criteria for when the model results fail to match up reasonably well with the actual results. When any criterion is violated, there should be transparent follow-ups, such as re-fitting the model, a complete overhaul of the model, or requiring add-ons to the model.

CCAR requires banks to produce three 9-quarter projections for operational risk losses based on different scenarios with the "baseline" describing typical losses, the "severely adverse" describing highly stressed losses, and the "adverse" somewhere in between. So, a possible backtesting criterion for CCAR is for a model's forecasts for severely adverse losses being higher than actual losses in a benign economy. Also, modelers should check how their model would have performed had it been in use prior to the 2008 financial crisis.

LDA models produce distributions of losses rather than conditional expected loss forecasts, but this allows for ample backtesting. Practitioners should compare rolling sums of actual four quarters of losses to the LDA annual loss distribution, and set up "tests" that would lead to further analysis of the model. For example, the annual losses of a bank with ten years of data should exceed the 80th percentile of the LDA results approximately twice. If more than two years exceed the 80th percentile, the bank should investigate whether the model is underestimating losses, and should make changes accordingly. Banks can use similar analysis with stress testing exercises paying particular attention to the losses that occurred during the crisis period.

If actual losses consistently match up with high percentiles of the theoretical distribution, the model likely needs to be redeveloped.

13.4.2 Sensitivity Analysis

Sensitivity analysis means testing and challenging the inevitable assumptions in any model (Pannell, 1997). Econometric models must make simplifying assumptions to make sense of complex processes, and sensitivity analysis provides credence that these assumptions are reasonable. So, sensitivity analysis must cover a broad area of potential issues and, therefore, does not have a definitive definition. But, for operational risk modeling, sensitivity analysis is paramount in making model output meaningful and useful. Sensitivity analysis should be used liberally and continuously, and individual models will require unique sensitivity analysis. The novelty of operational risk modeling demands ample sensitivity analysis: Uncertain dates, very large losses and small samples mean that sensitivity analysis must be used to justify all models in operational risk. When assessing operational risk regression models, model developers and validators should explore, at a minimum, whether model results change in response to (1) using different loss dates (i.e., occurrence date vs discovery date vs accounting date); (2) using different lags for explanatory variables, such as GDP growth; (3) using different segmentations of operational losses (e.g., modeling all operational losses together vs modeling losses by Basel event type); and (4) using different scenarios for the future path of explanatory variables. Within LDA models, sensitivity analysis is also critical. At a minimum, practitioners should assess how results change (1) when different severity distributions are used; (2) when different segmentations of the data are used; (3) when different correlation structures are assumed; and (4) when additional, conceivable large loss events are included or when un-repeatable large loss events are excluded.

Performing sensitivity analysis does not imply that worse case scenarios should replace model results. Even in the context of significant uncertainty, modelers should strive to identify which model design best reflects loss exposure. But sensitivity analysis is critical to foster understanding of model uncertainty and potential limitations. Given the relative infancy of the field and the fast evolving nature of operational risk models, we believe practitioners should engage in a wide-range of sensitivity analyses and use these results to better understand and communicate model estimates.

13.4.3 Benchmarking

The Federal Reserve defines benchmarking as "the comparison of a given model's inputs and outputs to estimates from alternative internal or external data or models."[23] Curti et al. (2016) explore benchmarking techniques in operational risk models and recommend extensive use of benchmarking for both AMA and CCAR models to improve confidence in model results and communication with relevant stakeholders. Often, simple comparisons that adjust for a bank's size provide useful benchmarks that allow banks to judge their capital position relative to peers and increase confidence that the models are producing reasonable results. For example, many US banks compute the ratio of AMA capital estimates (available through Pillar III disclosures) to total assets across the industry. For the June 30, 2016 quarterly reporting, the reporting AMA banks look as follows in Table 13.8.

Table 13.8. ***Descriptive statistics on operational risk assets.***

Bank	Operational Risk Capital ($000s)	Total Assets ($000s)	Op Risk Capital / Total Assets
US Bank	4,891,000	438,463,000	1.1%
Northern Trust	1,376,170	121,509,559	1.1%
Goldman Sachs	10,400,000	896,870,000	1.2%
Wells Fargo	22,902,000	1,889,235,000	1.2%
Morgan Stanley	10,243,000	828,873,000	1.2%
JP Morgan Chase	32,000,000	2,466,096,000	1.3%
State Street	3,554,908	255,396,733	1.4%
Citigroup	26,000,000	1,818,771,000	1.4%
Bank of NY Mellon	5,818,000	372,351,000	1.6%
Bank of America	40,000,000	2,189,811,000	1.8%

[23] www.federalreserve.gov/bankinforeg/srletters/sr1107a1.pdf

Table 13.9. *Ratio of operational risk stressed projections. BHC Stress Loss Projections / Total Assets.*

Percentile	Ratio
10th	0.24%
25th	0.46%
50th	0.63%
75th	0.84%
90th	1.24%
Average	0.69%
Sample Size	31

Table 13.10. *BHC stress loss projections / maximum nine quarters losses.*

Percentile	Ratio
10th	0.6
25th	1.1
50th	2.0
75th	3.7
90th	5.5
Average	2.8
Sample Size	31

Regulators can produce similar ratios for CCAR projections as detailed in Curti et al. (2016), which provided the following statistics in Table 13.9 around the ratio of the BHC operational risk stressed projections divided by total assets:

Using Federal Reserve's Y-14Q data, we can produce benchmarks that use operational loss data of banks. A simple benchmark to consider is a comparison between banks' stressed loss projections and maximum losses that banks have experienced in nine consecutive quarters. Table 13.10, taken from Curti et al. (2016), presents the descriptive statistics for this ratio:

Given that BHC stress loss projections are supposed to cover losses under severe macroeconomic conditions plus bank-specific severe operational vulnerabilities, in most cases these projections should be higher than the largest historically experienced losses. Twenty-five out of thirty-one banks in our sample have stress loss projections higher than their largest nine consecutive quarter losses.

A bank's loss data can also be used to produce more sophisticated benchmarks using bootstrapping techniques. The bootstrapping benchmark we propose uses an LDA framework, but with unique assumptions to ensure comparability across banks. Curti et al. (2016) calculated this benchmark for all US AMA banks. Calculation of this benchmark begins by separating each bank's losses into the seven Basel event types. Then, like a traditional LDA, loss frequency and severity are modeled separately for each event type and assumed independent. Loss frequency is assumed to follow a Poisson distribution. The intensity parameter is calculated from the average loss frequency over a four quarter window. Loss severity is assumed to follow the historical empirical distribution of loss severities. Then, we employ a Monte Carlo simulation to obtain the distribution of annual operational losses for each event type. Finally, to calculate the 99.9th quantile of annual total operational losses to benchmark AMA models, we assume perfect dependency across event types; thus, we simply sum the 99.9th quantile of each event type. The descriptive statistics for the ratio between AMA capital and this benchmark are presented in Table 13.11.

Given that empirical bootstrapping assumes that the largest historical loss event that has been observed in the bank's data is the largest loss event that can occur and that banks have on average little more than ten years of data, this benchmark likely underestimates the true 99.9th percentile. Thus, banks' models should cover the empirical

Table 13.11. ***AMA capital / 99.9th quantile empirical bootstrap.***

Percentile	Ratio
10th	0.8
25th	1.0
50th	1.5
75th	2.7
90th	3.0
Average	1.7
Sample Size	14

bootstrapping benchmark. The models of nine out of the fourteen US AMA banks meet this criterion.

13.5 Conclusion

Operational risk modeling is a new discipline that has made significant progress in the last two decades. In response to the AMA and stress testing requirements, banks have developed and implemented operational risk models that have greatly increased understanding of operational risk leading to more rigorous attention to operational losses at the executive level. The discipline has advanced through analysis that explores communalities in risk exposure across the industry. New analytic techniques have been refined while disproven methodologies have been displaced. This feedback loop should be encouraged. Operational risk analytics advances through an accumulation of studies, so industry practitioners, academics and regulators must continue to develop new analytical techniques and refine existing methods. Banks must invest in improved operational risk data collection including collecting potential loss drivers so more useful modeling can be developed. Operational risk has never been better understood, but there is room for improvement.

Analytic practitioners must follow two steadfast rules when faced with data issues, extreme events, and small sample sizes. First, practitioners must unflinchingly communicate the uncertainty inherent in the results. Far too often, modelers overstate the accuracy of their models or communicate nothing at all regarding uncertainty, which often leads model users to develop an unrealistic faith in the accuracy of the models and ultimately to poor decision making. Second, practitioners must provide ample sensitivity analysis such that model users understand how results would change if different assumptions were made. Modelers must work closely with managers to communicate the uncertainty in the model, ensure that the effects of that uncertainty are understood and accurately state the degree of confidence that the modelers have in the results.

Losses associated with operational risk have increased since the 2008 financial crisis. The business news has been replete with embarrassing stories of banks failing to manage their operational risk effectively: the mortgage settlements, the manipulation of the FX and LIBOR markets, the London whale, the money laundering losses, and the most recent cross-selling scandal at Wells Fargo. Rather than seeing more chief executive officers proclaim their ignorance before Congress, we must improve management of operational risk to ensure a bank's success and even survival. Proper management of operational risk must balance analytic analysis with qualitative assessments. Analytic practitioners must improve on communicating the strengths and weaknesses of their analysis, and non-analytic practitioners must learn how to better use the information garnered from the models to align risk incentives appropriately. The best operational risk managers will think abstractly while simultaneously sorting through the abundance of information operational risk models provide. The banks that successfully fuse analytic analysis with qualitative assessments of operational risks will thrive, while those that fail will face greater risk of insolvency.

References

Abdymomunov, A., Curti, F., and Mihov, A. (2015). U.S. Banking Sector Operational Losses and the Macroeconomic Environment. Working Paper, Federal Reserve Bank of Richmond.

Admati, A. (2014). Statement for Senate Committee on Banking, Housing and Urban Affairs Subcommittee on Financial Institutions and Consumer Protection. Hearing on Examining the GAO report on Expectations of Government Support for Bank Holding Companies.

Akerlof, A., and Romer, P. (1993). Looting: The economic underworld of bankruptcy for profit. *Brookings Papers on Economic Activity* 2, 1–73.

Aliber, R., and Kindleberger, C. P. (2005). *Manias, Panics, and Crashes: A History of Financial Crises*. Wiley.

Ames, M., Schuermann, T., and Scott, H. (2015). Bank capital for operational risk: A tale of fragility and instability. *Journal of Risk Management in Financial Institutions* 8(3), 227–243.

Campbell, S. (2006). A review of backtesting and backtesting procedures. *The Journal of Risk* 9(2), 1–17.

Chernobai, A., Jorion, P., and Yu, F. (2011). The determinants of operational risk in US financial institutions. *Journal of Financial and Quantitative Analysis* 46(6), 1683–1725.

Cope, E., and Carrivick, L. (2013). Effects of the financial crisis on banking operational losses. *The Journal of Operational Risk* 8(3), 3–29.

Cope, E., Mignola G., Antonini, G., and Ugoccioni, R. (2009). Challenges and pitfalls in measuring operational risk from loss data. *The Journal of Operational Risk* 4(4), 3–27.

Curti, F., Ergen, I., Li, M., Migueis, M., and Stewart, R. (2016). Benchmarking Operational Risk Models. Finance and Economics Discussions Series, Federal Reserve Board.

Danielsson, J. (2002). The emperor has no clothes: Limits to risk modeling. *Journal of Banking & Finance* 26(7), 1273–1296.

Gabaix, X., and Laibson, D. (2008). The Seven Properties of Good Models, *The Foundations of Positive and Normative Economics: A Handbook*. Oxford University Press.

Heckman, P. and Meyers, G. (1983). The calculation of aggregate loss distributions from claim severity and claim count distributions. *Proceedings of the Casualty Actuarial Society* LXX, 22–61.

Hess, C. (2011). The impact of the financial crisis on operational risk in the financial services industry: empirical evidence. *The Journal of Operational Risk* 5(2), 43–62.

Hoenig, Thomas. (2016). A Capital Conflict. Speech to the National Association for Business Economics (NABE) and the Organization for Economic Cooperation and Development (OECD) Global Economic Symposium, Paris, France. May 23.

International Monetary Fund. (2014). Global Financial Stability Report – Moving from Liquidity to Growth-Driven Markets.

Ioannidis, J. (2005). Why most published research findings are false. *PLoS Medicine* 2(8), e124.

Kahneman, D., and Lovallo, D. (1993). Timid choices and bold forecasts: A cognitive perspective on risk-taking. *Management Science* 39(1), 17–31.

Leamer, E. (1983). Let's take the con out of econometrics. *The American Economic Review* 73(1), 31–43.

Leeson, N., and Whitley, E. (1996). *Rogue Trader: How I Brought Down barings Bank and Shook the Financial World.* Little Brown and Company.

Mignola, G., and Ugoccioni, R. (2006). Sources of uncertainty in modeling operational risk losses. *The Journal of Operational Risk* 1(2), 33–50.

Nešlehová, J., Embrechts, P., and Chavez-Demoulin, V. (2006). Infinite mean models and the LDA for operational risk. *The Journal of Operational Risk* 1(1), 3–25.

Opdyke, J. and Cavallo, A. (2012). Estimating operational risk capital: The challenges of truncation, the hazards of maximum likelihood estimation, and the promise of robust statistics. *The Journal of Operational Risk* 7(3), 3–90.

Pannell, D. (1997). Sensitivity analysis of normative economic models: theoretical framework and practical strategies. *Agricultural Economics* 16(2), 139–152.

Schorfheide, F., and Wolpin, K. (2012). On the use of holdout samples for model selection. *American Economic Review 102*(3), 477–481.

Sekeris, E. (2012). New frontiers in the regulatory advanced measurement approach, *Operational Risk: New Frontiers Explored*. Risk Books.

Stewart, R. (2016). Bank fraud and the macroeconomy. *The Journal of Operational Risk 11*(1), 71–82.

Velleman, P. (2008). Truth, damn truth, and statistics. *Journal of Statistics Education 16*(2), 2–15.

14 Statistical Decisioning Tools for Model Risk Management

BHOJNARINE R. RAMBHARAT*

14.1 Introduction

Empirical strategies for managing model risk in bank operations use principles from both quantitative and qualitative rubrics to facilitate effective decision-making. Probability theories underpin the inferential framework in areas such as market, credit, operational, and compliance risk, where standard model evaluation metrics are leveraged to assess the usefulness of a given model; however, uncertainty in model evaluation has consequences for model-based decision-making, yet this concept is usually overlooked. If different models are estimated using the same data set, goodness-of-fit (GOF) measures might only reveal slight differences. Or, if there are material differences, idiosyncrasies with respect to a given model may not be apparent in GOF measures. Consequently, a model developer could be faced with additional uncertainty in model evaluation. Rather than make a sub-optimal model choice, a more structured model selection framework that results in robust model risk management strategies could be pursued.

Utility theory provides a structured rubric to guide decision-making in model risk management where, in addition to GOF-based metrics, "rewards" associated with models can be analyzed. A reward can be a benefit or a cost, depending on the specific modeling problem. For example, suppose that two models are marginally close to each other based on common GOF measures like the AIC (Akaike Information Criterion) or BIC (Bayesian Information Criterion). If the model developer employs a statistical decision-theoretic approach, insightful differences between the two models could be revealed through utility computations

* B.R. Rambharat is a subject-matter expert (Statistics) at the U.S. Office of the Comptroller of the Currency (OCC). The views expressed in this paper are solely those of the author and do not reflect the opinions of the OCC. The author would like to acknowledge all reviewers whose comments have improved the content of this paper. Any residual errors are the sole responsibility of the author.

that take into account salient features of the model – e.g., model parameter estimates. Specifically, given a justifiable utility-based framework, model selection exercises have an opportunity to be enhanced.

The relevance of decision theory in applied statistical work is evident from the seminal research of leading scholars such as Savage (1972), DeGroot (1970), and Berger (1985). The foundations developed by them paved the way for applications of decision theory to statistical inference. Model developers can leverage a decision-theoretic framework to supplement modeling and analysis. A potential opportunity arises with respect to quantitative applications in model risk management. While discerning between models can be reliably accomplished using standard GOF metrics, model choice is unclear if differences in a given metric (like AIC or BIC) are subtle or if certain idiosyncrasies cannot be reconciled. Specifically, assume that a metric like AIC points to a choice of model A versus model B; however, there may be some advantages to model B that may not be apparent from the evaluation of a single statistic; however, these benefits of model B might become more apparent in a utility-based framework.

Model evaluation (and model selection) are important components of the analytical work that quantitative specialists perform in financial institutions when developing and validating models. Quantitative modeling is but one component of managing risk in these areas. A significant challenge for model developers concerns model choice, particularly in light of the uncertainty associated with a model. The areas of model uncertainty and model selection criteria are well-documented in the literature, for instance in the noteworthy contributions of Clyde and George (2004), Kadane and Lazar (2004), Claeskens and Hjort (2008), Bannör and Scherer (2014) and Rao and Wu (2001). We believe that model developers and evaluators can leverage statistical decision theory to help compare (and question) models that are used to better understand risk in financial institutions.

This chapter describes another application of statistical decision theory to modeling and analysis, but with a more narrow focus on model risk management in financial institutions. We compare model evaluation criteria: one that is a standard model assessment metric and another that is based on maximizing expected utility. This study is organized as follows: Section 14.2 describes the risk modeling problem. Section 14.3 argues for a ranking of models based on utility optimization.

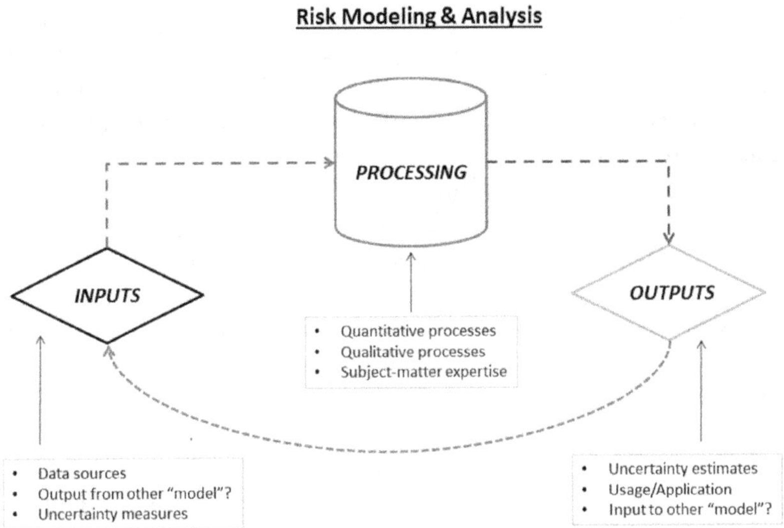

Figure 14.1 A schematic of risk modeling as *1) inputs, 2) processing* and *3) outputs*, where some relevant issues are listed for each component.

Section 14.4 presents an empirical application in the context of fair-lending – specifically, assessing potential disparate impact using a home mortgage data set where we reconcile varying complexities of statistical modeling. Next, Section 14.5 discusses model comparison and evaluation. Finally, Section 14.6 provides concluding remarks.

14.2 Risk Modeling

Risk modeling in financial institutions uses basic principles that underpin modeling and analysis. Figure 14.1 shows that risk modeling can be assessed, from a high level, in terms of three basic components: 1) inputs, 2) processing, and 3) outputs.[1] A brief overview of each of these components will illustrate some of the concerns that model developers face when addressing model choice and uncertainty.

The inputs to a model will likely include sources of uncertainty. First, the quality of the underlying data sets (as well as the data sources) ought

[1] This framework is also found in the supervisory guidance on model risk management, which is jointly published by the OCC (as Bulletin 2011–12) and the Federal Reserve Board (as SR 11-7).

to be recognized. Moreover, inputs to a model could include outputs from another model (e.g., a hierarchical paradigm), and relevant measures of uncertainty of such intermediate output should be taken into account. Second, the processing stage includes quantitative and qualitative elements, where statistical and judgmental sources of uncertainty might arise. Finally, a model's output produces key statistics that help developers with evaluation. Output measures highlighting quality of fit and measures of variation (e.g., of relevant coefficient estimates) are important to a model developer's assessment. Each of these three components of risk modeling can warrant advanced statistical analysis in its own right, but it is not within the scope of this study to pursue this issue. Rather, this chapter aims to highlight how statistical decision theory can supplement the overall risk modeling architecture illustrated in Figure 14.1.

When comparing across alternative models, it is not uncommon to find that statistics that assess the quality of model fit have only marginal differences. Moreover, even if there are appreciable differences in these evaluation metrics, they may neglect nuances of a specific problem that are important to a developer. Section 14.3 describes the role that utility theory can play as a supplement to the standard metrics used to evaluate model performance and model risk management.[2]

14.3 Utility Analysis

The definition of a utility function, taken from DeGroot (1970), is stated next.

Definition 3.1 *DeGroot (1970). A utility function is a real-valued function such that for two probability distributions, P_1 and P_2, P_1 is "not preferred" to P_2 if, and only if, $E[U(\cdot)|P_1] < E[U(\cdot)|P_2]$, assuming the expectations exist. For a given reward R, $U(R)$ is denoted as the utility of the reward R.*

The quantity $E[U(R)|P]$ denotes the expected utility of a reward R and is usually referred to as the "utility of the reward R," but it is more precisely the utility of the reward R to be *expected* under the probability distribution P, which, according to DeGroot, motivates the

[2] The point here is to note that a utility-based approach only acts as a *supplement* and in no way substitutes for the use of standard model evaluation metrics.

expected-utility hypothesis that stipulates the existence of a utility function U. Indeed, the expected-utility hypothesis and the definition of a utility function U further motivates a ranking approach for models based on evaluation of their (expected) utility.

A statistical decision-theoretic framework provides methods to enlarge the scope of evaluation for model developers. Evaluating the utility of rewards allows analysts to potentially assess idiosyncrasies in models that may not be apparent in standard evaluation metrics. Therefore, model users can leverage a decision-theoretic framework to make more robust conclusions about models used by financial institutions.

The choice of a utility function in the context of modeling and analysis in financial institutions will likely depend on the specific problem. Typically, a *concave* utility function could facilitate the work of a model tester or auditor since the marginal utility of rewards would arguably "diminish" with increasing rewards because enough evidence would be gathered to motivate a more exhaustive review of the model's implications. Figure 14.2 shows an illustrative, concave utility

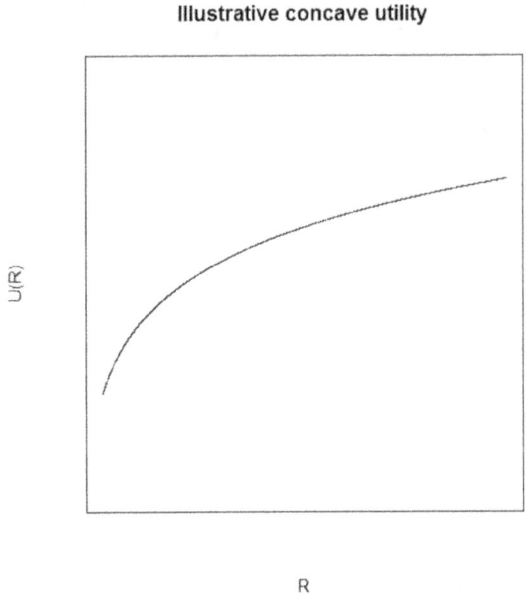

Figure 14.2 An illustrative concave utility function, which graphically shows that the marginal utility from rewards "diminish" as rewards increase. The analysis in this paper assumes a concave utility function.

function. Common examples of concave utility functions are $U(r) = \sqrt{r}$ or $U(r) = \log(r)$. In the following analysis, we adopt the convention that the utility function U is concave.

Assumption 3.2 *The utility function, U, is assumed to be concave and monotonically increasing. Consequently, the marginal utility of an incremental reward $U'(R) > 0$ (and $U''(R) \downarrow$ as $R \uparrow$).*

Motivating a ranking framework based on utilities of rewards requires an understanding of how rewards are constructed. As noted above, this depends heavily on the context of the problem. We next state and prove a lemma that motivates a utility-based ranking rubric. The lemma postulates that, on average, the utility of a *fixed* reward is at least as great as the utility of a model-based reward that is *uncertain*.

Lemma 3.3 ***Risk aversion:*** *Let U be a concave utility function, R a reward, and assume a probability law P. On average, the utility of a fixed and certain reward is at least as great as the utility of an expected reward conditional on the probability distribution P. Specifically:*

$$U\left(\underbrace{E(R)}_{fixed}\right) \geq E\left[U\left(\underbrace{E(R|P)}_{random}\right)\right] \tag{14.1}$$

or, equivalently,

$$E[U(E(R)) - U(E(R|P))] \geq 0. \tag{14.2}$$

Proof. This lemma requires one to prove that the utility of an unconditional expected reward R is at least as great as the model-averaged utility of an expected reward conditional on a given model P, or equivalently, that the lower bound on the average maximal gain in utility from the elimination of uncertainty is non-negative (see Eq 14.2). Since U is concave, Jensen's inequality implies that $E[U(R)] \leq U(E(R))$. Inspecting this inequality through conditioning,

$$E[U(R)] = E\{E[U(R)|P]\} = \int E[U(R)|P]dP \leq \int U[E(R|P)]dP \tag{14.3}$$

$$\leq U\left(\int E(R|P)dP\right) = U(E[E(R|P)]) = U(E(R)). \tag{14.4}$$

Both inequalities above are achieved through appealing to Jensen's inequality.[3] Regarding the claim in the lemma, Equations 14.3 and 14.4 show:

$$U(E(R)) \geq \int U[E(R|P)]dP = E[U(E(R|P))]. \tag{14.5}$$

Lemma 3.3 motivates an evaluation of these models using (expected) utilities as articulated in Definition 3.1, but this motivation is not in discordance with how models are typically assessed using standard metrics. The issue of how to establish a reward R, which is typically user dependent, finds natural applications in modeling and analysis problems in the context of financial institutions.

Section 14.4 discusses an application of utility-based rankings for models in a hypothetical consumer compliance problem where the reward R relates to a model's ability to uncover incidences of disparate impact. We argue for a rank-ordering of the models based on expected utilities where inferences with less uncertainty (or a higher degree of precision) are preferred.

14.4 Empirical Application

A concrete example of how to apply the result in Lemma 3.3 arises in home mortgage applications where models can be used to assess the possibility of disparate impact. Below, we describe the underlying data and specific modeling problem where the objective is to model approvals versus denials, as well as gradations in between, for the case of mortgage loans.[4] The results from three standard generalized linear models (GLM) are presented for a public home mortgage data set that consists of HMDA/LAR data across nine banks. We use data from multiple banks in order to: (1) protect the identity of a single bank

[3] DeGroot (1970) provides details on Jensen's inequality, both for conditional and unconditional expectations.

[4] By "gradations" we mean the various "action taken" categories in the HMDA Loan Application Register (LAR) – "approve / not accepted," "denied," "withdrawn," etc.

LOAN/APPLICATION REGISTER
CODE SHEET

Use the following codes to complete the Loan/Application Register. The instructions to the HMDA-LAR explain the proper use of each code.

Application or Loan Information

Loan Type:
1 – Conventional (any loan other than FHA, VA, FSA, or RHS loans)
2 – FHA-insured (Federal Housing Administration)
3 – VA-guaranteed (Veterans Administration)
4 – FSA/RHS (Farm Service Agency or Rural Housing Service)

Property Type:
1 – One to four-family (other than manufactured housing)
2 – Manufactured housing
3 – Multifamily

Purpose of Loan:
1 – Home purchase
2 – Home improvement
3 – Refinancing

Owner Occupancy:
1 – Owner-occupied as a principal dwelling
2 – Not owner-occupied
3 – Not applicable

Preapproval (home purchase loans only):
1 – Preapproval was requested
2 – Preapproval was not requested
3 – Not applicable

Action Taken:
1 – Loan originated
2 – Application approved but not accepted
3 – Application denied by financial institution
4 – Application withdrawn by applicant
5 – File closed for incompleteness
6 – Loan purchased by financial institution
7 – Preapproval request denied by financial institution
8 – Preapproval request approved but not accepted (optional reporting)

Applicant Information

Ethnicity:
1 – Hispanic or Latino
2 – Not Hispanic or Latino
3 – Information not provided by applicant in mail, Internet, or telephone application
4 – Not applicable (see App. A, I.D)
5 – No co-applicant

Race:
1 – American Indian or Alaska Native
2 – Asian
3 – Black or African American
4 – Native Hawaiian or Other Pacific Islander
5 – White
6 – Information not provided by applicant in mail, Internet, or telephone application
7 – Not applicable (see App. A, I.D.)
8 – No co-applicant

Sex:
1 – Male
2 – Female
3 – Information not provided by applicant in mail, Internet, or telephone application
4 – Not applicable (see App. A, I.D.)
5 – No co-applicant

Type of Purchaser

0 – Loan was not originated or was not sold in calendar year covered by register
1 – Fannie Mae
2 – Ginnie Mae
3 – Freddie Mac
4 – Farmer Mac
5 – Private securitization
6 – Commercial bank, savings bank or savings association
7 – Life insurance company, credit union, mortgage bank, or finance company
8 – Affiliate institution
9 – Other type of purchaser

Reasons for Denial (optional reporting)

1 – Debt-to-income ratio
2 – Employment history
3 – Credit history
4 – Collateral
5 – Insufficient cash (downpayment, closing costs)
6 – Unverifiable information
7 – Credit application incomplete
8 – Mortgage insurance denied
9 – Other

Other Data

HOEPA Status (only for loans originated or purchased):
1 – HOEPA loan
2 – Not a HOEPA loan

Lien Status (only for applications and originations):
1 – Secured by a first lien
2 – Secured by a subordinate lien
3 – Not secured by a lien
4 – Not applicable (purchased loans)

Figure 14.3 HMDA Loan Application Register (LAR) code sheet. Additional details can be found at www.ffiec.gov/hmda/pdf/code.pdf.

(or HMDA reporter), and (2) gather HMDA decision outcomes across financial institutions of varying sizes.[5]

14.4.1 Home Mortgage Data

Enacted into law in 1975, the Home Mortgage Disclosure Act (HMDA) mandates that financial institutions provide basic information to the public summarizing outcomes in the loan application process.[6] Figure 14.3 shows the information collected on every loan.

This analysis explores potential underwriting disparities where the outcome is the "Action Taken" field, and the effects of ethnicity, race, and gender on this outcome are considered. We also control for "loan amount" and "income" as these are also available in the public

[5] The following illustrative empirical work is a stylized example and is not intended to represent actual supervisory oversight and/or implementation of the Community Reinvestment Act of 1976.

[6] Additional details about HMDA and relevant data sets are available on the website www.ffiec.gov/hmda/.

HMDA data.[7] The HMDA data set also contains information related to "reasons for denial," but this is an optional reporting variable and we do not include it in this illustrative analysis; however, a more elaborate model could take this information (including the lack of it) into account.

14.4.2 Disparity Analysis

Using three statistical models : (i) logistic regression, (ii) ordinal logistic regression, and (iii) multinomial logistic regression, this illustrative study uses 2015 loan dispositions from reporting institutions based on their HMDA/LAR files. The three models vary based on how the outcome variable ("Action Taken") is modeled. In the case of logistic regression, we collapse the "Action Taken" outcome to a binary one: originated or not. We use this approach to be as consistent as possible with the other two modeling frameworks (i.e., to use the same data sets).[8] Concerning the ordinal logistic regression case, we organize the "Action Taken" outcome as (1) *originated*, (2) *mixed*, and (3) *denied*, so the other categories apart from originated ("Action Taken" = 1), approved/not accepted ("Action Taken" = 2), or denied ("Action Taken" = 3) are designated as "mixed" or unclear outcomes. Finally, in the multinomial logistic regression model, which has been used in the literature to model HMDA data (e.g., see Cherian (2014)), we do not collapse any of the "Action Taken" categories, but we drop the "Action Taken = 6" (or "Loan purchased by financial institution") as this is indicative of origination. We further subset the data comprised of conventional loans for home purchase that are owner-occupied and are one to four-family properties. After sub-setting, the sample across the nine banks has 42, 482 applications. When making comparisons, protected class racial categories are compared to non-Hispanic Whites,

[7] As this is an illustrative exercise, we focus on relevant, available covariates in the public HMDA data set. More refined models could be estimated using an augmented data set with additional, non-public information on applicant profiles.

[8] We did the standard logistic regression analysis using just "originated" vs "denied" and the coefficients that show strong statistical significance are the same in both cases; however, we preferred to incorporate the other "Action Taken" features not symptomatic of origination and thus use *originate* vs *not originate*.

Table 14.1. ***Results from HMDA data collated across nine banks where the statistical significance of protected-class variables are highlighted. Recall, the outcome is originate / not originate, using a*** **standard logistic regression model** ***with ethnicity, race, gender, loan amount, and income as covariates.***

Variable	Estimate (SE)	*P*-value
Hispanic	0.343 (0.0440)	**<0.001**
odds ratio	1.409	
Am. Ind./Alas.	0.1607 (0.209)	0.440
odds ratio	1.175	
Asian	0.1611 (0.0354)	**<0.001**
odds ratio	1.175	
Black / Af-Amer.	0.607 (0.0664)	**<0.001**
odds ratio	1.835	
Hawai'i/Islander	0.714 (0.165)	**<0.001**
odds ratio	2.042	
Female	0.0236 (0.0289)	0.414
odds ratio	1.024	

females are compared to males, and Hispanics are compared to non-Hispanics.

14.4.3 Model Estimation Results

Table 14.1 shows the results of the standard logistic regression. We see that all of the protected class covariates, apart from American Indian/Alaskan Native and Gender, are strongly statistically significant. Recall that these specifications model the "Action Taken" outcomes as either "originated" or "not originated," which simplifies the outcomes, but may arguably be a sub-optimal approach to signal disparate impact.

Next, Table 14.2 shows the results of a slightly enhanced modeling approach where the "Action Taken" outcomes are "ordered" as *originated*, *mixed*, or *denied*, thus assigning an ordering from an outcome of least to most "severe." The model also estimates thresholds that demarcate the boundary between the three outcome categories. The protected class results for the ordinal logistic

Table 14.2. ***Results from estimating potential HMDA underwriting disparities, where the outcome is originate/mix/deny, using an ordinal logistic regression model with ethnicity, race, gender, loan amount, and income as covariates.***

Variable	Estimate (SE)	*P*-value
Hispanic	0.352 (0.0438)	<0.001
odds ratio	1.422	
Amer. Indian/Alas.	0.158 (0.208)	0.447
odds ratio	1.171	
Asian	0.187 (0.0353)	<0.001
odds ratio	1.206	
Black / Af-Amer.	0.581 (0.0658)	<0.001
odds ratio	1.788	
Hawai'i/Islander	0.713 (0.163)	<0.001
odds ratio	2.040	
Female	0.0175 (0.0288)	0.544
odds ratio	1.018	
Threshold orig|mix	1.727 (0.0252)	<0.001
Threshold mix|deny	1.965 (0.0259)	<0.001

regression are similar to those of the standard logistic regression; however, the ordinal scale organizes potential disparities on a continuum.

Finally, in Table 14.3, we show the results of modeling all of the "Action Taken" categorical outcomes in the HMDA data set[9] and the statistically significant results are highlighted. Thus, for each of the outcomes shown in Table 14.3, we estimate the protected class effects with respect to the corresponding baseline.[10]

Interestingly in the multinomial framework, we find that, in addition to the protected class effects noted in the models above, additional effects for other categories arise. Notably, American Indians/Alaskan Natives, Asians, African-Americans, and Hawaiians/Pacific Islanders all show

[9] In our data set, action outcomes 7 and 8 did not appear and we dropped the action outcome 6 (Loan purchased by financial institution) as this predicts origination, which is also noted in the analysis of Cherian (2014).

[10] Recall that the baselines are such that protected class racial categories are compared to non-Hispanic Whites, females are compared to males, and Hispanics are compared to non-Hispanics.

statistically significant disparities in non-Denied (but non-approved) categories, although some of these are inverse disparities, which means the baseline (non-Hispanic White) group could have potentially been adversely impacted. The ethnicity category, Hispanics, also shows a statistical significant effect in a non-denied/non-approved category.

The more granular findings from the multinomial model are not immediately apparent in the two other specifications, but they could be of importance to internal (or external) compliance agents. Overall, we could reasonably infer that all three modeling frameworks generally agree. Nonetheless, it should not be surprising to uncover disagreement between modeling specifications. Additionally, where a multinomial framework is used in formal analysis, the binary independence assumption (or the independence of irrelevant alternatives, viz., IIA) ought to be ascertained. Cherian (2014) shows that the IIA assumption holds in an application of the multinomial logit model to HMDA data. We explored the Hausman–McFadden (HM) test-statistic for assessing IIA, developed in Hausman and McFadden (1984), and conclude that the IIA holds in the data set we used. Specifically, we compare the fully specified multinomial model to a reduced model where one of the "Action Taken" categories in Figure 14.3 is removed in order to assess the effect on the estimated coefficients for the "deny" action relative to the "loan originated" baseline we specify. The estimated coefficients and the variance–covariance matrix of the aforementioned estimates in both the full and reduced specifications reveal that the IIA holds as per the guidance in Hausman and McFadden (1984) and as described in Cheng and Long (2007).[11]

14.5 Model Evaluation

14.5.1 Comparison Metrics

A common model comparison metric often used is AIC (Akaike Information Criterion), which is a metric based on a trade-off between the fit of a model and the number of parameters in the model. Specifically,

[11] As is documented in the literature, IIA tests have shortcomings. Cheng and Long (2007) provide a useful discussion of some IIA tests, including the HM test, in an applied context.

Table 14.3. *Results from estimating potential HMDA underwriting disparities, where the outcome is all actions, apart from loan purchase, from the HMDA code sheet, using a* multinomial regression model *with ethnicity, race, gender, loan amount and income as covariates.*

Variable	Approved/Not Accepted	Denied	Appl. Withdrawn	Closed/Incomplete
Hisp: *est.(se)*	0.386 (0.110)	0.400 (0.0501)	0.0502 (0.107)	0.0209 (0.0174)
odds ratio	1.471	1.492	1.051	1.021
p-value	**<0.001**	**<0.001**	0.639	0.229
AI/Al: *est. (se)*	0.238 (0.0102)	0.115 (0.246)	0.342 (0.0177)	−7.505 (3.883e−07)
odds ratio	1.269	1.122	1.408	5.503e−04
p-value	**<0.001**	0.640	**<0.001**	**<0.001**
Asian: *est. (se)*	−0.0406 (0.0969)	0.312 (0.0399)	−0.353 (0.0905)	−0.396 (0.0344)
odds ratio	0.960	1.366	0.703	0.673
p-value	0.675	**<0.001**	**<0.001**	**<0.001**
Blk/AA: *est. (se)*	0.308 (0.187)	0.587 (0.0774)	0.830 (0.126)	0.724 (0.0132)
odds ratio	1.361	1.799	2.293	2.063
p-value	0.100	**<0.001**	**<0.001**	**<0.001**
Hw/Is: *est. (se)*	0.866 (0.0143)	0.710 (0.184)	0.677 (0.0164)	−7.633 (3.402e−07)
odds ratio	2.377	2.034	1.968	4.842e−04
p-value	**<0.001**	**<0.001**	**<0.001**	**<0.001**
Fem: *est. (se)*	0.0321 (0.0617)	−0.00129 (0.0309)	0.101 (0.0499)	−0.139 (0.155)
odds ratio	1.033	0.999	1.106	0.870
p-value	0.672	0.969	0.116	0.600

Table 14.4. ***The AIC metric for three models, logistic regression (originated vs not originated), ordered logistic regression (originated, mixed, deny), and multinomial regression (all relevant HMDA action codes modeled).***

Model	*AIC*
Standard logistic	**37,546.42**
Ordered logistic	44,385.03
Multinomial	49,825.84

$$AIC = 2p - 2 \times \log(\hat{L}), \tag{14.6}$$

where, p is the number of parameters in the models, and $\hat{L}$ is the estimated likelihood of the model.[12] Thus, the AIC evaluates a model in terms of its goodness-of-fit (via the likelihood) and its parsimony (parameter dimension). Figure 14.4 compares the three models using the AIC metric. Judging purely from the AIC, it appears that the standard logistic regression model, where the outcomes are "loan originated" versus "not originated," is the best model since it has the minimum AIC. The other two models have more parameters, especially the multinomial model since it models various gradations of non-origination categories, while the standard logistic regression model conveys potential signals of disparate impact more parsimoniously.

Despite the seemingly definitive feature of the AIC metric, valuable information about the outcomes and their associations with model covariates could be masked when data are collapsed as in the standard logistic and ordered logistic models. Therefore, varying degrees of disparate treatment against consumers may not be apparent in a simplified model and could possibly add to the uncertainty associated with that model. Nonetheless, the value in more detailed granularity of a model may vary from one application to the next, and such issues have been addressed in deeper strands of decision-theoretic research work.[13] We now discuss a decision-theoretic approach to further study the nuances of the modeling frameworks outlined above.

[12] Additional details about the AIC as a model-comparison metric can be found in Brockwell and Davis (1999).

[13] See, for example, DeGroot (1970) or Berger (1985), among others.

14.5.2 Quadratic Reward Specification

The notion of a reward in the context of modeling, analysis, and model selection will depend on the model user and the specific applications. The analysis presented here, where we analyze data on home mortgage loan decisions, could be of interest to insured depository institutions.

Assuming that $\beta \in R^k$ is the vector of coefficients in a model, the analytical frameworks above provide information on the statistical significance of a given coefficient – e.g., whether or not females (or males, the gender reference group) could be adversely impacted. However, the choice of a modeling paradigm affects how granular one can assess that potential impact. While the multinomial framework provides the most granularity of the three models, the AIC comparison metric deems it the least preferable owing to the number of parameters. An alternative, possibly more flexible model evaluation approach could be facilitated by calculating the expected utility of a "reward" based on the model output. A reward function where R is a function of the estimated model coefficients, or $R(\hat{\beta})$, could be utilized where that function quantifies the severity of the disparate impact. We discuss an example of this construction of a reward function in the next example.

Example 14.5.1 One natural choice of a reward function is a quadratic form in the coefficients that model the effects on specified characteristics (race, ethnicity, gender, etc.) scaled by the standard error of the coefficient. Under suitable mathematical conditions, quadratic forms have appealing analytical tractability and may lead to known statistical distributions of the reward.

Let $w = \left[\frac{\hat{\beta}_1}{\hat{\sigma}(\hat{\beta}_1)}, \ldots, \frac{\hat{\beta}_k}{\hat{\sigma}(\hat{\beta}_k)}\right]$, and let the reward function R be a quadratic form in w so that

$$R(\hat{\beta}) = w \cdot w^T = \sum_{i=1}^{k} \left(\frac{\hat{\beta}_i}{\sigma(\hat{\beta}_i)}\right)^2, \qquad (14.7)$$

where $\hat{\beta}_i$ is the model-estimated coefficient of the ith covariate and $\hat{\sigma}(\hat{\beta}_i)$ is its standard error. Since $\hat{\beta}_i \sim N(\beta_i, \sigma^2(\beta_1))$, each of the summands has a non-central chi-squared distribution with degrees-of-freedom (d.f.) equal to 1 and non-centrality parameter $\lambda_i = \left(\frac{\hat{\beta}_i}{\hat{\sigma}(\hat{\beta}_i)}\right)^2$. Since the

Example 14.5.1 *(cont.)*

$\hat{\beta}_i$ are correlated, the sum in Equation 14.7 will have a generalized non-central chi-squared distribution.[14] However, noting that each summand in Equation 14.7 has a non-central chi-squared distribution and the reward function is a linear form in the noncentrality parameter λ_i, Monte Carlo simulation can generate draws from the reward $R(\hat{\beta})$ in order to facilitate an expected utility calculation.[15]

14.5.3 Utility Comparisons

The expected utility using the reward function described in Example 14.5.1 (see Section 14.5.2), assuming that the utility is $U(r) = \sqrt{r}$, is:

$$E\left[U\left(R\left(\hat{\beta}\right)\right)|P\right] = \int \sqrt{r} f\left(r|\hat{\beta}\right) dr, \tag{14.8}$$

where r represents the quantity $R(\hat{\beta})$ as expressed in Equation 14.7, and $f(r|\hat{\beta})$ is its probability density function (pdf). As noted above, this pdf will have a generalized non-central chi-squared distribution. However, since each summand in $R(\hat{\beta})$ has a non-central chi-squared distribution with degrees-of-freedom equal to 1 and non-centrality parameter equal to λ_i (again, see Example 14.5.1 in Section 14.5.2), we can compute the conditional expectation in Equation 14.8 using the following Monte Carlo simulation routine.

Routine 14.5.2 Monte Carlo simulation of $E\left[U\left(R\left(\hat{\beta}\right)\right)|P\right]$.

For $n = 1, \ldots, M$:

- *Compute* $\lambda_i = \left(\frac{\hat{\beta}_i}{\hat{\sigma}(\hat{\beta}_i)}\right)^2$.
- *Generate a draw,* $\chi_1(\lambda_i)$, *from a non-central-chi-squared distribution with d.f. = 1 and non-centrality parameter equal to* λ_i, *where* $i = 1, \ldots, k$.

[14] Since estimates of the $\hat{\beta}_i$ coefficients are derived from the input data set, they will be correlated. See, for example, Weisberg (1985) for details.

[15] Additional details about distributions of quadratic forms, as discussed in this example, can be found in a text by Mathai and Provost (1992).

(cont.)

- *Compute the quantity* $\sum_{i=1}^{k} \chi_1(\lambda_i)$.
- *Calculate* $U(R(\hat{\beta})) = \sqrt{\sum_{i=1}^{k} \chi_1(\lambda_i)}$ *and store as* U_n.

Monte Carlo estimate: $U_{MC} = \frac{1}{M} \sum_{n=1}^{M} U_n$.

Routine 14.5.2 can be applied to evaluate the expected utility of three models used in the illustrative empirical exercise (recall Tables 14.1–14.3). We compute the reward based on coefficients that are statistically significant. Note that the shades (or gradations) of the outcome variable are different for each model with the logistic model being the simplest and the multinomial model being the most granular. Indeed, it is arguable that with more gradations in the outcome, there is less variability (and less uncertainty) in terms of assessing the extent of possible disparate impact. Table 14.5 highlights this observation based on the utility calculations using the Monte Carlo simulation procedure in Routine 14.5.2. In addition to tabulating the estimated expected utilities, we also recall the AIC results from Table 14.4.

As the table shows, in contrast to the AIC outcomes, the expected utility analysis suggests the opposite! Specifically, the expected utility for the multinomial model is highest of the three, even though for comparative purposes, we base its calculation using the coefficients

Table 14.5. ***An assessment of the three models, logistic regression, ordered logistic regression, and multinomial regression estimated in Section 14.4.3 based on expected utility calculations using Routine 14.5.2 with*** **M =** ***10,000*** **Monte Carlo simulation runs. We only compute the expected utility for the denial** ***category in the multinomial model to demonstrate its utility just using this most negative action outcome.***

Model (P_j)	*AIC* (P_j)	*Expected utility* (P_j)
Standard logistic (P_1)	**37,546.42**	13.644 (9.964e-03)
Ordered logistic (P_2)	44,385.03	13.883 (9.916e-03)
Multinomial (P_3)	49,825.84	**14.142** (9.950e-03)

for the "denied" category.[16] Given that the loan decision is more nuanced in the multinomial model, this reduces variability in the outcome (i.e., "Action Taken") and thus reinforces the observation from Lemma 3.3 about expected utility and orderings based on variability.

If a model evaluator wants to focus solely on the most negative outcome for an applicant (the "denied" applicants), it is arguable that one might proffer a logistic regression framework using approved versus denied outcomes, but this ignores other features of the HMDA/LAR data frame. The results in Table 14.3 show that a multinomial framework is more comprehensive in evaluating all "Action Taken" outcomes in the HMDA data set since it effectively captures the stratification inherent in the outcomes, thereby benefiting from the reduction in outcome variability. The multinomial framework can also be used to hone in on other disparity categories by jointly modeling the outcome categories, and this can help refine subsequent marginal analysis of the data.

14.6 Discussion

We outline a specific problem where a utility-based approach to evaluate models (and model risk) could possibly supplement model assessment exercises. Standard model evaluation metrics (such as the AIC) may not account for certain nuances of a model that have value. While it is compelling to seek models that offer goodness-of-fit and parsimony, more complex models should not be dismissed especially where they could offer more insights into model risk.

Another approach not addressed here is to view the optimization problem in terms of minimizing "loss," rather in contrast to maximizing "rewards." Additional material on the use of loss functions in the decision problem can be found in DeGroot (1970) or Berger (1985). We also did not evaluate the comparative advantage of one model over another in terms of forecast qualities. Our concern here is *ex post* model evaluation, but an adaption of a rubric like the Diebold–Mariano (DM) Test (Diebold and Mariano, 1995) can be used to

[16] Given the greater number of coefficients in the multinomial model, it would not be surprising that the reward is greater based on the number of statistically significant parameters, so we compute a "partial" expected utility using the most egregious outcome. A similar reasoning can also be applied to the ordinal logit, so we based the reward on the protected class coefficients.

assess which model better predicts signals of disparate impact. Arguably, the multinomial model could well be more efficient in that regard since, by construction, it accounts for a wider range of loan application outcomes.

The multinomial framework adds complexity to the modeling problem in this exercise. Nevertheless, the expected utility analysis shows that it has potential value. The multinomial approach could also be used as a road map to a simpler approach if we consider a hierarchical framework. For example, the first stage of the hierarchy could use a multinomial model and, given the results from this stage, further modeling steps could be considered (e.g., a more fine-tuned logistic regression model) to hone in on better signals of disparate impact, which could possibly better assess risk in a Fair-Lending application as studied here (or any other modeling application).

An objective of this study is to illustrate the use of utility analysis as another evaluation approach, assuming it is suitably justified, and is not meant to emphasize any specific data-analytic problem – e.g., fair-lending or any other facet of consumer compliance. Additional insights can be achieved from further empirical studies addressing model risk at financial institutions

References

Bannör, K. and Scherer M. (2014). Model risk and uncertainty – illustrated with examples from mathematical finance. In C. Klüppelberg, D. Straub, and I. Welpe (Eds.), *Risk: A Multidisciplinary Introduction*, Chapter 10, 279–306. Springer International Publishing.

Berger, J. (1985). *Statistical Decision Theory and Bayesian Analysis* (2 ed.). New York: Springer.

Brockwell, P. and Davis R. (1999). *Introduction to Time-Series and Forecasting* (2 ed.). New York: Springer-Verlag.

Cheng, S. and Long J. (2007). Testing for IIA in the multinomial logit model. *Sociological Methods & Research 35*(4), 583–600.

Cherian, M. (2014). Race in the mortgage market: An empirical investigation using HMDA data. *Race, Gender & Class 21*(1–2), 48–63.

Claeskens, G. and Hjort N. (2008). *Model Selection and Model Averaging.* Cambridge: Cambridge University Press.

Clyde, M. and George E. (2004). Model uncertainty. *Statistical Science 19*, 81–94.

DeGroot, M. (1970). *Optimal Statistical Decisions*. Hoboken: John Wiley & Sons, Inc.

Diebold, F. and Mariano R. (1995). Comparing predictive accuracy. *Journal of Business and Economic Statistics 13*, 253–263.

Hausman, J. and McFadden D. (1984). Specification tests for the multinomial logit model. *Econometrica 52*(12), 19–40.

Kadane, J. and Lazar N. (2004). Methods and criteria for model selection. *Journal of the American Statistical Association 99*, 279–290.

Mathai, A. and Provost S. (1992). *Quadratic Forms in Random Variables*. New York: Marcel Dekker, Inc.

Rao, C. and Wu Y. (2001). On model selection. In IMS Lecture Notes – Monograph Series, Volume 38.

Savage, L. (1972). *The Foundations of Statistics* (2 ed.). New York: Dover.

Weisberg, S. (1985). *Applied Linear Regression* (2 ed.). New York: John Wiley & Sons.

15 *Validation of Risk Aggregation in Economic Capital Models*

IBRAHIM ERGEN, HULUSI INANOGLU AND DAVID LYNCH*

15.1 Introduction

Economic capital modeling can be defined as a set of methods or practices that financial institutions may use in order to consistently assess "total risk" in terms of capital requirements across business lines within a firm (BCBS, 2009). Essentially, different types of risky activities within a business line must be aggregated before its economic capital can be compared to other business lines' economic capital and, consequently, a bank-wide risk measure can be estimated. This typical silo approach tends to tackle complex issues by dividing them into small components and addressing each component, one at a time. That is, financial institutions classify their economic activities into main risk categories, namely credit, market, interest rate and non-financial risks (operational risk, reputational risk, etc.) and measure these standalone risks so that they can manage and monitor the risks separately. To the extent that these risk types are quantifiable, there is still a major task – how to aggregate the risks to arrive at the total risk of a business line, and consequently to estimate the total risk of the financial institution. Economic capital modeling has adopted several techniques to address this difficult task.

* Ibrahim Ergen co-authored this chapter while he was a Senior Financial Economist with the Quantitative supervision and Research unit at the Federal Reserve Bank of Richmond, Baltimore, MD, ibrahim.ergen@gmail.com. Hulusi Inanoglu, Principal Economist, Quantitative Risk Management, Federal Reserve Board of Governors, Washington, D.C., hulusi.inanoglu@frb.gov. David K. Lynch, Deputy Associate Director, Quantitative Risk Management, Federal Reserve Board of Governors, Washington, D.C., david.k.lynch@frb.gov. The authors thank Ross Podbielski for excellent research assistance. The authors also thank the editors for valuable comments and discussion. The opinions expressed in this manuscript belong to the authors and do not represent official positions of the Federal Reserve Bank of Richmond, the Federal Reserve Board or the Federal Reserve System.

While economic capital is defined as the "total risk" for a given entity, economic capital modeling does more than estimate the "total risk"; it also serves a critical role in breaking down the barriers among risk types. In other words, economic capital modeling looks into interactions among risk types and aims to explain the co-movements of risk types that are crucial to financial institutions' businesses. Thus, much of economic capital modeling is mainly about dependence modeling to the extent that standalone risk types are well modeled and stable. Due to this fact, the validation of economic capital models boils down to the validation of dependence modeling among different risk types.

In this chapter, we first review the literature on economic capital models and summarize the recent international and US guidance on model validation. Then, we implement a statistical framework for validation of economic capital models via copula methods. This framework includes statistical information criteria, analytical and visual goodness-of-fit tests and backtesting of economic capital estimates using a suite of penalty functions for forecast evaluation. We also perform stability analysis of economic capital estimates in response to realized new loss observations and stress testing of economic capital estimates in response to hypothetical extreme loss observations.

15.1.1 Literature Review

BCBS (2009) provides a summary report on international range of practices and issues in economic capital frameworks. It discusses five risk aggregation methods: simple summation, a fixed diversification percentage, variance–covariance approach, copula approach, and full modeling of common risk drivers through factor models.[1] BCBS (2009) describes the modeling of common risk drivers as theoretically most appealing and potentially the most accurate. However, in practice, it is the most demanding in terms of input, time, and technology requirements. Therefore, other methods are more commonly used in the industry.

[1] While Brockmann and Kalkbrener (2010) also classify this approach as a distinct category in risk aggregation methods and refer to it as "multi-factor approach," they also argue it is a subset of the copula-based approach. That is, instead of modeling dependence across all risk factors, the multi-factor approach maps risk factors to economic factors which are believed to explain the majority of the changes in the risk factors. After this step, a joint model is constructed for the economic risk factors via copulas.

A year after, BCBS released another report (BCBS 2010) which described the latest developments in modeling risk aggregation used by firms and regulators. This report highlights the differences in modeling intra-risk and inter-risk diversifications across different jurisdictions. This report lists three main approaches in risk aggregation, namely:[2]

(1) variance–covariance approach (aka square root formula);
(2) copula approach;
(3) scenario-based aggregation.

The variance–covariance approach is the most simplistic approach which uses pairwise correlations of risk types in an analytical formula. Mathematically, economic capital (EC) is:

$$EC = \sqrt{\sum_{i=1}^{N} w_i^2 r_i^2 + \sum_{i=1}^{N} \sum_{j=1, i \neq j}^{N} w_i w_j r_i r_j corr(i,j)},$$

where r are the risk types, *corr(i,j)* is the correlation between risk types i and j, and $w(i)$ are the weights of each risk type in the firm-wide exposure. The formula is a generalization of the variance of the sum of independent normally distributed random variables (i.e. when each risk type is proxied by its own volatility, the total volatility of independent risks is the square root of the sum of the squares of each risk's volatility). Therefore, the use of this analytical formula is limited to elliptical distributions, and dependencies across risk types are represented by a single number, namely the Pearson's correlation. This approach has many well-known weaknesses. For example, it is well documented that the distributions for most risk types exhibit skewness and a high degree of excess kurtosis, which violates the elliptical distribution assumption. Moreover, the Pearson's correlation can only measure the linear dependence between risk types whereas nonlinear dependence is omitted. Finally, Pearson's correlation gives equal weight to observations in the body and in the tails, resulting in an average dependence measure. Consequently, the body of the distribution dominates the calculated

[2] Simple summation and fixed diversification approaches were considered as aggregation methods in BCBS (2009) but BCBS (2010) only considers the empirical and statistical models driven by data and analytics as the main aggregation approaches.

average. Therefore, this approach fails to account for stronger tail dependencies among different risk types which lead to significant over-estimation of diversification benefits.

In contrast to the variance-covariance approach, the copula approach is a distribution-based aggregation. It uses entire loss distributions (i.e. risk types) as inputs to the aggregation process as opposed to a single correlation statistic (BCBS 2010, p17). In doing so, copula-based aggregation can capture tail-dependencies more accurately. Copula functions can be thought of as multivariate distributions which join marginal distributions. Hence, they provide flexibility in dependence modeling. A modeler can select from a suite of alternative copula functions using statistical criteria such as information criteria and goodness-of-fit tests. However, when the sample sizes are limited as in most banks, the selection process can be more of an art rather than a science and it can be very subjective. Despite this drawback, the copula approach has become more widespread due to its flexibility in dependence modeling and has been the workhorse of risk aggregation.

The third approach – scenario-based aggregation – determines the state of the firm under specific events and sums profits and losses for the various positions under the specific risk event (BCBS 2010, p18). As this approach is more applicable to insurance firms which use actuarial loss distributions, we refer the reader to the survey report for more details.

In addition to these two BCBS reports, there are quite a few research papers on economic capital modeling. We will briefly summarize the notable ones here and contrast them to what we plan to do in this chapter. Rosenberg and Schuermann (2006) is one of the most well-known economic capital modeling papers which uses copula models as a risk aggregation method for credit, market and operational risks. Similarly, Inanoglu and Jacobs (2009) use the copula approach for aggregating accounting-based risk proxies, but add two more risk types, namely interest rate and liquidity risks, in defining firm-wide economic capital. We follow the general idea in these two studies. However, we make several important improvements. First, we excluded liquidity risk from economic capital modeling as liquidity risk has been recently addressed in the context of Basel III liquidity requirements instead of capital requirements. Second, we enhanced the risk proxies by using supervisory confidential bank data for market and operational risks rather than relying on publicly available bank holding company data. We believe that using confidential realized loss data from major US banks for market and operational risks captures dependence structures across risk types much better than the earlier studies in the literature. Third, we conducted our analysis to follow the latest supervisory guidance on model validation such as the supervisory letter 11-7 (SR11-7) by Federal Reserve. Finally, we include both analytic and visual goodness-of-fit tests for copula model selection.

Drehmann et al. (2010) demonstrate that it is fundamental to measure the integrated impact of credit and interest rate risk jointly. Alessandri and Drehhmann (2010) show that ignoring the interactions between the credit and interest rate risk distorts economic capital estimation. These results are generally consistent with the findings in this chapter. However, in contrast to our study, these two papers do not include market and operational risks and do not make use of copula models.

Using data from 881 Austrian banks, Li et al. (2015) compare the performances of simple summation, the variance–covariance approach, and the copula approach. The authors find that the simple summation approach overstates the risk while the variance–covariance approach understates the risk. They propose the copula approach as the future major trend for risk aggregation in banks. Li et al. (2015) also report that the student's t-copula with a single digit degree of freedom is a good choice to capture tail dependence. Li et al. (2015) were not able to estimate correlations between the risk types due to sparse data. Instead they made assumptions based on preliminary data analysis and provided support for their results through sensitivity analysis. These results confirm our understanding of the state of the art in economic capital modeling; hence we will focus on copula models as the primary tool for economic capital estimation in this chapter. However, unlike Li et al. (2015) we will not make any assumptions for parametrization of copula models. Instead, we will use more reliable statistical estimation methods to infer copula model parameters.

The weaknesses in dependence model parametrization are not unique to the Li et al. (2015) study. Almost the entire literature[3] leverages the co-movement of asset price indices or similar proxies that

[3] Rosenberg and Schuermann (2006), Maciag et al. (2015), Yi et al. (2012), Liang et al. (2013), Inanoglu and Jacobs (2009).

are thought to be representative risk factors to parametrize the dependence among those risk factors. We would like to reiterate that our study significantly contributes to the literature on risk aggregation for economic capital modeling with the use of proprietary supervisory confidential loss data that eliminates the need for proxies.

15.1.2 Validation of Economic Capital Models

As economic capital models have evolved in a short period of time, in 2013, the BIS provided a set of principles to strengthen banks' risk data aggregation capabilities (BCBS, 2013). The first principle for effective risk data aggregation prescribed by BCBS (2013) is the strong governance requirement around risk data aggregation. This includes independent validation of risk data aggregation and reporting processes (BCBS 2013, paragraph 29-a). Per BCBS (2013) guidance and to follow the theme of the handbook of model validation, we will focus on regulatory expectations for model validation in this chapter. Before we delve into the validation of economic capital models, it is important to pay attention to the model validation guidance issued by US regulators, i.e. SR 11-7. The supervisory letter SR 11-7 includes three core elements for an effective validation framework:

(1) evaluation of conceptual soundness, including developmental evidence;
(2) ongoing monitoring, including process verification and benchmarking;
(3) outcomes analysis, including backtesting.

The first element includes providing empirical evidence supporting the methods used. Basically, the model reviewer assesses the choice of the variables/parameters and evaluates the relevance of the data used to build the model. Evaluation of models includes two tests that have a clear distinction but usually are somewhat integrated; namely sensitivity analysis and stress testing. Sensitivity analysis aims to check the impact of small changes in inputs and parameter values on model outputs while stress testing aims to check performance over a wide range of inputs and parameter values, including extreme values, to verify that the model is robust. Stress testing of the model for robustness should not be confused with supervisory stress test exercises that intend to assess whether firms have sufficient capital during times of economic and financial stress.

The second element includes benchmarking analysis which is the comparison of a given model's inputs and outputs to estimates from alternative models. Model reviewers should compare alternative models to test for the reasonability of the model under consideration.

Finally, outcomes analysis compares model outputs to corresponding actual outcomes. Outcomes analysis typically relies on statistical tests or other quantitative measures. Backtesting is one form of outcomes analysis. Backtesting can be transparent and be easily implemented for some models such as market risk VaR models that compare realized trading revenue (profit or loss) with the VaR model forecast over a short time horizon. On the other hand, this is not the case for operational risk models which do not have a sufficient time series to perform this kind of comparison for backtesting purposes.

This chapter is organized as follows. In Section 15.2, we describe our data from five major US banks and construct a hypothetical large bank to protect the confidentiality of the supervisory data. Then, we provide descriptive statistics in the form of graphical analysis. In Section 15.3.1, we provide a discussion of various risk aggregation frameworks. As we focus on the validation of different dependency assumptions along the SR 11-7, we examine the impact of alternative copula models on the diversification benefits of our hypothetical bank. In doing so, we apply goodness-of-fit tests for copula models and evaluate statistical information criteria as well. In Section 15.3.2, we perform an in-sample backtesting exercise with alternative penalty functions for forecast evaluation. Finally, as part of a coherent model validation process, we include stability and sensitivity analysis in Section 15.3.3 and stress testing in Section 15.3.4. Section 15.4 makes concluding remarks.

15.2 Data and Descriptive Statistics

To preserve the confidentiality of proprietary data, we constructed a hypothetical bank by summing up the credit, market, interest rate and operational risk data across five major US BHC's.[4] Our investigation of dependencies across risk types within each BHC, is in line with the

[4] These five BHC's are JP Morgan Chase, Citi, Bank of America, Goldman Sachs and Morgan Stanley.

hypothetical BHC's dependence structures across risk types. The use of a hypothetical bank is merely for anonymizing the confidential data.

We follow Inanoglu and Jacobs' (2009) approach in constructing loss data for risk types by using accounting-based proxies. However, we deviate from the aforementioned paper whenever we have access to confidential supervisory data for certain risk types. This was the case for operational and market risks.

For operational risk, we used Y-14Q reports that contain data on operational losses of firms. We aggregate the individual event level loss data to obtain quarterly total operational losses. By using banks' confidential operational loss data, we hope to capture the dependencies between operational risk and other risk types better. For market risk, we rely on data from a supervisory data collection exercise. This market risk data consists of individual bank historical daily trading revenues (P&L) and bank 99% VaRs provided to the Federal Reserve Board from major US banking institutions. Since we have this market risk data only for the five major firms that are materially active in the trading business, we restricted our sample to these firms. To proxy market risk, we have calculated a quarterly Value-at-Risk (VaR) number for the hypothetical bank using the bank submissions of daily VaRs for each firm. Banks noted that the interaction between market risk and credit risk was more important than previously had been recognized (BCBS 2010, p.16). By using banks' confidential trading book data, we intend to proxy the market risk better and capture the interaction between credit and market risk better as well.

We continue to use quarterly gross charge-offs to proxy credit risk and interest rate gap (interest expense on deposits minus interest income on loans) to proxy interest rate risk in our analysis following the work of Inanoglu and Jacobs (2009).

15.2.1 Variables for Risk Types and Hypothetical Bank Construction

In this section, we provide further details of our data sources, variable construction for each of the four risk types and the construction of a hypothetical bank from the five banks in our sample.

Credit and interest rate risk proxies: We used Y9-C report data and supplemented it with data from Bloomberg to construct our credit risk and interest rate risk proxies. Several data transformations were performed on the Y9-C data prior to supplementation with Bloomberg data to assure consistency. For example, most income and revenue variables in the Y9-C data are year-to-date variables and, therefore, we converted them to quarterly variables. We retrieved Y9-C report data at the BHC level for the five primary firms in our sample and also for the firms that merged into or were acquired by these five primary firms during the sample period. We need data on these latter firms in order to generate pro forma financials with the assumption that merged or acquired firms were already integrated into the primary firms prior to their merger or acquisition date.

Bloomberg data are used to supplement any potential missing values that may exist in the Y9-C data. Bloomberg provides balance sheet data from several sources. It is important to note that a firm like Merrill Lynch, which was acquired by Bank of America, has never filed Y9-C reports and therefore all of the data available for that firm is Bloomberg-sourced data. The mapping between the Y9-C and Bloomberg data fields is presented in Appendix A.

Once missing values from the Y9-C report are supplemented with Bloomberg data, we back-merge the firms that merged into or were acquired by the five primary firms during the sample period. The back-merging involves the summation of variables for the primary firm and its merged or acquired firms, prior to the actual quarter of the merger or acquisition. For example, the asset size of Bank of America in the quarters preceding its merger with Countrywide and Merrill Lynch is the sum of assets for these three firms in those quarters. This method removes the previously existing spikes in the primary firm's data due to a merger or acquisition. As a result of this step, we obtain pro forma financials. The list of mergers and acquisitions we used are presented in Appendix B.

We use gross charge-offs to proxy credit risk following Mester (1996). The data is sourced from the BHCK4635 field in Y9-C data and the FDIC_GROSS_CHAREGEOFFS field from Bloomberg data.

To proxy interest rate risk, we use net interest income following Jorion (2006). The data is sourced from BHCK4074 field in the Y9-C data and the CF_NET_INT_INC field in Bloomberg data. Following Inanoglu and Jacobs (2009), we also take the difference of net interest income from its expectation calculated as the average net interest income of the preceding four quarters. This variable is also multiplied by −1 to change the interpretation to a loss as opposed to a gain.

In the construction of the hypothetical bank, we sum up both credit and interest rate risk proxies across the five primary firms.

Operational risk loss: We use the operational loss data submissions in FR Y-14Q reports to source the data. Our sample of data contains 189,005 individual loss events from the five primary BHCs for the period 2001-Q1 through 2015-Q4. This sample is substantially richer than publicly available operational loss data sources. Since banks have different data collection thresholds, we truncate data using a common threshold set at $20,000. For each of the five primary firms, we aggregate event level loss data to obtain quarterly total operational losses. Firms are required to submit the pre-acquisition operational losses of acquired firms and therefore, Y-14Q data doesn't require further processing to generate pro forma losses. In the construction of the hypothetical bank, we sum up operational losses of five primary firms.

Market risk loss: The market risk data consists of individual bank historic daily trading revenues (P&L) and bank 99% VaRs provided to the Federal Reserve Board from five major US banking institutions. The daily VaRs are used by banks in managing market risk for regulatory capital purposes. Bank data starting dates begin in the early 2000s and extend through all major market events. Banks predict day-ahead VaR using market factor histories at daily frequency. VaR is updated daily based on the new end-of-day positions. Exposures are typically estimated for factors by geographical region, industry and factor type. It is possible for individual-name exposures to be represented by an aggregate market index. Risk factors used in calculation of the VaRs can be several thousand or more. VaR estimation involves application of historical or analytically simulated market factor distributions to the current end-of-day exposures. Calibration of market factor distributions generally relies on historical windows between one and five years with an average window of approximately threeyears. Market factor histories are updated with a frequency that ranges from one day to one quarter with an average lag of approximately one month. Bank VaRs measure risk only for mark-to-market positions while daily P&L includes fees, commissions and interest income as well.

In construction of the hypothetical bank, we sum up both the P&L and VaR variables across all five primary firms. Then, we aggregate the daily frequency data and transform it to quarterly data. To obtain quarterly P&L, we sum up the daily P&Ls. To obtain quarterly VaR, we calculate the average daily VaR for the quarter and multiply it with the square root of the number of trading days in that quarter. To proxy market risk, we have chosen to use this quarterly VaR number. This implies that we rely on the bank's internal models in calculating a risk measure. Given that we have the raw P&L data available; it is probably preferable to develop our own model to generate a risk measure. However, this would be beyond the scope of this paper because we specifically would like to focus only on the risk aggregation problem. Therefore, we have chosen to follow the simpler method of using the readily available VaR data from the bank submission.

15.2.2 Graphical Analysis

We begin the analysis of dependence among different risk types with scatter plots of the loss data for the hypothetical large bank constructed as described above. As another layer of protection in preserving the anonymity of banks and confidentiality of data, we map quarterly dollar losses for each risk type to the unit interval based on their ranks as follows:

$$U_{r,t} = \frac{R_{r,t}}{N+1}, \tag{15.1}$$

where the subscript, r and t stand for the risk type and the quarter, respectively. Further $R_{r,t}$ denotes the rank of loss in quarter t for risk type r in the entire history of quarterly losses for risk type r, i.e., the largest loss quarter will have $R_{r,t} = 1$, the second largest loss quarter will have $R_{r,t} = 2$ and so on. Finally, $N = 60$ is the number of quarters in our dataset and is typical of the amount of data banks have available to model economic capital. Simply put, we map quarterly dollar losses to the unit interval such that they become unitless and lose their dollar interpretation. In essence, the above transformation is the empirical cumulative distribution function and therefore the transformed variables $U_{r,t}$ are uniformly distributed by construction. As discussed in Genest et al. (2009), this probability integral transform is commonly used in the copula modeling literature and the extra quarter in the denominator aims to avoid limit values of 0 and 1 for the transformed variables.

The above transformation in Equation 15.1 is also closely linked to the concept of rank correlation. There are two main measures of rank correlation: Kendall's tau and Spearman's rho. Spearman's rho can be simply thought as a Pearson correlation for the ranks of data. In other words, Spearman correlation can be defined as:

$$\rho_S(X_1, X_2) = \rho(U_1, U_2).$$

On the other hand, Kendall's tau can be understood as a measure of concordance. Two observations of bi-variate random variables are said to be concordant if $(x_1 - x_1')(x_2 - x_2') > 0$. As the degree of co-movement increases between the two variables, they are more likely to have more concordant observations rather than discordant observations which is defined as $(x_1 - x_1')(x_2 - x_2') < 0$. Kendal's rank correlation is defined as the difference between the probability of concordance and discordance. It can be shown that it is equal to

$$\begin{aligned}\rho_\tau(X_1, X_2) &= E\left[sign\left(\left(X_1 - X_1'\right)\left(X_2 - X_2'\right)\right)\right] \\ &= E\left[sign\left(\left(U_1 - U_1'\right)\left(U_2 - U_2'\right)\right)\right].\end{aligned}$$

As can be inferred from the definitions, both Kendall's tau and Spearman's rho are only dependent on the copula of the bi-variate distribution. They can be calculated using the ranks of data alone, i.e. actual numerical values of the sample are not needed.

A matrix of scatter plots from the transformed losses is presented in Figure 15.1 on the lower triangle with their rank correlations on the

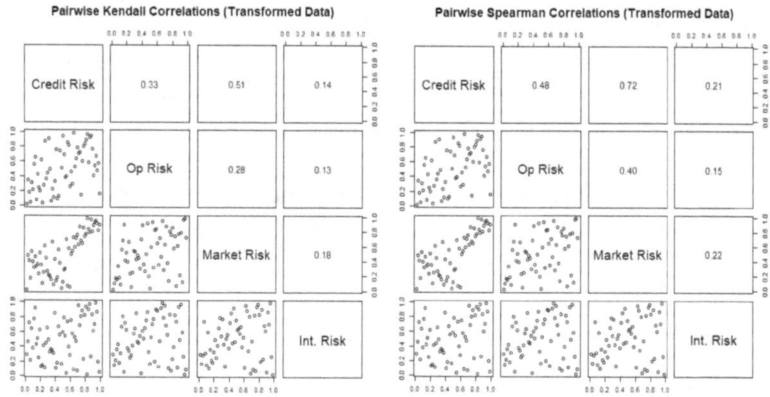

Figure 15.1 Scatter plot of transformed losses for four risk types: credit, operational, market and interest rate risks. Upper panel presents the Kendall's tau and Spearman's rho dependence measure for each pair of risk types.

upper triangle. Credit and market risks clearly exhibit strong dependence both on the body and tails of the distribution. Credit and operational risks exhibit moderate dependence in the body of the distribution and strong dependence on both tails of the distribution as the clustering on the upper right and lower left corners of the scatter plot indicates. The same is true for market and operational risks, but to a lesser extent. The interdependence of interest rate risk and other risk types is less clear. Although some clustering is observed on the joint tail corners, there is also some clustering on the lower right corner which indicates quarters where interest rate risks were low despite high risk in other areas. Despite being weak, overall dependence of interest rate risk with other risk types is generally positive. All these observations from the scatter plots are also consistent with the rank correlation estimates presented in the upper triangle of the plots. Credit and market risks exhibit strong rank correlation followed by credit-operational and market-operational risk pairs. Interest rate risk exhibits positive but somewhat weaker rank correlation with other risk types.

Time series plots of transformed loss variables are provided in Figure 15.2 for each pair of risk types. Figure 15.2 basically shows the time dimension of the correlation between the risk types. Credit and market risk show significant dependence regardless of the level of losses. Operational risk is idiosyncratic as expected but it has significant overlap with credit risk during the downturn periods. Spikes in operational risk in 2002 and 2008 correspond well with the spikes in credit risk. Operational risk and market risk spikes in the financial crisis period, 2008–2009, also correspond well with each other. The interest rate risk loss proxy does not show the same level of strong dependency with the other three risk types, but a moderate level of positive association is visible from the plots. Overall, the observations from time series plots are consistent with the scatter plots.

Our graphical and descriptive statistical analysis shows that the dependence between different risk types is much stronger than what has been presented in previous literature. As mentioned earlier, most studies in the earlier literature leverages the co-movement of asset price indices or similar proxies that are thought to be representative risk factors to estimate dependence parameters. These approaches fail to capture the real strength of dependency among the risk types. The use of confidential realized loss data for operational and market risks

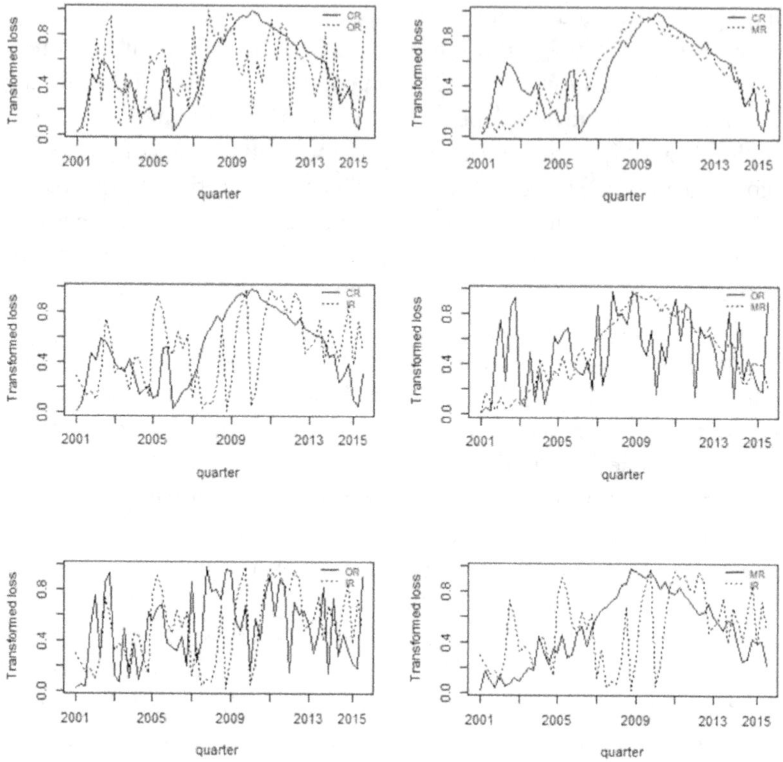

Figure 15.2 Time series plots of transformed losses for four risk types: credit risk (CR), operational risk (OR), market risk (MR) and interest rate risk (IR). Plots are generated for each pair of risk types for better visualization of dependence.

together with very reliable publicly available proxy for credit risk (charge-offs from Y9.C) enables us to uncover the true strength of tail dependencies among different risk types.

15.3 Empirical Methodology and Results

As discussed in the introduction, copula models have become the standard tool across the banking industry for the purpose of risk aggregation and economic capital estimation. In this section, we provide a conceptual overview of copula modeling methods and the benchmark copula models used in this study. We describe and implement empirical methods for parameter estimation and goodness-of-fit testing. Finally, we provide descriptions and results of our backtesting, stability testing and stress testing applications.

Copulas are useful modeling tools to focus on the analysis of the dependence between variables because they allow for the separation of marginal distribution modeling from dependence modeling. By Sklar's (1959) theorem, multivariate distribution functions can be separated into their marginal distributions and a function known as the copula which captures the dependence among the variables. If $X = (X_1, X_2, \ldots, X_d)$ is a d-dimensional continuous random vector with a joint distribution function F, then the copula representation of F is given by:

$$F(x_1, x_2, \ldots, x_d) = C(F_1(x_1), F_2(x_2), \ldots, F_d(x_d)),$$

where $F_1, F_2, \ldots F_d$ are the marginal distribution functions for the individual variables. A copula is a mathematical function from the d-dimensional unit cube to the unit interval. In other words, it is a d-dimensional cumulative distribution function with uniform margins on the unit interval. Nelson (2006), Trivedi and Zimmer (2007), and McNeil et al. (2005) provide excellent discussions of copula modeling and its financial applications.

15.3.1 *Benchmarking: Alternative Copula Models*

While choosing a copula model for risk aggregation and economic capital estimation, it is very important to test alternative benchmark specifications and choose the final model based on sound statistical criteria supported by intuitive business judgment in order to reduce model risk. Therefore, we include four different copula models in this study. We fit the Gaussian, T_4, Clayton and Gumbel copulas to the data.[5] The Gaussian and T_4 copulas are elliptical models and therefore the right and left tail dependence are the same. On the other hand, the Clayton and Gumbel copulas can capture asymmetric dependence between the right and left tails of the joint distribution. Choosing alternative benchmark models that can capture different characteristics of the data is another important method of reducing model risk as it is not possible to know a priori whether the dependence is symmetric or asymmetric.

[5] For t copula we used 4 degrees of freedom rather than estimating it. Ideally, the degrees of freedom can also be estimated jointly with the correlation matrix. However, due to numerical problems in goodness-of-fit testing, we decided to fix this parameter to an integer value. When estimated from the data, the degree of freedom turns out to be 4.26.

In addition to including five alternative copula models, we use two different parameter estimation methods. Maximum likelihood estimation (MLE) has become the predominant methodology for estimating the parameters of risk aggregation models. However, parameter estimates can be quite sensitive to the choice of estimation method especially when the sample size is small. Thus, it is important to explore the use of alternative estimation methods to address the benchmarking and sensitivity analysis requirements of SR 11-7. In addition to MLE fitting,[6] we also use the method known as the inversion of Kendall's tau matrix. This method, in essence, is a method of moments estimation as it calibrates the model parameters to match the empirical estimates of Kendall's tau matrix as closely as possible.

15.3.1.1 Statistical Assessment Criteria

As mentioned earlier, sound statistical criteria should be employed in model selection for risk aggregation. In this paper, we compare models both by statistical information criteria and also by goodness-of-fit test results. As statistical information criteria, we use the Akaike Information Criteria (AIC) and the Bayesian Information Criteria (BIC) which are commonly used in econometrics literature for model selection. AIC is defined as

$$AIC = 2 \times N_{parms} - 2 \times Log\text{-}Likelihood.$$

The likelihood function measures the probability of observing the empirical data if the data was truly coming from the estimated model. Therefore, higher likelihood value indicates that the model provides a good representation of the observed data. The AIC penalizes the logarithm of likelihood with the number of estimated parameters because all else equal more parsimonious and simpler models are preferable. It is possible to fit models with numerous parameters to achieve higher likelihood values and such models may provide better fit to the in-sample data. However, this raises the concern of over-fitting which results in bad performance in out-of-sample forecasting.

The Bayesian information criteria has similar theoretical underpinnings and empirical implications with AIC. The BIC is defined as

[6] In the maximum likelihood fitting of Archimedean copulas, we used exact formulas for the generator derivatives driven by Hofert, Machler and McNeil (2012).

$$\text{BIC} = \log\left(N_{sample}\right) \times N_{parms} - 2 \times \textit{Log-Likelihood}.$$

The difference from the AIC is the size of the penalty for additional parameters. While AIC penalizes each additional parameter by 2 units, the BIC penalizes each additional parameter by the logarithm of sample size which is log(60) for our sample of data. Lower values of AIC and BIC (lower number of parameters and higher likelihood values) indicate better models to represent the empirically observed data.

As for goodness-of-fit tests, we implemented three analytical and one graphical goodness-of-fit testing methods in order to evaluate the model fit to the data. The three analytical tests rely on the bootstrapping methods described in the seminal review paper by Genest et al. (2009)). Two of them are Cramér-vonMises type statistics and one of them is an Anderson–Darling type statistic. For the graphical goodness-of-fit test, we follow Hofert and Machler (2013) .[7]

In terms of CvM tests, we use the SnB and SnC test statistics proposed in Genest et al. (2009). To perform these tests, we first apply the Rosenblatt (1952) transformation to the data using the hypothesized copula. Rosenblatt's transformation of a copula C assigns a vector $(\mathrm{e}_1, \mathrm{e}_2, \ldots \mathrm{e}_\mathrm{d})$ to every vector $(\mathrm{u}_1, \mathrm{u}_2, \ldots, \mathrm{u}_\mathrm{d})$ where

$$e_1 = u_1$$

and

$$e_i = \frac{\partial^{i-1} C(u_1, u_2, \ldots, u_i, 1, \ldots, 1)}{\partial u_1 \ldots \partial u_{i-1}} \bigg/ \frac{\partial^{i-1} C(u_1, u_2, \ldots, u_{i-1}, 1, \ldots, 1)}{\partial u_1 \ldots \partial u_{i-1}} \forall i > 1.$$

The Rosenblatt transformation is a well-known probability integral transform which provides a simple way of decomposing a random vector with any given distribution into independent components that are uniformly distributed on the unit interval. If the hypothesized copula, C, provides a good fit to the data u, then we would expect the independence copula $C_\perp$ to provide a good fit to the Rosenblatt

[7] All four goodness-of-fit tests we implement in this paper are readily available as part of the R package "copula." We performed both parameter estimations and the goodness-of-fit tests using the functionalities of this source.

transformed data, e. The SnB and SnC test statistics are defined in Genest et al. (2009) as

$$S_n^{(C)} = n \int_{[0,1]^d} \{D_n(e) - C_\perp(e)\}^2 dD_n(e)$$

$$S_n^{(B)} = n \int_{[0,1]^d} \{D_n(e) - C_\perp(e)\}^2 de,$$

where D_n denotes the empirical copula for the Rosenblatt transformed data and $C_\perp$ denotes the independence copula. Therefore, these test statistics are the sum of squared distances between the independence copula and the empirical copula of the Rosenblatt transformed data.[8] Although this makes them Cramér-vonMises type statistics, their limiting distributions depend on both the hypothesized copula under the composite null hypothesis and its unknown parameter values. Therefore, asymptotic distributions cannot be tabulated and probability values can be obtained only via parametric bootstrapping procedures that are described in Genest et al. (2009).

We also perform an Anderson–Darling type test that was originally proposed by Breyman et al. (2003). The idea was first to apply the Rosenblatt transform using the hypothesized copula to obtain independent uniform margins, e, and then define

$$\chi_i = \sum_{j=1}^{d} \left\{\Phi^{-1}(e_{ij})\right\}^2, \quad where\ i \in \{1, 2, \ldots, n\},$$

where Φ is the standard normal distribution function. As this is a squared sum of IID normal variables, Breyman et al. (2003) argued that the set of all χ_i should generate a chi-squared distributed sample and proposed to test it via the Anderson–Darling test. However, using tabulated values of the Anderson–Darling statistic ignores the

[8] The only difference between the SnB and SnC test statistics are their integration measures. The SnB test statistic is simply an equally weighted average of squared distances between the empirical copula and the independence copula. On the other hand, the SnC test statistic applies weights to those squared distances. The parts of the distribution with high values of empirical copula's density receive more weight thereby rewarding the closeness to independence copula most at the denser parts of the distribution.

Table 15.1. ***Information criteria and goodness-of-fit tests results for all benchmark copula models.***

Model	AIC	BIC	SnB P-value	SnC P-value	AD P-value
Normal.mle	−44.70	−32.14	0.124	0.106	0.246
Normal.itau	−43.30	−30.73	0.210	0.188	0.258
T4.mle	−49.59	−37.02	0.179	0.191	0.882
T4.itau	−48.10	−35.53	0.180	0.214	0.893
Gumbel.mle	−22.93	−20.84	0.023	0.184	0.012
Gumbel.itau	−18.14	−16.04	0.179	0.227	0.289
Clayton.mle	−18.04	−15.94	0.018	0.149	0.008
Clayton.itau	−1.39	0.70	0.426	0.362	0.186

composite nature of the null hypothesis where the limiting distribution of the test statistic is a function of both the hypothesized copula and its unknown parameters. Dobric and Schmidt (2007) raised this point and showed that the Breyman et al. (2003) test based on tabulated values of the Anderson–Darling statistic has essentially no power and does not even hold its level. Consequently, Dobric and Schmidt (2007) proposed a bootstrapped version of this test. In this chapter, we use this bootstrapped test which is also included in the power study of Genest et al. (2009).

The AIC and BIC statistical information criteria as well as the probability values from the analytical goodness-of-fit tests are presented in Table 15.1. Based on both statistical information criteria, elliptical copulas provide a much better representation of the data compared to Archimedean copulas. Among the elliptical copula, the T4 copula with MLE fit has the lowest AIC and BIC scores closely followed by the T4 copula with ITAU fit.[9] In terms of goodness-of-fit tests, the MLE fits of Archimedean copulas perform very poorly as they are rejected based on both SnB and AD tests. All other models pass all three goodness-of-fit tests at a 95% confidence level, i.e., using a 5% rejection threshold for p-values. In general, the T4 copulas pass the goodness-of-fit tests with relatively higher p-values, especially the Anderson–Darling test.

[9] For ease of reference, we will refer to the method of moments fitting methodology by inversion of Kendal's tau matrix as the ITAU fit of the copula model.

It is important to note that the MLE fit of any copula provides better statistical information criteria (AIC, BIC) compared to the ITAU fit of the same copula. This is true just by construction since the MLE parameters maximize the likelihood function and the number of parameters is the same regardless of the fitting method. Therefore, an analyst or model developer making model selection decisions solely based on statistical information criteria would never select a model estimated with ITAU fitting method. However, a quick review of the p-values from the goodness-of-fit tests shows that ITAU fits of Archimedean copulas provide a better fit to the data compared to the MLE fits of the same copulas. It is not surprising to obtain differing rank-ordering of models based on differing selection criteria since the different objective functions capture different aspects of the quality of fit. Therefore, it is very important to have multiple statistical assessment criteria and multiple fitting methods which provide different perspectives. It is crucial for a model developer to understand each criterion well, interpret results accordingly and inform model selection based on both statistical and economic intuition.

Finally, we also implement the graphical goodness-of-fit test proposed by Hofert and Machler (2013). This test also relies on the Rosenblatt transformation like the other three analytic tests. However, it fundamentally differs in the methodology of testing the independence for the transformed data. Instead of transforming the entire data vector and testing the independence of all variables jointly, Hofert and Machler (2013) propose applying Rosenblatt's transformation and testing the independence for each pair of variables.[10] Graphically, the authors propose displaying a matrix plot of the Rosenblatt-transformed data together with the probability values of the pairwise independence tests encoded as a background color. They develop methods to derive a global p-value as well. The results of the graphical goodness-of-fit test are provided in Figure 15.3. Probability values from each pairwise independence test are coded as shown in the legends. Probability values greater than 5% are

[10] They use the independence test from Genest and Remillard (2004) for testing pairwise independence.

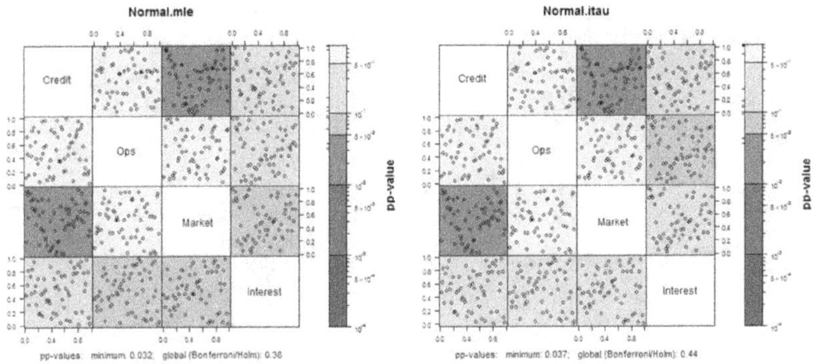

Panel A: Normal copula (MLE fit on the left and ITAU fit on the right)

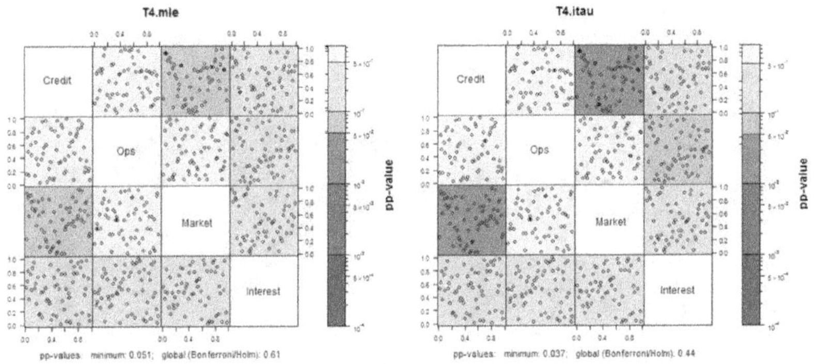

Panel B: T4 copula (MLE fit on the left and ITAU fit on the right)

Figure 15.3 Graphical goodness-of-fit test from Hofert and Machler (2013) applied to our data. Panel A for normal copula, Panel B for T4 copula, Panel C for Gumbel copula, and Panel D for Clayton copula. In each panel, MLE fit is on the left and ITAU fit is on the right. Scatter plots for every pair of variable shows the Rosenblatt transformed data for that pair. The methodology tests for independence of this transformed bivariate data. The three lightest grey shadings indicate p-values greater than 5% and failure to reject the null hypothesis of independence. The three darkest grey shadings indicate p-values smaller than 5% and rejection of null hypothesis.

shown with the three lightest grey shadings, and indicate failure to reject the null hypothesis, i.e. they imply a reasonable fit to the data. Probability values less than 5% are shown with the three darkest grey shadings indicate rejection of the null hypothesis, i.e., an

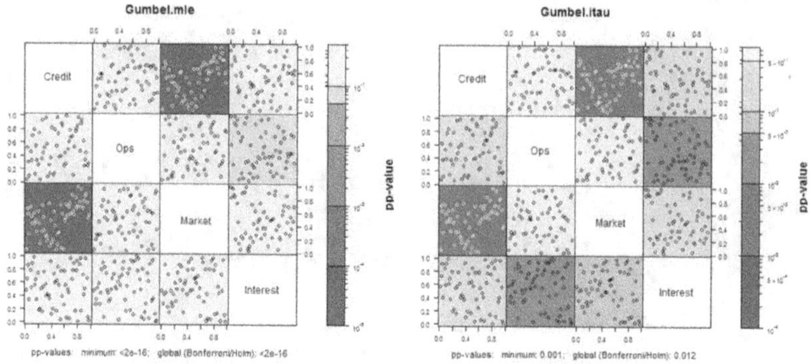

Panel C: Gumbel copula (MLE fit on the left and ITAU fit on the right)

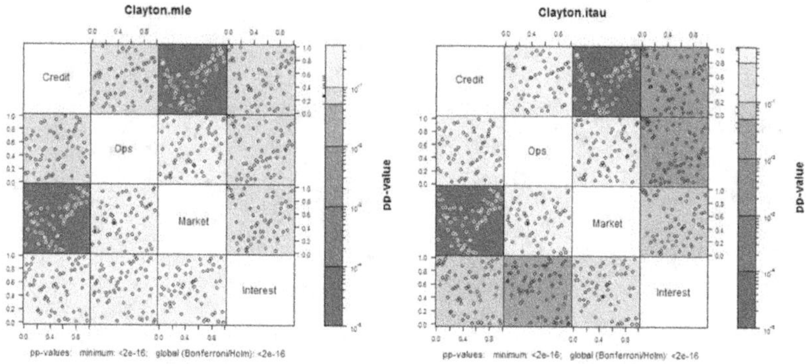

Panel D: Clayton copula (MLE fit on the left and ITAU fit on the right)

Figure 15.3 (*cont.*)

unacceptable fit to the data.[11] The global (Bonferroni/Holm) probability values are also reported under the plots.

Archimedean copulas, in general, perform worse than the elliptical copulas indicated by the grey shading. The unfavorable goodness-of-fit is also reflected by very low global (Bonferroni/Holm) p-values for Archimedean copulas. The T4 and normal copulas both provide reasonable goodness-of-fit which is reflected by both the pairwise grey shadings and the global p-values. The T4 copula with MLE fit is particularly very good as it is the only model for which the null hypothesis is not rejected for any of the pairs and it provides the

[11] Not every color has to exist in each plot due to varying probability values across different copula fits. So, legends look somewhat different across different plots but they use the same color convention.

highest global p-value. Based on the graphical goodness-of-fit test, T4 copula with MLE fit is the best model and T4 copula with ITAU fit is the second best model. These observations are mostly consistent with the statistical information criteria and the goodness-of-fit statistics presented in Table 15.1.

15.3.2 VaR Estimation and Backtesting Analysis

Under the Basel III regulatory regime, banks are not permitted to benefit from diversification for the purpose of regulatory capital calculation. Instead, they sum up the regulatory capital for each risk type to arrive at the total regulatory capital at the firm level. This can be considered an undiversified VaR estimation. However, for the calculation of economic capital, firms build dependence models and calculate a diversified VaR. This generally involves the estimation of a copula model and of marginal distribution functions for each risk type.

15.3.2.1 VaR Estimation

In this study, we will use only a copula dependence model and rely on the empirical distribution functions for the marginal loss distributions. In other words, we simulate loss amounts from each risk type from the historical realized losses rather than from a parametric distribution fit to the data. This ensures that our results are not impacted by the choice of a particular parametric marginal distribution and we focus entirely on the impact of dependence modeling.

We follow the procedures below to estimate the diversified VaR:

- We estimate parameters for each of the four copula families (Gaussian, T4, Gumbel and Clayton) with both estimation techniques (MLE and ITAU fit). This provides a total of eight benchmark models.
- We simulate a four dimensional random vector (u_1, u_2, u_3, u_4) from each of the eight benchmark copula models with parameters estimated from above step.
- Each of the random variables, u_i, generated in the above step are uniformly distributed in the unit interval [0,1] and correspond to quantiles of quarterly loss distributions for each risk type: u_1 for credit, u_2 for operational, u_3 for market and u_4 for interest rate risk. We pick these corresponding quantiles from the sixty quarters of

realized historical loss data for each risk type and sum them up to obtain an observation of quarterly total loss.

$$TotalLoss_i = \sum_{r=1}^{r=4} quantile([QLoss_{1,r}, QLoss_{2,r}, \ldots, QLoss_{60,r}], u_r,).$$

- Repeating the above procedure 100,000 times results in the simulated distribution of aggregate quarterly diversified losses. We use high quantiles of this distribution as the VaR estimate:

$$VaR_{q,Diversified} = quantile([TotalLoss_1, TotalLoss_2, \ldots, TotalLoss_{100,000}], q).$$

The simulation procedure described above is similar to the methodology used in Abdymomunov and Ergen (2017) where the dependence between different operational loss event types was modeled.

The diversification benefit is a measure of the impact of dependency modeling on the VaR estimates relative to the base case of perfect dependence among losses of different risk types. The diversification benefit is defined as:

$$DB_\alpha = 100 \times \frac{VaR_{q,Undiversified} - VaR_{q,Diversified}}{VaR_{q,Undiversified}},$$

where $VaR_{q,Undiversified}$ is estimated with assuming perfect dependence among credit, market, operational and interest rate risks and is calculated as a sum of VaRs for each risk type. On the other hand, $VaR_{q,Diversified}$ incorporates imperfect dependence among losses from different risk types. Therefore, the diversification benefit given above simply calculates the percentage reduction in VaR with respect to the benchmark case of perfect dependence.

We do not report the VaR estimates as they have dollar interpretation. Instead, we report the diversification benefit results from each of the eight benchmark models. Our data is from a hypothetical bank that is constructed by combining the five major US banks in our sample and anonymity of individual banks is already preserved with this strategy. On top of that, we do not report any numbers with dollar units as a secondary layer of protection for the confidentiality of supervisory data. Table 15.2 reports the diversification benefits from each of the eight benchmark models at several high quantiles.

The Clayton copula provides significant diversification benefits that range from 26% to 32% when estimated via MLE and from 23% to 29% when estimated via the ITAU method. On the other hand, the Gumbel copula provides the lowest diversification benefits ranging between 8% to 13% with ITAU estimation and 13% to 18% with MLE estimation. These results are intuitive since the Clayton copula captures only left tail dependence, whereas the Gumbel copula captures only right tail dependence. Clayton copula can provide a good representation of data if all large gains tend to happen simultaneously but not all large losses happen at the same time. On the contrary, Gumbel copula can provide a good fit to data if all large losses happen simultaneously but all large gains do not happen at the same time.

Normal and T4 copulas provide more moderate diversification benefits ranging between 15–18% for the T4 copula and 16–19% for the normal copula. These results are intuitive since normal and T4 copulas are elliptical and therefore they exhibit symmetric dependence in the right and left tails. Also, they provide similar diversification benefits at lower quantiles but the T4 copula provides lower diversification benefits at higher quantiles because it captures asymptotic tail dependence in both tails. In other words, the T4 copula provides a good representation of the data if all large losses tend to happen simultaneously as well as all large gains. The normal copula provides a good fit if neither all large losses nor all large gains happen simultaneously.

We should also state that our results provide some support for regulators' hesitation to recognize diversification benefits for the purpose of regulatory capital estimation. As it can be seen, the potential diversification benefits cover a wide range of values between 8% and 32%. This range can be even be wider if parametric distributions are used to model marginal loss severities for each risk type. Also, there is a great deal of uncertainty given the low sample sizes used in estimation of dependence models. Therefore, exercising conservatism for regulatory capital makes economic and intuitive sense. However, dependence model selection and estimation of diversification benefits is still an important academic and practitioner problem for the estimation of economic capital.

Table 15.2. *Diversification benefits in percentage terms for each model at different quantiles.*

Quantile	N.mle	N.itau	T4.mle	T4.itau	G.mle	G.itau	C.mle	C.itau
0.95	17.04%	16.91%	16.7%	16.27%	18.37%	12.96%	26.12%	22.96%
0.96	16.89%	16.84%	16.38%	15.95%	17.12%	11.46%	26.87%	23.56%
0.97	17.56%	17.64%	16.7%	16.34%	16.84%	11.63%	28.27%	24.77%
0.98	19.18%	18.82%	17.65%	17.09%	16.82%	11.69%	30.36%	27.19%
0.99	18.68%	18.08%	15.93%	15.35%	13.96%	8.64%	32.55%	29.23%

15.3.2.2 Backtesting Analysis

SR 11-7 defines backtesting as "one form of outcomes analysis; specifically, it involves the comparison of actual outcomes with model forecasts during a sample time period not used in model development and at an observation frequency that matches the forecast horizon or performance window of the model." If a long time series history is available, this can be done by continuously monitoring the VaR violations over time, which involves comparison of *ex ante* VaR forecasts to *ex post* realized losses. This is generally performed for market risk models using a rolling-sample methodology as in Kuester et al. (2006) and Ergen (2015) but this strategy requires a long time series history at daily frequency.

Due to the limited sample size with sixty quarterly observations in this study, we cannot perform such out-of-sample backtesting. Instead, we will perform in-sample backtesting that involves the comparison of VaR estimates obtained from modeling the entire sample of data with realized losses during that same sample period. We acknowledge that this involves a look-ahead bias. The main comparison we will make in this analysis is the comparison of actual VaR violations ($Loss > VaR$) with expected number of VaR violations. Due to the in-sample nature of this analysis, it doesn't satisfy the backtesting requirement described in SR 11-7.[12] Therefore, we refer to it as "in-sample backtesting" to be clear about the distinction. To perform our in-sample backtesting analysis, we estimate VaR at the 0.95th, 0.96th, 0.97th, 0.98th, and 0.99th quantiles, we compare the estimates with realized quarterly total losses and identify the violations/breaches of VaR.[13] The number of violations for each model and quantile are reported in Table 15.3. The quantiles q are reported in the first column and the expected violation count is reported in the last column which is calculated as $60*(1-q)$.

[12] SR11-7 is quite strict in the requirement that the backtesting has to be out-of-sample. It further states that, "Analysis of in-sample fit and of model performance in holdout samples (data set aside and not used to estimate the original model) are important parts of model development but are not substitutes for backtesting."

[13] This practice is consistent with SR 11-7 which states that, "Along with measuring the frequency of losses in excess of a single VaR percentile estimator, banks should use other tests, such as ... checking the distribution of losses against other estimated percentiles."

Table 15.3. ***Backtesting results. Realized and expected violation counts for each model at different quantiles.***

Q	N. mle	N. itau	T4. mle	T4. itau	G. mle	G. itau	C. mle	C. itau	Expected
0.95	4	3	3	3	4	2	6	5	3
0.96	2	2	1	1	2	1	5	5	2.4
0.97	1	1	1	1	1	0	5	3	1.8
0.98	0	0	0	0	0	0	2	1	1.2
0.99	0	0	0	0	0	0	0	0	0.6

The Clayton copula underestimates the VaR resulting in higher violation counts than expected at almost all quantiles. In general, the violation count is 1.5–3 times its expected value and this is true regardless of fitting methodology. Please also remember that the Clayton copula provides the highest diversification benefits as shown in Table 15.2. As it turns out, those diversification benefits are overestimated due to VaR being underestimated.

According to Table 15.3, the Gumbel copula with ITAU method of estimation is the most conservative model with the realized violation count always below the expected value. Starting with the 97th quantile there are no VaR violations while other models still result in at least one violation count. So, it is likely that the Gumbel model with ITAU fitting method overestimates the VaR. Please also remember that the Gumbel copula with ITAU fitting method provides the lowest diversification benefits as shown in Table 15.2. So, those diversification benefits are likely underestimated due to VaR being overestimated.

The normal copula, T4 copula and Gumbel copula with MLE estimation seem to be relatively more accurate than other benchmarks. There are differences among these plausible options as well. However, it is hard to make strong conclusions from this backtesting exercise due to limited sample size as well as limited number of quantiles for which Var is estimated. With only sixty quarters, the expected violation counts above the 98th and 99th quantiles are only 1.2 and 0.6. If we were to produce confidence intervals around these point estimates, they would certainly include 0. That being said, low sample size as a limitation shouldn't be a reason for not performing the analysis. Keeping this limitation in mind, we need to complement this analysis with other performance testing exercises. Therefore, we take a step further and develop penalty functions based on the difference between the realized and expected violation counts. This enables the performance measurement and model comparison to be made at a finer grid of quantiles. In what follows we estimate VaR at fifty different quantiles in the interval [0.95, 0.999] with equal intervals of 0.001 and develop penalty functions using the difference between the realized and expected violation count as an error. As in every forecast evaluation exercise, it makes sense to start with the analysis of mean squared error and mean absolute error. In this context, the mean squared error (MSE) and mean absolute error (MAE) penalty functions can be written as:

$$MSE = \frac{1}{50} \times \sum_{i=0}^{i=49} \left((60 * (1-q)) - Count(Loss > VaR_q)\right)^2$$

$$MAE = \frac{1}{50} \times \sum_{i=0}^{i=49} \left|(60 * (1-q)) - Count(Loss > VaR_q)\right|,$$

where $q = 0.95 + i * 0.001$.

Although these metrics can be useful in evaluating model performance, they have a common drawback that they are symmetric. The majority of the forecasting literature uses symmetric penalty functions; i.e., negative and positive errors are penalized equally. However, asymmetric loss functions are often relevant. For example, the cost of arriving ten minutes early at the airport is quite different from arriving ten minutes late. We have the same issue in VaR estimation. The cost of an undercapitalized large bank to the financial system and the society can be in the form of ultimate failure and potential financial and economic crises. This is quite different than the cost of an overcapitalized large bank to the financial system and society in the form of inefficient use of capital. Before developing an appropriate asymmetric penalty function, we first would like to introduce an extreme version of it where we penalize only underestimation. The mean squared underestimation (MSU) and mean absolute underestimation (MAU) can be defined as:

$$MSU = \frac{1}{50} \times \sum_{i=0}^{i=49} \left(min\left[0, (60 * (1-q)) - Count(Loss > VaR_q)\right]\right)^2$$

$$MAU = \frac{1}{50} \times \sum_{i=1}^{i=49} \left| min\left[0, (60 * (1-q)) - Count(Loss > VaR_q)\right] \right|,$$

Where $q = 0.95 + i * 0.001$.

When the expected violation count is larger than the realized violation count indicating overestimation of VaR, the MSU and MAU functions do not apply a penalty for that particular quantile. Therefore, all the weight is distributed to those quantiles where the VaR is underestimated.

The check-loss function is one of the prominent examples of asymmetric cost functions. It is widely used in quantile regression literature since it is the objective function that is minimized to obtain the quantile estimate as in Koenker and Bassett (1978). It can be written as:

$$CL(e) = [\alpha - 1(e < 0)] \times e,$$

where e is the forecast error, α is the quantile of interest in the quantile regression context and the function 1(.) is an indicator function which takes a value of 1 if its argument is true and 0 otherwise. It is easy to see the function becomes a symmetric penalty function when $\alpha = 0.5$. In fact, it reduces to the mean absolute error. As it is well known, the median regression is a special case of quantile regression and it minimizes the MAE, so this shouldn't be surprising. When $\alpha = 0$, only the negative errors are penalized which is an extreme case of asymmetric cost function similar to our MAU function which penalizes only underestimation.

In our context, the differences of the expected VaR violation from realized VaR violation can be considered as the forecast error. Also, we need to set $\alpha = 1 - q$ so that underestimation of Var is weighted more than the overestimation. Therefore, our mean check-loss (MCL) penalty function can be written as:

$$MCL = \frac{1}{50} \times \sum_{i=0}^{i=49} ((1-q) - 1(e < 0)) \times (e),$$

where $e = (60 * (1-q)) - Count(Loss > VaR_q)$ and $q = 0.95 + i * 0.001$.

This construction makes economic and intuitive sense. First it takes the form of a mean check-loss function across all fifty quantiles on our grid. Second, it penalizes underestimation a lot more than the overestimation in line with our earlier arguments for an asymmetric penalty function. Third, the weight given to underestimation keeps increasing as the VaR quantile increases. This latter feature also makes sense from a business perspective because undercapitalization would be a lot more concerning during more extreme market crashes. In addition to these empirical and economic arguments, Giacomini and Komunjer (2005) have theoretically shown that the minimization of the check-loss function is the natural choice for quantile forecast evaluation by developing an encompassing test based on it. Considering all the advantages, we think that the mean check-loss penalty function is superior to the other penalty functions we discussed earlier. The results of our analysis with all alternative penalty functions are presented in Table 15.4.

The results of this analysis are mostly consistent with our earlier discussion. The Clayton copula regardless of fitting method and the Gumbel copula with ITAU estimation have the largest penalty values based on MSE and MAE indicating bad backtesting performance. Among the other five benchmarks, the two normal copulas seem to perform better than the others based on MSE and MAE penalty functions. However, based on MSU and MAU, which penalizes only underestimation, the T4 copulas perform better than the normal copulas. Based on these penalty functions, the Gumbel copula with ITAU fit has absolutely no penalty. This may seem counter-intuitive at first but it is driven by the realized violation count being always greater than the expected violation count at all quantiles across our grid. Please remember that both MSU and MAU penalize only underestimation of VaR. Therefore, the zero-penalty value based on MSU and MAU, in our opinion, is a clear indication of overestimated VaR. This is consistent with the results shown earlier in Table 15.3 where

Table 15.4. ***Backtesting results: Penalty function values.***

	MSE	MAE	MSU	MAU	MCL
Normal - MLE	0.699	0.726	0.004	0.018	0.035
Normal - ITAU	0.707	0.734	0.003	0.013	0.030
T4 - MLE	0.785	0.774	0.002	0.012	0.031
T4 - ITAU	0.879	0.824	0.001	0.007	0.029
Gumbel - MLE	0.847	0.820	0.074	0.085	0.099
Gumbel - ITAU	1.661	1.170	0	0	0.046
Clayton - MLE	3.779	1.552	3.751	1.481	1.428
Clayton - ITAU	1.957	1.062	1.887	0.916	0.881

Gumbel copula with ITAU fit consistently had less violations than expected. If the sole objective of the economic capital estimation exercise was conservatism, one could simply select the Gumbel copula with ITAU fitting method. Although conservatism is a very important principle to keep in mind for model selection, we do not think that the Gumbel model with ITAU estimation is a viable option. Its statistical information criteria (AIC/BIC) and goodness-of-fit test results indicate a bad fit to the data and backtesting results indicate unnecessary conservatism. Also, one should note that the T4 copulas are also providing conservative estimates judging by their low MSU and MAU penalty values. Considering its statistical performance presented in Table 15.1, the T4 copulas seem to strike a better balance between conservatism and goodness-of-fit to the data.

All of these observations are also confirmed by our most preferred mean check-loss penalty function. The elliptical copulas clearly outperform the asymmetric copulas based on MCL results in Table 15.4. Gumbel with ITAU estimation performs worse than the elliptical copulas. So, based on MCL function, elliptical copulas can even beat the conservatism aspect of Gumbel copula with ITAU estimation. Please remember that MCL function already penalizes underestimation a lot more than overestimation. Among the elliptical copulas, the T4 copulas perform marginally better than the normal copulas when compared across same estimation methodologies. Overall, T4 copula with ITAU estimation provides the best backtesting performance among all eight models.

To visualize this backtesting methodology and our penalty functions better, consider below Figure 15.4, where the X-axis shows the quantile q for which VaR is estimated. The solid line represents the expected violation count given by $(1 - q) \times 60$ and the dotted line represents the actual violation count which is a step function since the actual count is always an integer. The forecast error at each quantile is measured by the distance from the solid line to the dotted line. The MSE (MAE) provides an equally weighted average of squared (absolute) forecast errors. The MSU (MAU) first caps the forecast errors at 0 and then provides an equally weighted average of squared (absolute) forecast errors, i.e., an error is possible only when the solid line is below the dotted line. The MCL penalty function provides a weighted average of these forecast errors. When the solid line is below the dotted line, i.e., the error is negative, the weight is $(1 - q)$ and when the dotted line is below the solid line, i.e., the error is positive, the weight is equal to

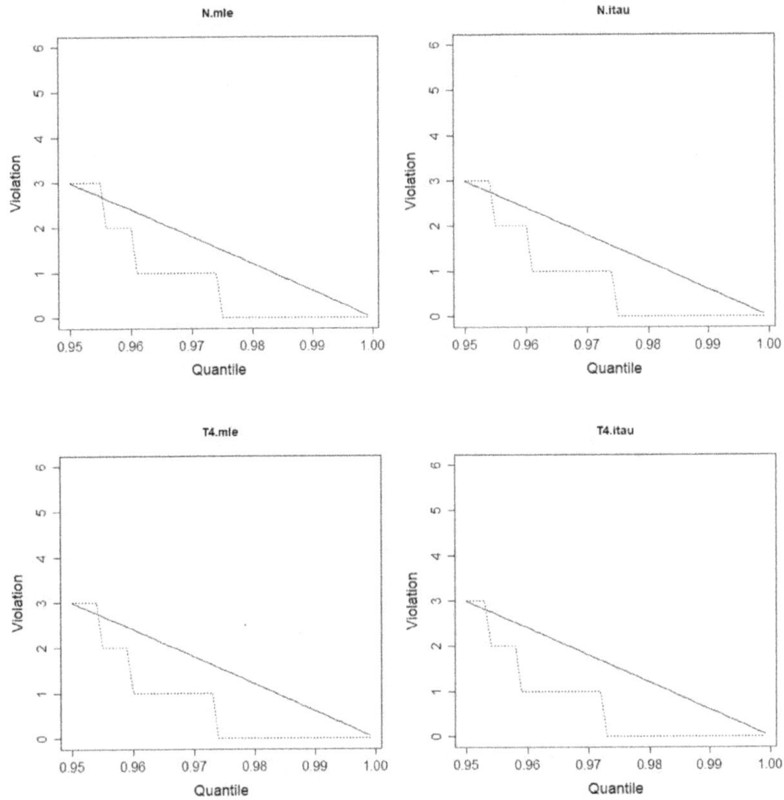

Figure 15.4 Expected violation count is shown with the solid line whereas the realized violation count is shown with the dotted step function. Violation is defined as a quarterly loss greater than the estimated VaR. Expected violation count is a straight line because it is equal to 60*(1–q) where 60 is the number of quarters in our sample and the quantile in X axis of the plots is the quantile for which VaR is estimated. The realized violation count is a step function because realized count can only be an integer.

$(-q)$. With this loss function, nominal values of errors are used, i.e., no absolute value or squaring is used so that a positive penalty value is obtained after multiplying with the weight.

The results on Table 15.4 and the graphs are consistent. The Clayton copula results in significant underestimation of VaR and the Gumbel copula with ITAU estimation leads to significant overestimation at all quantiles. The two normal copulas, the two T4 copulas and the

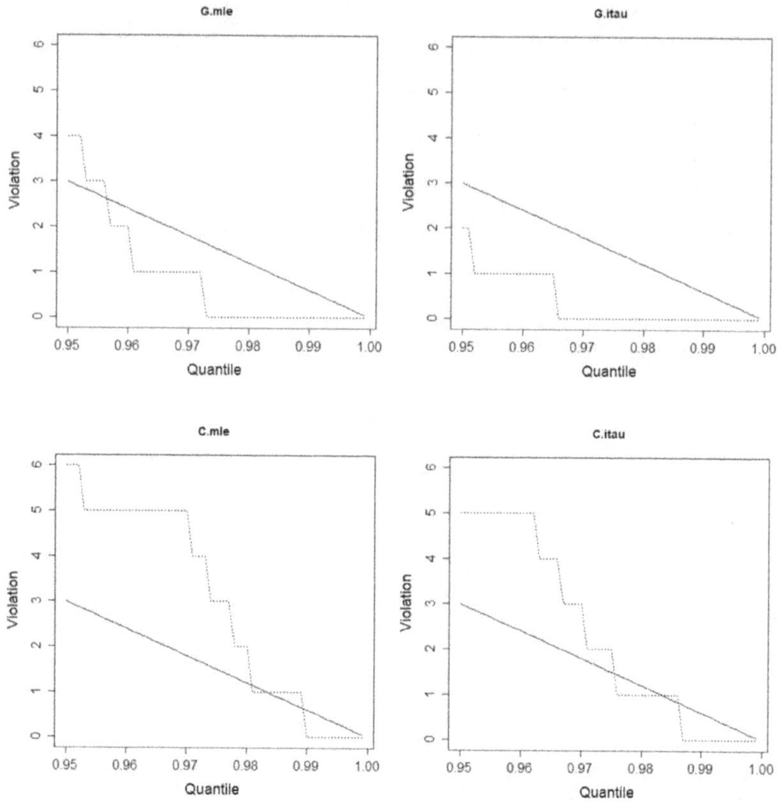

Figure 15.4 (*cont.*)

Gumbel copula with MLE method have reasonable backtesting performance. While Gumbel with MLE has both positive and negative errors, the elliptical copulas are more conservative. Due to the lower sample size posing significant uncertainty, incorporating some conservatism to the selected model is preferable. Therefore, the T4 copulas seem to be a better choice. This choice would also be consistent with the information criteria and the goodness-of-fit results presented in Section 15.3.1.

15.3.3 VaR Stability

Supervisory letter SR 11-7 cites model stability among the criteria used to measure model quality alongside precision, accuracy, power and robustness. It requires the robustness and stability of the model to be checked periodically through sensitivity analysis. Further it states that, "Where appropriate to the particular model, banks should employ sensitivity analysis in model development and validation to check the impact of small changes in inputs and parameter values on model outputs to make sure they fall within an expected range. Unexpectedly large changes in outputs in response to small changes in inputs can indicate an unstable model."

Following this guidance, we check the stability of the VaR estimates over time by analyzing the sensitivity of VaR estimates to the addition of new data. More specifically, we exclude the last eight quarters from our sample. Instead of using all sixty quarters until the end of 2015 Q4, we use the fifty-two quarters until the end of 2013 Q4 to estimate the VaR at several quantiles (0.95, 0.96, 0.97, 0.98, and 0.99). Then, we start adding one quarter of data at a time and re-estimate the VaR. Normalizing the average VaR to $100 as of 2013 Q4 for all models, we generate a time series plot, in Figure 15.5, showing the evolution of average VaR over the time horizon from 2013 Q4 to 2015 Q4.

It is very intuitive that the VaR is reduced for all models as new data points are added to the sample. Adding most recent quarters to the sample reduces the relative weight of the 2008–2009 financial crises in the data. Therefore, the dependence among different risk types gets weaker, which in turn leads to lower VaR estimates. Until 2014 Q2, the reduction is more consistent across all models but in later quarters they diverge from each other in a significant way. The VaR estimates from the normal and the t4 copulas do not decrease as fast as the VaR estimates from the asymmetric copulas. It seems that the elliptical copulas provide better stability. In particular, the T4 copula model with ITAU estimation exhibits strong stability over time.

15.3.4 Stress Testing

As a stress testing exercise, we add a hypothetical stress quarter to our dataset where extremely large losses in all risk types are observed simultaneously. We develop this test directly from the SR 11-7 excerpt stating that, "Banks benefit from conducting model stress testing to check performance over a wide range of inputs and parameter values, including extreme values, to verify that the model is robust." For each of the four risk types we insert a hypothetical quarter of extreme losses defined as

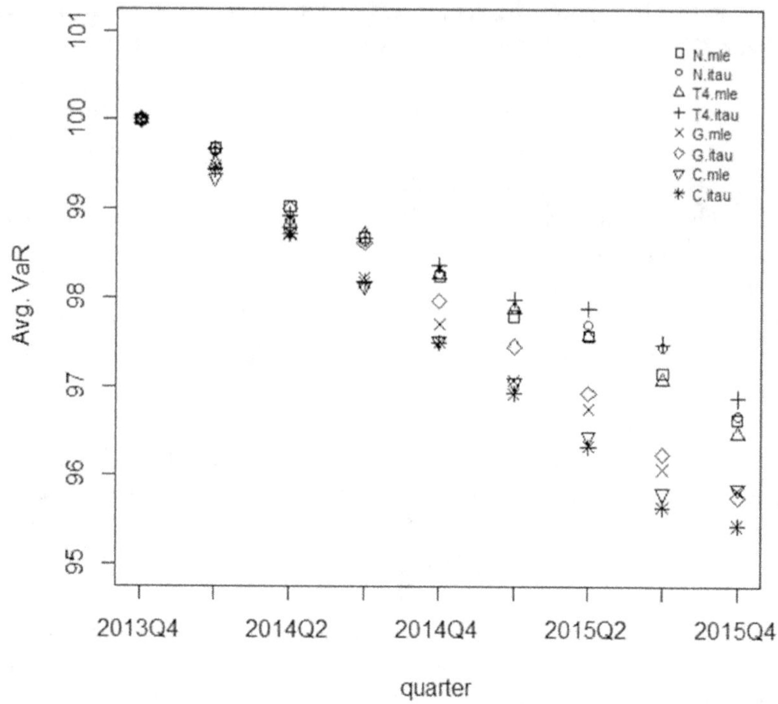

Figure 15.5 The evolution of average VaR for all benchmark copula models from 2013 Q4 to 2015 Q4. All models are renormalized to have VaR = 100 as of 2013 Q2 in order to facilitate the assessment of model stability and robustness.

$$Loss_{hyp,r} = \mu_r + k \times \sigma_r,$$

where μ denotes the average quarterly historical loss, σ denotes the standard deviation of historical quarterly losses, k determines the severity of the hypothetical stress quarter and the subscript r is used to designate the risk types such as market and credit risks. We recalculate the VaR estimates at each quantile (0.95, 0.96, 0.97, 0.98, and 0.99) for eight different values of k (0.5, 1, 1.25, 1.5, 1.75, 2, 2.25, 2.5). Averaging the VaRs across all quantiles and normalizing the unstressed VaR to \$100 for all copula models, we obtain the below plot in Figure 15.6.

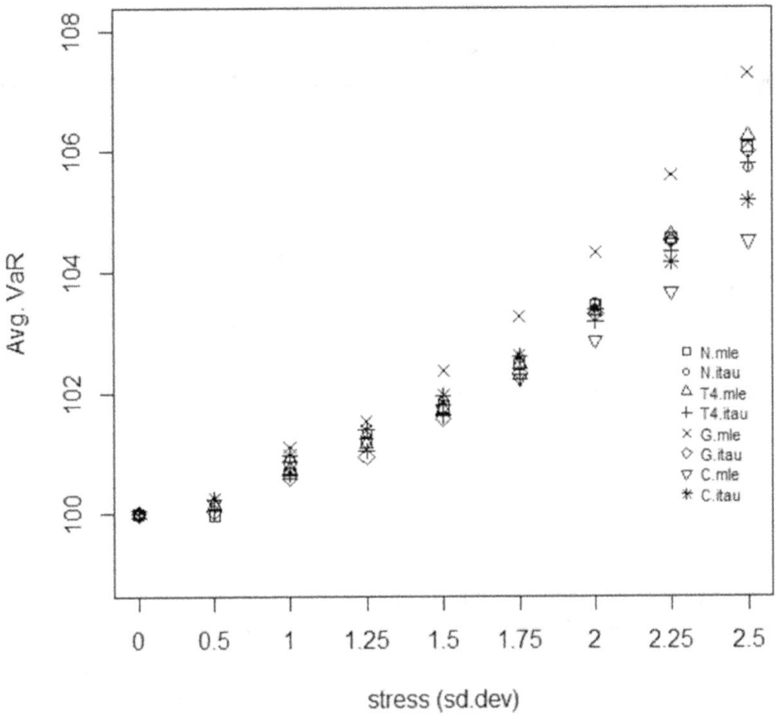

Figure 15.6 The response of average VaR to a hypothetical stress quarter for all benchmark copula models. All models are renormalized to have VaR = 100 when there is no stress in order to facilitate the assessment of stress sensitivity.

It makes intuitive sense that the VaR estimates increase for all models as the severity of the stress, k, increase. Occurrence of extremely large and simultaneous losses in all risk types lead to stronger dependence which is captured by the copula model parameters and increases the VaR estimates.

The Gumbel model with MLE method is the most sensitive to stress, followed by the T4 copula with MLE method and normal copula with MLE method. It should be noted that sensitivity to stress is a desired property. Therefore, there is a trade-off between the objectives of model stability and stress sensitivity. For example, the Gumbel copula didn't perform well in the stability test but it is very responsive to a stress quarter in the stress testing exercise. This result is expected and reflects the trade-off between stability and stress-sensitivity which is a tough problem to deal with for many financial institutions.

15.4 Conclusion

In this chapter, we proposed an empirical statistical framework to test the performance of alternative benchmark models for economic capital estimation following the principles laid out in the SR11-7 supervisory letter for managing model risk. The model selection should be a function of information criteria, goodness-of-fit tests, backtesting performance, model output stability, stress sensitivity criteria and conservatism.

With our hypothetical bank data, the T4 copula both with MLE and ITAU estimation performs well and strikes a good balance among all the different desired properties. For example, the T4 copula with MLE estimation is the top model according to AIC and BIC information criteria, it passes all three analytic goodness-of-fit tests and ranks high based on the probability values. Also, it is the best model according to the graphical goodness-of-fit test, it provides good backtesting performance and incorporates reasonable conservatism. It also ranks third according to both the stability criteria and the stress sensitivity criteria which are conflicting objectives. The T4 copula with ITAU estimation method also seems to be a reasonable model. It is the second-best model based on statistical information criteria, passes all three analytic goodness-of-fit tests with high p-values. It is the second-best model based of graphical goodness-of-fit test. It provides very good backtesting performance ranking top according to mean check-loss penalty function. It is the most stable model in terms of VaR variability over time in response to new data and it has reasonable performance in stress testing.

It is important to understand that we do not make a recommendation to use T4 copula as the dependence model in economic capital calculation. The results we presented in this paper are valid for the data we use in this study. That said, T4 copula should provide a reasonable benchmark for economic capital models to check reasonableness.

Appendix A: Mapping between Y9.C and Bloomberg variables

The first column displays the variable names. The second column provides the variables from Y9-C report and the remaining columns, two through five, provide the variable names from Bloomberg sources. The Bloomberg data was collected with the use of the Bloomberg Market Wizard Excel add-in.

When Y9.C data is not available, we fill it with the Bloomberg1 variable. If that is also not available, we fill it with the Bloomberg2 variable and if that is also not available, we fill it with the Bloomberg3 variable.

Table 15.A1. ***Mapping between Y9.C and Bloomberg variables.***

	Variable Names from Sources			
Variables	Y9-C Report	Bloomberg 1	Bloomberg 2	Bloomberg 3
Total Assets	BHCK2170	FDIC_TOTAL_ASSETS	BS_TOT_ASSET	ARD_TOT_ASSETS
Total Liabilities	BHCK2948	FDIC_TOTAL_LIABILITIES	ARD_TOT_LIABILITIES	BS_TOT_LIAB2
Loans and Leases	BHCK2122	BS_TOT_LOAN	ARD_TOTAL_LOANS	
Trading Assets	BHCK3545	FDIC_TRADING_ACCT_ASSETS	ARD_TRADING_SECURITIES	
Trading Liabilities	BHCK3548	FDIC_TRADING_LIABILITIES	ARD_TRADING_LIABS	
Net Interest Income	BHCK4074	CF_NET_INT_INC	NET_INT_INC	
Interest Income	BHCK4107	FDIC_TOTAL_INT_INC	INTEREST_INCOME	IS_INT_INC
Non-Interest Income	BHCK4079	FDIC_NON_INT_INC	NON_INT_INC	FDIC_TOTAL_INTEREST_EXPENSE
Charge-Offs	BHCK4635	FDIC_GROSS_CHARGEOFFS	ARD_GROSS_CHARGE_OFFS	
Recovieres	BHCK4605	FDIC_RECOVERIES		
Non-Performing Loans	BHCK5525 +BHCK5526	BS_NON_PERFORM_LOANS	FED_NONPERF_LOANS	
Non-Performing Assets	BHCK5525 +BHCK5526 +BHCK2150	BS_NON_PERFORM_ASSET	FED_NONPERF_ASSETS	

Appendix B: Mergers and Acquisition list

Transactions		
Acquirer	Acquiree	Date
Bank of America	Merrill Lynch	2009Q1
Bank of America	Countrywide	2008Q3
Bank of America	MBNA	2006Q1
Bank of America	Fleet Street Boston	2004Q2
Bank of America	BANA	2008Q1
J.P. Morgan Chase	Bear Stearns	2008Q2
J.P. Morgan Chase	Bank One	2004Q3
J.P. Morgan Chase	Washington Mutual	2008Q3
J.P. Morgan Chase	J.P. Morgan Inc.	2000Q4

References

Abdymomunov, A. and Ergen, I. (2017). Tail dependence and systemic risk in operational losses of US Banking Industry. *International Review of Finance*, *17*(2), 177–204.

Alessandri, Piergiorgio and Drehmann, Mathias. (2010). An economic capital model integrating credit and interest rate risk in the banking book. *Journal of Banking and Finance*, *34*, 730–742.

Basel Committee on Banking Supervision. (2009). Range of practices and issues in economic capital frameworks. Bank for International Settlements, Basel, March.

(2010). Developments in modelling risk aggregation. Bank for International Settlements, Basel, October.

(2013). Principles for effective risk data aggregation and risk reporting. Bank for International Settlements, Basel, January.

Breymann, W., Dias, A., Embrechts, P. (2003). Dependence structures for multivariate high-frequency data in finance. *Quantitative Finance*, *3*(1), 1–14.

Dobric, Jadran and Schmid, Friedrich. (2007). A goodness of fit test for copulas based on Rosenblatt's transformation. *Computational Statistics & Data Analysis*, *51*(9), 4633–4642.

Drehmann, Mathias, Sorensen, Steffen and Stringa, Marco. (2010). The integrated impact of credit and interest rate risk on banks: A dynamic framework and stress testing application, *Journal of Banking and Finance*, *34*, 713–729.

Ergen, Ibrahim. (2015). Two-step methods in VaR prediction and the importance of fat tails. *Quantitative Finance*, *15*(6), 1013–1030.

Federal Reserve. (2011). Supervisory guidance on model risk management, *SR Letter* 11–7.

Giacomini, Raffaella and Komunjer, Ivana. (2005). Evaluation and combination of conditional quantile forecasts. *Journal of Business & Economic Statistics*, *23*(4), 416–431.

Genest, Christian, Remillard, Bruno, and Beaudoin, David. (2009). Goodness-of-fit tests for copulas: A review and a power study. *Insurance: Mathematics and Economics*, *44*(2), 199–213.

Genest, Christian and Remillard, Bruno. (2004). Test of independence and randomness based on the empirical copula process. *Test*, *13*(2), 335–369.

Hofert, Marius, Machler, Martin, and McNeil, Alexander J. (2012). Likelihood inference for Archimedean copulas in high dimensions under known margins. *Journal of Multivariate Analysis*, *110*, 133–150.

Hofert, Marius and Machler, Martin. (2013). A Graphical goodness-of-fit test for dependence models in higher dimensions. *Journal of Computational and Graphical Statistics*, *23*(3), 700–716.

Inanoglu, Hulusi and Jacobs, Michael. (2009). Models for risk aggregation and sensitivity analysis: An application to bank economic capital. *Journal of Risk and Financial Management*, *2*(1), 118–189.

Jorion, P. (2006). *Value at Risk: The Benchmark for Managing Financial Risk*, Third Edition, New York, N.Y.: McGraw Hill.

Koenker, Roger, and Bassett, Gilbert. (1978). Regression quantiles. *Econometrica*, *46*(1), 33–50.

Kuester, Keither, Mittnik, Stefan, and Paolella, Mark S. (2006). Value-at-Risk prediction: A comparison of alternative strategies. *Journal of Financial Econometrics*, *4*(Winter), 53–89.

Li, Jianping, Zhu, Xiaoqian, Lee, Cheng-Few, Wu, Dengsheng, Feng, Jichuang, and Shi, Yong. (2015). On the aggregation of credit, market and operational risks. *Review of Quantitative Finance and Accounting*, *44*, 161–189.

Liang, Changzhi, Zhu, Xiaoqian, Li, Yilin, Sun, Xiaolei, Chen, Jianming and Li, Jianping. (2013). Integrating credit and market risk: A factor copula based method. *Procedia Computer Science*, *17*, 657–663.

McNeil, Alexander J., Embrechts, Paul, and Frey, Rudiger. (2005). *Quantitative Risk Management: Concepts, Techniques and Tools*. Princeton: Princeton University Press.

Mester, L.J. (1996). A study of bank efficiency taking into account risk-preferences. *Journal of Banking and Finance*, *20*(6), 1025–1045.

Nelson, Roger B. (2006). *An Introduction to Copulas*. New York: Springer-Verlag.

Rosenberg, J., and Schuermann, T. (2006). A General approach to integrated risk management with skewed, fat-tailed risks. *Journal of Financial Economics*, *79*, 569–614.

Rosenblatt, Murray. (1952). Remarks on a multivariate transformation. *The Annals of Mathematical Statistics*, *23*(3), 470–72.

Sklar, Abe. (1959). Fonctions de répartition à n dimensions et leurs marges. *Publications de l'Institut de Statistique de l'Université de Paris*, *8*, 229–231.

Trivedi, Pravin K. and Zimmer, David M. (2007). Copula modeling: An introduction for practitioners. *Foundations and Trends in Econometrics*, *1*(1), 1–111.

Yi, Shanli , Li, Jianping, Zhu, Xiaoqian and Feng, Jichuang. (2012). Mutual information based copulas to aggregate banking risks. *Proceedings of the Fifth International Conference on Business Intelligence and Financial Engineering.*

16 *Model Validation of Interest Rate Risk (Banking Book) Models*

ASHISH DEV

16.1 Introduction

Banking book interest rate risk is the risk of interest rate movements in a balance sheet (of a financial institution) consisting of assets and liabilities which are not marked to market (i.e., accrual accounting is applied to those assets and liabilities). It is a common practice amongst financial institutions to manage the balance sheet interest rate risk at the top of the house. This process is known as asset–liability management (ALM) or balance sheet management (BSM).

Every asset and every liability has principal cash flows and interest cash flows till its maturity (a bullet instrument is a special case where there are no intermediate interest cash flows). A bond has no principal cash flow till maturity and has interest cash flows every six months. An instalment loan has both principal and interest cash flows every month. A non-maturity deposit does not have a contractual maturity – behavioral assumptions have to be made about the amortization of the non-maturity deposit.

At the heart of ALM is the modeling of principal and interest cash flows – positive cash flows for assets and negative cash flows for liabilities. The unit of time commonly used is a month. In any large financial institution, there are a very large number of loans and deposits (as well as other financial instruments). For ALM purposes, each transaction is not modeled individually; instead they are bucketed by bands of weighted average coupon and weighted average *remaining* maturity.

ALM is sometimes referred to as IRRBB (interest rate risk in the banking book). IRRBB is the risk of losses resulting from movements in interest rates and their impact on future cash-flows.

In this chapter we will use a broader definition of IRRBB. IRRBB includes Funds Transfer Pricing (FTP) as well as ALM. FTP is a charge (for assets) or a credit (for liabilities) that is charged (credited) by the corporate treasury to the business unit in order to isolate the business unit from market interest rate fluctuations for the life of the asset (liability).

16.2 Earnings at Risk

One of the most common measures of risk for ALM purposes is Earnings at Risk. Each bank specifies movement (up or down) of interest rates as a parallel movement of all points of the yield curve. For example, they could be instantaneous shocks of +/− 25bps, +/− 100bps and +/− 200bps. Earnings are calculated as the interest cash flows, over the next twelve months, of all assets and all liabilities for the base case scenario and then for each of the shocked scenarios. The difference between the earnings in the shocked case scenario and the base case scenario is the Earnings at Risk (EaR). For example,

$$\text{EaR (100bps)} = \text{Earnings (+100bps)} - \text{Earnings (base case)}.$$

$$\begin{aligned}\text{Earnings} = {} & \text{interest cash flow, over next 12 months, summed over all assets} \\ & - \text{interest cash flow, over next 12 months, summed over all liabilities}\end{aligned}$$

Most banks use a stair-step movement of the yield curve instead of instantaneous shocks.

Earnings (and Earnings at Risk) includes new production over the next 12 months. Generally, the new production comes out of the business unit plans. Mostly the plan is assumed to be the same in the base case and in the shocked case. But in some banks, the business units are asked to provide a separate plan for the shocked cases.

Validation of Earnings requires generating the interest cash flows of all assets and liabilities in the shape of a separate code. Generally, the interest cash flows of individual products are generated (and will be discussed in the following sections pertaining to each individual product).

A fixed rate asset (or liability) has the same interest (coupon) cash flows for the base case as for the case of shocked interest rate. Therefore, its EaR is zero.

A floating rate asset (or liability) typically has its coupon as a function of 3 mo. Libor (Libor + xxx bps). In the case of a positive shock, the coupon is higher than the coupon in the base case. Thus the EaR is positive (negative in case of liabilities) for a positive shock.

EaR is also defined for larger shocks like 200 bps or 300 bps.

16.3 Economic Value of Equity

Accounting Equity is the difference between book assets and book liabilities. Economic Value of Equity (EVE) is the difference between the discounted present value of asset cash flows and the discounted present value of liabilities cash flows. In this case, the relevant cash flows are both interest and principal cash flows. Instantaneous shocks (+/− 25bps, +/− 100bps, +/− 200bps) are applied to the interest rates and valuation of assets and liabilities are done. The difference between the EVE in the shocked case scenario and the base case scenario is the EVE at Risk.

$$\text{EVE–at–Risk (100bps)} = \text{EVE (+100bps)} - \text{EVE (base case)}$$

EVE = Present Value of principal and interest cash flows over the life of the asset or liability.

EVE (and EVE-at-Risk) comprises cash flows of the existing book and ignores any new production.

16.4 Duration of Equity

Analogous to duration of a bond,[1] duration of equity (DoE) is defined as:

$$\text{Duration of Equity} = [\text{EVE}(-\gamma) - \text{EVE}(+\gamma)]/[2\gamma * \text{EVE (base case)}],$$

where γ is a small change in interest rate.

Duration of equity can be positive or negative.

Since the yield curve is upward sloping most of the time, the duration of equity is often targeted to a positive number (e.g. 2.5 years).

Analogous to convexity of bonds, a convexity of equity can also be defined. But we will not go into that in this chapter.

Both EaR and EVE-at-Risk should be measured as they are complimentary measures (EaR is short-term and EVE-at-Risk is long-term; EaR involves only interest cash flows while EVE-at-Risk involves both interest and principal cash flows). Typically risk appetite is defined as limits on both EaR and EVE-at-Risk. Essentially what ALM is doing is to set a limit on EaR (e.g. 1.5% for a 200 bps shock) subject to a

[1] The properties of duration of equity are not the same as those of duration of a bond.

constraint on EVE-at-Risk (e.g. 20% for a 200 bps instantaneous shock).[2] Secondly, EVE-at-Risk and DOE are different ways of presenting the same risk. EVE-at-Risk has both duration and convexity built into it.

Basel Committee (BCBS, 2016) has articulated this in Principle 3 and Principle 4:

Principle 3: *The banks' risk appetite for IRRBB should be articulated in terms of the risk to both economic value and earnings. Banks must implement policy limits that target maintaining IRRBB exposures consistent with their risk appetite.*

Principle 4: *Measurement of IRRBB should be based on outcomes of both economic value and earnings-based measures, arising from a wide and appropriate range of interest rate shock and stress scenarios.*

16.5 Governance of ALM

The IRR position is presented and discussed at a high-level committee called asset–liability committee (ALCO). ALCO is presided over by the CEO or the President of the bank. ALCO sets limits for EAR, EVE-at-Risk and DOE. There are some underlying constraints in defining these limits.

In some financial institutions, the Board of Directors sets IRR limits and ALCO operates with limits within the Board limits. The Basel Committee (BCBS, 2016) introduces Principle 2 which states:

Principle 2: *The governing body of each bank is responsible for oversight of the IRRBB management framework, and the bank's risk appetite for IRRBB. Monitoring and management of IRRBB may be delegated by the governing body to senior management, expert individuals or an asset and liability management committee (ALCO). Banks must have an adequate IRRBB management framework, involving regular independent reviews and evaluations of the effectiveness of the system.*

[2] Or the other way around, i.e., minimizing EVE-at-risk subject to a maximum EaR.

Thus, model validation should look at the articulation of risk appetite for IRRBB by the Board and check whether ALCO and the Treasury is acting within those limits.

On the directives of ALCO, the asset–liability manager or the Treasurer takes hedging positions in the book. Typically, IRR hedging is done by taking long positions in treasuries, residential mortgage-backed securities (RMBS) or collateralized mortgage obligations (CMO) tranches as well as positions in generic swaps, swaptions and IRR Caps and Floors. Hedging is for the purposes of reducing interest rate risk in the balance sheet. But sometimes, ALCO might take a speculative position[3] based on the members' consensus view on interest rate forecasts, especially Fed Funds movements. In theory ALCO could send directives to the business units to administer a product in particular ways (e.g. setting product rates on non-maturity deposits or change the mix of floating versus fixed rate loans) to minimize IRR.[4]

Governance over the ALM process thus involves whether the ALCO directives are faithfully recorded and acted upon (usually within a week or so) after an ALCO meeting. The asset–liability position is reported as a footnote in the Quarterly Reports (10Q and 10K) for public dissemination. Since a typically twenty-page ALCO report is synthesized into a half-page footnote, it is important what is actually included in the footnote as to be most transparent (at least to the security analysts) depiction of the IRR of the bank's balance sheet.

Considering the broader definition of IRRBB taken in this chapter, there is need to ensure that the FTP calculations are consistent with the ALM calculations including the assumptions in either case. Many an ALCO meeting goes by with no discussion of FTP. From a governance angle, this leaves a gaping hole, which is somehow rectified during business unit performance meetings.

Thus, part of the model validation of ALM consists of:

- Determine whether all significant functions of the bank are represented on the ALCO committee.

[3] This might be violating the recent Volker Rule under Dodd–Frank (2010), although it is not very clear yet whether it does or not.

[4] But in practice this is rarely done. It involves a lot of business managers to do something which is more difficult than taking positions, e.g., in Swaps and then unwind later if necessary.

- Review the reports and other information provided to the ALCO committee to determine whether it has the information necessary to properly manage its interest rate risk.
- Establish whether the ALCO committee meets on a regular basis and reviews the structure of the bank's balance sheet, profitability, interest rate risk and addresses other issues within its policies and procedures.
- Assess whether the board of directors is adequately involved in the ALCO function.

This governance part of model validation is quite a bit more than governance part of model validation of a single stand-alone large and complex model in the bank. In some banks this governance-related check is performed by internal audit but in others model validation performs this role.

A system like QRM provides the user many choices of models or setups and special care has to be taken during model validation to see that such choices have been exercised judiciously. Each bank is actually a different implementation of QRM. An exercise of *effective challenge* by the validator must take this into account.

16.6 Residential Mortgages

Residential mortgages are an important part of a bank's assets. Cash flow in mortgages follow an amortization – instalment loan amortization (as captured by the PMT function in Excel). The maturity is typically very long with original maturity of fifteen or thirty years. Residential mortgages have the embedded option of being prepaid at any time without any penalty. This option lies with the customer. The propensity to prepay is dependent on the current interest rate. The most important driver of prepayment is refinance incentive measured by the proportional difference between the contractual coupon and the current interest rate. The lower the current interest rate is the more likely the mortgage is refinanced and exits the books of the bank. Prepayment speed also depends on other factors like burnout.

Mortgage cash flows are not modeled as individual loan cash flows. Instead, mortgages are bucketed into weighted average coupon (WAC) and weighted average *remaining* maturity (WAM). For example, the cell defined by WAC of 6–6.5% and WAM of sixty to seventy-two months has the sum of outstanding balance of all mortgages that fall into that two-dimensional bucket.

Since the prepayment is rate dependent, and interest rates are stochastic, there is need to develop a term structure model (see the Section 16.14 on **Term Structure Modeling**) while modeling mortgages. Given the term structure model, there is the need of a prepayment model that generates prepayment along a rate path.

The prepayment model is often a third party developed model which seamlessly connects with the ALM system. One of these is Andrew Davidson (ADCO[5]) prepayment model. Some financial institutions have in-house prepayment models. Along each rate path (generated by the term structure model), the pool level prepayment is computed for each bucket defined by WAC and WAM ranges.

There are several stages of model validation for models used for mortgages. First is whether the stratification by WAC and WAM has been correctly done. This involves verification of data from the application system or the data warehouse as the case may be. It is part of process verification by checking random feeds from the application system and the veracity of the stratification (bucketing).

Second is the conceptual soundness of the mortgage cash flow generation. The cash flow formulae are well established (see Fabbozi, 2000) and can be verified by building a cash flow engine as a benchmark.

Third is the conceptual soundness of the prepayment model. The prepayment model is a "fourth" party model and a validator does not have access to all documentation. The factors can be verified for conceptual soundness from basic theory. But the coefficients on those factors are proprietary and cannot be verified easily. A service provider like Andrew Davidson & Co. uses a lot more data than a bank's own book of mortgage business. Building a bank's own prepayment model in order to validate ADCO is, therefore, sub-optimal. Another alternative is to subscribe to an alternative service provider (e.g. Polypath) and benchmark the results of the two mortgage prepayment models.

Lastly, the validation of the term structure modeling. This has been relegated in this chapter to Section 16.14 on **Term Structure Modeling.**

Home Equity Line of Credit (HEL) is another mortgage related product that most banks have. This is an off-balance sheet item and can be ignored for ALM purposes.

[5] ADCO is also the model underlying Bloomberg's mortgage prepayment.

16.7 Commercial Loans

Commercial or wholesale loans are an important asset class for all banks. Typically, the cash flows of commercial loans follow a twenty year maturity of the amortization with a bullet payment at the contractual maturity (which is typically much less than twenty years). Cash flow pattern of commercial loans is, thus, relatively easy to model. Since commercial loans have contractual prepayment penalty, prepayment is often assumed away. Alternatively, a non-rate dependent prepayment is assumed from historical behavior of commercial loans alongside prepayment penalty cash flows. Based on historical default behavior, a cumulative default rate (CDR) is introduced.

Commercial loans are also bucketed by WAC and WAM. A single monthly mortality (SMM) for prepayment and for default are computed for each pool, consisting of the bucket defined by WAC and WAM ranges. Commercial loan can be either a fixed rate or a floating rate instrument.

A fixed rate loan has the same interest (coupon) cash flows for the base case as for the case of shocked interest rate. Therefore, its EAR is zero.

A floating rate loan typically has its coupon as a function of 3 mo. Libor (Libor + xxx bps). In the case of a positive shock, the coupon is higher than the coupon in the base case. Thus, the EAR is positive for a positive shock.

From the perspective of model validation, conceptual soundness is simply to ensure that the cash flows are formulated according to what has been described above. These are simple formulae that can be worked out in excel to benchmark the cash flows.

Model validation extends to the derivation of SMM for prepayment and default rates. Prepayment is non-rate sensitive. Both prepayment and default rates are derived from historical behavior of the pool of commercial loans. These can be tested by a stand-alone code in excel.

16.8 Credit Cards

Credit cards are unsecured loans to individuals, which are administered assets. There are no contractual amortization and contractual maturity of credit card pools. However, internal data on credit cards enable a bank to come up with assumptions of amortization and maturity. Credit card customers are categorized as revolvers, transactors and balance parkers. A revolver is a credit card issuer term for customers who carry balances, paying off those balances over time, thus "revolving" them. The opposite of the revolver is the "transactor" – people who pay their credit card balances each month, avoiding interest charges. Balance parkers are those customers who transfer balances in one or more credit cards to a new credit card which is offering a teaser rate for some period of time. For each category of credit cards, separate assumption of maturity and coupon are made. Outside the teaser period the credit card issuer can change the interest charged at any time after notifying the customer.

Credit cards have a maximum line of credit and the difference between the maximum and the balance outstanding is the undrawn line. This is an off-balance sheet item and can be ignored for ALM purposes.

16.9 Other Retail Loans

These are automobile loans, automobile leases and student loans predominantly. These loans are first bucketed by WAC and WAM and then cash flows of each of these buckets generated. The coupons for these loans are fixed. The principal amortization follows the instalment loan amortization (as captured by the PMT function in Excel) schedule. A non-rate dependent prepayment is assumed based on past history of the portfolio.

The model validation consists of data verification about the two-dimensional stratification, cash flow generation which can be replicated in excel and then also a validation of the prepayment rate again using excel.

16.10 Wholesale Liabilities

Banks issue senior or subordinate bonds in the capital markets to fund their activities. These issues are sufficiently large on their own – so no bucketing is done. Bond interest cash flows are generally once in six months and the principal payments are at the maturity of the bond. Some of the bonds are callable. The call feature requires additional modeling as to whether it pays to exercise the call.

Prices of corporate bonds can be observed. But most of bank-issued corporate bonds do not trade in a very liquid market. Therefore, it is necessary to model the cash flows internally. From a model validation perspective, the market-observed bond prices can be used as benchmarks for the wholesale liability modeling in the ALM process.

The conceptual soundness of the wholesale liability modeling can be tested by replicating the cash flows in excel. Cash flows of callable bonds require use of if-then statements or a computer code.

16.11 Certificates of Deposit

Certificates of deposit (CDs) are customer deposits with a contractual maturity. Some CDs pay a lump-sum at maturity, some pay interest semi-annually and others pay interest monthly. CDs typically pay a fixed rate of interest (product rate).

The cash flows of CDs are relatively simple to replicate for validation purposes. CDs permit the holder to "break" the CD and take early payment. There is a break-funding charge to the customer. It is customary to assume no prepayment on CDs and if a CD is broken before its scheduled maturity, a break funding charge is imposed by the Treasury to the business unit in the FTP system, which is in theory collectible from the customer.

Traditionally CDs are classified as > $100,000 and < = $100,000. Within each of these two categories, the CD portfolio is stratified by WAC and WAM. Part of model validation for CD modeling consists of data analysis to see if the stratification is done correctly.

16.12 Non-maturity Deposits

Retail and wholesale deposits (other than certificate of deposits, CDs) are bank deposits which the customer can withdraw any time. Therefore, there is no pre-determined maturity of these deposits. Further, the product rates paid on these deposits are administered by the bank. That is not to say that the product rates are arbitrarily set. Most non-maturity deposits have their product rate as a function of the Fed Funds rate while the money market non-maturity deposits follow the Donahue index. But there is an asymmetry between the up movement and the down movement. For example, when the Fed Funds rate goes down, the product rate instantaneously goes down while when the Fed Funds rate goes up, the product rate follows with a significant lag.

For ALM purposes, non-maturity deposits are not modeled as individual transactions. They can be categorized typically into: interest checking, regular savings, demand deposit (personal), demand deposit (public), demand deposit (corporate) and money market. Non-maturity deposits are modeled at these category levels.

Within each category, the deposits are divided into core and non-core components. for most banks this division is ad hoc. the non-core amortizes within one month. the core amortizes over an assumed longer period of five to ten years. the product rate (same as coupon) is a function of fed funds rate or one-year libor for money market deposits. typically, the product rate is a linear function of the projected fed funds (o/n) rate with different slopes for rising versus falling rates.

Non-maturity (also called indeterminate maturity) deposits constitute about an $11 trillion of banks' liabilities in the usa. yet the assumptions made in most banks in the modeling of non-maturity deposits are such that one can drive a truck through it. There is enough micro-level data available with the large banks to model them more rigorously.[6] Model validation can raise the expectations in this regard and guide and encourage the ALM function to devote more effort in modeling non-maturity deposits.

16.13 Investment Portfolio

banks invest part of their assets in the capital markets. the investment portfolio typically consists of treasuries, residential mortgage-backed securities (rmbs) and collateralized mortgage obligations (cmo). treasuries are easy to model. securitized products like rmbs and cmo require creation of cash flow waterfalls. For almost all banks, the waterfall comes from a third-party provider called Intex. Intex generates the cash flow waterfall in accordance with the details in the prospectus of each deal. For ALM, the investment portfolio is modeled by each stand-alone instrument.

For RMBS and CMO, apart from Intex, a prepayment model and a term structure model are required. The seamless integration of QRM and Intex has the disadvantage that the cash flows from the underlying collateral and the cash flows in the waterfall cannot be directly

[6] Granted that banks administer their non-maturity deposits in patterns that change all the time.

validated. The best that can be done is to code, in a different system, cash flows from the underlying mortgages and the cash flow waterfall (by meticulously going through the several hundred pages of the prospectus and replicating them in the cash flow code). Then compare the valuation of the RMBS or CMO tranche with the valuation of QRM. The comparison can be done for a sample of the investment portfolio. The prepayment model and the term structure model are kept constant by invoking the "Single instrument module" in QRM which runs the same term structure model as well as the same prepayment model as the main QRM engine.

Investments should also be looked upon as instruments of hedging IRR. Other instruments of hedging IRR are derivatives like generic swaps, swaptions, caps and floors. These derivatives are accounted for as "accrual" and their cash flows need to be accounted for in the ALM calculations. Typically, a proposal of these hedging instruments that brings the EaR to within the limits is put up before ALCO which discusses and approves them. Treasury acts upon the approved proposal by taking (or unwinding) positions in interest rate derivatives.

16.14 Term Structure Modeling

The interest rate term structure model is the generation of random paths of the short rate into the future, given the yield curve and the interest rate volatility. From the yield curve, the zero curve is constructed using interpolation, from which the forward curve is derived. there are various methods of interpolation of which the cubic spline method is the most common.

QRM has three options for interpolation: linear interpolation, cubic spline and maximum smoothness. They are all conceptually sound. however, it is rather difficult to validate the last one. Linear interpolation and cubic spline can be validated by writing a separate code and run both QRM and the code for the same yield curve. Alternatively, one can subscribe to a common and relatively inexpensive system like FINCAD and benchmark the results of QRM with the results of FINCAD. The Curve Generation process leads to a Zero curve interpolated at all monthly term points, such as shown below in Figure 16.1

From the zero (also known as par) curve, a forward curve is first derived through no arbitrage formulae. These formulae can be easily validated by calculating them in excel.

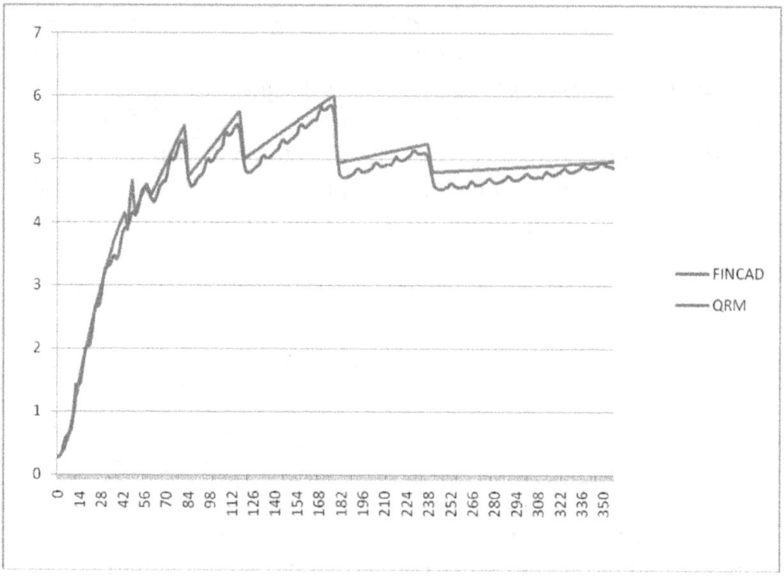

Figure 16.1 Comparison of curves generated from FINCAD vs QRM.

Given the Forward curve (or equivalently the discounts), and the term structure of volatility, the future short rate term structure can be derived through Monte Carlo simulation using one of several short rate propagations. QRM offers the choice of Black–Derman-Toy, Black–Karazinski, Hull & White and Heath–Jarrow-Morton models. These are all published academic models and, from a validation perspective, they are all conceptually sound. Although QRM provides short documents on each of those models, they are not sufficient. In this chapter we will not go into the description of each of these four term structure models (see Fabozzi, 2002). Instead, we focus on the model validation of the term structure model chosen.

The prices of Interest rate Caps and Floors are observable. Caps can be decomposed into Caplets. From the derived prices of the Caplets, using the closed-form Black–Scholes model, a term structure of implied volatilities can be obtained. As this is a closed form computation, it can be easily benchmarked and hence is easy to validate.

The model developers need to justify why they have chosen the particular term structure model (out of Black–Derman-Toy, Black–Karazinski, Hull & White, Heath–Jarrow–Morton). Banks do not do a good job of this. Often the model is chosen based on a discussion with QRM. QRM has recently introduced a regime-switching term structure model, which uses one model when the interest rates are close to zero (e.g., Black–Karasinsky) while using a different model when the interest rates are sufficiently above zero (e.g., Hull & White).

Model validation generally does not replicate and compare the rate paths directly. It is impossible to replicate the random number generator or the antithetic method adopted as a variance reduction technique. Instead, selected interest rate options (swaptions) of various maturities are valued in an outside term structure model as well as in QRM terms structure model and the valuations compared. If the valuations are close, the QRM term structure model passes muster. If the valuations are not close then further investigation is required.

16.15 Summary of Model Validation for ALM

From the perspective of model validation, ALM model validation poses a conundrum, as almost all large banks use a complicated system called Quantitative Risk Management (QRM) provided by a third party. Smaller (community) banks and credit unions also use third-party vendor-developed systems like Sendero, BancPath or ZMdesk. As vendor developed platforms go, QRM is more transparent than most. But it is still a vendor developed system and there are proprietary models within it that are not transparent.

According to SR 11-7 (of the FRB; same as OCC 2011-12), "*Vendor products should … be incorporated into a bank's broader model risk management framework following the same principles as applied to in-house models, although the process may be somewhat modified*"…. "*Vendor models are often designed to provide a range of capabilities and so may need to be customized by a bank for its particular circumstances. A bank's customization choices should be documented and justified as part of validation*". This is particularly true of QRM. There are many possible choices at various levels within QRM. The group running QRM needs to be knowledgeable about each of those choices so as to document and justify the particular setting. The model validator also needs to get into the reeds of QRM to see how and when those choices are made and whether the cash flows generated by QRM are consistent with the choices. This is time-consuming but not an impossible task. Another aspect of model validation is to check whether the ALM personnel in the bank have asked QRM for developmental evidence, appropriate testing results that show their product works as expected, ongoing performance monitoring and outcomes analysis and what they have received from QRM.

According to FDIC Supervisory Insights (FDIC, 2013) "*when assessing their IRR frameworks, banks should keep in mind that effective IRR management need not be overly complex, nor should it rely exclusively on third parties.*" The reality on the ground is that almost every bank is using a third-party vendor model for purposes of ALM. This increases the burden of backtesting and benchmarking in the validation process, since the vendor may be unwilling to provide background and detailed documentation about some of their proprietary analysis.

In an Interagency Advisory on Interest Rate Risk Management: Frequently Asked Questions (OCC, Jan 2012), the following question and answer are noted:

Question: "*Most institutions use third-party tools to measure IRR. Can independent Certifications/ validations commissioned by model vendors satisfy supervisory expectations for model validations?*"
Answer: "*No. Financial regulators expect each financial institution to ensure that the selected model is appropriate for its IRR profile by conducting an independent review and validation and performing ongoing monitoring and backtesting to confirm model appropriateness. Although a useful tool, model certifications/ validations commissioned by vendors would likely not completely satisfy supervisory expectations regarding validation of the use of vendor products. As part of the validation process, institutions need to ensure that the mechanics and mathematics of the IRR model are functioning as intended. The advisory recognizes that most community institutions use largely standardized vendor-provided models, and in such cases validations provided by vendors can be used to support the model mechanics and mathematic calculations. For models that are customized to an individual institution or in situations where the vendors are unable or unwilling to provide appropriate certifications or validations, management would be responsible for validating the mechanics and mathematics of the model work as expected.*"

Thus, each bank is expected to perform its own validation of the vendor-developed system in use for ALM purposes. In case of small (community) institutions, for validation of the model mechanics and mathematical/statistical calculations, validations provided by vendor can be used. Presumably this is not acceptable in case of large banks. Large banks are expected to build benchmark models and test the cash flow and valuation models (including prepayment) within the ALM platform.

Ongoing Monitoring consists of confirming that the model adequately captures and measures the specific risks to which the bank is exposed. This would entail a review of the types of assets and liabilities the bank holds on its balance sheet with verification that the model is both capable of handling all instruments and is currently configured to handle them properly. The requirement can be met by following these steps:

- On an annual basis, the ALCO needs to formally compare the model's "intended use" and modeling capabilities to the bank's balance sheet. Does the model capture the risk that the bank is taking? Are all of the holdings on the bank's balance sheet (including new account types) handled properly by the model? The discussion should be documented in meeting minutes.
- On an annual basis, the ALCO should verify that any applicable new regulations have been accounted for in the modeling and reporting process.
- The bank should require the model developer to provide a change log for any significant changes to model assumptions as well as a list of all manual overrides. Any unusual or recurring overrides could be a sign of model weakness.

The Basel Committee (BCBS, 2016) has enunciated the following two principles relating to model validation in the IRRBB space:

Principle 6: "*Measurement systems and models used for IRRBB should be based on accurate data, and subject to appropriate documentation, testing and controls to give assurance on the accuracy of calculations. Models used to measure IRRBB should be comprehensive and covered by governance processes for model risk management, including a validation function that is independent of the development process.*"

The model validator needs to assess the accuracy of data from the application system or data warehouse. The accuracy of output of the stratification routine also needs to be validated. Starting with the technical documentation provided by the vendor, the modeler is expected to write extensive documentation on the model methodology and mathematical calculations of the ALM system. However, being a vendor-developed system, some elements may be proprietary with very little documentation available. In this case, more than usual emphasis has to be placed on benchmarking and backtesting of the models in the system.

Principle 5: "*In measuring IRRBB, key behavioral and modelling assumptions should be fully understood, conceptually sound and documented. Such assumptions should be rigorously tested and aligned with the bank's business strategies.*"

In QRM each account has to be set up by spelling out how the coupon rate behaves as a function of a market-observed rate (like Fed Funds, Libor, etc.) and how the principal amortizes, whether as a function of rates or not. The two most important behavioral assumptions (embedded options) are rate-dependent prepayment in mortgage-related products and the maturity and amortization of non-maturity deposits.

FRB SR 11-7 states that:

"*Banks should consider risk from individual models and in the aggregate. Aggregate model risk is affected by interaction and dependencies among models; reliance on common assumptions, data, or methodologies; and any other factors that could adversely affect several models and their outputs at the same time.*"

The ALM platform (vendor developed) comprises several models. QRM, for example, has a plethora of models within its platform as well as models or systems to which it seamlessly connects (e.g. Intex and ADCO). In most banks, QRM is the largest platform of models by far. Therefore, the model validators have to pay special attention to how interaction and dependencies among individual models play out in the version of QRM which is run in the bank. Validation of models individually is not enough. For example, the prepayment model interacts with the rate paths generated by the term structure model and generate stochastic cash flows.

17 Validation of Risk Management Models in Investment Management

AKHTAR SIDDIQUE*

17.1 Introduction

For regulated financial institutions in the USA, the Supervisory Guidance on Model Risk Management – Supervisory Release 11-7 (SR 11-7) for the Federal Reserve and Bulletin 11–12 for the OCC) and Europe – the EBA issued GL/2014/13 on Supervisory Review and Evaluation Process (SREP) that included expectations for validation of models used for investment management. For example, SR 11-7 refers to "models for . . . managing and safeguarding client assets" as within the scope of models that need to be looked at within model risk management.

However, validation of investment management models has not historically gotten as much attention as models used in other lines of business. In part that was because model risk management has been stronger within institutions regulated by banking regulators and a very large proportion of the investment management business lies outside those parameters. Because of changes in the regulatory landscape, with not only banks and bank holding companies but asset management businesses as well coming under greater regulation, validation of investment management models is likely to gain greater prominence in the future. For example, regulated financial institutions face enhanced expectations to ensure that models that are used to manage their client assets, even in third party contexts, are validated. Beyond the expectations of regulated institutions, validation of models is useful to ensure that risk management is carried out appropriately.

The obscurity of model validation for investment management models persisted in spite of the role that certain investment management activities played in the Financial Crisis. Most prominently,

* The views expressed in this chapter are those of the author's alone and do not represent those of the Comptroller of the Currency or other US regulators. They do not establish supervisory policies, requirements or expectations.

money market funds breaking the buck and their sponsors having to step in was identified by the Financial Crisis Inquiry Commission as one of the major milestones of the Crisis.[1]

More recently, in 2018, the Securities and Exchange Commission focused on portfolio allocation models used by AEGON USA Investment Management, an asset manager with $106 billion in assets under management. The SEC issued a cease and desist order and imposed nearly $100 million in penalties against AEGON USA Investment Management, Transamerica Asset Management, Transamerica Capital, and Transamerica Financial Advisors. SEC complained that the representations regarding the models were misleading because the advisers and broker-dealers "launched the products and strategies without first confirming that the models worked as intended and/or without disclosing any recognized risks associated with using the models."

At the outset, it is important to note the role of the risk budgeting process in investment management models and its interaction with the validation of the risk models. Typically, the risk of the portfolio is distributed among various asset classes with the objective of maximizing total portfolio returns while keeping the total portfolio risk at a given target. Thus, how risk across various asset classes aggregate is an important consideration.

In this chapter, we begin with a discussion of the issues that are encountered in the validation of risk management models for investment management. We also contrast these models with models used in other lines of business such as sales and trading. We then discuss a stylized example of how validation of models may be used in the investment management context.

17.2 What Makes Validation of Investment Management Models Different?

Validation of models typically follow one of several well-known paths that have become de rigueur across different risk stripes. Industry practices have converged on these paths. The paths depend on the objective of validation, i.e., where errors in the model arise and how that error is minimized. Validation of risk in investment management models do not seem to have reached the same level of convergence.

[1] Report of the Financial Crisis Inquiry Commission, pages 253–255.

Diversity in validation approaches is observed. This diversity arises from diversity in investment management approaches as well as the large number of models used within the investment management businesses. Some of the models in the asset management industry which may be validated more easily include models that are similar to the models used in the trading businesses.

For valuation models, used most heavily on trading desks, where there are observed market prices, validation typically analyzes how the modeled values differ from the market prices. For risk models on the trading desk, such as for the greeks (delta, gamma, vega) for derivatives, the validation traditionally assesses how closely using the modeled greeks in a valuation model matches the observed market prices. As an example, in attribution analysis, validation typically examines whether the changes in greeks would have explained the change in the market prices. Frequently, the highest risk in such applications is the use of greeks from a liquid market in pricing less liquid financial instruments. In contrast, risk in investment portfolios is typically measured as volatility, an unobservable time-varying variable, and consequently difficulties arise.

For forecasting models as varied as credit scoring models, Value-at-Risk models, mortgage prepayment models, validation relies extensively on backtesting. In these contexts, the forecast error is the object of analysis. The forecast errors could be for either the actual portfolios or hypothetical portfolios. Mincer and Zarnowitz (1969) provide a framework for such forecasts.[2]

As observed above, models in investment management seemed to have remained quite heterogeneous. It may also be useful to differentiate between models that can be validated conventionally versus those that are not amenable to conventional validation. Another important criterion is that for investment management models, expert judgement tends to play a very large role.

Equity portfolio risk models are perhaps the most heavily developed risk models in investment management. These can be classified into several different types based on how the portfolios are formed: variance–covariance methods; historical models; factor models; Value-at-Risk models; statistical models; and Monte Carlo techniques.

[2] Jacob A. Mincer, Victor Zarnowitz, Evaluation of Economic Forecasts, NBER, 1969.

Variance–covariance methods go back to Modern Portfolio Theory and Markowitz (1959) and Sharpe (1963). The primary problem with such models is that these tend to not allow for the analysis of sources of risk. Additionally, the underlying assumptions may be too restrictive. Advances have allowed for some of these assumptions to be relaxed as well as permit the incorporation of assets with nonlinear payoffs.

Other types of risk model are based upon this fundamental approach. For example, both prespecified and statistical factor models decompose the historical co-variance matrix in terms of a parsimonious set of factors. The former, as the name implies, relies on prespecified factors. The underlying idea is that certain prespecified factors have earned long-term risk premia and represent systematic sources of risk. A very large body of academic research has identified these factors such as value/growth, size, momentum, etc. and portfolios are formed where the allocations represent exposures to the factors. Blackrock estimates that factor investing may grow to $3.4 trillion by 2022.[3]

In contrast, statistical factor models represent an attempt to identify the factors using data-driven approaches. Statistical models such as principal component methods produce statistical factors that drive the returns of the portfolio. These factors can be hard to estimate and require large amounts of data.

Value-at-Risk models come from the perspective of how much an investor could lose at a given level of probability? The estimates can be either parametric (or Monte Carlo) based methods or non-parametric methods such as historical simulation. The most important issue with Value-at-risk models tend to the observation that risk attribution is difficult, i.e., it is hard to pin down what part of the Value-at-Risk comes from a given risk factor.

A very large literature has developed around the use of Monte Carlo techniques to measure portfolio risk. These include both parametric (i.e. with specific distributions) as well as non-parametric method. These techniques use large numbers of randomly generated scenarios to model the possible outcomes and the consequent risk.

Validation of risk models for investment management involve both investigation of conceptual soundness as well as assessing the implementation of a given model. For example, with portfolio allocation models that may rely on variance–covariance optimization, it can be

[3] www.blackrock.com/us/individual/investment-ideas/what-is-factor-investing.

important to assess the deviation from normality and the impact of these deviations. In the same spirit, it can be important for the validators to assess the appropriateness of the historical data as well as whether any proxy data are being used.

In the same vein, factor models tend to rely on econometric tools and thus are amenable to the methods used to assess the validity of the econometric methods. There is also a very large academic literature that have examined whether the empirical findings are spurious or not.[4] These research findings have bearing upon the conceptual soundness of models that measure the risk of factor models.

In assessing the implementation, an important consideration is to delineate where quantitative/data-based elements end and where expert judgement begins. As a concrete example, in the use of investment signals in a portfolio construction process, multiple signals are used. If the signals are derived from econometric models, then the standard tools of validation that are used for such methods can be applied. However, the weights given to the signals are quite often from expert judgement rather than quantitative models that can be subjected to standard validation.

17.3 Asset Management Models That May Be Validated Using Methodologies for Similar Models Used for the Bank's Own Assets

In many cases, the valuation models used in asset management are almost identical to those used by the sales and trading businesses. However, given the requirements that are unique to the asset management businesses, some of the uses for the valuation model can be different.

Separation of the design function from the validation function. Valuation in asset management also typically relies significantly on valuation by independent third parties. It is also important to note the common overlaps between independent verification of inputs and validation.

Another set of risk in investment management models involve tracking errors. Tracking error is typically defined as the standard

4 See for example, Harvey, Campbell R. and Liu, Yan, Lucky Factors (April 8, 2021). Available at SSRN: https://ssrn.com/abstract=2528780 or http://dx.doi.org/10.2139/ssrn.2528780.

deviation of the difference between a portfolio's actual return and the return of its benchmark. Given that it can be measured *ex post* or *ex ante*, there can be both *ex ante* and *ex post* tracking error models.

Prudent validation would judge the suitability of the benchmark chosen as well as how the tracking errors are being measured.

An important example of where the distinction between components that can be validated versus subjective judgement is the adaptation of validation to investment strategies. It is important to emphasize that this is a highly stylized and simplified example.

The investment manager starts with an asset allocation model whose output then gets modified based on subjective information. The subjective information cannot be validated. However, the asset allocation model could be validated.

For example, if an investment strategy promises returns with a 5% shortfall risk. Then the following validation process can be carried out.

1. A binomial test for a model for generating asset allocations for investors:
   a. generate the efficient frontier for the model that produces the asset allocation for each year;
   b. select a performance target such as 0% return and identify the portfolio that would produce that target with a given probability say 5%;
   c. compute the realized return on the target portfolio;
   d. by repeating this process, a series of forecasted and actual returns on a given target is produced;
   e. assess whether the underperformance of the realized return series is around 5%.

17.4 Conclusion

What this short chapter on validation of risk management models for investment management highlight is that there is room for significant improvement in the practice of validation of these models. At the same time, given that investment management relies on models that are similar to various other risk areas, models taken from those areas can be brought to use in investment management.

Index

For EU product safety concerns, contact us at Calle de José Abascal, 56–1°,
28003 Madrid, Spain or eugpsr@cambridge.org.

www.ingramcontent.com/pod-product-compliance
Lightning Source LLC
LaVergne TN
LVHW011657200926
848484LV00004B/965

* 9 7 8 1 1 0 8 4 9 7 3 5 0 *